A Calculus of Color

# A Calculus of Color

## The Integration of Baseball's American League

### ROBERT KUHN MCGREGOR

McFarland & Company, Inc., Publishers

*Jefferson, North Carolina*

McGregor, Robert Kuhn, 1952–
A calculus of color : the integration of baseball's American League /
Robert Kuhn McGregor.
p.   cm.
Includes bibliographical references and index.

**ISBN 978-0-7864-9440-8 (softcover : acid free paper)**∞
**ISBN 978-1-4766-1868-5 (ebook)**

1. American League of Professional Baseball Clubs—History.
2. Baseball—United States—History.   3. Major League Baseball
(Organization)—History.   4. Racism in sports—United States—History.
5. Discrimination in sports—United States—History.   I. Title.

GV875.A15M34 2015          796.357'640973—dc23          2015005733

BRITISH LIBRARY CATALOGUING DATA ARE AVAILABLE

On the cover: Cleveland Indians center fielder
Larry Doby (National Baseball Hall of Fame
Library, Cooperstown, New York)

Printed in the United States of America

*McFarland & Company, Inc., Publishers
Box 611, Jefferson, North Carolina 28640
www.mcfarlandpub.com*

For Deborah, subjects in the mirror

# Table of Contents

# Acknowledgments

I have been very fortunate in my academic career to have enjoyed the comradeship and support of a great many superior colleagues at the University of Illinois-Springfield. Among those especially interested in this project were Bill Bloemer, Bill Siles, Heather Bailey, Peter Shapinsky, David Bertaina, and Kristi Barnwell. Cecilia Cornell provided a nuanced perspective on civil rights; Ethan Lewis pays more attention to my writing quirks than is probably good for him. Baseball fans one and all, though I am dubious of their respective team loyalties.

Amanda Winters was very helpful in unsnarling the usual computer snafus, while graduate assistants Michelle Montgomery and Amanda Dahlquist were astonishingly determined and productive at turning up obscure journal and newspaper articles. They now know *ProQuest* as well as anyone. The University Library staff was also most helpful in this regard, especially inter-library loan wizard Carol Reese.

Critical to the entire process were the dozens of students who took the history of baseball course I offered three times at UIS. The classroom is the place to work out ideas, find ways to express the themes plainly, discover the flaws. My students were perceptive and enthusiastic participants, and learned, I think, a great deal more about American history than they suspected.

I floated the prototype for this effort at the 2009 Cooperstown Symposium on Baseball and American Culture, where Jim Gates, Hall of Fame librarian, and William M. Simons, professor of history at the State University of New York-Oneonta, were especially encouraging. My subsequent researches at the A. Bartlett Giamatti Library were greatly assisted by librarian Freddy Berowski, archivists Sue MacKay, Mary Bellew, Jenny Ambrose and Sarah DeGaetano, and research interns such as Kyle Austin, who tracked down the really obscure stuff and mailed the copies on to me.

Perhaps the most entertaining aspect of this project was selecting the photographs from the vast Hall of Fame archives. Reference librarian Cassidy Lent was exceedingly helpful in my examination of the files, while assistant photo archivist John Horne offered substantial support and assistance in the final selection process.

The project came to fruition with the enthusiastic support of the good people at McFarland.

My children were not so closely associated with this effort as they were the works of our younger days. Scattered across the country, Molly, Leaf, Blue, Janna, and Bran still shared in the effort, kept the old man reasonably spry.

Most of all, there is Deborah. Most every day, we soldier off to our respective studies, to wrestle for hours with essentially the same questions, approaching the problem from vastly different perspectives. I can only hope to have helped her half as much as she has helped me. This work is dedicated to her, and our life together.

# Preface

To offer a new monograph on the subject of baseball's integration is to venture into a well-mapped but daunting minefield. The geography may be well known, but there are a great many traps lurking for the unwary. There is also no chance of completely pleasing anyone; the only sane course is to make as honest an assessment as possible and seek a fuller understanding of a difficult subject. I have chosen to explore this minefield for two reasons. The first is to fill what seems to me an awkward gap in the scholarship of baseball and race. Certainly there are outstanding books on the exciting yet grim history of the Negro Leagues—books chronicling the great players, the excellence of play, the difficulties of management. There are also any number of striking books on the integration of the major leagues, ranging from close studies of Jackie Robinson's ordeal to critical analyses of Boston's stonewall reluctance. But there really is no book uniting these two subjects in any but a superficial way. What I intend at least to suggest is the relationship that existed between segregated black and white baseball, the unequal parallels that would subsequently shape and severely limit efforts to end the discrimination. The separation was a product of an America we would as soon forget—Jim Crow at his most extreme, the menacing impact of near-apartheid conditions this nation tried so hard to establish. The Negro Leagues existed because a color line was enforced not just in the South but in the industrial North and Midwest, making black separatism a necessity. By the time America belatedly came to realize that Jim Crow was a costly and tragic error, the influence was too pervasive to escape. Efforts to challenge the color line in even a small fashion brought awkward consequences.

My second reason for writing this book is to focus on the American League. Generally, studies of baseball's integration tend to concentrate on the Senior Circuit. The National League story, familiar though it now is, is still compelling. Then follows the happier success story, peopled by some of the greatest players of all time—Campanella, Mays, Aaron, Banks, Clemente. The American League can seem the weaker partner in such a narrative. Larry Doby was every bit as courageous as Jackie Robinson, and in some ways more a victim, but he did not possess Robinson's fiery personality, his crusading determination. Too often, Doby becomes the footnote. And fewer significant black players followed him onto American League rosters. (Satchel Paige is the obvious exception, but he was 41 by the time he debuted in the majors, and the pitcher would compile fewer than 500 innings as an American Leaguer.) In 1959, when the Red Sox finally capitulated, becoming the last major league team to integrate, just 19 black players took the field for the eight American League clubs. Fifty-five blacks played in the National League that year.

In an odd way, this comparative failure makes the American League the more obvious circuit to consider in any discussion of integration and its attending issues. The league, a show-case of pioneering innovation in its youth, had become reactionary after a half-century of existence. No challenge was too large to ignore. Whatever forms of reluctance baseball's owners may have embraced to resist integration, they were clearly and shamefully exhibited in the Junior Circuit over 12 long years. The foot-dragging. The excuses. The chest-pounding righteousness. The evasions. The very history and organization of the league created the conditions that made integration so difficult.

In the 21st Century, no researcher would begin such a book as this from scratch. The scholarship of race and baseball is far-reaching and intimidating, though not without a flaw or two. Early efforts to capture the history of the Negro Leagues, including Robert W. Peterson's *Only the Ball Was White* and the several books by John Holway, provide priceless material saved from oblivion by the authors' efforts. But they do tend to romanticize a bit, to paint a picture far more in keeping with the happy endings of integration than the bitter truth of Jim Crow days. John Holway argues that black baseball existed from the beginning to prepare against the time integration would inevitably come. A far too romantic interpretation, it is not at all fair to the entrepreneurs who tried so hard to establish an independent black enterprise in the face of severe discrimination. More realistic is Neil Lanctot's *Negro League Baseball*, an unflinching examination of black baseball's realities. That book, along with Leslie Heaphy's *The Negro Leagues, 1869–1960*, Dick Clark and Larry Lester's *The Negro Leagues Book*, and Lester's *Black Baseball's National Showcase*, inform much of the more recent scholarship.

Adding dimension to what might otherwise become a dangerously simplistic understanding of baseball and race is a consideration of the Latino players who dented the color line—both before and after Larry Doby and Jackie Robinson. Adrian Burgos, Jr., in *Playing America's Game*, provides a subtle and perceptive treatment of the issue. Rob Ruck's *Raceball* examines the effects of Major League Baseball's "imperial will" on Caribbean baseball (and the Negro Leagues), while *Far from Home*, by Tim Wendell and Jose Luis Villegas, celebrates the impact of the great Latino players.

Any discussion of baseball's integration begins with Jules Tygiel's *Baseball's Great Experiment*. Tygiel, examining events largely through the experience of Jackie Robinson, does concentrate on events in the National League. Rick Swaine's *The Integration of Major League Baseball* includes an encyclopedic consideration of each of the 16 clubs in existence between 1947 and 1960. Whenever my understanding of a transaction seemed amiss, consulting Swaine's work helped to set me straight. For the more exacting details regarding rosters, transactions, playing time, individual performance and even batting orders, I have relied heavily on *Baseball Reference.com*, supplemented by textual sources such as the *ESPN Baseball Encyclopedia* and *Total Baseball*. As we shall see, every team has its biographers, and almost every significant executive and player.

The information is certainly out there. The problem is trying to figure out what all this history is telling us about ourselves. We will need some understanding of what race means in an American context. And some knowledge of baseball's economic side. And a great deal of history. Above all, we need to understand that this history is a world we live in, one that shapes our daily existence. William Faulkner, a man deeply haunted by issues of race, understood this well. "The past is never dead," he warned. "It's not even past."

Let us try to capture a glimpse of ourselves.

# Introduction

## *The Costs of Racism*

---

The winter of 1960 seemed an appropriate moment to take stock. In the year just ended, major league baseball completed a process begun more than 12 years before, finally integrating all 16 franchises. Major strides had come in other professional sports as well—most NFL and NBA teams relied on black players, while the barriers were weakening in tennis and even golf. *Sport* magazine, widely respected for its energetic reporting, probing interviews, and often spectacular photography, chose to devote the March 1960 issue to a special topic, "The Negro in American Sport." The centerpiece of the issue was a roundtable discussion featuring Jackie Robinson, Larry Doby, Bill Davis, Buddy Young, Althea Gibson, and Sam Lacy. Some of the names remain readily recognizable a half century down the road; a few have faded with time. What they discussed in conjunction with the editors of *Sport* amounted to an assessment of the early years of professional sports integration, a perceptive and cautious summation of victories won since 1945, and of more work extending into an infinite future. Traditionally, historians have chosen to present just those years, from the end of World War II through 1960, as a definable era: the Golden Age, the Era of Integration. It is as well to remember that for blacks and whites playing together on major league ball fields, the era was no more than a beginning, and a shaky one at that.

Larry Doby, the pioneer black player in the American League, was a forceful presence in the *Sport* discussion. 1959 was his 13th year playing major league ball, and as matters turned out, his last. What Doby chose to emphasize as he looked forward was the need for blacks to be better educated—about life, about the wider world, about the history of his race. He recalled the shock of his first real exposure to the world of virulent, hate-filled racism, playing exhibition games with the Cleveland Indians in several Southern cities. Nothing he had learned in school remotely prepared him for that, and the onslaught, he felt, hurt him as a player. Doby played in the Negro Leagues before joining the Indians, but never a day in the minor leagues. That lack of seasoning did not hurt him as a player—he hit .301 in his first full season with Cleveland—but it did hurt him as a human being. Throughout his career, Doby found himself trying to assess the people he met, determine their degrees of acceptance, of tolerance, of bigotry. He never mastered the task to his satisfaction. If you were black, there was a lot more to professional baseball than stroking the ball.

The discussion broadened to consider the perceptions of the black fan supporting athletics in 1960. The group gathered around the table generally concurred that there had been a change in black fan behavior, a healthy change. Back in the 1940s, and for a long time thereafter, blacks following major league baseball had not so much rooted for teams; they cheered for individual players—Jackie Robinson, Larry Doby, Hank Thompson, Luke Easter, Satchel Paige et al. These men were not so much followed as participants in a sport, but as symbols of racial accomplishment, a source of tremendous pride. Which team won hardly mattered, as long as those particular players performed well. That kind of fan loyalty was slowly fading as black players grew in number and took places on every team roster. It was true that many black fans were rooting for teams where black players had a greater presence, but the panel seemed reasonably certain that such a tendency would diminish as the numbers of black players on each team evened out. No one at the table could imagine a team where black players would outnumber and dominate the whites—this was America, after all.

Insofar as life in the locker room went, the participants could agree that some kind of positive change had occurred and was continuing, though prejudice had by no means disappeared. As Jackie Robinson noted, some people were just going to remain bigoted, no matter what. For the greater part, white players seized the opportunity to see and play with black teammates as individuals, rather than as stereotypical members of a different race. That determination broke down a lot of barriers, though serious problems remained. On the black side of the equation, the panel argued that with greater numbers of blacks on each team, a preference to form cliques had unfortunately developed—the black players too often kept to themselves. This would never do. Pointing to his own experiences with the Dodgers, Jackie Robinson argued that players, black and white, should seek out teammates who shared their interests and their pastimes, be it card playing or duck hunting or whatever. This would do more to dissolve racial walls than anything.

That race continued to inhibit the mature growth of athletic competition there was no doubt. Blacks had achieved a limited access to the playing field—a few on each team, but no more. There were no black managers in 1960, and no blacks in important front office positions. The discussants were uncertain whether black salaries measured up to white, but it was obvious that white stars took home more money—they earned thousands of extra dollars in advertising endorsements, opportunities blacks almost never saw.

What the achievements of the era amounted to was a breaching of the walls Jim Crow had constructed, the establishment of a strong foothold. Black players had demonstrated beyond all doubt that they could play at the very highest levels. Sheer ability, supported by enormous social and political pressure, had resulted in the integration of every major league team, though sometimes grudgingly and with token effort. But black players still remained a special category. Teams counted to make sure they did not have too many and considered carefully to make sure they had the right ones, in terms of both ability and character. What black players would do after baseball remained a mystery. None had been invited into the ranks of management; there was just one black coach. In 1960, Jackie Robinson was an executive with the Choc Full O' Nuts Coffee Company. A few highly publicized doors had swung open in baseball, but several really important ones remained firmly closed. Race was by no means a dead issue, in baseball or in American society, as events soon proved.[1]

The breakdown of racial barriers in the American League, painful and protracted as it was, proved no more than a single chapter in the long story of race relations in baseball. There was no other way it could be. Race—racism—is in the very threads of the American fabric. No matter how we embroider the cloth, it will always be there.

A few months after Barack Obama took office as President of the United States, *Newsweek* chose to head the magazine's cover story with the very provocative question, "Is Your Baby Racist?" The burden of that feature was an essay detailing recent psychological research indicating that babies respond to differences in appearance—skin color being an obvious example—at a very early age, suggesting that such discriminating tendencies are present from birth, hardwired in the genetic makeup. Discrimination is a tricky word, a harsh word. At its most innocent, the word means merely to note a difference; historically it means to withhold civil rights on the basis of color. That babies note difference is not at all surprising. It seems that the ability, the desire to categorize and create divisions out of whatever set of phenomena presents itself is a basic human trait, a survival mechanism. As the article explains, psychologists know this as essentialism, the basic thinking skills we all share. We use such skills to separate, to consider obvious difference, to puzzle over possible meanings. Show a baby pictures of people of different colors, and they will note the difference. And this is not racism, whatever *Newsweek* may want us to think.[2]

Difference is everywhere. Difference in color, in sex, in language, in ethnicity, in age, in belief, in just about every human quality and every human ability imaginable. Difference is quite healthy, and it is a useful thing to discern difference, to move toward the friendly and familiar, to be aware of what is troubling. Racism is qualitatively different. Racism takes that essential discrimination as a first step, constructing out of the difference an intellectual hierarchy—that because two things are different, one plainly must be the superior of the other. The superior deserves all the privilege—the right to rule, to grow rich, to dominate the social landscape. The lesser deserves nothing, or at least as little as possible. No rights worth having, as little economic wherewithal as keeps body and soul together. The racist sees superiority as normal, innate, God-intended, forever. Equality lies outside the natural order of things. Discrimination moves from the benign recognition of difference to a determined enforcement of caste. Skin color becomes the primary measure of a human's abilities. Individuals exist only within each race, their qualities dictated by genetic inheritance. The racist believes, and acts on the belief, that no matter how hard they try, the inferior folks, defined by color, will never equal the greater in intellectual pursuit, athletic performance, or anything else.

Racism is vicious. It is not something babies are born with. No amount of staring at pictures of people of differing colors will lead babies to conclude they are biologically better than one or the other. Racism is a learned behavior, built on false premises, fueled by constant cultural reinforcement. At the least harmful it is a patronizing warping of the soul, at its worst a blind hatred for the other. Racism is the essentialism at the core of American history.

It began long before independence, born in a dilemma that has haunted the American economy ever since. In the early years, the Colonies, desperate for labor, indentured poor white people to do the heavy lifting. Eventually the situation grew volatile. As the laborers grew poorer while the masters got rich, rebellion filled the air. The answer was to stop importing whites to work hard; the wealthy shifted to black slave labor, creating a system where the slavery was permanent, the condition was heritable through the female, and the slaves had no rights any white was bound to honor. That was grim enough, but in their determination to maintain control, the wealthy promoted the idea that the blacks were enslaved because of their essential racial inferiority. No matter how poor or wretched any poor white laborer might be, he was still white, and that alone made him the superior of any black person. Racism was infused into the American way of life to support a social system justifying an overbearing oligarchy. Racism prevented poor black and poor white from seeing their common ground; both were being exploited by the wealthy few. This same wealthy few, bearing names such as Washington, Jefferson, and Henry, were deeply involved in American independence. American slavery and American freedom are inextricably intertwined.[3]

Buck O'Neil, long a source of memory for the days of Negro Leagues baseball, recalled an incident in Charleston, South Carolina, that weighed heavily on his mind. O'Neil was in Charleston with the legendary Satchel Paige, the first Negro Leagues player inducted into the Baseball Hall of Fame. Their hotel rooms not yet ready, so Paige proposed they take a journey—to Charleston Harbor, and back in time.

> Well, we went on over to an area near the harbor called Drum Island. That was where they had auctioned off the slaves, and there was a big tree with a plaque on it, marking the site of the old slave market. Satchel and I stood there, silent as could be, for about ten minutes, not saying anything, but thinking a whole bunch of things. Finally, Satchel broke the silence.
> "You know what, Nancy?" he said.
> "What's that, Satchel?"
> "Seems like I been here before."
> "Me too, Satchel."[4]

Right there was the essence of the story. Three-quarters of a century after the Civil War brought an end to slavery, every black person in America felt they had been on Drum Island.

America's Civil War is, in a strange way, a much underappreciated event in the nation's history. Everyone grasps that the war was a watershed in determining America's path—the end of slavery, the triumph of industrialization, the future dominance of the national government. Less acknowledged is the war's enduring influence on human emotions, feelings that would do much to shape racial boundaries. Black slaves came away from that war with freedom and not much else; no one fully thought through the issues facing a suddenly freed people possessing almost no property, no money, and no education. Dislocation was the best they could hope for. In the North, the war victors were understandably angry over their losses of blood and treasure. The South, they felt, richly deserved full punishment for those losses. The desire for revenge is never a wholesome emotion, but war does bring that out in people. Northern anger persisted for generations. In the South, white people tasted not merely the bitterness of defeat and the loss of a cultural tradition built on black labor, but pretty much the decimation of their entire political economy. Southern whites were lost, angry, and resentful. A war had been won, a war had been lost, and no one, black or white, was feeling very sanguine.[5]

There is a school of historical thought which contends that race relations immediately after the Civil War were reasonably positive, more so than at any other time in the 19th Century. The slave system was destroyed forever, Southern whites were beaten to their knees, and Northern officials extended concerned hands to assist the freedmen to a new life. Such interpretations mask a much harsher reality.

Slavery might have been dead, but racism survived to flourish anew in an atmosphere of white anger and vengeance. Surely some well-intended people gave their all to a spirit of real reconstruction, the creation of a new South where both black and white could prosper. But in the end, Reconstruction became a sorry sham. For Northerners, reconstruction was an opportunity to exact the revenge they wanted so badly, to deprive the white South of their property and their governments. That blacks might benefit from such policies was more incidental than purposeful. Southern whites deeply resented reconstruction, naturally enough. They blamed Northerners for their continued sufferings, and they blamed the blacks—the supposed beneficiaries of reconstruction policy—into the bargain. In 1877, when the North grew tired of enforcing construction, tired of nursing their anger, it was very easy to abandon Southern blacks to their fate. Union troops withdrew, Southern whites "redeemed" their states, and segregation took shape uninhibited. Very occasionally, signs suggesting some spirit of cooperation did appear. When agrarian populism gained momentum in the late 1880s, poor farmers black and white joined together to fight a common enemy: the railroad trusts. The partnership was all too brief. To maintain newfound power, white populist politicians turned their backs on the blacks who supported them, ushering in an era of renewed repression.[6]

Whites north and south were willing to shove the black population into near serfdom by a very simple justification: very nearly everyone believed—had never stopped believing, even during the War and Reconstruction—that blacks were naturally inferior, not quite human in the accepted sense. The nation's economy was built on that belief, and most white people never doubted it was true. They looked at the lives of black people—the menial toil, the poverty, the bondage, the lack of proper cultural expression—and they chose to believe all this had happened because black people were less human, less capable. Scientific inquiry worked very hard to bolster the belief. Early anthropologists such as Josiah Knott constructed a social science to "prove" black inferiority, while Philadelphia physician Samuel George Morton measured hundreds of human skulls before pronouncing that blacks had smaller brain capacities than whites. By unconsciously fudging data and refusing to accept that context influenced social condition, such researchers supported a notion that most white Americans wanted to be true. Whites, they so much believed, were biologically superior to blacks. Americans sharing and acting on that assumption included Thomas Jefferson, Abraham Lincoln, Ralph Waldo Emerson, Elizabeth Cady Stanton, and, as time moved on, Theodore Roosevelt, Henry Ford, Woodrow Wilson, Charles Lindbergh, and several million others.[7]

The Civil War freed the slaves. Reconstruction gave some of them property and political power, very little of which survived past 1877. But the War did nothing to alter American perceptions of race. Blacks were seen as inferior long before the first cannon's roar. Many cannons later, that belief had not changed in the least.

The thing was, Americans were especially sensitive on questions of race. Even in the 18th Century, America was perceived as a nation of mongrel descent, with immigrants from Anglo-Saxon England, Celtic Scotland and Wales, various portions of Germany, and some from France and Holland and Ireland dotting the landscape. Europeans were already squabbling over just how many races of people coexisted on their continent. At least three was the common thinking, maybe more. For certain there were the Germanics with their virile Viking backgrounds, the folks who populated the parts of England that counted, along with the German states and Scandinavia. Next in this highly bigoted construction were the Celts, a lesser type peopling Scotland, France, and other unhappy places. Beyond that were the Eastern Europeans—the Slavs, from whom the very word slavery derived—and maybe some of the Mediterranean peoples, if they were white at all in such a scheme.

For alleged science, it was all very hazy and imprecise, yet somehow very important. It was not enough merely to categorize peoples in this haphazard fashion; they had to be ranked. Each race had its attributes, positive and negative. According to the system of values applied, one group's stereotypes would outshine all the others, thereby becoming the best, the truly *white* race. American white thinkers were so worried about which of the American peoples descended from the true whiteness that they never questioned the assumption of white superiority over black. Who were the true whites, the true and blue, the real Americans? Who was fit to lead, to establish true civility and cultural hegemony?[8]

These were questions that had real meaning on a ball field. Abner Doubleday notwithstanding, baseball as we know it developed in urban surroundings, nurtured by young, aspiring, middle class males seeking gentile forms of exercise. Baseball began as a gentleman's sport reflecting white civilized values and the ideal of sportsmanship. It is not whether you win or lose, but playing by the rules without even a thought of cheating, and so forth. The umpire was an honored gentleman sought out by the contestants, men who would never resort to the bad form of questioning a call. The vocabulary of the game reflected Victorian civility. A man who walked took his base; his effort did not count for or against him. He had not earned his base in a manly way by striking the ball fairly, but he had not gotten there by dishonorable means either. In the records, there had been no at-bat at all, a Victorian nicety that persists to this day. If, on the other hand, a batter reaches base because of a fielder's mistake, that is not a respectable achievement. The batter is charged with an at-bat without a hit (an out that did not quite happen), and the fielder is charged with an error. Shameful. Baseball was a game of values—values defined by middle class whites, values that defined whiteness.[9]

The question of whiteness was important enough before the Civil War. There was a good dollop of the Anglo-Saxon race spread across the map, in old Virginia, in parts of the Mid-Atlantic, and especially in New England. There were a lot of Celtic descendants, who were careful to delineate themselves from the Irish by calling themselves the Scots-Irish, the Ulster Irish, or some such. There were a fair number of Germans, who were regarded as being essentially all right because they shared a Germanic heritage with the Anglo-Saxons. Though they have had some doubts about one another, these three groups comprised what most regarded as the true American race, the people born to think and to rule. The white race. On the outside stood the Irish—Catholic and obviously not possessed of the proper virtues—and the blacks.

The last half of the 19th Century complicated the race picture without really changing it. Immigration came to a complete halt during the Civil War. When the flow of people began again, the immigrants no longer came in large numbers from Britain, Germany, France, or even Ireland. The new people were neither Germanic nor Celtic, but Southern and Eastern Europeans—Italians, Slavs, Russian Jews. Racial definition and debate intensified. The American race—the *white* race—now had to articulate American values, real American culture, more fully and carefully. Russians, Poles, Czechs, Croats, and so many more could never become really white, but they could be Americanized through education and patriotic display. The older American race became increasingly sensitive and worried about American values. They also became slightly more expansive. The Irish became white.[10]

Again baseball reflected the subtle shiftings in American cultural understanding. Baseball began as a gentleman's game with civilized values, but one of the values the American race (Germanic or Nordic or whatever it was) most honored was competitive superiority. The whole point of racial classification was to determine dominance, and might does go a long way toward making right. The Germanic folks did not point back to their Viking forebears with pride because they were kindly shipbuilders. Winning was important, and winning came to mean finding the best players, even if you had to search outside the gentile middle class.[11]

As baseball began to professionalize seriously in the years immediately after the Civil

War, many of the professionals were working class Irishmen. The values defined by amateur sportsmanship largely disappeared as a win-at-all-costs attitude came to dominate. Umpire-baiting became an expected facet of the game, along with roughhouse and sometimes overtly violent play. Fan decorum dissipated amidst coarse language and open gambling, and very soon the ballpark was no place to bring a family. One of the goals of the National League at its founding in 1876 was to restore the Victorian values, but the intent was soon lost in the competition with rival leagues for attendance. No matter the race or class, money always speaks the loudest. It took until the early years of the 20th Century, and the efforts of the upstart American League, for baseball to clean up the worst of its act and become a family game. When the National and American Leagues joined forces to pressure virtually all of the minor leagues to accept the principle of the standard contract and the reserve clause, organized baseball established a monopoly over players, over play. By this time baseball had far outrun its adversaries to become the athletic expression of American culture. America's game. The white man's game.[12]

Baseball's appeal was never limited to white people, no matter how much they tried to monopolize the game and its style. Blacks embraced the game very early on; there are indications that slaves played some form of base ball. A very small number of blacks managed to find places on professional rosters during Reconstruction and shortly after. All-black professional teams were playing by the 1880s. The early history of black baseball is to some degree a barometer of race relations in the latter half of the 19th Century. Relations were not good. That so few black professionals won places on the very large number of professional teams would indicate that racial barriers were set very high from the beginning, a probability supported by the rapid appearance of the all-black teams. By the late 1880s the barrier was complete. The National League and its competitors routinely shut out all black players. Organized Baseball was to be an exclusively white operation, expressive of those superior white values the race scientists always harped on, the ones Theodore Roosevelt, Woodrow Wilson, and Henry Ford so firmly defended. For America to survive, the Germanic, Anglo-Saxon ideals would just have to dominate.[13]

Most Americans probably paid little attention to the subtleties of scientific racism. Just how many races there were, or how precisely they were defined, did not much matter. What did matter, late in the 19th Century and on into the 20th, was that America was for Americans, and there were too many foreigners about. These "hyphenated Americans" spoke strange, impenetrable languages, worked too cheaply, lived together in crowded urban ghettos, and stoutly resisted efforts to make them see the superiority of the American way. Just who or what comprised a real American was a little difficult to pin down, and the definition slid with time, but the notion was very real. The Irish were firmly American by this time, part of the mainstream and a real political power. The later immigrant Germans were eyed suspiciously, but by contrast with their eastern European cousins, they were in. (When Johannes Wagner, a son of German immigrants, became a star with the Pittsburgh Pirates early in the 20th Century, the newspapers were flummoxed by his un–American name. After wrestling a good while, they settled on the nonsense moniker "Honus"—the handle Wagner carried into the Hall of Fame.) Very gradually, society bended to accept people of Slavic, Jewish, and Italian background, although these groups were often disparaged as "hyphenates" during the Great War.[14]

In a land that could not quite define what white was, even if everyone understood that whiteness—true whiteness—was very important, black people had no real chance at all. The legacy of the Civil War soldiered on in the South, where whites still smarted from the vengeance meted out by the North, and took it out on the blacks. Whatever small toeholds the black population established during Reconstruction disappeared almost completely. With almost no property, no education, and no money, and possessing very little understanding of the larger capitalist world, most black people soon slipped back into a world they understood. Slavery was gone, but in its place emerged sharecropping, a kind of peonage where blacks rented farmland from white landlords, pledging a share of the crop—inevitably cotton—as payment. Somehow the bills always exceeded the value of the crop, to be carried over to the next year. The difference from slavery was hard to distinguish.

What had emerged in the South was a world of peculiar accommodation, on both sides of the racial ledger. The blacks lived in a society dominated politically and economically by whites, even in places where blacks were a majority of the population. White treatment of blacks ranged from toleration to exploitation to outright hatred, yet the whites had to be realistic. Poor as they were, the blacks were still a profitable cog in the Southern economy. More important, blacks were everywhere—farming in the countryside, doing the menial work in towns, serving in white households. The blacks had been suddenly thrown, wholly unprepared, into a world of merciless economic competition. It was a world largely created by the whites, and a world the two races now had to share, if unequally. There was no escape from one another.

If the two races had to live together in one community, the whites were determined that it be a community they would fully control. Segregation was in some respects impossible in the South—blacks were too many to be ghettoized, isolated from the whites—but such segregation as was possible became rigidly enforced. Jim Crow in his Southern incarnation separated blacks and whites in public transportation, in dining establishments and hotels, and in schools. In 1896, in *Plessy v. Ferguson*, the United States Supreme Court ruled that such segregation was legal, so long as "separate but equal" facilities were maintained for each. Jim Crow's reach grew rapidly. Beneath the legal decisions, the legislative actions, and the executive enforcement that defined Jim Crow, there bubbled the element that made him so sadistically powerful: domestic terrorism. The South averaged dozens of lynchings each year from 1877 to 1900, a ferocious spasm of hatred that made an arbitrary and often invisible color line all too real. Black men walked carefully in the South; they did not bother white women, and they did not try to vote. Black women could do little more than endure.[15]

Fenced in by lynching and Jim Crow legalisms, trapped into debt peonage, handicapped by limited education, blacks lived a life defined by race, in a nation that measured itself by race. Some Northerners were uncertain that Southern whites really qualified as white in the "scientifically" accepted meaning of the word, which leaves a pretty good idea of where the black people stood. There had to be some answer to the black dilemma. By the early years of the 20th Century, three possible alternatives commanded attention.

The first, perhaps most appealing, certainly most unrealistic possibility was to leave. Before the Civil War, manumission societies had tied abolition to migration, advocating black colonization in Africa or Latin America. A few free blacks embraced such schemes, and American blacks did establish a settlement in Liberia, on Africa's western coast, in the 1830s. But there were two impediments—several million blacks lived in the United States; transporting them across the ocean would be fabulously expensive, and most would refuse to go. American blacks were Americans, even if they retained some qualities of African culture. Hateful though it often was, America was home. Black leaders occasionally advanced African colonization ideas during Reconstruction and later, but they attracted little attention. Early in the 20th Century, quite another kind of migration really would alter the landscape of American race relations.[16]

As the vast majority of black people were determined to remain in the United States, they obviously needed some kind of strategy to escape the fences Jim Crow built around them. By the early 1900s, two strong-willed men had developed competing strategies to forward the fortunes of American blacks. Two men born in the same country could hardly have come from more different circumstances, contributing heavily to the differing visions of black America they delivered nearly at the same time. Booker T. Washington observed that "I must have been born somewhere and at some time," but was genuinely unsure about the specifics. He was born into slavery in western Virginia not long before the Civil War, experiencing at first hand the uncertainties of the war and the hardships of reaching adulthood with no money and little opportunity. He managed to find education, displaying talents that won him the opportunity to establish an industrial school for blacks at Tuskegee, Alabama. The school became the model and hope for the black future in the South, providing a practical education leavened with instruction in skills such as farming, animal husbandry, and brickmaking. In his highly influential autobiography, *Up from Slavery*, published in 1901, Washington adopted a deceptively deferential tone to argue for a conciliatory strategy for blacks in the immediate future. To his mind, the essential task for blacks was to create a sound economic base by mastering material crafts critical to the Southern economy—farming, blacksmithing, carpentry, and again, bricks. Such skills would enable blacks to weave themselves into the productive heart of the South. Legal and political rights would necessarily follow. Washington was opposed to pressuring for such rights, just as he was opposed to black education for the professions or higher learning. His experiences suggested that blacks would best prosper by joining with whites at a basic economic level, while posing no visible threat to white political control.[17]

W. E. B. DuBois took a more aggressive stand. DuBois was born in kinder circumstances, as a free black in western Massachusetts in 1868. The Civil War and Reconstruction made only remote impressions on his sensibilities, and he took advantage of opportunities that Southern blacks rarely saw. In 1895, DuBois became the first black man to receive a Ph.D. from Harvard University. Soon after, he was teaching history and economics at Georgia's Atlanta University. DuBois wrote extensively on black culture and history, but it was his 1903 publication, *The Souls of Black Folk*, that effectively challenged Booker T. Washington's strategy. DuBois devoted a chapter to Washington's career, acknowledging the value of his work and the hope he inspired, yet laying bare the severe limitations. By neglecting the liberal arts in favor of narrow industrial education, Washington, in DuBois's view, was abetting whites in confining blacks to second-class citizenship. Through a series of varied explorations, social and historical, DuBois painted a picture of the Southern black trapped in a degrading web that offered no hope of escape. To improve themselves, blacks would have to seize the initiative, achieve a real understanding of the larger world, and insist on the rights belonging to them. DuBois even doubted the continued value of the skills Washington's school emphasized. They were crafts geared toward a rural economy, taught in a nation that was rapidly urbanizing.[18]

DuBois did his best to invest action in his words, establishing a National Negro Business League in 1900, the Niagara Movement in 1905, and co-founding the National Association for the Advancement of Colored People in 1909. Washington, whose own political influence with Presidents Roosevelt and Taft belied his accommodationist philosophy, did his best to undermine DuBois's efforts. Yet the men agreed on the point that would most affect black economic development in the 20th Century. For blacks to gain traction in American society, they had to achieve real economic independence. Money was power. As events unfolded, the frivolous world of professional baseball became an essential proving ground to test the validity of this position.[19]

Even as the ink was drying on both men's books, trends were taking shape that would have a profound influence on their philosophies. Beginning nearly at the start of the new century and accelerating rapidly in the years through World War I, one of the greatest population movements in history saw nearly a half-million black people leave the South for the urban North. As with all mass movements of population, this Great Migration was a product of push and pull factors. In the South, the boll weevil had entered the cotton fields, devastating a monocrop economy. Independent black farmers and sharecroppers were ruined directly, and a subsequent shift to other, less labor intensive crops lessened the demand for black agricultural labor. Add economic ruin to the prevailing atmosphere of Jim Crow and outright terrorism; there was little incentive to stay. A series of catastrophic floods hastened the diaspora.

Northern industrialists wanted the black people to migrate for reasons good and bad, and always self-serving. Continued industrial expansion had created a job market that the native white population and the supplement of European immigrants proved unable to fill. Factory owners were willing to hire blacks and pay decent wages. But they also imported blacks to serve as strike breakers, creating a mutual mistrust that would keep black and white working class folk suspicious and hateful for decades to come. Industrialists certainly understood that a large influx of black workers might well create a labor surplus, depressing wages for everybody. The labor unions understood that, too.[20]

The Great Migration altered America's racial equation fundamentally. When both Washington and DuBois wrote their most influential words, black racial issues were perceived as a wholly Southern problem. There were free blacks living in every Northern city, but in numbers so small that the dominant population could isolate and completely ignore them, spending their time arguing over who was really white. The black migration forced white Northerners to respond to black presence for the first time. Respond they did, developing their own variety of Jim Crow, every bit as segregationist as anything the South ever invented. And more isolationist.[21]

In the South, complete separation of black and white was a practical impossibility; for better or worse, the fortunes of both were intertwined. In most Northern cities before 1900, the small populations of black citizens tended to concentrate in well-defined enclaves—neighborhoods or ghettoes. As black populations in these cities began to expand, white population sought every means—including some very drastic ones—to confine blacks to those old neighborhoods, a wrinkle in Jim Crow's persona developed in the North, rather than the South. A simple table illustrates the change taking place:

**Table 1.122**

### Populations of Selected Northern Cities, 1900 and 1940

| CITY | 1900 POPULATION* | % BLACK | 1940 POPULATION* | % BLACK |
|------|------------------|---------|------------------|---------|
| New York | 3437.2 | 1.8 | 7891.9 | 9.5 |
| Cleveland | 381.8 | 1.6 | 914.8 | 16.2 |
| Boston | 560.9 | 2.1 | 801.4 | 5.0 |

| CITY | 1900 POPULATION* | % BLACK | 1940 POPULATION* | % BLACK |
|------|-----------------|---------|------------------|---------|
| Chicago | 1698.6 | 1.8 | 3620.9 | 13.6 |
| Detroit | 285.7 | 1.4 | 1849.6 | 16.2 |
| Washington | 278.7 | 31.1 | 802.2 | 35.0 |
| Philadelphia | 1293.7 | 4.8 | 2071.6 | 18.2 |
| St. Louis | 325.9 | 4.4 | 802.2 | 17.9 |

*times 1,000

In each of these cities, the population grew at a breathless pace, in most places doubling and more, reflecting the general trend toward urbanization. But in most of these cities, the growth of the black population was far more rapid. In New York City, the number of black residents increased by more than 700 percent in 40 years. With the development of the automobile industry, Detroit's total population grew by a factor of almost six, but the black population expanded from 4,000 to more than 149,000, a 37-fold increase. What in the 19th Century had been viewed as a Southern problem had become a Northern issue, and a volatile one. Enough blacks found relative success moving northward to feed a tide of rising expectations, always a dangerous moment when the dominant population is determined to squelch those dreams. Confident people fight back.[23]

The First World War became a turning point in America's racial history, and not a pretty one. Fighting overseas gave Americans a taste of internationalism, and they recoiled in horror. With every suspicion of malicious foreign influences seemingly affirmed, self-appointed "real Americans" went after Bolsheviks, Red Communists, hyphenates, Wobblies, Catholics, Jews, New Negroes, and anybody else who did not meet the criteria for American whiteness. It was a long list. 1919 would see the "Red Summer," as blood literally flowed in riot-torn streets. Attorney General Mitchell Palmer grasped at excuses to attack organizations he considered un–American, while the Ku Klux Klan was reborn. The sheets emphasized their whiteness. Danger lurked everywhere in the land of the free, so the ones in control did their best to make freedom a very narrow privilege.[24]

The riots were nothing new. Race riots had shattered American tranquility at several junctures in the years following reconstruction, as tensions rose to boiling point in such scattered places as Wilmington, North Carolina (1898), New York City (1900), Atlanta (1906), Springfield, Illinois (1908), East St. Louis (1917), and Philadelphia (1917). The riot erupting in Chicago in 1919 took an ominously different shape—less of a riot, more of a race war. In the two years leading up to the mass outbreak, white gangs bombed 26 black homes, determined to drive away blacks with the methods of terror. When tensions exploded in July, white gangs, mainly Irish, attacked black neighborhoods, determined to dictate the boundaries of black living space and turn back recent expansions. Blacks fought back just as ruthlessly, often using sniper fire to blunt attacks. A bloody stalemate ensued; 38 people died, hundreds suffered wounds, hundreds more saw their homes burned out. A vicious response to a Great Migration.[25]

Quickly taking stock, the land where whiteness (however defined) counted so much responded to its fears. Radical labor unions were quickly and sometimes violently repressed, new immigration laws severely restricted the flow of people deemed not white enough in appearance or thought, and Jim Crow slithered northward. New laws and covenants segregated housing, transportation, food and lodging, medical services, and education. In the North, though black populations continued to grow, they remained small minorities in most cities. Laws fenced them into urban ghettoes; Jim Crow did his best to seal them off. New waves of anti-black restriction swept the nation, supported by the findings of racist pseudo-science. More than ever, blacks were seen as inherently inferior, a lesser product of uncompromising biology. America chose to embrace the racist traditions at the core of their history, strengthening a set of federal, state and local policies that together spelled nothing less than apartheid. D. W. Griffith's "Birth of a Nation" became the primary propaganda film. (Woodrow Wilson loved it.) "Hyphenated" immigrants experienced little better, as society and a determined educational system sought to stamp out any trace of foreignness. The true America was supposed to be not just white, but a certain specific form of white. Xenophobia reigned. Not to put too fine a point on America's past, the country went dangerously nuts.[26]

It was against this weird backdrop of ugly, self-defined self-pride and galloping insecurity that modern baseball took shape, for both black and white. The eight cities listed in the pre-ceding table of populations were not chosen capriciously; they were the eight towns hosting American League ball clubs in 1903. Adding Cincinnati, Brooklyn and Pittsburgh would pro-vide a list of *all* the cities with major league teams between 1903 and 1953. After a long stretch of competitive instability, baseball had finally achieved the dream of its owners: a stable monopoly. Big league baseball in the first half of the 20th Century would be confined to the northeast quadrant of the nation, played in just ten cities along the eastern seaboard and extend-ing as far west as Chicago and St. Louis. St. Louis, along with Washington D.C., was baseball's south. When blacks migrated northward, it was into major league baseball territory they trekked (not that this was the intention). It was in those northeastern cities that urban ghettoes developed, racial tensions swelled, Jim Crow assumed new meanings, and apartheid took shape. Maybe baseball was America. Surely the racism that gripped the sport was a product and a reflection of American culture.[27]

Much has been made of the strange tale of baseball's integration, how the public and peaceable admission of black players to major league rosters smoothed the path in many walks of life. There is a grain of truth in this, but only a grain. The Great Migration of blacks from the South changed the nature of racial tension in America. The movement of blacks to North-ern cities and the maturation of major league baseball were very different, almost unrelated expressions of the same historical development: the urbanization of American culture, led by determining elements unfolding in the large Northeastern cities. The major league cities con-trolled baseball across America, just as the big cities came to control cultural expression as modern newspaper, advertising, and electronic media took shape. Blacks came north just in time to stand at the periphery of profound change.

In *The Souls of Black Folk*, W. E. B. DuBois spoke eloquently of a black sense of two-ness, "an American, a Negro, two souls, two thoughts, two unreconciled strivings; two warring ideals in one dark body whose dogged strength alone keeps it from being torn asunder." At once, blacks longed to grow into the full measure of their humanity, yet be fully accepted in their rights and responsibilities as American citizens. DuBois himself had advocated full black participation in the Great War, believing that this sacrifice would open the door to full accept-ance. The postwar reaction crushed his hope, leaving blacks in greater ambiguity than ever. Such answer as remained seemed to lie in the strengthening of black community, the matura-tion of independent black enterprise. Blacks would be two: residents of America, but in control of their own separate identity, financial and cultural.[28]

Baseball enters here. There were black baseball teams long before 1920, and failed attempts to establish leagues. But after the War, as Jim Crow spread the miasma of two-ness across the country, black players and entrepreneurs glimpsed a grim future of barriers and opportunity. Organized baseball was not going to allow blacks to play—not then, probably not ever. Blacks would have to go their own way. Yet blacks identified heavily with mainstream American culture, especially the more middle-class blacks who had established themselves in Northern cities before the Great Migration began. Baseball was one of the more esteemed elements of that culture. The skill blacks exhibited on baseball fields became an enormous source of black pride, a demonstration of aptitude for a supposedly white man's game. Barred from participating with whites, blacks developed parallel institutions, Negro Leagues that played in much the same set of cities, eventually in many of the same parks. Baseball was cultural expression, and it was also financial opportunity. The Negro Leagues became one of the most visible of all black business enterprises in the first half of the 20th Century.[29]

The story of baseball's integration is not a parable of America's brutal desegregation saga. The integration of baseball was a localized, Northern event, with very few immediate repercussions in the South. Jim Crow in major league baseball was a product of the shifts in the nation's race relations developing after 1900. The Great Migration for the first time made race an urban issue and a Northern issue. The separate playing fields of professional baseball mirrored urban racial confrontations, scenes that inflated Jim Crow's shadow. Baseball's eventual integration reflected efforts to face these Northern, urban problems, to reverse course on just one of America's many roads to apartheid. The obstacles thrown in the path of this one simple act suggest just how deep the roots of American apartheid had grown.[30]

The story of baseball's integration is in some ways a familiar one, enriched by a wide-ranging investigative literature. This volume looks to address the question of black opportunity in professional baseball—how chances briefly opened, firmly and unalterably closed, and then slowly reopened once again. The chapters to follow trace the parallel developments of black and white baseball, the efforts first to keep them apart and then draw them together, and the eventual breakdown of the racial barriers maintained by the eight American League teams, a process that occurred in essentially three phases.

Why the American League? First of all, to simplify a very complicated story just a bit—the machinations of eight clubs are easier to trace and explain than 16. There is greater room for telling detail. The forces, the concerns, the prejudices that made integration so complicated in the American League were much the same for the National—at several points, the responses of the leagues were interwoven. The story of one is much the story of the other. Yet the American League is generally the stepchild in such histories. Integration in the National League was largely a success story—Jackie Robinson, followed by Roy Campanella, Willie Mays, Henry Aaron, Ernie Banks, Roberto Clemente, and so many others. The American League came off a poor second when it came to claiming black stars. The American League was also home to the last team to integrate, leaving the impression, justified or not, that the junior circuit was the more reluctant when it came to race. More reluctant, and more inept.

We shall see.

# I

# The Negro Leagues

## *Baseball by and for Black People*

There is no adjective sufficient to embody the storied history of America's Negro Leagues, no word adequate to capture the spirit of those strange times. At once, the Negro Leagues stand as a testament to glorious baseball, and as an indelible reminder of American social convention at its very worst. The Negro Leagues lie at the very heart of America's ambiguous past. They were, at least at times, among the most successful of black capitalist ventures, an ongoing exhibition of surpassing baseball skills that rollicked and entertained, bringing joy to thousands. They existed because the American people, faced with hard choices grown out of their troubled racial past, chose segregation as the path to the future. Too often, the men who operated this black baseball were little more than crooks, gamblers who preyed on the desperate dreams of their own people. Occasionally, the Leagues depended on the help of white people who actually cared, who wanted to see black baseball succeed simply because it was good. Supreme athleticism, petty greed, calculated entertainment, personal tragedy, and competitive triumph were all ingredients of the experience. There was nothing straightforward about the Negro Leagues, even if the concept was very simple. Black men (and one woman) joined together to play professional baseball on mostly black-supported, black-operated teams, simply because they were barred from playing anywhere else.

Looking back from the perspective of old age, players recalled their Negro League days with a telling mix of emotions. Some were angry, recognizing that they had sold their skills in segregated venues for precious little, while white athletes with no better ability won far greater recognition and reward. "The only thing I regret," Sug Cornelius allowed, "is that I wasn't given a chance. My skin was black and that denied me the right to play in the majors." Others recalled the joy of Negro Leagues play, the camaraderie, the fun, the amazing level of play that the major leagues seemingly could not match. "I'll say this," Ted Page offered. "I'm not bitter. I think I'm very lucky to be able to say that I played with all the great ballplayers, with and against them. This is something that is unusual."[1]

There was bitterness and regret, often trumped by satisfaction and good humor. There was quiet resignation. "I'm not bitter about missing the big leagues," Webster McDonald confided. "What were you going to do at the time? You know what the situation was." Cool Papa Bell said much the same thing: "I've got no kicks, no regrets. Of course it would have been nice to play in the Majors, but I have my memories." The black baseball leagues were a bundle of strange contradictions: some great players making the best of the poorest possible circumstances. "There were great players back then," Crush Holloway remembered. "But nobody knows about us anymore.... It's just the past, that's all." The Negro Leagues stir fond memories, yet no one regrets their disappearance. They are the well of so much understated emotion. The story of baseball's eventual integration begins here.[2]

Like everything else, the Negro Leagues did not come into existence of their own making. The Leagues were a product of many things, some good and many bad. There was the racial trajectory of an American history that made a strict color line segregation so possible, so likely. Black people had emerged from the Civil War clinging to a small ray of hope, a faith that the country freeing them might give them a fair chance. Then came Southern redemption and Northern indifference; black hope was pretty much gone by 1877, certainly by 1900. If black people were going to benefit from the opportunities offered by American enterprise, they would have to invent their own institutions. White America barred them from any share of what was already out there—professional baseball included.

There was also the trajectory of baseball itself—a history that began with a child's game transformed into manly recreation, then competitive recreation, too soon a professionalized operation, and then a profit-seeking business. The evolution of black baseball followed much the same pattern, a parallel evolution that carried players from chance pick-up games to the eventual emergence of black professional leagues. Like their white counterparts, black ballplayers would come face to face with the realities of capitalism: they became paid laborers in an entertainment business that sought to monopolize its product and control the workers. The Negro Leagues were black and separate, but they were still very American in pattern. They existed not to be different, but to be as close as possible to the standards evolved within the white community, a shadow drawn into existence purely by discrimination. Blacks wanted to play baseball; they wanted to make money at it, just as white Americans did. Excluded from playing with the whites, black players and entrepreneurs created corresponding institutions as best they could.

There may be the faintest glimmer of truth to the argument that post–Civil War racial prejudice took shape over a lengthy period, that minimal discrimination immediately following the war grew more vicious as racial borders hardened. Reconstruction governments did try to give the newly freed slaves a fair shake, but racial prejudice had been a constant in American life since at least the 1670s. The vast majority of white Americans continued to see the freedmen and women as a separate and inferior race to themselves. Too many hated and feared what they saw. Baseball diamonds were not free from this kind of attitude; racial exclusion came very quickly to innocuous recreation. In 1867, the National Association of Baseball Players voted to reject a membership application from the Pythians of Philadelphia, a black team. In fact, the nominating committee unanimously reported "against the admission of any club which may be composed of one or more colored persons." Three years later, the New York State Base Ball Association legislated a similar ban, leading a reporter from the *New York Clipper* to recommend that black players organize their own national association.[3]

The writing was on the wall, just five years after the passing of the 14th Amendment. Powerful baseball associations in the two most populous Northern cities had fashioned racial policies that members overwhelmingly accepted as good and right. In the Philadelphia case, the decision was aimed primarily at an all-black team, a very good indication that segregation was already at work on the field. Black players had joined together to form the Pythians, their own separate team, and were petitioning to play against all-white teams. Hardly a case of racial integration. Separatism was already the norm.

A very few black players did manage to catch on with professional baseball organizations during the last decades of the 19th century. They were the exceptions that came to emphasize the rules. Sol White, pioneer black professional player and eventual manager, chronicled their mostly unhappy careers in his *Official Base Ball Guide*, published in 1907. White credited Bud Fowler, pitcher and second baseman from (of all places) Cooperstown, New York, as "the first colored ball player of note playing on a white team." Fowler began his career in 1878, playing with various teams in Massachusetts and then throughout New England and the Midwest. For a while, his talent trumped his racial identity, but acceptance came harder and harder as he bounced from one team to another. By 1894 Fowler was helping to organize the Page Fence Giants, a very successful all-black team from Michigan. White baseball had shut him out.[4]

Several black players tried to follow Bud Fowler's path. By 1887, there were at least 20 players playing in what was becoming organized ball, including six in the International League and three in the Ohio League. Fleetwood Walker, a catcher born in Mount Pleasant, Ohio, proved the most successful black player of his time, reaching the major leagues with the Toledo Blue Stockings of the American Association in 1884. (Walker's brother Weldy also briefly caught on with the team, appearing in six games.) Fleetwood Walker was batting .263 when injury ended his season, and Toledo folded at year's end. He moved on to play with teams in the Western League and the International League over the next four years. Quitting after 1889, Walker eventually became an advocate of the Back to Africa movement.[5]

Walker suffered the misfortune of becoming a visible lightning rod for growing racial hatred in organized ball during the 1880s. That hatred was personified in the crude belligerence of Cap Anson, star player for the Chicago White Stockings, who loudly refused to play against Walker on three different occasions between 1883 and 1887, simply because of race. The biggest confrontation occurred in Newark, New Jersey, in 1887, when Anson successfully balked at playing against Walker and Newark pitcher George Stovey, black and very skillful. This and similar incidents fed a growing resistance to black participation. Both the National League and the American Association completely banned blacks before the next year, establishing a color line that lasted 58 seasons. From 1889 onward, the history of blacks in professional baseball becomes a separate story.[6]

Cap Anson is targeted with the lion's share of the blame for Jim Crow in baseball. Anson was apparently a nice man in other respects, though he probably still deserves every measure of contempt that attaches to his racism. But Cap Anson was not the culprit, not him alone. Major league baseball began in 1871. Four different major leagues and at least 32 top drawer teams appeared over the next several years, each fielding at least a 12-man roster. There were hundreds of major league players, but just one black who made any impact—for part of one season. Sheer numbers tell an obvious story. The professional teams by and large resisted black players from the beginning. The major leagues were overwhelmingly, ridiculously white long before they were exclusively white. Cap Anson may have been a loudmouth, but he was merely symptomatic of a prejudice that ran deep in his profession.[7]

By the late 1880s, the future was very plain. If blacks were going to play professional baseball, they would be forming their own teams and playing primarily against other black teams. Exhibitions against white teams would be acceptable, so long as the racial divide was honored and no black team attempted to enter the rapidly crystallizing white professional leagues. For black teams, barnstorming and semi-organized competitions against other black teams were all that anyone could expect.

Probably the most notable of the early all-black teams were the Cuban Giants, the first fully professional black nine. Stories of the team's origins are almost mythological. The organizer was a hotelman, one Frank P. Thompson, who moved between Florida and New York State with the seasons, managing luxury hotels and providing entertainment for the wealthy and influential. Supposedly the first team members were a pick-up nine chosen from among the black employees of Thompson's hotel in Babylon, New York, organized to provide exhibition baseball against local teams. Games became increasingly competitive, and Thompson cast a wider net, looking for the best black talent available. In the autumn of 1885, the Cuban Giants emerged, the first fully professional black team. That winter they played several all-black teams in Florida, then departed northward to face new competition. The team became a black version of the 1869 Cincinnati Reds, the first travelling all-professional team. Sol White, one of the original Cuban Giants, assures us that the players "were not looked upon by the public as freaks, but they were classed as men of talent." In 1887, the men of talent posted a record of 107–54.[8]

White later recalled that the players were "neither giants nor Cubans, but thick-set and brawny colored men." That they called themselves Cubans says a great deal about race relations in the United States in 1885. The most famous story told about the team reinforces the image. The Cuban Giants, so legend claims, spoke to one another on the ball field—yelled signals and so forth—in a gibberish that they supposedly hoped would pass as Spanish, enhancing their claim to foreign ancestry. Recent historians have cast justifiable doubt on this legend: how stupid can anyone think people were, even in 1885? Perhaps the Cuban Giants did the gibberish as a joke, an entertainment. It is the kind of myth that can be twisted into a larger and sadder kind of story, one that becomes only too believable. Why were the Cuban Giants supposedly so determined to pass themselves off as Cubans? So they would not be seen by predominantly white crowds as American black men, fit for the cruelest forms of recrimination. Better to be Cuban than American black.[9]

More black professional teams quickly followed the Cuban Giants' lead. The Gorhams of New York City fired up in 1886, with the Pittsburgh Keystones and the Norfolk Red Stockings following soon after. By 1888 the four teams were competing in New York City for the "colored championship of the world." At much the same time, all-black baseball leagues attempted to take shape, first the Southern League of Colored Base Ballists in 1886, followed the next year by the National League of Colored Baseball Clubs, centered in Louisville, Kentucky. Neither league lasted more than a couple of weeks. The National League tried to eliminate the flaws of the Southern League by including clubs only from large (and mostly northern) cities, but it was too soon. Northern black populations were still tiny, and Jim Crow was just coming into his own. In 1887, the newly-crowned (white) National League World Champion St. Louis Browns refused to play an exhibition match against the Cuban Giants. The Browns were nearly unanimous and very clear on the issue, stating that the players "had no objection to playing against a white club, but they drew the color line strongly." The team held firm even when the Browns' owner threatened to release each and every player.[10]

But black baseball continued to grow, supplying an entertainment need within the increasingly segregated black community, providing an opportunity for black men to compete at the highest athletic levels their country would allow them. The most influential were the travelling teams, organizations that gypsied from town to town seeking competition and the funds to keep going. The strength of black baseball began to shift toward the Midwest, with its somewhat larger black resource base. In Adrian, Michigan, a local all-black team reached a sponsorship agreement with a local manufacturing company, becoming the Page Fence Giants. Bud Fowler assembled the squad, carefully choosing players not addicted to alcohol. These Giants began to travel in 1894, quickly developing a powerful reputation. There were also the Chicago Unions, later to morph into the Union Giants, and the New Orleans Pinchbacks—powerhouse teams doomed to roaming the countryside, occasionally meeting up with another for a more serious contest. New management took over the Cuban Giants, and soon there were two teams, the better players becoming the Cuban X Giants and extending their yearly tours beyond the East Coast to take on teams from the Midwest. By this time, the team name "Giants" had obviously become a codeword indicating that the team coming to town was composed of black players, unless they came from New York and were managed by John McGraw.[11]

Such growth was very exhilarating. And frustrating. Sol White counted nine fully professional American black teams operating on the East Coast in 1906, along with two teams of real Cubans, the Havana Stars and the Cuban Stars. The lack of formalized leagues or sanctioned championship playoffs meant that any number of black teams could claim to be the greatest of them all. Sometimes good teams would even avoid playing each other, unless they could dictate home field conditions so favorable that the opponent would deny the outcome had any meaning. In 1896, organizers set up a series of games pitting the best teams against one another, offering a top prize of $1,000. Even then, the Page Fence Giants (soon known as the Columbia Giants) and the Cuban Giants managed to avoid squaring off against one another. An East-West Colored Championship continued sporadically over the next two decades, but no one was really satisfied with the outcomes. There were too many asterisks.[12]

Deciding who was best was an important consideration for the men playing the game, but it was a small thing compared to the issues that really hampered black baseball. Black teams were experiencing some of the same problems that had beset organized baseball in its early years. White baseball (and it was purely white after 1889) had arrived at a competitive and financial system that would provide stability for the major and minor leagues for the next three-quarters of a century. For better and worse, organized baseball, with its leagues composed of stable teams from large cities, its formalized schedules, and its national labor agreement, would become the model that black baseball tried very hard to emulate. Things never went well for very long.

Sol White put his finger on the exact trouble. "The colored ball player should always look before he leaps," White wrote. "He is not in a position to demand the same salary as his white brother, as the difference in the receipts of their respective games are decidedly in favor of the latter; thousands attending games of the whites to hundreds of the blacks."[13] Simple demographics were the inescapable writing on the wall. The thousands of whites paying attendance at major league games guaranteed a capital flow that insured profits, paid respectable salaries, and built very large ball yards that attracted still greater attendance. Blacks, perhaps ten percent of the American population (and much the poorest), would never generate that kind of capital. Salaries would remain minimal, profits thin to vanishing, and large, black-owned venues a dream. Demographic reality not only made black baseball poor, it made it weak, subject to predatory scavenging by the white community. The color line never blocked the movement of money. With Jim Crow in full force by 1900, black baseball had no choice but to try and organize itself, for cooperation, for mutual protection, and for profit.

Organized baseball was the obvious model to work from. That model was purely a business proposition; major league owners sold baseball in the same way Carnegie sold steel and Swift sold sausages. At least a dozen fully professional teams took shape following the dominating procession of the Cincinnati Reds in 1869; the National Association of Professional Base Ball Players emerged just two years later. Leagues organized and as quickly floundered, bedeviled by management-labor issues that encouraged anarchy. Players jumped contracts and moved from team to team, chasing the best offers with impunity. Scheduling was a nightmare, as teams with larger fan bases often refused to return visits to smaller franchises for lack of financial incentive. Teams would break up in the middle of a season, unable to meet contract obligations. Playing conditions varied considerably from town to town. Even as popularity boomed and city populations came to identify more fully with the operations of home teams, making money became increasingly challenging.

The answer was monopoly, and a little thing called the reserve clause. In 1876, business magnate William Hulbert, owner of the Chicago White Sox, joined forces with pitching star and emerging sports entrepreneur Albert Spalding to force teams from eight cities to join the National League of Baseball Clubs. This was an amalgamation of clubs, not players—a crucial difference. The purpose was to stabilize baseball as a business proposition by guaranteeing the power of the club owners. Only clubs from larger cities would participate, and the teams would play official games against other league teams, no one else. League officials drew up season schedules, and teams failing to play scheduled games faced very heavy penalties, including expulsion. Most importantly, the teams agreed to honor one another's player contracts. Very soon, the National League would dictate a national agreement with the large number of smaller, minor leagues springing up across the country, obligating their team owners to honor player contracts as well. From this point forward, players became hired labor, contracting to perform athletic entertainment for club owners reaping the profits from the enterprise.

Rival leagues and player rebellions would challenge this arrangement over the next three decades, but the essential model survived them all. Organized baseball became the property of team owners, while players became salaried labor unable to control their own destinies. Club owners in fact strengthened their hold over the players by developing what was called the reserve system. The idea began in 1879 with an agreement among the ten club owners that each could identify five players on their season-ending rosters who would continue with the team the next year. No other team could negotiate with these designated players. The system expanded quickly, in two ways. Instead of just five players, the reserve came to include any and all players an owner wanted to retain. Any player, once signed to a contract, was reserved to that team for as long as the owner wanted him, whether the player signed additional contracts or not. One contract made the player the team's property for as long as they wanted him; there was no escape while national agreements held.

Formation of the National League brought a large measure of stability, though not complete peace. Rival leagues rose up to challenge the monopoly, with limited success. The players themselves, outraged by a classification plan that would severely limit their salaries, formed their own league in 1890; the circuit lasted a single season. The National League was in many ways its own worst enemy. Apart from the classification idea and other goofy plans to increase profits while destroying competition, the League allowed one of its most important articulated goals to slide: the ballpark experience. Baseball in the immediate post–Civil War had become a rough and tumble activity. Gambling was open and pervasive, game-fixing a serious problem, and crowds attending games often came to resemble mobs, threatening umpires and visiting players. Language got coarse, and only ladies of dubious virtue dared attend. The National League promised to clean up such vulgarity, and did so for a time, demonstrating the possibilities of baseball as a clean, family-oriented operation.[14]

Faced with rivals, faced with intensifying competition, National League baseball soon descended into roughness. Kicking—intimidating umpires, players, and opposition fans—became a common practice. The Baltimore Orioles of the 1890s, with Ned Hanlon as the manager and "Muggsy" McGraw the sharpest player, became masters of the art. The National League itself grew arrogant. The League in 1892 emerged the sole survivor from a clash of major leagues, absorbing clubs to create a 12-team circuit. They almost immediately began to behave as an unchecked monopoly, discarding four clubs and seriously entertaining plans to operate the League as a syndicate, with all the owners holding interests in all the clubs. The door was opened for yet another challenger, and one more bidding war for player contracts.[15]

The challenger was Ban Johnson, a former newspaper reporter who worked with castoff National League franchises operated by Charles Comiskey and Connie Mack in the 1890s to create the Western League, a high minors organization. That was just a preliminary. Drinking whiskey at a saloon in Cincinnati, Ban Johnson thought over the rowdyism and intimidation characterizing National League ballparks, and saw an opening. In 1901, he announced the transformation of the Western League into the American League, where play would be wholesome and clean, umpires respected, and families welcome. Over 100 National League players jumped to the eight American League clubs, and baseball war resumed. Peace came in just two years, as the National and American Leagues met and hammered out a new National Agreement. Monopoly was re-established, extending over two leagues and 16 teams residing in ten northeastern cities. The monopoly possessed a three-headed tyrant: the presidents of the two leagues and a third individual, chosen by agreement of the presidents. Ban Johnson was the real power. Major league baseball assumed a shape that would survive without real change for the next 50 years. If stability was the essential ingredient to a successful baseball business, the major leagues had undeniably achieved just that. One part of that stability was keeping the black players out. The new National Agreement did not simply form a major league monopoly that barred black participation; the pact wedded practically every small-town minor league team to that same policy. Ban Johnson saw no problem with that.[16]

The major leagues naturally became the system against which black baseball had to measure itself. Early in the 20th century, the black clubs were experiencing very much the same run of problems that had plagued organized baseball. Black players jumped contracts without reservation as more lucrative opportunities beckoned. Games at times became rowdy, both on the field and in the stands. Each team attempted to do its own scheduling; there was no central governance, no penalties for failure to keep agreements. The more powerful, financially-supported teams took unmerciful advantage of poorer local squads. Some teams abruptly disappeared, unable to meet obligations.

Closely related and critical to the problem of scheduling was the matter of booking. Very few black teams owned their own ball parks; most were dependent on fields ranging in quality from near pastures in remote rural settings to the occasional game in the large, newly constructed major league parks. The problem was that any venue large enough to provide the promise of a profitable attendance was controlled by a booking agent, a white booking agent demanding an exorbitant percentage of the gate. As long as black teams remained unorganized and independent, they could not muster enough muscle to face down the power of the agents, and profits, never plentiful, suffered much.[17]

There were other problems too, problems particular to the status of blacks in American society. The largest was media access. The early 20th century was the heyday of big city newspapers. Every major city had competing dailies, and their editors quickly learned that baseball sold papers. Game accounts, box scores, feature stories—every paper had them, pulling out all the stops to support the fortunes of the home team. The home white team. Black teams got almost no coverage in the metropolitan dailies—the team standings and schedules that tracked the fortunes and futures of major league clubs never extended to include black teams. Media indifference made it difficult for black clubs to build the fan base so critical to financial success. A few black newspapers tried to track the performance of leading black teams, but even that coverage was hit and miss. Leading black newspapers such as the *Pittsburgh Courier* and the *Chicago Defender* published weekly rather than daily, and sought a nationwide reading audience. There was little of the local rooting that boosted white teams. Black newspapers did not regularly assign reporters to cover games, and clubs often would not report if they did not win. Something as basic as a team's win-loss record was often a mystery. How many wins? Against which teams? How many losses are going unreported? Which games count, when it comes to identifying the best team? The white guys had a World Series and an identifiable, undisputed champion at the end of each season, beginning with 1905. Black baseball never achieved such finality.[18]

At first glance, the record-keeping problem may seem superficial, a disappointment more than an aggravation. Not so. Statistical tracking and increasingly sophisticated statistical analysis became woven into the fabric of baseball very early on. It took some time to develop such tried and true measures as the batting average, the RBI, and the earned run average, but all were in place by 1920, readily available to major league fans. Tavern arguments over who's better, who's best, generally hinged on such statistics. The inability to derive such measures reliably, much less get them printed in the black newspapers, hurt greatly. To this day, black performance is grounded more in legend than in actual numbers.[19]

Transportation and accommodation were further issues as Jim Crow grew new muscles early in the new century. Train travel made professional baseball possible, providing teams the opportunity to move from city to city to take up challenges. But trains were particular targets for "separate but equal" notions—white players rode in high style, while black teams were relegated to conditions anything but equal. It would take a lot of money to rectify that indignity. And hotels were a horror, bastions of Jim Crow segregation that guaranteed blacks second class or worse. A black player on a travelling team needed a tough temperament and a lot of patience; Jim Crow was militating against him with more and greater determination. Defeating his schemes seemed beyond possibility; it would take a lot of organization just to fight him to a standstill, to lead a respectable life.

Separate but equal. Society had fastened on that as the answer to the race question. What that meant, if you were a black man trying to establish professional baseball, was establishing a set of black institutions, patterned after the organizations that had stabilized the major league game. Blacks would have to have their own leagues, separate and maybe truly equal.

Most sources maintain that the initial black baseball leagues appeared in 1906, presumably meaning that these were the first leagues that actually survived longer than two weeks. The first grew out of the issues facing the more successful Eastern teams. The league, officially entitled the International League of Colored Baseball Clubs in America and Cuba, originally featured six teams centered mainly in New York and Philadelphia, including the Cuban X Giants and the Philadelphia Quaker Giants, along with two touring Cuban teams and two white teams. Clubs began to shuttle in and out almost immediately, but six teams did complete a schedule of games leading to a World's Colored Championship, won by Philadelphia. That October, the league assumed a different shape as the National Association of Colored Baseball Clubs of the United States, formed in Brooklyn and including some of the same teams. This too was a purely Eastern organization, created mainly to force members to honor one another's contract agreements and put an end to player jumping. "Property rights" was the operative phrase, as owners sought to emulate the reserve arrangements fully matured in organized ball. It was no go. Players continued to jump to teams outside the league, putting a strain on relationships among the league clubs. The National Association persevered for a few seasons, even extending their schedules to include games in Cuba and the Midwest, but there was too little cooperation, too much self-interest, and too much com-

petition from outside the ranks. By the close of the 1912 season, the first reasonably successful black league was dead.[20]

In the years leading up to the First World War, black baseball was a much healthier enterprise in the Midwest than in its original homes on the East Coast. Conditions were more favorable for one thing—black populations in New York and Philadelphia were still markedly small, while numbers in Chicago and other Midwestern cities had begun to grow with the Great Migration. Add to that a developing tradition of high-level competition among several teams; what emerged was the climate for a separate professional black league. The possibility was at once exhilarating and deeply depressing. A separate league represented a tantalizing opportunity for black enterprise and a surrender to the apartheid taking visible shape across America. The situation required a firm and determined organizational hand, someone who could break down the walls of self-interest that limited cooperation among the clubs and create an institution that might inspire the black community.

Enter Rube Foster.

Andrew Foster's career in black baseball tells the story of his sport in miniature. He was born in Texas in 1879 and

**Rube Foster, race man. Owner and manager of the Chicago American Giants, Foster long opposed the organization of any black baseball league. The Chicago race riots changed his mind. His Negro National League would seek complete separation from all white baseball institutions. (National Baseball Hall of Fame Library, Cooperstown, New York.)**

began his professional pitching career at age 18. There are those that claim he was the best pitcher of the 20th century; certainly he was just about unhittable on his best days. Reputation and popularity growing steadily, Foster came north in 1902, joining the best of the Midwestern teams: Frank Leland's Chicago Union Giants. Leland and Foster did not get on, and Foster soon left for an obscure opportunity in Otsego, Michigan. By 1903 he was in Philadelphia, mowing 'em down for the Cuban X Giants. The next season he jumped to the Philadelphia Giants, underscoring the most severe internal problem among the black teams, the inability to maintain a stable roster. As the game's best pitcher, Foster could change teams at will. Three years later, along with a few teammates, Foster found his way back to Chicago, rejoining Leland's Union Giants as player-manager. Ambitious and astute, Foster soon divided Leland's team in two, assuming control of the better players, rebuilding the roster (in part by stealing players from other teams) and embarking on a challenging but very lucrative barnstorming campaign. He was a very persuasive man; his teams never got less than half the gate for any game they played. By 1911, Foster's team, renamed the Chicago American Giants, were the powerhouse of Chicago. That year found Foster and Leland in court, disputing the distribution of profits from their divided enterprise. Resorting to a tactic that would become quite familiar, Foster aired his side of the story by writing an essay for the *Indianapolis Freeman*, advocating the need for greater organization while accusing Leland of "low, dirty, undermining tactics." Foster concluded by emphasizing a willingness "to co-operate with all in doing anything to uplift Negro baseball."[21]

In 1911, Rube Foster established himself as power broker in black baseball. Foster and white business partner John Schorling, a tavern-keeper who married White Sox owner Charlie Comiskey's daughter, purchased Comiskey's old ballpark at 39th and Wentworth when the Sox opened the new steel and concrete Comiskey Park, which seated 28,800. Initially renamed Schorling Park and later known as American Giants Park, the all-wooden venue grew from 9,000 seats to eventually hold 18,000—tiny for a major league franchise, enormous for a black club. With that kind of clout, Foster was able to become his own booking agent, dictating schedules while ensuring a larger profit margin. He continued to strengthen his roster, at the same time lending money, players, and advice to help launch other black franchises. By this time, Rube Foster was more businessman than player, a well-to-do owner and agent as well as manager. Pitching less and less with each passing season, he finally gave up the mound for good in 1917. Black baseball was flourishing; there was steady talk of establishing a league. Much of that talk revolved around Rube Foster's power.

Beauregard Mosely, another business associate of Foster, tried to pull together a league of eight Midwestern black teams as early as 1910, but the effort never got off the ground. Every year brought new rumors, new advocacies. Black teams continued to derive large amounts of cash playing white semi-pro teams, but the desire to create a completely separate race enterprise grew with each season. Peering into the future of black baseball in 1916, *Freeman* reporter David Wyatt foresaw a league where "No white men are to have anything pertaining to a controlling interest." It was a vision Rube Foster did not share. In an interview with the *Freeman* published in May 1914, Foster held out the hope that "Before another baseball season rolls around colored ball players, a score of whom are equal in ability to the brightest stars in the big league teams, will be holding down jobs in organized baseball." In 1914, the appearance of the Federal League, vying to become a third major league, created a brief yet brisk demand for quality players. Might such a demand open the market to blacks? Sure that integration was on the near horizon, Foster was not about to encourage black separatism.[22]

The aftermath of the First World War shattered his illusion.

Those years proved pivotal for Jim Crow. Black soldiers returned from Europe disillusioned and angry. Drafted to serve their country, they were segregated into service and supply units, placed in danger zones yet barred from combat. Returning home expecting a recognition of their rights, they met instead a more determined resistance than ever. Woodrow Wilson's government suppressed leftist radicalism—including any stand for racial equality—while the Ku Klux Klan got going again. Lynchings mounted. The message was clear and stark: the color line would not only persist, it was clawing its way still deeper into America's essence. American apartheid. A series of ugly race riots ensued, the most infamous the deadly 1919 confrontation in Rube Foster's Chicago. Thirty-eight people died in explosive mob scenes, punctuated by a series of bombings in black neighborhoods. Segregation, violently enforced, etched itself into Chicago's soul. The hopeful sojourners of the Great Migration, together with their sons and daughters, would be caged in a ghetto on the Southside. Illinois Governor Frank O. Lowden saw such separation as a solution to the violence. Black people read the message scrawled on the tenement wall. Very soon, Northern blacks were reasserting their own faith in separatism, inspired by Marcus Garvey's Back to Africa campaign and the Universal Negro Improvement Association, along with the cultural explosion of the Harlem Renaissance.[23]

Rube Foster and his Chicago American Giants were barnstorming in Michigan when the Chicago race riot broke out early in July. Scheduled to return to the city, Foster instead led his team farther east in search of games. There was reason. The State Militia, called out after several days of unabated violence, manned strategic points close to the battle zone fronting Wentworth and Indiana Streets. One contingent was stationed at American Giants Park, at 39th and Wentworth. Race war was bivouacked in Rube Foster's front yard.[24]

Foster wrote several pieces for the *Chicago Defender* in the winter following the Chicago riot, fervently advocating creation of a black league. Though he never once referred to the summer's violence, to argue that his thinking was not affected by events would be to strain belief in coincidence beyond any reasonable breaking point. Hopes rooted in the Great Migration, the flood of new industrial jobs, and the opportunities for war heroism were entirely smashed; Jim Crow stalked Northern streets, mocking any talk of equality. Foster let go his optimistic faith that blacks would find their way into Organized Ball. There was no other choice, not in 1920. Rube Foster became a Race Man.[25]

Modern scholars, influenced by the triumph of integration after World War II, try very hard to sugarcoat the turn in Rube Foster's thinking in 1919, often citing (without provenance) his observation that "We have to be ready when the time comes for integration." Supposedly, Foster "urged blacks to maintain a high level of play so that when the white doors were open at last, they would be ready." To make Rube Foster a hero to modern eyes, analysts do their best to portray him as an ongoing advocate of integration, even as he molded black baseball into a separatist entity. Understandable though it is, the argument is a shaky one, more a willful refusal to acknowledge the force of American apartheid than an effort to understand Foster's motivation. Beginning in 1919, Foster worked night and day to establish a viable, independent enterprise on his side of the color line, a fully black business venture such as Booker T. Washington or W. E. B. DuBois might well applaud. If Rube Foster was organizing a Negro baseball league to prepare blacks to play with the white guys, he hid that purpose exceedingly well. In the winter of 1919–1920, he outlined several essential reasons to create a Negro National League. Never once did he mention prepping black players for Organized Ball.[26]

A number of large contingencies coincided to make a black baseball league really possible in 1920, after so many failures. Chief of these was the Great Migration itself, a massive shifting of the black population into concentrated Northern urban settings, where they formed a nucleus of support, a market for black teams. By World War II, half of America's black population lived in Northern cities. At the same time, for completely unconnected reasons, white semi-pro baseball was dying out. World War I enlistments broke up many teams, and most did not revive after 1918. Exhibitions against these semi-pro teams had been a major item in black team ledgers; they needed an alternate source of income. Attendance at black team games had fallen off; some kind of spark to draw the fans was imperative. There were in 1920 enough viable franchises to create a firm financial footing for a black league. The owners gathered at meetings in Chicago and Detroit to discuss the possibilities.[27]

While negotiations ensued, Rube Foster outlined the problems facing black ball clubs, and the potential benefits of a league, in a series of articles "written exclusively for the *Chicago Defender*," entitled "Pitfalls of Baseball." He pulled few punches. Operating costs were high; American Giants Park required more than $1,300 a week just to maintain, and half the gate went to the visiting team. Player salaries cost a bundle because owners were foolish enough to offer players exorbitant salaries to jump contracts. (Foster understood the attractions of jumping exceedingly well, having jumped a few times himself.) A league where the teams agreed to honor one another's contracts would bring an end to jumping, but would also assist players by promoting financial stability. Better business practices could only benefit all concerned. "Only in uniform strength is the permanent success," Foster warned, "organized effort our only salvation."[28]

Day to day practical business issues meant much to Foster, but there were more important considerations at work. If the current morass of black baseball organization were to continue, he warned in early January, most of the future profits would find their way into white people's pockets. For black baseball to survive, there would have to be some serious investment, in player salaries, in equipment, in advertising and record keeping, in ballparks. A black league would create a more stable vehicle to attract and secure black investment. Without that outlay, much of the necessary money would come from white entrepreneurs, booking agents especially.

The following week, Foster warmed to this theme. Black baseball owed its fans a continued and larger success, "based solely on their loyalty to the Race." Foster drove the point home, emphasizing that "I have fought against delivering Colored baseball into the control of whites, thinking that with a show of patronage from the fans we would get together." A league may have been a logical business step, but the alliance was equally a step forward in determining the future of black people. Foster used the last essay in the *Defender* series to underscore the "lack of cooperation" between the Midwestern teams, largely controlled by black operators, and the Eastern teams, under the thumb of white booking agent Nat C. Strong. The choice of futures could not be made more clear.[29]

By strength of will, determination, diplomacy, and persuasion, Foster managed to construct a black league on the foundations of his growing baseball empire. The Negro National League, generally recognized as the first successful black league, organized in Kansas City in February 1920. Foster, along with Indianapolis owner C. I. Taylor, was the driving force. The League originally numbered eight mostly Midwestern teams, including clubs located in Dayton, Ohio, Detroit (another team Foster actually owned), Indianapolis, Kansas City, St. Louis, and two from Chicago. The eighth team, the Cuban Stars, had no home base. Foster himself became

League president while maintaining active control of the Chicago American Giants. Fan response was heartening—as many as a million patrons may have witnessed Negro National League games in 1920.

Rube Foster was very determined that the NNL would be a black operation. If the races had to be separate in Jim Crow America, Foster would make them really separate—with equal opportunities. The League would control its own players, its own scheduling, and above all, its own booking. The profits would flow to black ownership, a race enterprise free from white parasites and white meddling. Foster was so determined on the issue he tried hard to keep the Kansas City Monarchs out of the League. Apart from the American Giants, the Monarchs were the most successful black team operating, a powerful and popular force that commanded respect throughout the Midwest. An alliance including Chicago and Kansas City would make the NNL the most powerful entity black baseball could create, but Foster had his doubts. The Monarchs were owned by a white man, a shrewd entrepreneur named J. L. Wilkinson.[30]

Apart from his color, there was nothing to be said against Wilkinson. Like Foster, Wilkinson maintained a first class operation, travelling in Pullman cars and staying in the best places possible. He always insisted on complete professionalism, enforcing a dress code and assessing fines for poor behavior. Wilkinson entered professional baseball in 1911, operating a travelling novelty "All Nations Team" that included blacks, whites of various religions and nationalities, and one female player, christened "Carrie Nation." When the Great War and its aftermath altered the racial landscape, Wilkinson (with the help of Casey Stengel) adjusted by recruiting some skillful black players. The Monarchs were the best black team outside Chicago in 1919, and unusually loyal to their owner. Wilkinson had earned a widespread reputation for honesty and fairness, paying top dollar for good play. Foster reluctantly acknowledged the value of a competing and well-run Midwestern powerhouse, and eventually he bowed to necessity, inviting Kansas City to join the League as a charter franchise. Wilkinson (initially misidentified as J. W. Wilkerson in the *Chicago Defender*) became league treasurer. That there was reluctance to include him was a measure of the racial chasm America had created for itself by 1920. Wilkinson was the only white owner in Foster's Negro National League. Apparently, Foster never discovered that Wilkinson's business partner, Tom Baird, was a registered member of the Ku Klux Klan. Probably Wilkinson did not know either.[31]

Rube Foster proved to be the Negro Leagues' greatest friend and its greatest burden, setting a pattern of operations that would hobble all the subsequent black leagues. He strove to make the NNL as exclusively black as he could, though an effort to use only black umpires frustrated him. His power as a booking agent was an enormous asset. With the combined buying power of eight teams behind him, he was able to negotiate far better terms for stadium fees than any of the teams could have commanded alone. Three of the league teams (including his own) made serious money that first season, and Foster came to the assistance of floundering franchises, sometimes reaching for his own wallet. There is not the slightest doubt that the league president wanted to see every team succeed. And yet, the Chicago American Giants somehow seemed to benefit from league operations just a little bit more than anyone else. As early as 1922, newspapers were decrying his "czar-like methods." Each league team had to buy its equipment through Foster, presumably to establish economies of scale. Foster got ten percent of the gate for every league game, as a league maintenance fee. Foster went so far as to dictate when teams could use their best pitchers, always reserving them for Sundays, when crowds were largest. When it came to player availability, league decisions always seem to funnel the best to Chicago. The American Giants won the first three Negro National League championships. The league schedule did not hurt, either. For inexplicable reasons, the American Giants played more home games than any other team, and almost never visited Kansas City. Competing owners suspected Foster's real aim in running the league was to establish his own booking empire through the Midwest and the South, rivaling Nat Strong.

Forming a league created a union of strengths that enabled black teams to combat the myriad problems each had experienced, but it did not put an end to them. There was still the issue of uneven scheduling: in 1920, the American Giants posted an official record of 32–13, while the last-place Chicago Giants went 4–24, a difference of 17 league games played. Game coverage was sporadic at best as the major dailies simply ignored league contests and black newspapers made uneven efforts, resulting in poor publicity and poor attendance at some venues. The eight teams made some efforts to honor one another's contracts at least during the season, but maintaining a roster was still a challenge. Eastern teams raided NNL teams at every opportunity. In the middle of it all stood Foster, his league a success in no small part because of his personal popularity, bounded with troubles at least partially his own making. Rube Foster the league president was unable to control Rube Foster the team owner and general manager, and that fostered understandable resentment.[32]

The Negro National League rode the nation's wave of prosperity through the first seven years of its existence. Encouraged by the success in the Midwest, Nat Strong persuaded six Eastern teams to try again, forming the Mutual Association of Eastern Colored Baseball Clubs late in 1922. Ed Bolden's Hilldale Daisies proved the dominant force among the eight eventual entrants, outlasting teams from Brooklyn, New York City, Atlantic City, Baltimore, Washington, and Harrisburg, Pennsylvania. Several of these franchises were white-owned, inspiring Rube Foster to disparage the league's lack of racial purity and the opportunities for white exploitation. He did not hesitate to steal players for his own league. The champions of the Negro National League and the Eastern Colored League did manage to play a championship series amidst much wrangling in 1924, 1925, and 1926, interpreted as a sign of "race progress." Even some white newspapers gave space to these contests.[33]

The championships illuminated yet another problem black baseball could not fully address: regionality. Unlike the two major leagues, each with teams spread throughout the northeast from Boston to Chicago, the Negro Leagues tended to maintain separate regional identities, seldom travelling into one another's domains to match up. The major obstacle was transportation costs—even Jim Crow cars came expensive—and poverty posed still another problem. Team owners calculated that most patrons in their home venues could not afford to buy tickets for more than one game, so each championship series moved from city to city, wandering the landscape in search of a gate. More than anything, the championships seemed to underscore an element of regional jealousy black baseball found difficult to overcome.[34]

For the breadth of a moment, it seemed these black leagues were an answer properly fitted to the realities of American society. True, the gains were uneven, the leagues a little unstable, the problems persistent. All new institutions suffer growing pains. Surely with the economy booming and northern black urban populations expanding, black baseball could continue to develop the economic possibilities a racist society could offer. Separate certainly, without any real equality at all, but still an opportunity, a chance to provide skilled athletic entertainment to fans black and white, and to make real money in a legitimate enterprise.

American prosperity in the 1920s was an illusion. So was the success of the first Negro Leagues.

Just as Rube Foster's baseball enterprise mirrored the race determination of blacks during the Roaring Twenties, so too his sudden demise reflected the fortunes of his community. In 1926, Foster suffered a grim accident, inhaling large quantities of gas from a leaking pipe at an Indianapolis hotel. He recovered, but was never quite the same afterward, displaying increasingly erratic behavior. Brain damage perhaps, exacerbated by the pressures of running a baseball league that had begun to bleed money. He became a danger to himself and others, and friends committed him to the Illinois State Mental Asylum in Kankakee in 1926. In November 1930, Frank Young, writing for *Abbot's Monthly*, warned that "the man who gave his time, money and health for the upbuilding of the national game among his own people today is a sick man." Young made no mention of Foster working in any way for integration. His legacy was a black baseball league, run by and large by black people, for the profit and enjoyment of black society. Andrew "Rube" Foster died a Race Man, in December 1930.[35]

His league died beside him. Not because its founder and leader was gone, though that was crippling enough. The Negro National League began to list as early as 1926, as the less financially successful teams found the going harder and harder. Shaky franchises weakened the structure of the whole; the league scrambled to meet obligations. Then the stock market crashed. Blacks, always the last hired, were often the first fired. The disaster struck hardest at the most defenseless, and black people, black enterprises, were especially vulnerable. Disposable cash mostly disappeared, attendance at ball games dropped like a stone, and already strapped ball clubs faced dissolution. The Negro National League struggled to keep going, but with a third of the nation out of work, the situation was hopeless. The Negro National League evaporated in 1932.

The Depression proved an enormous disaster for all forms of recreation, white and black. The major leagues struggled on, reducing salaries, shaving expenses, doing all they could to protect the structure. Those leagues survived, but they did not much change, just holding on to what they had. The Negro Leagues, so much closer to the edge, had no chance. The Eastern Colored League disintegrated before the Depression even struck. The death of the Negro National League was a staggering blow black ball had to absorb. A few black teams kept going by relentless barnstorming, making a few dollars wherever they could, playing games against local teams throughout the hinterlands, amateur, pro, and semi-pro, black or white, so long as people were willing to pay something to watch. The games could be delicate affairs. The travelling teams fielded players no local nine could possibly match, but it was in the interests of the barnstormers to keep the scoring low, the games competitive. No hard feelings, no racial animosities. A few teams resorted to clowning to broaden the spectacle, though black players generally abhorred the idea. Clowning—tap dancing, funny shoes, acting out in whiteface— was demeaning and stereotypical, just what audiences expected of black entertainers on the road. Most black clubs and ballplayers took their game very seriously. Satchel Paige was highly entertaining and provocative, but he never clowned.[36]

J. L. Wilkinson's Kansas City Monarchs, four-time champions of Foster's Negro National League, withdrew after the 1930 season to survive as a travelling independent, proving exceptionally adept. Their competitive reputation served them well on the long, long road, and Wilkinson improved their marketability by developing a system of portable lights, enabling them to become the first top-level team to feature night games. Working people could attend.

The lights doubled and tripled potential attendance, and often made it possible for the Monarchs to play two road games in one day. Wilkinson somehow made enough money to meet every payroll during black baseball's long drought, while his lights pointed to baseball's future.[37]

If times were tough for team owners, imagine what it was to play under conditions so harsh. Judging from the large number of oral memoirs gathered through the years, black baseball was a hard-nosed sport starting off, with beanballs, spike-high slides and rough tags all part of the fun. Willie Wells, one of the greatest shortstops of the 20th century, began his career in 1925. "Oh, it was rough when I came along," he remembered. "See, that's the way we played. Those guys would spike. Decent slides? There were no decent slides." Wells became the first professional to experiment with a batting helmet, after he got beaned in 1937. Newt Allen, who began playing second base for the Monarchs in 1926, agreed with Wells. "I was pretty bad playing ball," he admitted. "Yes, I was pretty bad—run over a man, throw at him. I did a lot of wrong things." The thing was, Newt Allen had a reputation for being *less* rough than most.[38]

Add to the rough play the grueling demands of constant travel on back roads through town after rural town, sometimes on dilapidated buses, sometimes in ancient and beaten automobiles. Getting to the next town close to midnight, then spending hours finding places to sleep, what with Jim Crow already in residence. Sometimes the Kansas City Monarchs camped out. It was a hard life, and it bred a rugged kind of player, rough and tumble guys given to hard vices—heavy drinking, gambling, skirt-chasing. "Those other guys would get them a bottle of whiskey and they'd go off to the racetrack," pitcher Ted Page remembered. The great Buck Leonard was still more pointed. "Ballplayers a long time ago, their characters were low, they'd do anything to win," he said. Later in the same interview, Leonard became more specific. "But if you could play ball, regardless of your character, you could come in our leagues. You could be a drinker, you could be staying with another man's wife, you could be gambling, whatever you wanted to be—if you could play ball, you could stay with us." Baseball was deep in the blood; no one less than fully in love with the game would commit himself to such a gypsy existence. Sometimes it took a lot of medicine just to get to the next day.[39]

The search for the next dollar, the next meal never ceased. Lots of folks travelled the country during the Great Depression, searching for always elusive work, searching a little for adventure, some of them. Black barnstormers at least had a skill to sell, but the chase never seemed to end. After a spring, a summer, and an autumn spent swallowing road dust and playing games before all kinds of crowds, many players made their way southward for the winter, playing ball some more. A few possessed no established home; travelling endlessly in the search for the next game, sometimes playing more than 250 in a year.[40]

Black players began pursuing winter ball opportunities long before 1920, initially in Florida, later in Cuba, then California. Sometimes entire Northern teams sought games in the warmer weather, Rube Foster's American Giants included. After winter ball, black teams would barnstorm their way north to begin a new season. These Southern exhibitions were important, not so much for the little money they brought, but for attracting new talent. Much of America's black population was still living in the South in the 1920s. Northern teams playing games in Southern towns was a way to advertise an opportunity.[41]

More often in winter, Florida teams would expand their rosters to take on a few of the more talented individual Northern players. Eventually, horizons expanded. A few players found their way to Cuba before 1900, blazing a trail that became steadily more attractive as Jim Crow ossified and the Depression dried up America's money supply. Familiarity with Cuban players toiling in the states helped to break down the natural reluctance to play in foreign climes, and American blacks soon found the tropical atmosphere a balm to their senses. Certainly there was racial discrimination in Cuba, but it was not so manifest on the ball field. Players of all shades played on the same teams with little rancor. Skill level was high, fans appreciative, games competitive—all in a winter paradise. "Before Castro, you couldn't beat Cuban baseball, couldn't beat it," Othello Renfro insisted. "That was the best, the strongest league you ever want to see." A few white Americans eventually joined the action, with remarkably few incidents. Life was not perfect—Cubans denied access to black people, native and American, at the finer restaurants and hotels, and the best beaches. The country was catering more and more to tourists. white American tourists. But Cuban ball was at least a little color-blind, especially in contrast to America's Jim Crow conditions. Pleasant winter ball experiences encouraged players to return. Blacks might play the Negro League season, then head south to collect more money, playing a full calendar year of baseball. Some American blacks left their native country altogether, finding greater opportunity—and some measure of equality—in Cuba or (later) in Mexico.[42]

What animosity existed in Cuba derived not so much from race prejudice, as from nationality. Black and white, American ballplayers were treated royally during their months in the Caribbean, often receiving significantly higher salaries than Cuban natives. The Cubans resented such discrimination, and made their point with a few headhunting incidents. When Ted Page managed two hits in two at-bats against Lefty Tiant (father of Luis), a Tiant fastball struck Page on the temple. "When we'd play the Cubans they would always throw at me," Page recalled. Years later, American blacks would remember that.[43]

Eventually, the attractions of Latin America became a threat to Negro Leagues baseball in the United States. Serious conflict initiated in 1937, when a baseball tournament in the Dominican Republic robbed the American black leagues of some of their best players in mid-season. Between May and July, at least 11 Negro Leagues stars, including Satchel Paige, Josh Gibson, Cool Papa Bell, Sam Bankhead, Showboat Thomas, and Chet Brewer, jumped their teams to accept paydays in the Dominican Republic. The pay scale ranged from $800 to $2,500. By the standards of the depression, these were huge mounds of cash, just for a few weeks playing in the tropics. Still, there was some danger involved. The tournament had political implications. "Unidentified backers" (the American Sugar Company) bankrolled the American ringers on behalf of Dominican dictator Rafael Trujillo, after his chief political rival hired a bunch of Cuban ringers, who were also playing in the American Negro Leagues. There were guns, and jails, and not-so-veiled intimidations. Satchel Paige was very glad to win and get out of town.[44]

Baseball in the Caribbean grew season by season, as more and more Latin American countries embraced the game and developed leagues. By the late 1930s, American blacks could choose to play for teams in Cuba, Mexico, Venezuela, Puerto Rico, Panama, or the Dominican Republic. A Caribbean World Series begun in the 1940s intensified the bidding for American stars. A few highly skilled players—the Satchel Paiges, Josh Gibsons, Cool Papa Bells of the black baseball world—eventually found baseball in Latin America more steady and more lucrative than any opportunity at home. One more threat to the survival of the Negro Leagues.[45]

Those Leagues began to resurrect themselves very soon after their deaths in 1926 and 1932, with some new management, a lot of the same old troubles, and some new issues that made matters still more controversial. Rube Foster's work had created a pattern of emphasis on racial pride that survived his passing; the new leagues would do their best to continue his model.

An East-West League organized in the vacuum left by the NNL in 1932, but folded after just half a season. That same year, a Negro Southern League tried to make a go, but that was sheer and utterly unjustified optimism. There were 11 teams, eight from Southern cities, including Atlanta, Birmingham, and Little Rock. Distances were long, expenses high. Truly crippling were the Jim Crow laws that prevented black teams from playing against whites in most Southern states. That killed the barnstorming that normally brought supplemental funds as teams moved across the map. Little Rock and Atlanta dropped out very early; the remaining teams played a schedule of roughly 40 games, then called it quits.[46]

A new Negro National League arose from the ashes in 1933, this time featuring teams from Chicago and Nashville (both refugees from the recently abandoned Southern Negro League), along with Pittsburgh, Baltimore, Detroit, Columbus, and Homestead. This was the first northern league to cast so wide a net, with teams from the East Coast and the Midwest attempting to compete. The distances between cities could only complicate logistical issues when money was tight, but the League did assume a more national flavor—for a brief moment.

Three teams dropped out after one year. Four others took their places, mainly from the East. The Negro National League would grind on for 15 more seasons, becoming more and more an exclusively Eastern enterprise. The Homestead Grays got thrown out midway through the first year, returning under new co-ownership two seasons later to dominate the league for nine straight campaigns. Beginning in 1940, the Grays would play much of their home schedule in Washington D.C., making Homestead one more East Coast team. Eventually the League would comprise the Grays, two teams from New York City, one from Newark, one from Baltimore and another from Philadelphia. What had begun as a national league in more than name had become one more incarnation of an East Coast Negro League. Teams played a league schedule usually of 50–60 games—official contests varied in number from season to season and team to team. The rest of the considerably long baseball season was devoted to barnstorming, playing the extra games that could balance a budget—sometimes two and, on Sundays, even three contests a day. Occasionally, scheduled League games got cancelled in favor of more lucrative exhibitions. The Depression may have eased after 1933, but the financial pinch certainly did not go away. Not for blacks teams trying to meet payroll obligations. With rosters carrying just 16 to 18 players, owners still paid out roughly $4,000 a month in salaries, while booking agents routinely skimmed ten percent of the gate.[47]

It was not simply the scarcity of cash that made the second incarnation of the Negro Leagues so different; it was the source of the new investment money that became available. The guiding genius of the new Negro National League was not a businessman with a strong standing in his community and a desire to finance wholesome entertainment, nor was he a former ballplayer with a fire to compete. Gus Greenlee was a bootlegger and a numbers man, a crook seeking legitimacy and public respect by sponsoring black professional baseball. He was clever, aggressive and very competitive, and he was tainted in a way that would much influence the eventual integration of organized ball.

Do not misunderstand. Whatever his antecedents, Gus Greenlee was an undisguised blessing for ball players and many others struggling to continue through the Depression. Based in Pittsburgh, Greenlee operated a numbers racket that generated as much as $100,000 a week. He had a payroll to meet and protection to maintain, but he also possessed a capital surplus, which made him a rarity among blacks in the early 1930s. He was a generous and influential man, genuine in his charity. The Crawford Grill, the club he opened on Pittsburgh's Wylie

Avenue, became a center for big-name black musicians in the heyday of jazz. He sponsored boxers as well as ballplayers, musicians as well as politicians. For a brief moment, Gus Greenlee stood at the center of black culture, bankrolling its possibilities, a much-respected man. It is more an indictment of American society that Greenlee and so many other black civic leaders had to accumulate their funds on the shady side of the law. It was pretty much the only side open to them.

In 1931 a local semi-pro black teams calling themselves the Crawfords approached "Mr. Big," asking Greenlee to sponsor them. Grasping an opportunity to add a veneer of respectability to his operations, Greenlee obliged—on a scale no one could have imagined. Within a year's time, he had financed—at a cost of at least $75,000—a complete renovation of the ball diamond, constructing a wholly black-owned steel and concrete stadium he called Greenlee Field. This was the first stadium to be fully equipped with lights—6,000 could watch a ballgame played at night. By this time, he was recruiting new talent for the Crawfords, players hailing from well beyond Pittsburgh. Some of the greatest stars in Negro Leagues history donned his uniforms—names such as Josh Gibson, Cool Papa Bell, Oscar Charleston, Judy Johnson, and Satchel Paige. The Crawfords quickly became a powerhouse, the nucleus of a revived Negro National League. Like Rube Foster before him, Greenlee developed enough muscle with his stadium and his connections to stare down the booking agents. That was the key to any league's success.

As League President, Greenlee was unable to avoid the same pitfalls that had so injured league operations under Foster. He set an ambitious agenda, striving to establish a professional élan comparable to the majors. He did his best to insist on fair and honest record keeping, but he remained a partisan and grimly determined team owner, and therefore a president who could never rise above the fray. He owned the Crawfords, he owned the Detroit Stars (who lasted one season), and he was assuredly propping up others with large infusions of cash. Every front office decision seemed to favor his teams, every adjustment made their chances of winning that much greater. In the new Negro National League's very first season, the Pittsburgh Crawfords contended to the very end, falling just short to Robert Cole's American Giants of Chicago. But wait! The American Giants had played a few league games that maybe should not count? Gus Greenlee, owner of the Crawfords, appealed the case to Gus Greenlee, President of the League. Sure enough, the president struck the questionable games from the record, making the Crawfords League champions.

That sort of thing went on for five seasons, until a double whammy brought a sudden end to the Greenlee domain. First was a business disaster of fearful magnitude—a popular betting number actually came in, forcing Mr. Big to pay out thousands and thousands in cash, crippling the racket. Then his best players deserted him for the Dominican Republic, drawn by the huge salaries the dictator Trujillo offered because he just had to win. Greenlee struggled to hang on, even banning the nomads from returning to his league. An empty gesture—how could you ban Josh Gibson or Satchel Paige when every owner knows they will fill the stands? Gus Greenlee was finished as a power by 1939. They even tore down his stadium.[48]

He did leave a legacy, a tradition that outlived his own power and gave focus and shape to black culture as the Depression wore on. In July 1933, two black journalists, Roy Sparrow and Bill Nunn, dreamed up the idea of a black All-Star Game, patterned after the newly-inaugurated major league contest. The two envisioned a North v. South game at Yankee Stadium, to support charity. Nothing came of that, but they did manage to sell Greenlee on the concept. He made it his own. Recognizing that the black fan base was much larger in the Midwest, Greenlee worked with Robert Cole, owner of the Chicago American Giants, to rent Chicago's Comiskey Park for a game on September 10. Profits would go to Greenlee and to Nashville Elite Giants owner Tom Wilson, who together were expending most of the cash to keep the Negro National League a going concern.[49]

The first East-West All-Star Game was a rousing success. From the beginning, this was more than a game, much more than an exhibition. Comiskey Park saw the origins of a cultural event as important as any in American black history to that time. Fans came from as far away as New York City, New Orleans, and Wichita, Kansas, to see the greatest assemblage of black baseball talent ever coaxed onto a ball field. The fans themselves elected the players, checking off thousands of ballots supplied by the nationally circulating black weekly newspapers, the *Chicago Defender* and the *Pittsburgh Courier*. Almost all the chosen players came out of the newly formed Negro National League, mostly from the Crawfords and the American Giants. Twenty thousand people, an audience almost entirely black, saw the duly elected stars play that first game, a tight contest that turned sloppy, the Western stars winning, 11–7.

The East-West Game very rapidly became the centerpiece for all the Negro Leagues represented. The Leagues themselves might be unstable and unpredictable, the ownership a little shady, the players occasionally disloyal, but for one day out of each season, the stars came out and the game glowed. This was black baseball's anchor. League championship series seemed mired in controversy and some indifference before and after play, but the All-Star Games in Chicago were completely serious business. The players came to play all-out, to show their talents to the nation, to win. And blacks came from everywhere to watch, enjoy, and celebrate a triumph for their race, when race meant everything. On the rare occasions when white America paid any attention to black baseball, it was the East-West Game that drew them. Whatever else may be said about Gus Greenlee, this game was his greatest invention.[50]

Greenlee's most obvious victim in his rise to influence and authority was Cumberland Posey, owner of the other Pittsburgh area black team, the Homestead Grays. Posey had started playing for black teams back in 1911, and gained financial control of the Grays in the early 1920s. The Depression drained him dry, and he sold several of his best players, including Josh Gibson, to Greenlee's Crawfords. Posey was instrumental in trying to organize the East-West League after the collapse of the old NNL, but 1932 was the very depth of the Depression. Only racketeers had money. Posey's Grays joined the new Negro National League the next year, but got accused of tampering with two Detroit Stars players. Greenlee not only tossed Homestead out of the League; he banned the remaining League teams from playing any games at all against the Grays.[51]

Cum Posey was nowhere near finished. He went out and found his own racketeer, one Sonny Jackson, by all accounts a very tough guy. With Jackson's deep pockets behind him, Posey began rebuilding and by 1937 the Homestead Grays were a force. Gus Greenlee stumbled. Cum Posey was there to repurchase Josh Gibson for the considerable sum of $2,500. Add Buck Leonard and Cool Papa Bell to the mix, and Posey had a team that would finish at the top of the Negro National League standings eight times in nine seasons through 1945. Though they remained the Homestead Grays, the team spread its wings, taking advantage of an offer to play half their home games at Washington's Griffith Stadium. Washington had the largest black population of any Northern city at the time; the Grays pulled in as many as 30,000 per game, often outdrawing the major league Washington Senators. Cumberland Posey profited,

Sonny Jackson profited, and the enigmatic Nationals owner Clark Griffith profited. Cum Posey was the most powerful man in black baseball by 1940, but he was every bit as ineffectual as Foster or Greenlee when it came to making the Negro Leagues fully professional. Too many owners still looked to self-interest first.[52]

Self-interest came naturally. Several team owners were accustomed to competing on much tougher playing fields than any grassy pasture surrounded by a fence. There was Tenny Blount, owner of the Detroit Stars, Baron Wilkins, who owned the New York Bacharachs, Dick Kent, with the St. Louis Stars, James Semler, operator of New York's Black Yankees, Tom Wilson in Nashville, Robert Cole, who took over the Chicago American Giants, Alex Pompez, and Abe Manley. All gambling men. In fact, every NNL team owner was somehow involved in the rackets. Most were well-respected individuals in their communities, and good to their players. Semler and Cole were the exceptions, hard-bitten guys no one could trust.[53]

Alex Pompez, a Florida native who spent most of his adult life in New York City, learned the essentials of numbers racketeering alongside Gus Greenlee in Cuba. Pompez supported a string of black baseball clubs, beginning with the Cuban Stars in 1916. He became especially adept at drawing Latino ballplayers to America's Negro Leagues, eventually attempting to monopolize their services. Opposing owners and journalists suspected his goal was to field an all–Latino team to square off against American blacks. In 1927, charges of racism flew. Depression setbacks forced Pompez to devote full time to his numbers. He dissolved the Cuban Stars in 1930, after trying for two years to sell the team. Five years of illegal gambling earned him enough to revive an interest in baseball. Pompez not only established a new team—the New York Cubans—but also lavished sums on refurbishing the Dyckman Oval, where his team played their home games. Apparently his rackets did a little too well, as Pompez had to take it on the lam to Mexico when New York State Attorney General Thomas Dewey began to scrutinize his activities. Pompez eventually turned state's evidence, testifying at length against the mob. After that, he limited himself to running his baseball team, very fortunate still to be drawing breath.[54]

Abe Manley, racketeer banker from Camden, New Jersey, began burnishing his public image by investing in local ball clubs in 1929. He threw in with the big-time in 1935, assuming ownership of the Newark Dodgers. Manley tried briefly and disastrously to move the team to Brooklyn's Ebbets Field before returning to New Jersey to become the Newark Eagles. Abe was a married man by this time, and even if Effa Manley was invariably careful to insist that her husband was primarily responsible for the team's success, her role should not be understated. If Abe Manley was the owner and the one intimately involved with the players' well-being, Effa was the general manager, overseeing the team's business fortunes. In 12 seasons, the Eagles finished below .500 in League competition just once (the worst war year, 1944), and finished first in the League's last two seasons, 1946 and 1947. By that time, major league teams were taking a considered interest in her top players. Effa Manley was an influential and sometimes irritating voice in NNL circles, taking stands to protect the players and professionalize the enterprise. She would have an essential role in the process of integration before all was said and done.[55]

Although the Negro National League operated at a net loss, attendance grew with each season between 1933 and 1937; plainly black baseball was as popular as people could afford. The hardscrabble survival of the League gave courage to Midwestern clubs doing their best to outlast the Depression. Barnstorming paid the bills, or most of them, but it was a hellish life, filled with uncertainty and soul-demeaning travel. The Chicago American Giants and the

Kansas City Monarchs, both independent of the NNL, made a huge impact on the East-West game in 1936—the West roster was made up entirely of players from those two teams. Perhaps heartened by such publicity, Midwestern team owners determined to try again to establish a black institution to equal the unapproachable majors.

Eight team owners met in 1937 to create the Negro American League. There was a little gambling money involved in this league too, though not nearly so obvious or influential as in the NNL. Kansas City, still owned by J. L. Wilkinson, was the most stable of the franchises, and therefore able to shape membership to some extent. Travel expense became the critical consideration. Wilkinson got the St. Louis Stars included so he would have someone to play on his way home to Kansas City, the westernmost of the participating cities. Teams from Cincinnati, Memphis, Detroit (a former NNL franchise), Birmingham, Indianapolis, and Chicago filled out the original eight. Teams came and went over the next 12 seasons. The fortunes of the Negro American League paralleled their NNL brethren, good times and bad. Kansas City, Chicago, and Memphis teams played every season, with Birmingham and Cleveland squads usually joining the competition. There were just six teams by 1939, and each year thereafter through 1946. Scheduling remained an unequal nightmare.[56]

The tenor of the East-West All-Star Games began to change with the arrival of the Negro American League. The game now became a contest between NNL players centered in the East, and NAL players from the Midwest. More a cultural extravaganza than ever, the game became the prize plum for journalists, the must-see icon for black fans from all walks of life. "It was a holiday for at least 48 hours," Sam Lacy of the *Baltimore Afro-American* recalled. "People would just about come from everywhere, mainly because it was such a spectacle." The game was the high water mark of black baseball's season, a barometer of Negro Leagues popularity and the growing affluence of black patrons. Between 1933 and 1937, attendance in Chicago averaged just over 25,000. The developing regional rivalry between the Negro National and American Leagues boosted average Comiskey Park attendance by about 20 percent between 1938 and 1940. A second game held at Yankee Stadium in 1939 drew 20,000. Then came the war years, when government spending finally revived the economy and thousands of blacks found steady work. The attendance boom reached a peak in 1943, when 51,723 filled the stands in Chicago. Attendance during the later war years might have been considerably higher had not the wartime government mandated travel restrictions. The event maintained its luster through 1948, then rapidly diminished, coming to an end in Chicago after 1953.[57] Let the figures speak:

**Table 2.1**

### Average Attendance, East-West All-Star Game, Chicago[58]

| | |
|---|---|
| 1933–1937 | 25,194 |
| 1938–1940 | 31,667 |
| 1941–1946 | 45,328 |
| 1947–1949 | 40,436 |
| 1950–1953 | 18,551 |

The East-West Game was the expression of black American culture, a reflection of the forces at work in society. There was a strong element of class values at work, as well as race. The small numbers of blacks living in the North before the Great Migration had greeted the influx of Southern black people with mixed emotions. The newcomers appeared raw and unsophisticated, hardly fit for life in Northern urban settings. The older residents, many of them professional people, set about mending the manners of the "country" folk, insisting on "proper" dress and behavior. When the East-West Game assumed the character of black cultural pageant, the patrons accentuated a display of those proper middle class values. The fans came in their Sunday best, and comported themselves accordingly.[59]

The All-Star Game began as a product of enforced separation—very American apartheid. It was a celebration of athleticism, heroism, and defiance, and from the beginning it was played in the shadow of larger issues. The All-Star Game showed what black ballplayers could do, and pointed out the essential question: these guys can play; why do they not play in the majors? Black journalists emphasized this lesson repeatedly; the few white journalists to attend wanted to deny that it was so. Floyd Lewis, a reasonably sympathetic reporter for the *Chicago Daily News*, allowed that black players were terrific at throwing and baserunning, though they tended to "showboat." "Only in batting are the Negro pros inferior," he informed his readers. "Lack of scientific training is apparent in their unsmoothness in wielding a bat."[60]

That kind of criticism raises an essential issue. Just what kind of baseball did they play in the Negro Leagues? The adjectives vary considerably, depending on the source, but the answer is very simple: the blacks played what was considered "inside baseball," today called "small ball." One author called it "a more thoughtful game," built around clever baserunning, the hit-and-run, the sacrifice, and frequent stealing. Cool Papa Bell called it "tricky" baseball. This was the older baseball of Ned Hanlon and John McGraw—subtle, quick, and just a little dirty. The major leagues had pretty much abandoned small ball by 1930 in favor of the big inning approach, inspired by the monster hitting of Babe Ruth, soon followed by Lou Gehrig, Jimmie Foxx, Hack Wilson, Hank Greenberg, and so many more. "Written baseball," Cool Papa Bell labeled it. While the majors played for the home run, Negro Leagues games continued to turn on close, one-run strategies.[61]

In part, this preference was dictated by the ball itself. After the First World War, the major leagues instituted a series of rules changes that commanded the use of a well made and pristine baseball. Doctored balls—scuffed, filed, nicked, torn, muddied, spat on—were gradually outlawed, and sullied balls came to be routinely tossed from play. This was a luxury the financially strapped Negro Leagues simply could not afford. "The ball we used just wasn't a major league ball," Buck Leonard lamented. "It was a Wilson 150 cc, and it wasn't as lively as the big-league ball." It was in fact cheap in every sense, so poorly made that a player with strong fingers could rip the cover as soon as it was tossed into play. Doctoring the ball was never outlawed in the Negro Leagues, either. Rube Foster supposedly used frozen baseballs. One legendary game played in 1930 became known as "the Battle of the Butchered Balls." Employing emery boards and tar, Smokey Joe Williams and Chet Brewer locked up in a duel that saw 46 strikeouts and a final score of 1–0.[62]

On average, black teams used maybe 40 balls over the course of a game. Soft, dinged, and dirty balls ruled the day, making long hits very challenging for anyone not named Josh Gibson or Home Run Brown. So, small ball. A lot of observers marked the difference in the styles of play when black players joined the majors. What they were watching was the spirit of John McGraw, brought to life by Jackie Robinson and Larry Doby. Major league baseball was patient and powerful; Negro Leagues ball was strategic and exciting.

One of the great ironies of Negro Leagues history is that they stumbled fatally just as they were starting to run. The late 1930s saw the waning of the Great Depression as the world staggered toward war and defense spending grew. Black organizations successfully pressured Franklin Roosevelt's government to guarantee blacks a share of the new employment opportunities. With discretionary cash available, attendance at Negro Leagues grew steadily. Yet problems remained—lots of problems, most of them familiar. Negro Leagues teams still possessed no large facilities of their own, making them overly dependent on outside booking agents to line up games in larger stadiums. That made for some unusual and draining spectacles, such as the four-team doubleheaders occasionally played at Yankee Stadium. These exhibitions made money and offered a varied entertainment, but they belied the kind of professionalism the Leagues wanted to establish. Transportation issues usually made such mass meetings of teams necessary—more economical to bring four teams to one large venue than for the teams to support extended travel in aging buses. Transportation was always near the front of owners' minds. In 1936, the Negro National League refused entrance applications from franchises in Cincinnati and Chicago—the distances were just too far for what had rapidly become an Eastern circuit, dependent entirely on bus travel. Soon after, the NNL turned down a Boston franchise application for the same reasons. The difference between a sustainable club and insolvency too often came down to a few gallons of gas. By the time the teams got their hands on a little more cash, the government was rationing gasoline as part of the war effort. Government officials, scrupulously fair, discriminated against the black teams by refusing to treat them differently. The clubs were denied exemption.[63]

Some real league leadership might have helped, some neutral authority who could rise above the petty bickering among owners, lay down some hard rules regarding player contracts, establish an equitable game schedule, and lend an air of professionalism. That never happened. The rise of the Negro American League just complicated matters. The two Negro Leagues tried to work together, holding joint annual meetings to sooth frictions and create unified policy. In 1939, team representatives ironed out an agreement covering booking fees for nonleague games, contract tampering, record keeping, gate guarantees, and championship playoffs. That they were still wrangling over these kinds of issues after 20 years of league experience speaks to the basic instabilities the teams faced.[64]

The wrangling never stopped. In 1940, leadership became the issue, with the six NNL team owners locked in a three-faction struggle over who would be the next president. Three years were not enough to resolve their differences, so there was no president. This made it difficult to face other matters. In 1941, the problem was players returning from Latin America. The Negro American League wanted such players banned for jumping contracts, but Negro National League teams were more than happy to sign them. The controversy very nearly ended the partnership between the leagues. Two years later, the Negro American League was in an uproar because officials had hired the Howe News Service, the longstanding but white-owned sports record company, to collect and manage league statistics. The NNL hired the Elias Bureau on significantly cheaper terms. Teams still found the going difficult and expensive, even if Elias was supplying the envelopes and the postage for mailing box scores. Clubs also continued to fight about ineligible players and games with suspended teams. And on and on. Small wonder that in 1946, officials wanted Happy Chandler, newly-crowned commissioner of organized baseball, to become Negro Leagues Commissioner too.[65]

They did try, very hard. The East-West Game was an enormous success through 1948, enough to attempt similar contests in New York, Cleveland, and Washington, with considerably smaller attendance. The two leagues overcame the differences of 1941 enough to initiate a

Negro Leagues World Series in 1942. This was a definite step toward equality with the majors, much handicapped by the realities of black baseball. Rather than playing the best-of-seven as a home and home series, owners again staged the competitions as a series of exhibitions moving from city to city, often amidst raging controversy. Champions were eventually crowned—four from the NNl and three from the NAL in the seven years of play—but the games never produced the impact (or the profits) of the East-West Game. The World Series was one of the first traditions to wither as the Negro Leagues faded after 1947.[66]

The Negro Leagues of the 1930s and 1940s grew from a peculiar nexus of absorbed self-interest and collective desperation. As individual ball clubs, the black teams lived very close to the edge, wondering if there was enough money out there to get to the end of a season. It was a test of survival, and owners did what they felt they had to do, stealing one another's players, fixing schedules, ignoring inconvenient agreements. Organizing into leagues simply made sense, the umbrella protection of the whole against the predation of the stronger individuals. That the predators too often ran the leagues for their own advantage was perhaps a necessary step on the way to maturity. Leagues needed money, power, and the respect of club owners to resolve the fundamental problems all the teams shared. The Negro Leagues never got the chance. More than anything else, prosperity destroyed them. Prosperity and guilt.

Black baseball prospered like never before during the years of World War II. Black populations in Eastern and Midwestern cities grew enormously during the Depression, and the defense work put money in their hands, enough to live on and a little to spare. Black attendance at ballparks boomed during the War, and team owners stopped worrying so much about expenses. Near capacity attendance at the East-West Games drove home the point. Black baseball had become an attractively profitable enterprise.[67]

Even as the wealth flowed in, and black baseball began to look like a viable enterprise, the world began to change. Back in 1920, white America, backed by tradition, fed by science, driven by hatred and greed, had decided separate but equal—unvarnished apartheid—was the only way to go. Then came World War II, and some very hard questions. How could Americans fight Hitler's racism while maintaining their own? Was the logic of Hitler's solution America's own eventual doom? How could America ask blacks to fight this war, and still refuse them their basic rights as citizens? Money and guilt can be powerful motivators, and they worked together to begin the making of a different America after World War II. Blacks would be integrated into society, encouraged to bring along their talent and their money. The process would be as slow and painful as racism could make it, but in the end, everyone would profit, with at least one notable exception: the owners of black baseball teams.

The sense of "twoness" W. E. B. DuBois so eloquently characterized in *The Souls of Black Folk* fully applies to the history of black baseball in America. During the heyday of the Negro Leagues, blacks could point to the success of black athletes and black entrepreneurs with a real sense of pride, yet at the same time feel the pain of exclusion, understanding that their achievements paralleled the dominant white culture rather than sharing in its experiences. When the opportunity for integration finally came, the "twoness" assumed new shape, a bitter choice between loyalty to black achievement and desire to become part of a greater American whole. That twoness persists in historical memory.[68]

Nostalgia and outrage are an odd mix of emotions. Both fully apply to the history of Negro Leagues baseball, an ambivalence, a contradiction that lies at the very heart of any understanding of American sports history. The Negro Leagues were the product of an extreme racism that sought from the beginning to define the national character, defying the principles etched in America's founding documents. That prejudice, that desire to create a separate and not really equal, was present at the birth of professional baseball and grew more rabid with each passing year. On the face of it, nothing could be more wasteful, more counterproductive than insisting on two independent and parallel developments of professional baseball, divided solely on the basis of color. Yet America insisted, because of all the options coming out of the Civil War, apartheid seemed the most attractive in the South, and after the Great Migration began, in the North as well. Jim Crow became the national clown who never smiled. Fence out the black people, he said. Keep them out of the hotels, the eating establishments, the trains, the buses, the stations, the neighborhoods. Don't let them drink from the same water fountains. And don't let them play on white baseball teams. If they feel they have to play, they can try to organize their own leagues. We can take their money.

These were the ingredients of a bad nightmare. The revulsion so many feel is a sense of common humanity, shared from the perspective of the 21st century. America would like to bury the fact that any of this injustice, this hatred ever had to happen. Revulsion is entirely justified.

Nostalgia is too. Blacks were justifiably angry and mystified over the long years of separate and not possibly equal, but they made the best of what American life offered, establishing a baseball tradition entirely their own. Baseball stood at the heart of black cultural expression, a genuine source of pride and inspiration that helped to sustain the faith of men and women staring down the worst of American apartheid. Negro Leagues baseball was resilient when black people needed a separate and positive identity. When that need altered with the march for civil rights, black baseball began to diminish. For a long time, the Negro Leagues were nearly forgotten as black stars made indelible marks in the big show. But, once upon a time, blacks produced their own memories in their own show, and with the passage of time, these have become their own kind of treasure. Black baseball was an expression of the spirit, an exuberant recreation played against impossible odds in difficult, sometimes sordid conditions. That the Negro Leagues survived, that they ultimately prospered, that they eventually awoke America to the fact that blacks could play the game—this was the triumph of an enduring culture. The Leagues were something of value beyond price. For America to be as it is, the Negro Leagues had to exist, and they had to fade into memory.

# II

# The American League

## *The Trials of a Major League*

---

In 1946, as Organized Baseball at long last shook itself free from the challenges of the Second World War, there was little doubt in more dispassionate minds that the American League was the superior of the two majors. True, a new era was emerging, and anything might happen, but the American League possessed the heritage and the star power to establish a reasonable claim. The Americans had won eight of the 12 All-Star games held since 1933, and 13 of the last 20 World Series. The New York Yankees alone won nine of those championships, becoming the most feared and envied franchise in baseball. Ted Williams, Hank Greenberg, Joe DiMaggio, Bob Feller—so many of the biggest stars competed on the American League side of the equation. If the League's owners and general managers displayed some arrogance as they looked down from the top of the heap, their over-confidence was understandable.

They were a well-entrenched group, the men who ran the American League. A couple of survivors had been deep in the mix when Ban Johnson engineered the startling coup that made the American a major league back in 1901. They had weathered storms then, and again in 1914, when the nascent Federal League tried unsuccessfully to force their own way to the top. In 1920, they somehow managed to escape the most deadly challenge of them all, when it became public knowledge that the eight "Black Sox" had thrown the 1919 World Series, and the much-loved Cleveland Indians star Ray Chapman was struck and killed by a pitched ball. Baseball was on its knees then, the American League facing the worst of that storm. An American Leaguer saved them, one Babe Ruth, who appreciated the majesty of the long home run and the value of constant publicity just as radio took hold. Ruth's swagger overcame the public doubts; baseball sailed on, renewed and emboldened. The National League became a stale, old-fashioned copy of Ruth's league.[1]

Then came the Great Depression, and the spinning of a great illusion. Back in 1903, as the dust settled on the National Agreement that made the National and American Leagues co-equal, the major leagues settled into the ten major cities in the Northeast, between the East Coast and St. Louis. It was an arrangement that made perfect sense at that moment, and for a couple of decades thereafter. Just about all the nation's most populous cities were included, and the transportation network supported ready movement from one to another. Any city outside the quadrant would have been difficult and expensive to reach, and probably would

43

not have people to support a team anyway. That was 1903. Baseball weathered 20 years of challenges in that configuration, and soon after, the Depression hit. The Negro Leagues were shaken off their foundations, and by 1932, major league baseball was in a desperate situation. Owners responded in the fashion of Depression Era businessmen, retrenching, cutting salaries and personnel, boarding up the windows, and refusing to risk capital on improvements. Putting the activity kindly, baseball stabilized, maintaining the practices that had made the sport national. To be more honest, baseball ossified, refusing to change anything for fear of sinking into the Depression. What made sound business sense in 1903 was still in place in 1945, no longer making as much sense.[2]

Pride does so often go before a fall, and the American Leaguers were about to endure some unhappy surprises as baseball adapted to the postwar world. Over-confidence breeds conservatism, a reluctance to alter what seems to work so well. But circumstances change, and conservatism can become a failure to adapt, even a failure to recognize that adaptation is necessary. Staying the course through the Great Depression, baseball postponed action on a lot of pressing issues, among them geographic expansion, labor relations, a declining infrastructure, and adjustment to the demands of a Cold War world. Integration was the most pressing of those demands.[3]

**Connie Mack. One of the pioneer managers in Ban Johnson's American League. Still owner and manager of the Philadelphia Athletics a half-century later, the pioneer had become cautiously conservative, resistant to change. (National Baseball Hall of Fame Library, Cooperstown, N.Y.)**

As befits a league that had not much changed since 1920, the American League owners' meetings in 1946 were populated by men who had not much changed since 1920. Ban Johnson was gone, dead since 1928, his wings clipped since 1920, when the owners made Kenesaw Mountain Landis Commissioner to save their necks. William Harridge, who became league president in 1931, made little impression. Two of Ban Johnson's fellow warriors in the making of the American League did remain deep in its councils more than 40 years on: Connie Mack, who became principle owner of the Philadelphia Athletics in 1937, and Clark Griffith, who took over the Washington Nationals in November 1919. Charles Comiskey, the real lightning rod of the Black Sox scandal, had been dead (supposedly of a broken heart) since 1931, but control of the Chicago White remained with his family. Grace Comiskey, Charley's widow, was running the show in 1946.[4]

The remaining five owners had not taken part in Ban Johnson's baseball revolution, but they were not for the most part fresh-faced newcomers, either. There was Alva Bradley, the respected but not terribly innovative owner of the Cleveland Indians, a team that had not won a pennant since 1920, the year Ray Chapman died. The Boston Red Sox in 1933 became the property of Tom Yawkey, heir to a lumbering fortune and a man with more money than was good for him. The Sox were his favorite toy. Walter O. Briggs, exploitive Detroit industrialist, had taken over the Tigers from longtime president and owner Frank Navin in 1936. Rebuilding his ballpark and changing the name to Briggs Stadium was his most daring ploy, though he did win several pennants with Hank Greenberg and Charlie Gehringer as his stars.[5]

Just two teams had undergone recent changes in ownership since 1936. The St. Louis Browns were the League's hot potato, changing hands often so the holder would not get burned too badly. The Browns were on their third owner in 12 years when Dick Muckerman got suckered into taking over in 1946. He fared every bit as well as his predecessors. At the other end of the spectrum from the Browns stood the New York Yankees, the wealthiest and most stable team in baseball. Brewery magnate Jacob Ruppert owned the team from 1915 to 1939, overseeing the team's rise from the second division to championship dynasty. Longtime General Manager Ed Barrow steadied the helm at Ruppert's death, but the ownership void persisted until Larry MacPhail ("the roaring redhead") partnered with Dan Topping and Del Webb to purchase the team in 1945. MacPhail's tenure was tempestuous but short, and the Yankees tradition survived intact. The truth was, even if the Yankees experienced the most tumultuous change in leadership in recent years, the franchise remained the embodiment of the American League's tradition. They were rich, they were arrogant, they were deeply influential, and they won an awful lot. They were not a presence to foster change readily.[6]

Taken together, the brain trust deciding the futures of the eight American clubs were hardly a dynamic lot. Shell-shocked from long years of Depression poverty, clinging desperately to tradition, the owners viewed change with a skeptical eye. Just two of their number could bring themselves even to consider innovation. Larry MacPhail, man with a maverick reputation, was very near the end of his run by 1947. Still thinking creatively, he was turning his peculiar genius to inventions intended to support the status quo. The second was Bill Veeck, a man with a flair for trying something new. The remaining owners hated him for that. In the American League of the late 1940s, rocking the boat was the unforgivable sin.

Yet change there would have to be. The landscape of American League baseball during the postwar era was an unplotted minefield, loaded with ticking bombs. Not just integration. The reserve clause began its slow march toward death as labor problems grew. Radio came of age, and television blossomed, while the minor leagues suddenly withered. Attendance numbers exploded and as quickly melted away. Teams scrambled to survive in a heady atmosphere of considerable rewards and incalculable risk. Sixty-some years down the road, memoirists try their best to portray those postwar seasons as a simpler time, a happier past when the game was still a game played for its own sake, unsullied by the business considerations that tarnish the modern era. Like most nostalgic longing, the memory is built on a past that never existed. The dice were every bit as loaded in 1947 as today, loaded to enrich the pockets of the powerful while maintaining the helplessness of the weak.

There is an old saying, that you have to spend a nickel to make a dime. The problem is getting your hands on the nickel in the first place. As baseball emerged from the trials of the Great Depression and the Second World War, a few teams had plenty of nickels in hand, while others had almost no nickels at all. The American League was a system that rewarded those able and willing to spend money, which pretty much doomed clubs with no access to that precious commodity. What emerged was a closed hierarchy engaged in unequal competition, producing all too predictable results. The integration question created a disturbance within that hierarchy, posed some new and pressing problems, but changed the inherent unfairness of American League baseball very little. Business remained business, and any study of integration needs to address how that business operated.

Looking back to the 1940s and 1950s, one essential quality seems to shape the character of American League baseball as played on the field. That quality was a steady and ineluctable change—a turning over, an impermanence—call it what you will. Despite the persistent myths of team durability and everlasting loyalty that supposedly shaped player mentality in those good old days, the fact was that clubs shifted their rosters constantly, with players moving more often than nomadic shepherds. No American League team ever fielded the same starting eight two years consecutively; as often as not two or three starting players from each team would change uniforms between seasons. Two of the five starting pitchers each season would be new to the rotation. The search for something better never slowed—even stars were subject to trade or shift as they faltered. Bill Veeck, who purchased the Cleveland Indians from Alva Bradley in 1947, and who was more humane than most owners he could name, put the issue perfectly:

> There is almost no such thing, I have found, as an untouchable player. When you trade a long-time favorite, the writers find kind words for such forgotten virtues as sentiment and loyalty and speak most darkly about front-office ingratitude. Three days later, they are back telling the manager how to run the ball club. The fans vow never to enter the park again; a few zealots even picket the park carrying banners proclaiming their unyielding purpose. The next time the Yankees are in town for a Sunday doubleheader, they're all there pleading for two tickets behind first base.[7]

Loyalty meant little to men armed with a reserve clause. Loyalty was for losers.

Never-ending change was the product of an inescapable condition of baseball life. Though there were just eight teams—just 64 guys needed to fill all the regular positions—no team could fill them all adequately. Always there were compromises: the shortstop who could not hit, the right fielder who could not throw. Every such compromise—and there were a lot of them—cried out for a change, an attempt at improvement—perhaps the shortstop with less range but more stick. The American League was a constantly turning mill, with eight organizations binding temporary aggregations of ballplayers to one-year contracts, as quickly breaking them down again. Players came and players went with such dizzying speed the fan had to buy a scorecard. There were players on other teams to be purchased or traded for, free agents mercilessly released from contracts, minor league prospects, the Rule V draft, the waiver wire. There were lots of ways to obtain new players, with prices to fit any budget. When baseball's integration finally took shape, the Negro Leagues became just one more venue for every general manager's ruthless, never-ending search for a better, cheaper ballplayer.

No team was an island. That was, and remains, the peculiar and appealing aspect of major league baseball. A group of largely selfish and highly competitive individuals controlled the teams, wanting nothing more than to humiliate their rivals in the win-loss column. Yet they saw themselves as members of an exclusive club advancing a common cause: the protection of baseball and their own profits, control over their players, and the elimination of outside interference from government, labor unions, maverick owners, the fans, or anyone else. When a Mexican League provided players a richer alternative to the American majors just after World War II, owners joined hands behind new Commissioner Happy Chandler to prevent the return of players who had jumped leagues. When players became interested in establishing a union, owners agreed to accept player representatives at meetings, guarantee minimum salaries, and establish a pension fund, thwarting any player organization's ability to exploit player unrest. What was at stake was the reserve clause, a very potent bit of legal chicanery born of baseball's dubious exemption from the nation's anti-trust laws. The reserve clause bound a player to whatever team contracted him, whether he signed a new contract with his team at the expiration of the old one-year deal or not. The owners very rightly feared a series of court challenges to the reserve clause in the labor-friendly atmosphere of the 1950s, believing mantra-like that the clause protected them from bidding wars, protected them from themselves. Given the hierarchical ladder that was baseball during the period, the perception was understandable. Unfair and protective of an unbalanced status quo perhaps, but understandable.[8]

Baseball existed as a business because there were eight teams in each league committed to performing 154 games for the sake of the profits derived from admission and frills. To entertain even the hope of making money, all eight teams needed all the others, even if the system virtually guaranteed the success of a few while denying the prize to others. The business was highly competitive but nothing like cutthroat; within the confines of the status quo, the richer teams helped the lesser to field a respectable team as much as they could. Baseball was an entertainment business; a team so bad that it failed to entertain was not simply a failure to the owner; such a team was a danger to the entire structure. Profitable teams owed their success to the existence of the less fortunate.

Begin with simple wins and losses. Table 2.1 is, at first glance, a celebration of the obvious. Everyone knows the Yankees dominated on-field competition during the postwar era, while the Athletics and Browns most emphatically failed to measure up. Do not cruise over this table lightly. Obvious though they are, the numbers encapsulate the entire story of American League baseball during the period. On-field results resulted from a far greater inequality in the fortunes of the eight ball clubs. In the postwar era, circumstances forged a hierarchy strikingly resistant to change. The American League had become a closed and layered system of haves and havenots. At the top of the ladder stood the wealthy, the teams that had money to spend, the teams that won. Wins and losses were the product of a larger inequality.

**Table 2.1**

### WINS and LOSSES, 1946–1954[9]

| Team | Cumulative Wins | Cumulative Losses | Win % | Ave. Wins/Year |
|---|---|---|---|---|
| New York | 868 | 515 | .628 | 96.4 |
| Cleveland | 815 | 572 | .588 | 90.6 |
| Boston | 789 | 597 | .569 | 87.7 |
| Detroit | 688 | 698 | .496 | 76.4 |
| Chicago | 663 | 721 | .479 | 73.7 |
| Philadelphia | 603 | 783 | .435 | 67.0 |
| Washington | 595 | 788 | .430 | 66.1 |
| St. Louis/Baltimore | 529 | 866 | .382 | 58.8 |

Between 1946 and 1954, the American League teams locked themselves into a ladder of three tiers. There were teams bound to win, teams sure to lose. Three teams—the Yankees, the Indians, and the Red Sox—comprised the privileged group, the wealthy elite. Going into a

new season, it was an understood thing that one of those three teams was going to win the pennant, that all three would almost certainly finish in the first division. The second tier—the White
Sox and Tigers—were reasonably competitive teams who could push into the first division or
sink to the bottom. (The Tigers finished second in 1946, 1947, and 1950; dead last in 1952.)
And then came the bottom filler. The Athletics and the Nationals may have enjoyed some days
in the sun in the distant past, and the Browns did manage to win a pennant during World War
II, but in the postwar era, these three teams entered each new season with no chance at all.
The Browns fielded any number of very bad teams; though the faces kept changing, performance did not. Washington and Philadelphia were little better. If one or more of the teams in
the upper tiers faltered a little, pausing to reload, one of these bottom three might feel the
modified joy of sneaking into the first division, but that was the best they or anyone else could
possibly expect. Their lowly fates were built into a financial arrangement that mandated eight
teams, but not eight good teams.

Twentieth century American life and the expectations constructed on market competition
fashioned the contours of major league baseball, and did much to shape the American League's
three-tiered ladder. The eight teams shared an identity and a common set of goals as purveyors
of sports entertainment, but each club stood on its own when it came to acquiring capital, accu-
mulating resources, and delivering the product. Financial inequality handicapped unfortunate
teams from the American League's very beginnings in 1901. Two teams—Milwaukee and Baltimore—failed immediately, while some others flourished and still others got by on reduced
budgets. Barring some form of revenue sharing, a team headquartered in New York was bound
to establish a better capital foundation than any team in St. Louis, especially if there was competition from the National League.[10]

What perpetuated the grim inequities of a league founded on the principle of every team
for itself were two cataclysmic historical events: the Great Depression and World War II. The
Depression simply tore apart the American economy; organized baseball was one more business
driven to the wall. Every team suffered at least a little, but the smaller markets—especially smaller
towns with teams in both major leagues—suffered most, losing customers, losing resources,
and losing the ability to compete. It was an old story often retold: a team that could not afford
good players could not attract a gate; without the gate, there was no money to pay a decent player,
even if one accidentally showed up. The poor just got poorer. Then came the war, which had
the temporary effect of evening the playing field (how else could the Browns win?), but in the
long run created a performance instability that persisted for years after 1945.

This was not a simple matter of ineptitude. The results on the field were more the product
of a fundamentally uneven distribution of resources than any athletic failing. There is a mountain of data on team operating expenses during the early 1950s, but a brief selection can stand
for the whole.

**Table 2.2**

### PROFITS and LOSS, 1952[11]

|                  | NY          | CLE       | BOS       | CHI       | DET       | WAS       | PHI       | StL     |
|------------------|-------------|-----------|-----------|-----------|-----------|-----------|-----------|---------|
| Media Income     | $475,000    | 452,650   | 366,500   | 261,202   | ?         | 169,905   | 168,595   | 8,935   |
| Total Income     | $3,996,665  | 2,963,481 | 2,301,487 | 2,208,262 | 2,255,849 | 1,393,297 | 1,536,901 | 999,831 |

|  | NY | CLE | BOS | CHI | DET | WAS | PHI | StL |
|---|---|---|---|---|---|---|---|---|
| **Player Salaries** | $561,420 | 523,934 | 413,029 | 324,464 | ? | 341,974 | 387,758 | 350,810 |
| **Total Expenses** | $3,066,181 | 2,621,496 | 2,484,384 | 1,855,091 | 2,282,114 | 1,112,303 | 1,548,249 | 1,274,188 |
| **Farm Team Subsidies** | $244,091 | +25,983 | -159,117 | -191,161 | ? | -170,653 | -40,089 | -55,280 |
| **Net Surplus or Loss** | +$223,943 | +204,088 | -342,014 | +65,052 | -26,265 | +58,471 | -51,437 | -329,637 |

This is largely the story told by the win-loss figures, presented in a more comprehensive format. No one should be surprised to discover that the New York Yankees in 1952 enjoyed an income of more than one million dollars, 26 percent higher than their nearest competitor (both on and off the field), the Cleveland Indians. The total income of the Senators, the Athletics, and the Browns combined did not quite equal that of the Yankees. Of course, New York paid out more in expenses than any other team, the price of winning the World Series four years running. Despite the hardhearted efforts of General Manager George Weiss to keep salaries down, the team paid out more than any of their League counterparts (including the supposedly much overpaid Red Sox). Their extensive farm system was also expensive. Yet, the team made money—more money than anyone else in the American League. The New York club was very rich in resources, and what was more important, knew how to take advantage of their position. New York's strength came from its very large fan base, coupled to the city's role as America's media capital. Add to this an inventive and aggressive management willing to seize the advantages offered by a rapidly changing minor league situation, and you have the juggernaut the Yankees came to be (yet again).

The Indians cleared almost as much as the Yankees, despite having a million dollars less to work with and the second highest player salary total in the American League. The Indians played in a much smaller market, but they had no National League competitor, and for a time they had Bill Veeck, the greatest innovator of them all. The team by this time recognized the money to be harvested from radio and television contracts, and somehow they were the only team in the League to show a profit from their minor league contacts. Boston, the third wealthiest team in 1952, lost the most cash of any team, mainly through paying very large salaries to a bunch who finished sixth with a losing record. Boston boasted good teams coming out of the War and still enjoyed the incomparably deep pockets of Tom Yawkey. Dropping more than $300,000 was just a bump in the road for Yawkey, who had inherited wealth from mineral and petroleum interests said to be worth more than $200 million. Yawkey could afford to lose, and lose he would, more and more.

Chicago and Detroit behaved very much as the middling teams they were, with moderate incomes and moderate expenses. Chicago was a team on its knees in the immediate postwar era, but unlimited trading and shrewd investment in youth by a new general manager eventually attracted customers in a larger market. The White Sox would prove that it was not impossible to move up the ladder. The team showed a modest profit after rising from the second division to finish a promising fourth in 1951, and third the next year.

Detroit, like Cleveland, was a smaller market with no competitor, governed by managements that oscillated between reckless venturing and extreme caution. The Tigers lost some money in 1952, but this was an aberration. The team was horrible that year, pulling off a panic-stricken trade and finishing dead last in the standings. Attendance dipped, but soon recovered as the team made efforts to improve with a youth movement. The Tigers chose not to report the salaries paid to their players, but the owner, Walter O. Briggs, was reputed to be the wealthiest and most generous in the American League (as long as the players were white).

As anyone might expect, the three bottom teams showed nothing but trouble. Washington player salary totals were 17 percent lower than Boston's, and 39 percent lower than the Yankees'. The Athletics and the Browns managed little better. The Senators shelled out a good deal of money trying to build up their farm system, yet managed to eke out a small profit by capping overall spending. In Philadelphia, the Athletics paid a tad more to the players, spent precious little on the farm system and lost a lot of money. Bad team, bad attendance, poor income. St. Louis was reeling, losing more than $300,000 the team could not afford, despite cutting costs to the absolute bone. The three bottom dwellers found it very hard to climb the competitive ladder, possessing few players worth mentioning and next to no resources even to try and improve. For St. Louis, Philadelphia, and Washington, the only lasting solution would be to change owners and move to newer, untapped markets.

An interesting item in the tabulations was the income teams derived from radio and television coverage. Still very small when compared to the fountain of money to come, media income was already an important item in almost every team's ledger, a counter to the funds lost with the decline in attendance. When radio began to make its presence felt in the 1930s, the owners did everything they could to oppose its growth, up to and including blackouts of local markets. The thought, of course, was that radio broadcasts would make potential patrons less likely to attend the games in person, thereby reducing attendance. That radio was a new form of moneymaking device, that there were exclusive contracts to be signed, advertising dollars to be had, promotions to be pushed, dawned very slowly. Above all else, radio attracted women to the game in unparalleled numbers, eventually bringing them to the ballparks, swelling attendance. American League teams derived $298,462 from radio and television in 1946. Just six years down the road, the seven teams reporting collected more than $1.9 million, an increase of more than 600 percent. The three top teams attracted by far the most cash, but all the teams gained financially except for those lovable Browns, who somehow managed to make $25,000 less in 1952 than in 1946. But even for the best teams, the money was little more than peanuts, at most about 20 percent of budgetary income.

Whatever else may be said concerning as venal a group as American League owners, they were not much for looking at new ways to make money. Attendance remained the essential measure of success. The break-even point for a healthy team was reckoned at one million fans. The late 1940s saw an enormous bubble in ballpark attendance (and concession sales), and it was this income that paid the bills.

Analysts posit two basic reasons for the postwar attendance upsurge. One was prosperity: the depression was over, the war was over; people had more leisure time and more money to spend. The second was night baseball. Introduced in Cincinnati in 1935, big league baseball under the lights became very popular in several cities during the War, as the large numbers toiling in defense plants could attend games after work. Yankee Stadium installed lights in 1946, Fenway Park in 1947, and Tiger Stadium in 1948, the last American League teams to do so. The trend enabled many thousands more to see their teams in action. Everyone's headcount rose for a few delirious years.[12]

# Table 2.3

## Attendance By City, 1946–60[13]

| | NY | % | CLE | % | CHI | % | BOS | % | DET | % | StL/BAL | % | WAS | % | PHI/KC | % | TOTAL |
|---|---|---|---|---|---|---|---|---|---|---|---|---|---|---|---|---|---|
| 1946 | 2,265,512 | 23.5 | 1,057,289 | 11 | 983,403 | 10.2 | 1,416,944 | 14.7 | 1,722,590 | 17.9 | 526,435 | 5.5 | 1,027,216 | 10.7 | 621,793 | 6.5 | 9,621,282 |
| 1947 | 2,178,937 | 23 | 1,521,978 | 16 | 876,948 | 9.2 | 1,427,315 | 15 | 1,398,093 | 14.7 | 320,474 | 3.4 | 850,758 | 9 | 911,566 | 9.6 | 9,486,169 |
| 1948 | 2,373,907 | 21.3 | 2,620,627 | 23.5 | 777,844 | 7 | 1,558,798 | 14 | 1,743,035 | 15.6 | 335,564 | 3 | 795,254 | 7.1 | 945,076 | 8.5 | 11,150,105 |
| 1949 | 2,283,676 | 21.3 | 2,233,771 | 20.8 | 937,151 | 8.7 | 1,596,650 | 14.9 | 1,821,204 | 17 | 270,936 | 2.5 | 770,745 | 7.2 | 816,514 | 7.6 | 10,730,647 |
| 1950 | 2,081,380 | 22.8 | 1,727,464 | 18.9 | 781,330 | 8.5 | 1,344,080 | 14.7 | 1,951,474 | 21.3 | 247,131 | 2.7 | 699,697 | 7.7 | 309,805 | 3.4 | 9,142,461 |
| 1951 | 1,950,107 | 22 | 1,704,984 | 19.2 | 1,328,234 | 15 | 1,312,282 | 14.8 | 1,132,641 | 12.8 | 293,790 | 3.3 | 695,167 | 7.8 | 465,469 | 5.2 | 8,882,774 |
| 1952 | 1,629,665 | 19.6 | 1,444,607 | 17.4 | 1,231,675 | 14.9 | 1,115,750 | 13.5 | 1,026,846 | 12.4 | 518,796 | 6.3 | 699,457 | 8.4 | 627,100 | 7.6 | 8,293,996 |
| 1953 | 1,537,811 | 22.1 | 1,069,176 | 15.4 | 1,191,353 | 17.1 | 1,026,133 | 14.7 | 884,658 | 12.7 | 297,238 | 4.3 | 595,594 | 8.6 | 362,113 | 5.2 | 6,964,176 |
| 1954 | 1,475,171 | 18.6 | 1,335,472 | 16.9 | 1,231,629 | 15.5 | 931,127 | 11.8 | 1,079,847 | 13.6 | 1,060,910 | 13.4 | 503,542 | 6.4 | 304,666 | 3.8 | 7,922,464 |
| 1955 | 1,490,138 | 16.7 | 1,221,780 | 13.7 | 1,175,684 | 13.1 | 1,203,200 | 13.5 | 1,181,838 | 13.2 | 852,039 | 9.5 | 425,238 | 4.8 | 1,393,054 | 15.6 | 8,943,071 |
| 1956 | 1,491,784 | 18.9 | 865,467 | 11 | 1,000,090 | 12.7 | 1,137,158 | 14.4 | 1,051,182 | 13.3 | 901,201 | 11.4 | 431,647 | 5.5 | 1,015,154 | 12.9 | 7,893,783 |
| 1957 | 1,497,134 | 18.3 | 722,256 | 8.8 | 1,135,668 | 13.9 | 1,181,087 | 14.4 | 1,272,346 | 15.5 | 1,029,581 | 12.6 | 457,079 | 5.6 | 901,067 | 11 | 8,196,318 |
| 1958 | 1,428,438 | 19.6 | 663,805 | 9.1 | 797,451 | 10.1 | 1,077,047 | 14.8 | 1,098,924 | 15.1 | 829,991 | 11.4 | 475,288 | 6.5 | 925,090 | 12.7 | 7,296,133 |
| 1959 | 1,552,030 | 17 | 1,497,976 | 16.4 | 1,423,144 | 15.6 | 984,102 | 10.8 | 1,221,221 | 13.3 | 891,926 | 9.7 | 615,372 | 6.7 | 963,683 | 10.5 | 9,149,554 |
| 1960 | 1,627,349 | 17.8 | 950,985 | 10.4 | 1,644,460 | 18 | 1,129,866 | 12.3 | 1,167,669 | 12.8 | 1,187,849 | 13 | 743,404 | 8.1 | 774,944 | 8.5 | 9,226,627 |
| Ave. | 1,790,869 | | 1,375,842 | | 1,101,071 | | 1,229,436 | | 1,316,905 | | 326,276 | | 652,364 | | 596,011 | | |
| | | | | | | | | | | | 964,785 | | | | 995,499 | | |

The attendance boom coincided with the initial stages of integration. Cleveland, the first American League team to integrate, enjoyed one of the largest attendance jumps, drawing an additional half-million fans in Larry Doby's initial season, and another million the next year, when the Indians won the championship. Probably a general increase in black attendance throughout the American League accounted for some portion of the boom, though this is impossible to prove. Certainly black attendance was not a constant. The Browns callously tried to attract black customers by simply adding two Negro Leagues players to their roster in 1947, but the results were very disappointing.

More than 9.5 million paying customers attended American League games in 1946. Attendance peaked at more than 11 million two years later, and then began to fall ominously.

If the years 1946 to 1948 were the best of times, the feeling surely came to some owners more readily than to others. Almost one-fourth of the entire American League audience went to Yankee Stadium, which drew more than two million every season through 1950. Cleveland's share grew mightily due to the unparalleled marketing genius of Veeck (and perhaps the additions of Larry Doby and Satchel Paige), coupled to the fact that the Indians won it all in 1948. (Cleveland's one million plus jump in attendance accounts for most of the League's record bulge in 1948.) Boston maintained pretty much a steady market through the entire 15-year period, falling off only in 1954 when Ted Williams broke his collarbone and the team was bad, and again in 1959 when the entire team went wrong. (The Sox added their first black player in 1959.)

In the second tier, Detroit enjoyed very good years from 1946 through 1950, then dipped by about 40 percent to a level they maintained over the next decade. They too were reluctant to sign black players. The White Sox, fielding poor teams in a divided Chicago market, did not much partake in the boom of the late 1940s. (The team had very nearly suffered bankruptcy as recently as 1941.) Attendance improved as the team gained respectability after 1950, when Minnie Minoso became a star attraction. Attendance improved dramatically when Bill Veeck came to town in 1959.

That leaves the lowest tier. The *combined* attendance of the Washington Senators, the Philadelphia Athletics, and the St. Louis Browns did not equal the attendance of *either* the Yankees or the Indians in 1948. Those three lowly teams together did not outdraw the Tigers or the Red Sox by much. They were very poor teams, in both meaningful senses of that word. They did not (for the most part) play well on the field, and people did not pay often to come and watch them. Each condition reinforced the other, creating a hole very difficult to escape.

The Senators began the postwar days with some promise, drawing a million fans for the first and only time and finishing fourth in the standings. But they were an old-fashioned team in many ways, slow to accept the accelerated patterns of postwar baseball. Owner Clark Griffith pitched in the majors as far back as 1884, began managing in 1903, and purchased the Washington club in 1920. The team was his livelihood; he had no independent income. His teams won three pennants (the last in 1933), but then settled into determined mediocrity, earning just enough money to meet a payroll that included his apparently innumerable relatives. Griffith was in some ways his own worst enemy. When night baseball first reached the major leagues in the 1930s, Griffith characterized the idea as "just a step above dog racing," seeing the trend not as an opportunity to draw a larger attendance, but instead to open the gates to unwashed barbarians. (His heir would carry this sorry notion a horrible step farther.) Griffith generally turned small profits by keeping expenses—player salaries especially—very low. (When Bob Porterfield, the team's best pitcher in 1953, wore out his cap, the team made him pay $7.50 for a new one.) The rot set in again in 1947: seventh place and an 18 percent drop in attendance. The desperate trades began, and very quickly Washington was seeing fewer than half a million patrons a year. All the while, Griffith danced around the possibility of integration, talking a good game but never placing an American black on his roster. The District of Columbia's population was one-third black.

The Athletics too possessed some cachet—a glorious past with some great players and some World Series victories. The team possessed a living and visible connection to that past in the venerable Connie Mack, manager and part-owner since 1901. Philadelphia hovered on the fringes of respectability in the late 1940s, coming in fifth two seasons running and then fourth in 1949, but the Athletics were not much fooling anyone, least of all the paying customers. Connie Mack was reputed to have said that the ideal season was a good and promising start to bring out the fans, and a poor finish so he would not have to give raises to his players. Attendance, almost one million in 1948, dropped by more than half after 1950. The Philadelphia days were numbered.

The Browns began the postwar era scraping the bottom, and managed to make things worse for themselves as the years flashed by. The club had been in serious financial troubles before the war, severely impairing their ability to put a respectable team on the field. In 1939, the other seven franchises even agreed to offer one player each to St. Louis, merely to improve the roster. Management advanced plans to move the operation to Los Angeles after the 1941 season, but Pearl Harbor put a stop to that happy thought. By 1947, the Browns organization was $2 million in debt. The team changed owners, with new owner Dick Muckerman ending up in hock to the American League to the tune of another $300,000. The next season the team held a fire sale, moving their best (and most expensive) players to the Red Sox and the Indians. Attendance dropped to little more than a quarter million patrons. By 1950, the Browns were hiring a psychologist to determine just why the remaining players had a losing attitude. A good use for the little money they had, undeniably.

The attendance boom of the late 1940s began to falter with the 1950 season. By 1953, fewer than seven million people paid their way into the American League parks, a drop-off of almost 40 percent in six short years. Although all the teams suffered losses, they did not suffer equally. The Yankees continued to outdraw everyone, hosting 22 percent of the total league attendance for 1953, and the Chicago White Sox were actually gaining ground, passing one million patrons in 1951, the first time since the war. The other teams held their own at reduced levels, but for the three clubs at the bottom of the ladder, the reduction spelled disaster.

A major component of the problem was the fact that major league baseball was confined to so few markets. Two teams shared the loyalty of Chicago, St. Louis, Philadelphia, and Boston, while three competed for the support of New York City's four millions. This became an increasingly intolerable situation in the smaller markets as attendance melted in the early 1950s. Boston, the third smallest market in baseball (1.17 million in 1950) was the first to break. The Braves, unable to compete against Tom Yawkey's relentless wealth, moved to Milwaukee after 1952. (Red Sox attendance actually dipped in each of the next two seasons.) St. Louis was the smallest market in all the majors (860,000), and the extraordinarily lousy Browns were trying to compete with the Cardinals, who won the World Series in 1942, 1944, and 1946 and owned the services of Stan Musial besides. Bill Veeck assumed control of the Browns in 1951 and managed to boost attendance to a half million, but it was not enough, once the Busch family with their unlimited pockets bought the Cardinals. The other American League owners forced

Veeck to sell out, and the team moved to Baltimore to become the Orioles, drawing more than a million there despite finishing seventh. But this move hurt the Senators, who labored in close proximity, forcing their move to Minneapolis in 1961. The Athletics meanwhile drew fewer than 400,000 in the mid-range Philadelphia market (1.8 million population) in both 1953 and 1954, the last nails in the coffin for the ancient Connie Mack and his barely competent sons. They sold off to construction millionaire Arnold Johnson, a very close associate of Yankees owners Del Webb and Dan Topping. Johnson moved the Athletics to Kansas City, touching off one of the strangest and most controversial interludes in American League history. The A's drew well at first, but a series of horrendous trades with the Yankees left the team rudderless and inept; support dropped by almost half. Johnson died suddenly in 1960, and new owner Charlie Finley eventually moved the team to Oakland.[14]

Every year, the deck was stacked. Every season, the prognosticators would sit down with pencil and paper to predict who would finish where in the American League standings. The race never was very difficult to handicap. Just eight teams, and just three or four with any real chance of winning, and three or four with an even chance of finishing in the cellar. The details might vary a little from year to year—the fortunes of the White Sox rose eventually into the top three, displacing mistake-prone Boston—but the storyline was very, very clear. Conditions and men constructed a ladder, built on the credo of every team for itself. Some good baseball resulted, and some very bad baseball, too. The competition for wins grew directly out of the competition for money, and the playing field was hopelessly uneven. The effects ramified through the entirety of each franchise, from the bottom to the top.

Once upon a time, all baseball was local. Transportation logistics confined the two major leagues to just ten cities in 1950, all in the northeast quadrant of the nation. St. Louis and Chicago were the western outposts. Folks out past the 100th Meridian or living in the Deep South might root for one major league team or another, but there was no immediacy about it. National media networks did not begin broadcasting games across the entire nation much before 1950. To actually witness and enjoy baseball, populations outside the big eastern towns supported a vast web of minor league teams—hundreds of them, spread across the nation.

Independent teams had once served as the essential source of talent. The web of minor leagues reached into every corner of the country, discovering (white) prospects, nurturing their ability, selling the best up the ladder to richer, better teams, until the very best landed in the majors. The big league teams needed deep pockets to pay minor league owners the market value for young players. Wealthier major league franchises enjoyed an obvious advantage, even then. But that was once upon a time. By the late 1940s, the independent minors were a vanishing breed. Rather than buying players, richer clubs had pretty much taken to purchasing entire minor league teams.

Major league clubs were both complicit in the destruction of the minor leagues and victims of the disaster. A few teams—the Yankees, Cardinals, Indians, Tigers, and Dodgers—spent a lot of money aggressively to incorporate minor league teams into their own organizations. A few such teams they purchased outright; with others they signed "working agreements." For the big teams, these farm outlets existed as proving grounds for their own prospects—the competitive fortunes of the minor league club did not matter a damn. Owners moved "their" players from team to team at will, often destroying a farm team's championship chances in the process. Local paying customers not surprisingly began to lose interest. If major league owners in distant Eastern cities did not care whether the local team won or lost, why should the local population? People stayed home by their radios, listening to major league contests, while the local teams (and entire minor leagues) collapsed for lack of support. Owners scratched their heads, wondering where future ball players would come from.

Creating a farm system required some serious cash investment. There were teams to be bought or rented, players to be found and signed, management to be organized and supported, ballparks to maintain. The payoff came in harvested talent; the more ballplayers a team found and trained for themselves, the greater the competitive advantage. Two ingredients were necessary to establishing a sound and productive farm system: aggression and money. Like everything else in the American League, these commodities were in uneven supply.[15]

Something as simple as a tally of each team's scouts provides a large clue to recruiting attitudes. William Marshall, in his excellent book *Baseball's Pivotal Era*, pinned down the numbers. The Boston Red Sox employed 23 scouts in 1947, more than any other American League team. The Yankees and Indians each had 21 men searching the country for talent, the White Sox 17, the Browns 13, the Tigers 10, the Athletics eight, and the Senators three—the three-tiered ladder in another form. Baseball did not institute an amateur draft until 1965. In the 1940s and 1950s, teams competed without limitations; the organization that found the most and paid the most got the most. Amateur free agent signings reflected the strengths of team scouting systems. Between 1948 and 1954, the Yankees signed 69 amateur free agents who eventually played in the major leagues—23 percent of the league total. Cleveland and Chicago signed 41 each, the Red Sox 48, and the Tigers 37. Then came the big fall-off to the last three teams: St. Louis and Washington each found 22 major league players, the Athletics 23. The Yankees alone found more successful amateurs than the three lowest teams combined.[16]

No matter how many scouts were on the lookout, there remained the problem of how to develop players once somebody found them. Judge Kenesaw Mountain Landis, baseball's first commissioner, did what he could to stymie what he saw as the pernicious growth of farm systems, deemed the invidious invention of that arch-demon, Branch Rickey, who then worked for the St. Louis Cardinals. But Rickey was simply working with a long existing concept, the idea that major league teams could use the vast web of minor leagues as a proving ground for franchise players. What Rickey did was to invest such a system with a very large infusion of cash. Other wealthy teams soon followed.

Landis did what he could to fight what he saw as a great evil, his reach extending to indict a number of American League teams. In 1940, the Judge declared 106 Tigers prospects free agents after Detroit played fast and loose with the rules. He also intervened in tampering cases involving the Cleveland Indians in 1936 and 1944. Such actions made management more circumspect, but did nothing to reverse the trend. The aggressive general managers—Branch Rickey with the Cardinals and later the Dodgers, George Weiss with the Yankees, Bill Veeck with Cleveland—gained enormous power. To keep pace, the rest of the major leagues would have to take advantage of minor league clubs ripe for the fleecing. They did just that, and nearly succeeded in killing off minor league ball. In 1949, something like 463 minor league clubs played in 59 leagues. Three out of every five teams were affiliated with a major league club. In the early 1950s, attendance in the minor leagues began to drop like a dead body off a cliff. By 1959, just 21 minor leagues remained, mostly supported by a large outlay of major league cash. Five teams out of every six depended on a big league affiliation—for players, for guidance, for money, for existence. Minor league team owners could no longer hope to earn money by selling independent players to the majors; the big leagues already had all the talent they wanted under contract.[17]

Another simple chart tells the story in stark numbers:

**Table 2.4**

### Minor League Affiliates, 1947–1954[18]

|       | 1947     | 1948     | 1949     | 1950     | 1951     | 1952     | 1953     | 1954     |
|-------|----------|----------|----------|----------|----------|----------|----------|----------|
| NY    | 20 (7)   | 23 (8)   | 21 (6)   | 15 (5)   | 14 (4)   | 10 (3)   | 11 (3)   | 9 (3)    |
| CLE   | 17 (7)   | 18 (6)   | 17 (7)   | 16 (2)   | 12 (2)   | 10 (3)   | 8 (3)    | 8 (3)    |
| BOS   | 10 (5)   | 13 (8)   | 9 (2)    | 8 (3)    | 8 (3)    | 6 (2)    | 6 (2)    | 6 (3)    |
| CHI   | 8 (2)    | 13 (5)   | 11 (6)   | 8 (4)    | 8 (2)    | 6 (2)    | 8 (3)    | 6 (2)    |
| DET   | 11 (3)   | 10 (4)   | 11 (6)   | 9 (7)    | 8 (4)    | 7 (4)    | 7 (3)    | 8 (3)    |
| WAS   | 6 (4)    | 11 (5)   | 9 (6)    | 10 (6)   | 6 (4)    | 8 (6)    | 7 (4)    | 6 (2)    |
| PHI   | 12 (7)   | 10 (9)   | 11 (8)   | 15 (8)   | 9 (6)    | 8 (6)    | 8 (3)    | 6 (3)    |
| St L  | 16 (6)   | 20 (5)   | 18 (5)   | 13 (2)   | 10 (1)   | 12 (1)   | 10 (1)   | 8 (1)*   |
| Total | 100 (41) | 118 (50) | 107 (46) | 94 (37)  | 75 (26)  | 67 (27)  | 65 (22)  | 57 (20)  |

NOTE: The first number in each space indicates the total number of minor league teams affiliated with each franchise. The number in parentheses indicates the number of minor league teams the franchise owned outright (a subset of the total affiliations).

*Franchise moved to Baltimore in 1954

Most obviously, the figures reflect the collapse of the minors. The number of American League affiliates peaked at 118 in 1948, and dwindled precipitously thereafter. By 1954, the number had dropped to less than half the peak. Minor league baseball was in serious trouble, and major league owners were not prepared to do much of anything about it. The number of teams owned outright dropped by 60 percent as owners consolidated and callously cut their losses. The minor leagues withered. By 1954, just 268 minor league teams remained. Major league clubs owned 48 outright, and controlled another 121 through working agreements. That left just 99 independents—36.9 percent of all teams.

Farm systems had been around for a while by 1947, but there was still enough novelty in the idea to create opportunity for assertive managements. In the table's early years, the Yankees and the Indians steadily outpaced their opponents, although the lowly Browns did try to keep up. The Browns were burdened with financial troubles; their ability to compete for prospects with the top of the ladder faded. Whatever prospects they did find rapidly disappeared, as they could not afford to pay them market value. The Browns stayed afloat by selling good young players to better teams—the Red Sox and Indians especially—thereby dooming themselves to the second division. The Athletics also tried to enlarge their farm system, but just as quickly contracted, unable to pay their bills. New York and Cleveland in the meanwhile were building powerhouse teams from within, drawing on large, efficiently managed systems. Between 1947 and 1954, the Yankees won six flags, Cleveland the remaining two. Farm system numbers largely mirrored the story of the ladder—teams on top grabbed the most and got the best. Not until the middle 1950s did the distribution of farm resources begin to even out.

But it was more than a question of resources. Even if a team could employ an infinite number of scouts to discover enough players to fill an infinite number of farm affiliates, there was still no guarantee that the operation would ever produce a major league baseball player. There remained the matter of actually training the players to play successful baseball, and that remained very much a hit and miss proposition.

Viewing the situation from 60 years or so down the line, it is quite puzzling to see just how lax most teams were when it came to instruction. The old attitude that great players were born, not made, seems to have prevailed, though it is difficult to understand why. As a rule, coaches did not coach much, and managers worked with whatever the general manager provided, rather than planning for the future. Coaching jobs were in too many cases a sinecure for the manager's pals, rather than a resource to train young players. Attitude was probably half the explanation, and money accounted for the rest. Training camps came expensive; any team paying just three scouts to find baseball players would not be wanting to spend much on teaching the prospects how to play the game. Presumably the kids knew how to play; that was why the overworked, much maligned scout had signed them in the first place. Scouts in fact played a very basic role in defining how the game was played "properly." Any prospect displaying an unusual approach to the game—an odd wind-up, a peculiar batting stance—found scouts very reluctant to sign him. There were expectations that had to be met, parameters to follow. Young black players with unusual swings or pitching motions ran up against this wall more than once.[19]

Like just about everyone else in mid–20th-century America, baseball scouts were both perpetrators and victims of the racial and ethnic understandings that had underpinned society. World War II dealt that world some sobering lessons about racial assumptions, but stereotypical vestiges remained, plainly influencing the ethnic makeup of the eight American League teams (along with so much else). Ethnicity was an issue important enough to the editors of the annual *Baseball Register* that the individual player sketches included a listing of nationality every year until 1956. The responses suggest something about the players' views on ethnicity. A handful, prescient and wise, chose to say simply that they were "American." Most answered as a race scientist would desire and expect, with some expression of their overseas background. A great many chose to emphasize that they were products of the melting pot, providing backgrounds such as "English-Irish" or "Swedish-English." The history of the 20th century meant something; many players were careful to ally their German forebears with something more socially acceptable. It was better in most cases to be "Irish-German," rather than "German-Irish." The ethnic amalgamations make it very difficult to establish the kind of racial categories the social scientists loved so much when most everyone believed that ethnicity spelled character. Still, taking just the first nationality each player provided, it is plain that American League baseball remained very much the province of the old immigration. Players of English, German, Scots-Irish, and Celtic (Irish, Scots, Welsh) account for more than two-thirds of the American League rosters. Scanning the ethnicities listed in the 1946 *Register* suggests that men of Eastern European descent had begun to make some inroads, though they still accounted for just 12 percent of the total. Other ethnicities remained suspect. There were just nine Italians in the American League in 1946, even if three of them—DiMaggio, Rizzuto, and Berra—were making a considerable impact with the Yankees. Despite some glorious seasons, Hank Greenberg stood as the only Jewish player in the League, and he would be sold to Pittsburgh in 1947. The racial barriers bended enough to allow eight players of American Indian descent entry, though just about all of them had to endure being called "Chief." (Allie Reynolds became "Superchief.") Of course there were no blacks (or "American Negro," as the *Register* would label them) until 1947. Nor were there many Latinos. In fact, just two players claimed any Spanish descent. The racial assumptions, the categories that governed society very much impacted America's game, consciously and unconsciously. "Traditional American" kids got more opportunity to attract serious attention; scouts viewed them more favorably. For Italians, for Jews, for Latinos, for

Native Americans, and especially for blacks, the road was all uphill. Racial stereotypes may have loosened, but they lingered in lots of shadowy places.[20]

No matter the prospect, one of the wealthy teams was far more likely to be assessing his talent—more scouts, more farm clubs, more and better coaching. The fact was, the top tier ball clubs were not only finding and developing their own players, they were essentially performing the same services for the three teams stuck on the bottom. The Browns, the A's, and the Nationals were the dependent stepchildren of American League baseball, unable to provide their own needs, looking to the tiers above them for the decent ballplayers they could not provide for themselves. The other teams provided.

**Table 2.5**

**Roster Players Acquired Through Transaction With AL Teams[21]**

**1946–1954**

**Players Acquired From:**

| Team | NYY | CLE | BOS | DET | CWS | WAS | PHA | SLB* | Total Acquired |
|------|-----|-----|-----|-----|-----|-----|-----|------|----------------|
| Yankees | X | 2 | 1 | 2 | 2 | 2 | 2 | 9 | 20 |
| Indians | 5 | X | 2 | 5 | 7 | 5 | 12 | 8 | 44 |
| Red Sox | 1 | 1 | X | 7 | 12 | 6 | 2 | 12 | 41 |
| Tigers | 1 | 4 | 7 | X | 6 | 2 | 1 | 9 | 30 |
| White Sox | 6 | 7 | 6 | 4 | X | 12 | 8 | 19 | 62 |
| Nationals | 9 | 9 | 12 | 2 | 14 | X | 2 | 12 | 60 |
| Athletics | 11 | 5 | 1 | 1 | 10 | 5 | X | 7 | 40 |
| Browns* | 16 | 9 | 13 | 13 | 13 | 9 | 5 | X | 78 |
| Total moved | 49 | 37 | 42 | 34 | 64 | 41 | 32 | 76 | 375 |

*moved to Baltimore to become the Orioles, 1954

There is a great deal to learn from this simple table. To begin with the most obvious, the New York Yankees were the team least dependent on the other American League clubs to fill their rosters, acquiring just 20 players from other AL teams over nine seasons. At the same time, they sent 49 major league ballplayers to the remaining seven teams, a net *loss* of 29 players. Three additional AL teams experienced tiny losses: the Red Sox (one), the Tigers (four), and the White Sox (two). New York, rich in talent from a very large farm system, was in the best position to give away quantity to acquire some quality, and they did just that.

Of the 49 players the Yankees sent away, 36 (near three-fourths) joined the rosters of the three teams at the bottom of the ladder. Much the same situation obtained in Cleveland, who moved 23 of 37 (62.1 percent) to the bottom dwellers, and in Boston, where 26 of 42 (61.9 percent) migrated downward. Clearly the top three teams were making an effort to stock the three resource-poor teams with enough decent players to maintain some semblance of competition. Add to this the fact that New York, Cleveland, and Boston all purchased players from the Browns at prices well beyond market value; what was happening was a kind of ad hoc resource redistribution, a barely disguised form of subsidy. The Browns would not win much, but the team would stay afloat.

The merest glance at Table 2.5 indicates that the St. Louis Browns, Chicago White Sox, and Washington Senators were changing their rosters at a far more reckless pace than the other five clubs. For the Browns, personnel change was a matter of sending away decent players the team could not afford to pay, and acquiring enough respectable, often very young or very old players to fill out the roster. That the resulting "team" was poor to lousy could not be helped. When a franchise is reconstructing at the rate of nine players from the other AL teams each year, and acquiring additional hopefuls from the National League, the independent minor leagues, and eventually the Negro Leagues, there is just not going to be much opportunity to mesh. Clark Griffith's Washington Nationals were not far different, taking on seven or more new players each year, while sending away four or five.

The White Sox were a little out of the ordinary. Doormats in the five seasons immediately following World War II, the club actually did possess enough resources to try to improve their win-loss record through some shrewd trading. Nellie Fox, Billy Pierce, Sherman Lollar, and Minnie Minoso all joined the White Sox from other American League clubs. The effort eventually succeeded. The White Sox reached the first division in 1951 and became a pennant contender thereafter. It may as well be admitted too that Frank "Trader" Lane, White Sox General Manager from 1950 to 1955, would have traded his own mother for the excitement of it, and thrown in his son-in-law to sweeten the deal.[22]

The Philadelphia Athletics, a proud old team operated by a very proud, very old man, did try to build from within, as their acquisition of just 40 players (second lowest over the period) attests. But Connie Mack was in a position no better that Clark Griffith, a position that would all too soon deteriorate to the desperate level of the Browns. Mack ended up accepting several players from the Yankees and the White Sox, giving very little in return.

Taken altogether, Table 2.5 is a visual representation of a league comprising rich, reasonably rich, decently well off, and desperately poor franchises. To maintain any legitimate claim to major league status, the Yankees, Indians, Red Sox, Tigers, and White Sox had to supply the glaring deficiencies of their weaker brethren. Those teams could afford it, so they traded their surplus young talent to the Senators, the Athletics, the Browns, receiving nothing like full value in return. The trading gave solid, slightly less skilled young players a chance to play every day, enhancing the overall quality of play and improving business for one and all.

The track record of acquisitions by team is one reflection of the larger and sad reality that manifested itself in every possible way. Some teams were bound to win, others sure to lose. Ethically speaking, the situation raised some interesting dilemmas. Should we see the Yankees and the Indians as muscle-bound villains, taking advantage of poorer neighbors and keeping them in their place? Or are Cleveland and New York the benevolent franchises, sharing their embarrassment of riches with less fortunate brethren, helping to maintain some semblance of competitive play despite the grinding poverty or pathetic negligence the lowest three teams continually exhibited? Such questions arise from a system grounded in a fundamentally unequal resource base.

Does a team need some good players? Obviously, yes. Not just to win, but to attract sufficient paying customers to the ballpark. The customers supplied the cash to pay the decent players on hand, find the players of the future, and train those players properly to do their jobs. The club has to hire perceptive scouts to scour the country, seeking players out. There has to be a large, well-organized farm system to provide prospects the necessary training and experience. Teams might even want some coaches who actually coach, so all that time and investment has a chance of actually producing someone who can play. In short, a team needs money, in very large amounts. In 1957, the Detroit Tigers management estimated that the cost of developing a single major league regular player—from the day he was discovered by a wide-ranging scout to the day he stepped onto the field at Briggs Stadium—amounted to $100,000. So, nine hundred thousand to field a starting nine from scratch. That was a lot more than some American League teams could afford.

If a team did not possess even a flicker of a chance, people simply would not come to the ballpark in sufficient numbers, making it difficult to pay the bills. The poorer teams facing this conundrum at the same time had to live with the knowledge that the Yankees, the Indians, the Red Sox had no trouble at all meeting expenses much higher than theirs. Victories cost money, but victories were the only real way to attract money. That nickel and dime thing.

The American League was a three-tiered world of haves and have nots, governed by a philosophy of one for all, and every man for himself. The owners would band together to fight off the incipient labor unrest posed by Mexican Leagues, fledgling unions, or court challenges to the reserve clause. They would agree to minimum player salaries, to player pension funds, to similar devices intended to mitigate potential player anger. But the eight owners would do nothing to alleviate the unequal playing field they had created among themselves. Revenue sharing, common media contracts, player drafts, these were all notions for the distant future, or for other sports altogether. Baseball in the 1950s was the American system at its best: everyone played by the same rules, had the same options, the same opportunities. The only flaw was that the necessary resources did not exist evenly across the map. Those who held the initial advantages kept them.

Beginning in 1947, the eight owners of American League clubs considered the prospect of integration in large part from just this business perspective. Would spending a nickel on a black ballplayer earn the team a dime down the road? Owners such as Bill Veeck, general managers such as Trader Lane, and managers such as Paul Richards saw Negro Leagues players as one of the most cost-effective investments available and plunged, with notable results. Color-bound traditionalists such as Connie Mack, Clark Griffith and Tom Yawkey would not see past their prejudices until it was too late. And George Weiss of the Yankees felt no need to parse his nickels; he had plenty to spare. Weiss could indulge his resistance to integration without fear of damaging his prospects, economic or competitive.

The story of the American League's integration is really eight stories at least, each with its own set of motivations, its own set of considerations, economic and otherwise. To ownership, integration was just one more wrinkle in the fabric of a predictable yet uncertain business—an annoyance, a burden, an opportunity. For Cleveland and Chicago (and eventually Baltimore), the talents of a newly opening labor pool would provide a welcome source of necessary talent to climb higher on the competitive ladder. For others—the Red Sox, the Tigers, the Athletics, the Senators—reluctance to integrate would allow their opponents to catch up to them and eventually pass them by.

American League baseball was an enterprise in motion, bounded by systemic inequalities, crawling reluctantly toward unwelcome change. There was no innocent past to recall with a nostalgic sigh. Black ballplayers gained entrance to an American League shaped by hard-nosed business types. Business considerations were always at the back of their decisions. Mostly they were trying hard to avoid losing too much. If blacks were going to play in the American League, owners had to believe that spending that nickel would earn them a dime.

# III

# The Masks of Separation

## *Why Integration Was Unlikely to Happen*

---

In the late autumn of 1943, Kenesaw Mountain Landis, Commissioner of Baseball for more than 20 years, announced that a joint meeting of National and American League representatives would receive a delegation from the Negro Publishers Association. As the national press release advised, "It will be the first time the race issue has come before the annual meeting." Very soon after, Judge Landis received a letter, with a copy of the newspaper announcement attached. The letter had this to say:

> Dear Judge
>   I certainly hope this does not mean you are planning to mix up Negroes and whites. No self respecting white man wants to live travel sleep and eat with a Negro—you will hurt the great game if you try to mix them—I am in favor of the Negro having the same things as the whites, but left to themselves. No mixing.[1]

Here was a sentiment that the Commissioner readily recognized and understood. The letter was no less than an expression of mainstream America, a heartfelt plea for a continuation of the policies that had made the nation what it was: a fortress of racial separation, where real freedom extended only to white people. Just how Judge Landis himself felt about that state of affairs was immaterial. What mattered was that he stood at the head of a vast organization of leagues and teams that many saw as the essential emblem of American culture. His job was to protect that image, to guarantee that baseball continued to reflect America's fundamental values, its embrace of freedom and equal opportunity. For white people only.[2]

As the United States reluctantly entered World War II, one condition of existence remained comfortingly certain: Jim Crow was alive and flourishing all across the nation. The dominant culture maintained control over any and all national institutions, and sought to siphon money from whatever institutions black people tried to create for themselves. The proposition that baseball embodied the essence of American culture was at that moment undeniably true—major league baseball was exclusively white. Completely separate Negro Leagues, burdened with ongoing financial woes and too often run by criminal elements, struggled to gain traction as the Depression slowly receded. Never was the color line more palpable, more emphatically expressed. Take the time machine back to 1941, when most Americans, black and white, expected such division to last into an indefinite future. Blacks would not vote or hold public office; they would be denied equal access to public transportation. Any facilities afforded them would be separate from whites, and plainly inferior in quality. They could eat only in their own establishments, sleep in their own hotels. Forever. Two Americas: a comfortable and accommodating situation for whites, a financially crippled and carefully fenced world for blacks. By 1941, apartheid had become a way of life.

Looking back from the 21st century, such an ugly state of affairs raises some knotty interpretive problems for historians. After all, this was just six years removed from 1947, when the first black players of the 20th century openly donned major league uniforms. What seemed so impossibly far away in 1941 was, as events played out, so very, very near. The juxtaposition of dates has created a profound influence on the way events are now recalled, how they are understood. If integration was that close to becoming reality in 1941, perhaps it was inevitable? Perhaps the determined racial separations of the 1920s and 1930s were some sort of aberration, a bump on the road to an eventual integration bound to occur? A dangerous and misleading assumption. Tracking the past backwards from the triumph of integration, the reader fashions a path filled with deceptive notions—that blacks fully expected the thing to happen, that every black person wanted integration above all else, that the Negro Leagues existed primarily to foster the process of bringing blacks into Organized Ball. In some instances, perhaps for some people, such propositions may have been true. But black baseball did not invent itself to become a conduit for the major leagues a quarter century down the road. The Negro Leagues were a black enterprise, one that had attracted the talent, the support, and the money of black people throughout much of America. The leagues were a growing source of cultural expression, an emblem of strength. They were built on hope and defiance, and they were a visible demonstration of black creative ability and black resources, in 1941, when black and white worlds existed on opposite shores of what seemed an unbridgeable and never-ending racial divide.

One stumbling block in interpreting the motivations of black baseball in the 1930s and 1940s is the relative lack of first-hand written material. There are lots of oral histories of black players, black owners, black fans, lots of memoirs, lots of observations—almost all written or collected sometime after 1947, when the triumph of Jackie Robinson pointed to a future constructed on integration. Black participants recalled their past in the context of that future, came to see themselves as cogs in an enterprise bent on obliterating the color line. Whether they saw themselves that way in 1920 or 1939 is another question. Certainly the powers operating Organized Baseball before the Second World War would not have seen them in that way. Black baseball was a world very separate from theirs. Just about everyone expected things to stay that way.

Perhaps the key source for understanding perceptions of black baseball as it really existed during the 1930s was the coverage offered by the black press. Just as baseball was racially divided into separate and unconnected worlds, so it was with American journalism. White newspapers had little to say about black events or black issues, unless something they deemed truly egregious occurred. Certainly the metropolitan dailies made no effort to cover the weekly grind of Negro Leagues baseball; the barest mention of the annual East-West Game was as good as they would do. Black newspapers came into existence to fill this void, providing news and commentary on issues affecting the black community. Tellingly, the black press never mentioned any events from major league baseball, limiting their baseball coverage to stories from the Negro Leagues. Several inescapable facts of life conspired to limit that coverage severely. Black people were one-tenth of America's population, more often than not the poorest tenth. Mostly they still lived in the rural South; black populations in Northern cities remained too small to support a daily newspaper. Black journals were not anchored to any specific local customer base, nor was there enough money to publish a daily paper. The great black newspapers of the 1930s and 1940s were weeklies aimed at a national reading audience. The chief of these, the *Pittsburgh Courier*, reached an audience of roughly 227,000 once a week. The *Chicago Defender*, the *Baltimore Afro-American*, the *Amsterdam News*, and the *Michigan Chronicle* were not dissimilar—papers with local names reaching for customers spread far and wide across the map. Reporting once a week, the black journals did little more than highlight the more striking action in Negro League play. Recording the daily contests, rooting for the home team were out of the equation. What the curious reader got from leafing through the back pages of the black weeklies was not so much a summary of Negro Leagues competition as an impression of black baseball's impact on the community. The impression was of a world far removed from the majors.[3]

Probably the elemental expression of black baseball's place in the culture came from the pen of Wendell Smith, sportswriter for the *Pittsburgh Courier*. Smith was generally considered to be the best of his generation, an influential voice who drew captivating word pictures of masterful play in the Negro baseball leagues. Wendell Smith joined the *Courier* in 1937. One year later, he was describing black baseball fans as "a strange tribe," cheering for major league clubs that did not want their patronage, failing to support Negro Leagues teams "filled with brilliant, colorful, dazzling players who know the game from top to bottom." Smith pointed to what he saw as harsh reality. "We have been fighting for years in an effort to make owners of major league baseball teams admit Negro players. But they won't do it, probably never will.... Oh, we're an optimistic, faithful, prideless lot—we pitiful black folk." A hint of militancy there, and not a lot of hope. At age 24, Wendell Smith was a black man living in a segregated black world, promoting black enterprise.[4]

Lacking a crystal ball, other notable black journalists took a similar line during the 1930s. Sam Lacy of the *Baltimore Afro-American* would later become one of the most determined crusaders for racial justice, but in 1939 he saw fit to print a collection of mostly discouraging opinions offered by Negro Leagues players. Misgivings included the fear that three-quarters of black players would lose their livelihoods if a few Negro stars went to the majors; that it would take a virtually impossible "universal movement" to achieve integration; that "bad actors" among the players would wreck the effort. Not an encouraging litany, but a sentiment widely echoed by black writers.[5] In 1941, Frank Young of the *Chicago Defender* was advocating construction of a large black-owned stadium in Chicago to free the Negro Leagues from dependence on white-owned Comiskey Park. Young lobbied heavily for Negro Leagues reform, worrying that black ball was "floundering around like a ship with a broken rudder in stormy seas."[6] Joe Bostic, writing for *The People's Voice* in New York City, declared in 1942 that "it would be criminal" to destroy the Negro Leagues. Bostic went on to argue that integration was a worthy ideal, but undesirable in the practical world.[7] Chester L. Washington, toiling for the *Pittsburgh Courier* in 1936, wrote of "the promised land of economic prosperity" for black baseball's future.[8] Ed Harris of the *Philadelphia Tribune* saw the 1941 East-West Game as "a triumph for Negroes."[9]

The cream of black sportswriters were generally a pessimistic group when it came to integration. They did articulate hope from time to time, decrying the injustice of segregation and emphasizing the formidable talent of black players. But they were not counting on any meaningful break in the color line, not soon. What they delivered to their audience was a celebration of the exciting and separate world of the Negro Leagues. By and large, they wanted to see those leagues prosper and grow, become an ever more powerful expression of black culture. If whites insisted on a racially separated America, black institutions would have to be independent and strong.[10]

Wendell Smith stood with his fellow black journalists in all these respects. But Smith also understood that try as they might, the Negro Leagues were never going to achieve the measure of major league ball—not in prestige, certainly not in money. Smith had personally tasted the bitter disappointment of losing out on the real glory—he had been denied a contract by a major league scout because of his color. Smith was not a man to allow near hopelessness to stand in his path. Very soon after joining the *Courier*, he began to use his position to push for integration. From the start, his campaign was consistent, pointed and clever. He took the fight to the enemy.[11]

Smith opened his campaign in 1939 with a column advocating formation of a chapter of the NAACP devoted to fighting the color line on behalf of black ballplayers. Individual efforts had achieved exactly nothing; it was time for organized, cooperative action to create leverage. But he continued to turn up the heat in his own fashion as well. His next step was an interview with Ford Frick, President of the National League, concentrating on race issues. Frick displayed some sympathy for Smith's cause, but argued that white America was in no way prepared for the changes integration would bring. Black players would suffer Jim Crow separations from their teams during spring training, Frick predicted, and during the season in towns such as St. Louis or Washington, D.C. Racially mixed teams would find it nearly impossible to function as a unit. Those were the realities blacks had to face.[12]

Ford Frick's explanations sounded very much like the standard excuses to Wendell Smith, so he decided to investigate their validity. Located in Pittsburgh, Smith had opportunities to speak with each of the National League managers over the summer and did so, sounding them out on the race issue. In a series of columns beginning on July 15, 1939, and running for eight weeks, he reported some intriguing results. The columns began on a positive note. Smith's first subject was Cincinnati Reds manager Bill McKechnie. The Reds were going unexpectedly well that season, and observers gave McKechnie much of the credit; he was considered perhaps the game's best manager. He was also a very decent man, supportive of his players and sunny in his outlook. He shared that optimism with Smith, smiling widely as he told the reporter, "I have seen at least 25 colored players who could have made the grade."

The following week's report was more sobering. "I do not think that Negro players will ever be admitted to the majors!" was New York Giants manager Bill Terry's reply. Smith was not surprised, having anticipated "Memphis Bill's" answer. "Terry is not the type that appeals to the fan," Smith advised. "There is nothing romantic or colorful about him." His reputation as a "conservative" on the race issue preceded him. Terry cited much the same arguments Ford Frick had mentioned, that Jim Crow would play havoc with travel and lodging. The Giants manager did agree that a few black players had the skills to play in the majors, though that was not the issue. The best thing for blacks, Terry believed, would be to organize one well-structured Negro League which would operate in parallel with the majors. In short, make Jim Crow just a little healthier.

The Bill Terry interview proved the low point of Wendell Smith's series. Terry turned out to be the only National League manager firmly opposed to hiring blacks, or at least the only one to say as much openly. Over the following six weeks, the remaining National League managers carefully followed Bill McKechnie's lead, praising the skills of black players, agreeing that several of the Negro Leagues stars could readily play for major league clubs. Later interviews grew more substantive as Smith probed beneath the surface to uncover the real roadblocks keeping black players out of the majors. Leo Durocher, the not-so-nice manager of the Brooklyn Dodgers, said he was ready to sign a black player who could improve his team, but the judgment was not his to make. "The decision as to whether or not they shall play is not up to the managers but ball club owners." (Durocher was telling the truth. When the Dodgers organization did commit to integration in 1947, he played a key role in staring down team opposition to the move.)

Ray Blades of St. Louis—the southernmost city in the majors—agreed that it was up to the owners to dissolve the color line, and thought that they would if there was enough pressure from fans. Not very likely in St. Louis, where seating at Sportsman's Park was still segregated. Both the Cardinals and the Browns played in that park, and not many fans came out to see either team in 1939. If anything was going to break down "the social prejudice that exists right now," it would be the possibility of bringing new fans to the ballpark in one of America's smallest major league cities.

The most thoughtful interview may well have come as a surprise to Smith and his readers. In 1939, Casey Stengel bore the reputation of hapless clown, a talkative but ineffective manager who had failed to get either the Dodgers or his current Boston Braves out of the second division. But, as he would later prove beyond doubt, Stengel was a shrewd baseball man, insightful into the game and the business. Back in 1919, he had recommended several of the players who formed the core of J. L. Wilkinson's Kansas City Monarchs. Stengel maintained an interest in black ball, readily identifying several players he felt could play in the major leagues. He was especially interested in two catchers—the position Stengel felt was key to the game. Josh Gibson's power hitting made him an attractive player, but Stengel was more drawn to Biz Mackey, "a marvel at working pitchers."

In his interview with Wendell Smith, reported on August 26, Stengel sounded what had by then become a familiar refrain. Integration was up to the owners and the owners alone. (The reader has to suspect a little collusion here—the managers surely recognized quickly that Smith intended to interview them all, so they agreed on a safe and stock answer: only the owners could decide.) Stengel refused even to speculate on when black players might be accepted on major league teams, not knowing how the owners felt about the issue. He had no doubt that there were blacks ready to play.

Stengel then dug a little deeper, indicating "that he was interested somewhat in the plight of organized Negro baseball." Blacks, it seemed to Stengel, did not take much interest in the Negro Leagues teams, did not follow their fortunes avidly. Smith explained that Negro Leagues teams played for the home fans only once or twice a week, making it hard to sustain interest, an observation that apparently satisfied the Braves manager. Stengel then wondered "if it would be profitable to admit Negroes to the majors." Would Negro fans follow them? This led to a larger discussion of the general role of ethnicity in the presentation of major league ball. With the exception of blacks, clubs ignored questions of ethnic composition. What mattered was putting a winning club on the field—fans of all stripes would pay to see a winner, whether the players were Mexicans, Greeks, or whatever. If teams composed their rosters on the basis of ethnic drawing power, Stengel pointed out, there would be very few minority players at all.

When it came to considering blacks, the situation appeared to be different. A calculus came into play—would placing blacks on white teams draw more fans to the ball parks? Black fans? Wendell Smith pointed out that if that was the reasoning, then surely the Yankees and the Giants "would almost be compelled to include Negro players, as their parks are right on the doorstep of Harlem, the largest Negro center in the United States." Stengel agreed with that line of reasoning, but remained uncertain. "I understand that there is a great deal of unrest within the Negro leagues themselves," Stengel observed. "Perhaps the owners feel that they may bring their troubles along with them into big league baseball, which would reflect on the game's name." Almost certainly, Stengel was thinking of individual character problems among Negro Leagues players—Sam Lacy's "bad actors." Wendell Smith instead chose to interpret the comment as a reflection on the poor organization and operation of the Negro Leagues as a whole. Smith could agree with that assessment. He could also point out that the major leagues' record was far from spotless, beginning with the Black Sox scandal. "The White Sox scandal is such a horror to them ... that they don't even want innocent black players," Smith shot back.

And so it went, a verbal chess match between a determined, fiery young writer and a quick-witted, loquacious career baseball man. Stengel demonstrated all the qualities that would later endear him to the writing community: his willingness to talk at length, his ability to express his thoughts on complicated issues, his readiness to spar, his essential ambiguity. Casey Stengel very seldom let on what he was really thinking, in 1939, or 15 years later, when he was in a vastly different, far more powerful situation. Where did Stengel really stand on the issue of race? There is ammunition in his conversation with Wendell Smith to argue any number of ways, for and against. He admired and coveted the ability of black players, but he did not flinch from citing obstacles to integration. Stengel left Wendell Smith and his readers feeling positive but unsure—just what he wanted.

Casey Stengel happened to be the last of the eight National League managers Wendell Smith interviewed. Smith chose not to present the interview pieces in chronological order, perhaps to shape the overall impact on his readers. He began with the brief and positive comments by Bill McKechnie, followed the next week by Bill Terry, the one wholly negative voice in the series. Several variations on McKechnie's themes follow before Casey Stengel holds forth, sandwiched between the even-handed responses of Gabby Harnett and Pie Traynor. Hartnett, manager of the Cubs, liked the idea of adding black players to his pathetic ball club, and hoped the owners would do something. Pie Traynor dreamed of Satchel Paige pitching for his Pirates, and thought there was a good chance blacks would play in the majors very soon. "Personally, I don't see why the ban against Negro players exists at all," Traynor advised. A good note to end the series.

Taken together, Wendell Smith's interviews with the major league managers provide a most accurate picture of baseball's position with respect to race before the War. No one who seriously understood baseball would deny the talent of the best black players—managers would readily find places for them. But none of the managers were prepared to address the deeper issue of separation because of race; they saw Biz Mackey and Satchel Paige as talented individuals, not as representatives of black America. More importantly, the managers told Wendell Smith that their opinions did not really matter. Answers to the race question rested squarely on the shoulders of the major league owners and their Commissioner. The playing fields did not matter. Integration would be resolved in baseball's board rooms, by men with business on their minds. It was a lesson Wendell Smith took to heart.[13]

Wendell Smith was an unusual voice in the America of the late 1930s. Twenty years of unrelenting Jim Crow machination, abetted by the poverty and fear born in the Great Depression, had severely deepened the long-standing racial divide. Baseball had become increasingly emblematic of that divide; the whites had their leagues, the blacks had theirs. A very long list of impediments to any form of baseball integration had grown increasingly plain. Three centuries of racist habits and racist thinking had woven themselves into the fabric of American life, spawning assumptions that warped every aspect of America's game, sometimes in peculiar fashion. Foremost was the issue of race itself, that us against them mentality that made skin color the sole measure of a human being.

Jim Crow was a habit taken for granted throughout the world of baseball. Segregated seating was the rule in most major league parks coming out of the Great War. As late as the 1940s, black patrons at Washington's Griffith Stadium continued to sit in the right field bleachers, even if the Jim Crow laws had been officially abolished. The park was the only desegregated entertainment venue in the District of Columbia. Jim Crow persisted at Sportsman's Park in St. Louis, home to both the Cardinals and the Browns, until 1944. Washington and St. Louis were the southernmost of the American League towns; there was not yet enough black attendance at the six additional parks to make seating much of an issue before World War II. What did exist was a fear of increasing black attendance, a prospect that weighed heavily on the minds of white owners trying to sell tickets. They could have had worse to worry about. In 1936, the Ku Klux Klan burned down the City Stadium in Omaha, Nebraska, one night after the Kansas City Monarchs came to town.[14]

Another strange incident drove home the point. On July 29, 1938, Bob Elson of Chicago radio station WGN interviewed Jake Powell, a reserve outfielder in town with the New York Yankees. Powell was in his sixth major league season, his third with New York. He had showed some promise with the Washington Nationals, hitting .312 in 1935, but had gone steadily downhill after the trade to the Yankees. Obviously Bob Elson was not expecting any headline event, just another interview with a second-line player on a July afternoon. Elson asked Powell what he did to stay in shape in Dayton, Ohio, over the winter. When Powell replied something like, "Oh, that's easy. I'm a policeman and I beat niggers over the head with my blackjack while I'm on my beat," all hell broke loose.[15]

Elson immediately terminated the interview. The following day, he wrote a statement published by the *Chicago Defender*:

> An incident occurred on my pre-game broadcast, which was very distasteful to me and, I know, to many of my radio listeners. I regret very much that player Jake Powell of the New York Yankees saw fit to make a remark which was entirely uncalled for and made without being anticipated in any way by me.... I want to repeat that the remark of Mr. Powell was as offensive to me as it was to many of my good friends.[16]

Art Rust, Jr., later a no-nonsense sportscaster and one of the first to write of baseball "from a black man's point of view," was an 11-year-old boy visiting his aunt in Chicago that summer. He heard Powell, and he recalled "feeling ill when I heard this."[17] Probably that was the best any black person could say. A few whites got angry too. Some, such as Yankees manager Joe McCarthy, were angry with Bob Elson for putting Powell in such an unscripted and unguarded situation where he could say something that stupid for all the public to hear. A few white newspapers tried to make excuses for Powell, claiming he was just a dumb Southern boy trying to make a joke. Commissioner Landis, shocked by a huge outpouring of black protest, tried to agree with McCarthy and the newspapers. The outcry from the black community grew so heated he no choice but to respond. Blacks were, after all, a significant component of the fan base. Powell got a ten-day suspension. The Yankees made him take a tour of black bars in Harlem to offer apologies. Some say he truly was remorseful, but given the mythology that quickly grew up around him, that is difficult to believe.

First of all, Powell was no ignorant Southern guy. He was born in Silver Spring, Maryland, and spent much of his boyhood in Ohio. He had in fact played professional baseball with black players several times on barnstorming tours. Negro Leagues star Ted Page recalled him as "quite a democratic individual." He was never a policeman in Dayton, either. Powell was what baseball men would call a scrappy player, the kind who would do anything his manager asked, right up to cheating and picking fights. Joe McCarthy loved him and was very resentful over the suspension, which came in the heat of a pennant race. Yankees management thought enough was enough after Powell's attempt at atonement, but the issue refused to die. Black community leaders and the black press pressured Yankees General Manager Ed Barrow to release him in the spring of 1939. Powell played—very sparingly—for New York in 1939 and 1940 before the team sold him to the Pacific Coast League for $12,000. Why the Yankees chose to keep him is another misty cloud in the mythology.

Some observers claimed that Powell remained a Yankee because Joe McCarthy wanted him around. If that was true, why did McCarthy allow him just 89 plate appearances over the entire 1939 season? Another possibility—one that has the appeal of making sense—was that the Yankees did try to move Powell, but found no takers willing to accept a chance on such value-damaged property. The odd thing was, the Yankees deployed him so rarely that black players registered false memories of what happened. Sug Cornelius recalled that three weeks after the fateful broadcast the Yankees sold Powell to Detroit, "and when he went over to Detroit, those fans over there threw so many balls and things at him that he was gone." It was true that black fans threw trash at Jake Powell—enough to stop the game several times—but the event took place in Washington. Powell was still a Yankee, fresh back from his suspension.

Powell was not gone in 1939, nor yet in 1940. World War II created a player shortage that brought him back to the big leagues in 1943, as an outfielder with the Washington Nationals. (Clark Griffith may have expressed a desire to play Josh Gibson during the war years; the man he did play was Jake Powell.) More trouble of his own making plagued Powell. Released when the veterans returned for the 1946 season, he drifted from trouble to trouble, passing bad checks and preparing to enter into a bigamous marriage. When police arrested him a second time in 1947, he shot himself to death. A troubled man, Jake Powell.

As Ted Page of the Philadelphia Stars long afterward observed, probably it "was a slip," that remark on a Chicago radio station that branded Jake Powell a racist of the worst kind.[18] He was not a Dayton cop with a blackjack, but a hard-nosed ballplayer with an attitude straight out of Jim Crow's America. For the most part, white America could not grasp what the rumpus was about—it was the kind of joke hurled across the racial abyss every day. Calling his words a slip underscored their context. It was an unthinking use of a common racist joke; the mistake was in using it when so many people, black and white, would hear. To white America, Powell's mistake was to say it on the radio. It was a little stupid, but let it die. He had never demonstrated any signs of overt prejudice before.

What was different about the Jake Powell incident was not so much what he said, nor the medium that broadcast his callousness and then cut him off, but the black reaction to his "slip." Leaders of the black community, particularly in New York, would not, could not let the matter die. This was too public, too egregious, too Jim Crow even for apartheid America.

Judge Landis was forced to agree. The Yankees tried to tough it out, but dared not play him much in 1939 or 1940. The times were disturbing. War had come to Europe; the forces of decency were standing up to Hitler's "scientific" racism. Sentiments in America were beginning to change, at least a little. Could a nation theoretically devoted to democratic principles allow institutional racism to continue? The consequence of that was a nation of Jake Powells, men who made sick jokes about keeping black people in their place. By 1939, the black community had endured more than enough.

Jake Powell was the man who exposed America for what it really was. Race abuse had become unthinking, casual, the stuff of dumb humor. Powell suffered a heavy price for failing to think, but he cracked open a door. Here was an incident repellant enough to provide ammunition to Jim Crow's opponents. In 1939, very few were willing for America to look this bad. Not in plain sight. Powell was the man who slipped and said too much.[19]

Racial discrimination wore different masks in 1939 America, depending on the region of the country. In some ways, the Northern cities where major league ball flourished were more obsessed than the South with delimiting the parts of the world where blacks could gain entry. Every city had its white neighborhoods, off-limits to blacks, and its black neighborhoods, the developing ghettos. In Southern towns, where black populations often outnumbered white and a degree of intermingling was an unavoidable way of life, there was greater emphasis on separate privilege for whites, and strict separation in institutions, services, and recreations. Jim Crow America expected Organized Baseball to maintain a visible color line in the North, and not even dream of allowing blacks to share spring training facilities down South. Nor would Southern whites countenance blacks playing on their minor league teams—one more issue for major league clubs owning farm franchises in the Southern Association, the South Atlantic League, or the Texas League.

Organized Baseball generally saw the whole race business as a nuisance. Not the color line itself—that was regarded as a normal and acceptable condition for living in America. The nuisance was that people had the temerity to keep calling up the race question, keep harping at it. Journalists were mostly responsible. Decisions might be made in baseball's board rooms, but the discussion would play out in public print.

In August of 1942, *The Sporting News* felt obligated to run an editorial entitled "No Good from Raising Race Issue." The weekly sheet was considerably more than an ordinary voice in the baseball wars. Run by J. G. Taylor Spink, *The Sporting News* functioned as the nation's central news source for major league baseball, and a guardian of all that was holy in the sport. News editorials spoke with the authority of scripture. This particular editorial began with a proposition straight out of the gospel according to Jim Crow:

> There is no law against Negroes playing with white teams, nor whites with colored clubs, but neither has invited the other for the obvious reason they prefer to draw their talent from their own ranks and because the leaders of both groups know their crowd psychology and do not care to run the risk of damaging their own game.

The editorial went on to castigate unidentified agitators pushing for integration for "their profit or self aggrandizement," maintaining that such people were attempting to force black players onto major league clubs against their will. An interesting interpretation of the situation, to be sure. The balance of the editorial drew heavily from the black press to justify continued separation, arguing that erasing segregation practices would ruin the Negro Leagues and subject black players to prejudiced taunting from players and fans at major league parks. The piece ended condescendingly with a very odd story about heavyweight boxing champion Joe Louis and pork chops. *The Sporting News* was not merely supporting the color line; it was guarding the border.[20]

In 1942, the Commissioner of Baseball, the unquestioned czar of Organized Ball, Kenesaw Mountain Landis, issued an unqualified statement regarding the hiring of blacks in the major leagues. "There is no rule, formal or informal, or any understanding—unwritten, subterranean, or sub-anything—against the hiring of Negro players by the teams of Organized Ball," Landis assured America's press. Six years later, after the debuts of Jackie Robinson and Larry Doby, *The Sporting News* thought it a good idea to republish the late commissioner's words, true or not, in the light of "the veritable tempest in a teapot Branch Rickey has stirred up." Larry MacPhail, then the president of the Brooklyn Dodgers, called the Landis declaration "one hundred percent hypocrisy!"[21] He was in a position to know. Fay Young, writing in the *Chicago Defender*, fleshed out the picture: "In other words, a Negro ball player is not out there because the owners decree that he should not be and these owners hide behind such a statement which Landis dishes out. In the meantime, Negro fans argue, fight, and go to see baseball as played by men who do not want you in the game—AND WON'T HAVE YOU."[22]

Certainly there was an understanding of some sort; the management structure of Organized Ball before 1945 was an essential and immovable obstruction in the path of baseball's integration. The best to be said regarding Landis is that he did not invent segregation in organized ball—the color line was established long before he became even a federal judge. But surely he did nothing to encourage any kind of change, and ignored more than one opportunity to abolish the practice. By the early 1940s, he was orchestrating a public relations campaign intended to stall any serious discussion of integration.[23]

Landis was far from alone. Whether from overt racist belief, hidebound conservatism, fear of public opinion, or too tight a grip on the purse strings, the owners of the 16 major league teams invariably backed the Judge. A few were undeniably racist in outlook. Others were less emphatic, but no one was pushing for change. If Kenesaw Mountain Landis wanted nothing to do with black players, the owners were ready to agree and more.

They kept one another informed. In January 1943, Eddie Collins, General Manager of the Red Sox, wrote to American League President William Harridge, enclosing the latest diatribe from Dave Egan, columnist for the *Boston Record*. Egan was making a habit of drubbing the Red Sox and Braves organizations for continuing to "discriminate against men because of the presence of a certain pigment in their skin." Clearly exasperated, Collins informed Harridge, "Here is another from our friend again." He thought Harridge would "enjoy" the reading [Collins's quotation marks].[24]

In December 1943, Washington Senators owner Clark Griffith sent a letter to the Commissioner. Attached was an editorial recently published in the *Baltimore Afro-American*, entitled "Can We Beat the Japs?" The column underscored the considerable support for the war effort undertaken by black people, both in the military and in domestic industry. Griffith marked off a sentence he felt the judge needed to share: "Not a word has been said at home about a new emancipation for the colored people, who are deprived of a vote and who are fettered with segregation," the writer lamented. That was too much for Griffith. "This will give you a good idea of what is *really* in the minds of the negro," he advised Landis.

The Commissioner wrote back.

Dear Mr. Griffith:

I have your letter of the 10th. The trouble with the whole thing is the misuse of the black man. Politicians, black and white, are exploiting him and they have been doing that thing since the first slave ship touched the west coast of Africa and sailed away with the first Negro bound and gagged— headed for slave labor in the western hemisphere.

A good Christmas to you, and give my love to your lady.[25]

Voting and desegregation, black people wanted. Next thing you knew, it would be major league baseball. The Commissioner was bemused.

As the racial situation began to change after 1941, a few maneuverings within the white baseball establishment punctuated their resistance. In 1943, riding on a storm of editorial pressure from black and white newspapers, Sam Lacy of the *Baltimore Afro-American* managed to wangle the invitation from Judge Landis for a delegation of black representatives to present their ideas at the annual owners' meetings. After considerable debate, Lacy, Wendell Smith, and other members of the Negro Publishers Association chose Paul Robeson, nationally renowned actor and athlete, to be their spokesman. Integration was obviously the topic of the day, although the black delegation included no one—player or management type—from the flourishing Negro Leagues.[26]

Howard Murphy of the *Baltimore Afro-American* outlined a four-step program to achieve full integration: currently eligible black players should be taken into Organized Ball immediately, all black players should be graded into the AAA, AA, A, B, and C classification employed for white players, prospective black players should be recruited employing the same system used for whites, and the white clubs should make public a policy of full integration.[27] Landis saw the event as an opportunity to diffuse criticism of Organized Baseball's de facto segregation policy without committing himself or the owners to any real action. He had already received letters from Roy Wilkins, Secretary of the NAACP, and Claude E. Burnett, head of the Associated Negro Press, praising his willingness to talk to the "Negro group."[28] Landis stage-managed the opportunity very carefully, issuing a formal invitation to the group, providing them a generous scheduling on the agenda, and giving them ample time to present their ideas. There would be no accusations of free speech denied.

What Landis understood was that the Negro Publishers Association had made a serious tactical error, choosing Paul Robeson as their spokesman. A towering figure in the black community, Robeson may have been respected among most whites, but he was also an avowed Communist. Fear of Communism ran deep among conservative businessmen; Commissioner Landis knew and understood his business-minded employers well. As Brad Snyder noted in *Beyond the Shadow of the Senators*, that fundamental fear of Communism would negate every word Robeson uttered, particularly in the minds of the game's old men, Connie Mack and Clark Griffith. The owners would perceive Robeson's plea for racial equality as Communist rhetoric; understand civil rights as Communism. After all, the *Daily Worker*, America's leading Communist newspaper, had been advocating baseball's integration for years. It was an insidious equation, one that would burrow deep into the minds of the status quo's defenders in the years to come.[29]

So the major league owners and general managers listened politely, perhaps with some interest, as Robeson and the others spoke. When the presentation ended, no one asked so much as a single question. That was that. The contingent was ushered out; the Commissioner moved on to the next item of the agenda. Landis and the owners delivered what they considered the perfect response: no response at all.[30]

**Clark Griffith. "The Old Fox," owner of the Washington Nationals from late 1919 until 1955, was instrumental in the founding of the American League. Like Connie Mack, he had grown conservative with age. Both men were willing to view civil rights as some kind of red radical plot. (National Baseball Hall of Fame Library, Cooperstown, N.Y.)**

Two years later, Sam Lacy tried again, appearing at the owners' annual meeting to urge formation of a committee to facilitate baseball's integration. Lacy had already written a letter outlining his ideas to several key officials, including Larry MacPhail, new owner of the Yankees, Mr. Quinn of the Boston Braves, and Eddie Collins, General Manager of the Red Sox. After reminding his recipients that he had organized the black delegation's presentation at the 1943 meeting, Lacy expressed his concerns.

> I have always realized that achievement of the goal is going to be a slow and tedious process, and one which will require a maximum of understanding and careful planning—from both the white and Negro angles. This being the case, it is quite possible you will find the suggestion I am about to make both timely and workable.
>
> A "pool" of the owners of one or both leagues or, for that matter, of two or three teams, may appoint a colored man to make a survey of Negro baseball to the end of thoroughly studying the possibilities, and finding the best way of ironing out the many ramifications that will attach to the employment of a Negro player, if and when that occurs.

Sam Lacy found the letter a difficult missive to write. After admitting that various measures undertaken to promote baseball's integration had not achieved anything like the desired effects, Lacy went on to say: "This is a sort of compromise for me as a colored man, in that it embraces the element of 'Appeasement,' but if it accomplishes anything I shall feel compensated in some measure for suggesting it. Certainly, it will be a step in the right direction."[31]

Two years earlier, this kind of letter might have inspired some sort of sympathetic and condescending reply, but surely nothing more. By the winter of 1945, however, the world had changed, and Organized Baseball was coming to the realization that their business was not changing much in response. For one thing, Kenesaw Mountain Landis was dead, his place taken by Albert B. "Happy" Chandler, former United States Senator from Kentucky. Surveying their world, baseball's owners saw that the conservative, stonewalling philosophy Judge Landis had engaged over so many issues was now threatening a peck of trouble. Throughout the nation, labor had organized and muscled up to obtain greater benefits, more representation, and better working conditions. Ballplayers would not be immune to the change in attitude. There were threats to baseball's immunity from monopoly legislation, both from within and from the outside. The Mexican League was actively encouraging players to jump their contracts. Major league attendance was down across the board, and ballparks, many of them built before the First World War, were showing signs of age. Then there was the race thing. Baseball decided to act, or at least to talk about taking action.[32]

Initial efforts misfired. The owners did agree with Sam Lacy enough to establish a committee along the lines he suggested, headed by Lacy, Branch Rickey of the Brooklyn Dodgers, and Larry MacPhail of the Yankees. The three were supposed to recruit further members, but the potentially volatile leaders never met. MacPhail expressed reservations, arguing that "any survey, report or recommendations would be entirely ineffectual unless it is recognized that the committee properly represents Baseball, the Press and the Public—both Negro and White." Branch Rickey was already pursuing his own secretive course, which culminated in the signing of Jackie Robinson. When representatives from the Negro Leagues refused to participate, the committee fell apart.[33]

Yet the problems remained. By the summer of 1946, the owners were meeting in special emergency session, trying hard to face the fact that it was no longer the 1930s. Precisely how the owners intended to deal with their problems was later shrouded in some mystery—understandable, considering some of the resolutions ultimately advanced. A few participants would later deny that anything much was done at all, but a "steering committee" was indeed organized and charged with considering the issues. Larry MacPhail was again named to the committee, along with Phil Wrigley of the Cubs, Sam Breadon of the Cardinals, and Tom Yawkey of the Red Sox, together with the presidents of the National and American Leagues. During July and August of 1946, the group met enough times to sift the issues and achieve a limited grasp of at least some of the problems. The subsequent "Report of the Major League Steering Committee For Submission to the National and American Leagues at Their Meetings in Chicago" was written entirely by Larry MacPhail. Testifying before Congress six years later, MacPhail stated that "It all represented my own personal views."[34]

There is no denying that there was a very personal dimension to the squabble over the possible integration of major league baseball, and that two prideful men were at the bottom of the pile: Branch Rickey and Larry MacPhail. Each was a very large personality, each convinced of his own reputation as baseball's most inventive innovator. Rickey had risen to prominence in the 1920s as architect of the modern farm system for the St. Louis Cardinals, which at one point operated 33 minor league teams. Rickey's ideal concept was to scoop up as many prospects as possible, contract them to the organization, and ship them out to the farms to see who was good enough. It was expensive, but it worked. Sheer volume insured the Cards enough good players to become annual pennant contenders, with enough left over to sell to other teams at a tidy profit. Rickey got a percentage of every sale. His reputation as a shrewd, cunning and ruthless trader grew rapidly. For all his sanctimonious palaver about Christian morals and responsibility, Branch Rickey was an operator to be watched carefully. Buyer beware. Men from Kenesaw Landis to Tim McCarver learned to loathe him.

Larry MacPhail got his start in baseball in large part because of Branch Rickey. MacPhail held the option when the Cardinals purchased the American Association's Columbus franchise; MacPhail became club president. He set about bolstering attendance, introducing night baseball and a host of attractions. His most daring maneuver was to try and build a winning team in defiance of Rickey's plans for the Cardinals farm system. That got him fired after just two seasons. He had done enough to build a reputation as a baseball man, and the hapless Cincinnati Reds hired him. MacPhail introduced night baseball to the majors in 1935 while building the Reds into a contender. Once again he managed to irritate the man who signed his paychecks, and once again he had to move on, this time to the Brooklyn Dodgers. Again he worked his peculiar magic, raising the Dodgers from the nearly dead. It was Larry MacPhail who promoted Pee Wee Reese, traded for Billy Herman, and made Leo Durocher his manager.

When MacPhail left the Dodgers organization to enter the United States Armed Forces in 1942, his place was taken by none other than Branch Rickey. The two had crossed swords a few times in the seasons after 1933; what had begun as a relationship of mutual respect had slowly degenerated into profound and mutual distrust. The two men had become baseball management's most profound competitors, strangely alike even as they were completely different characters. Rickey was placidly arrogant, secure in his own genius, and willing to educate the ignorant (almost everybody else) at impossible, preachy length. MacPhail was the "Roaring Redhead," insecure enough to lash out at the long line of dunderheads who continually crossed his path. He got into stupid fights; he regularly fired people important to him, rehiring them the next day. Each man was in his own way a genius, a daring innovator trapped in a chummy little club of conservative, completely unimaginative, gray little men: baseball's owners. And most importantly, both men were winners, masters at constructing competitive baseball teams.

When MacPhail returned to baseball in 1945 as part owner and president of the New York Yankees, he proved instrumental in the hiring of Happy Chandler as baseball's new commissioner. Chandler readily recognized MacPhail's talent and drive, making him an essential participant in the important committees as baseball faced up to its postwar challenges. As President of the Yankees, MacPhail now became the dominant voice for the American League in ownership meetings. The National League had Branch Rickey, who was receiving the lion's share of the credit for rebuilding the Dodgers, a work MacPhail had begun. The highly emotional chess match began anew. When Rickey established another frontier for innovation by signing Jackie Robinson to a minor league contract, MacPhail did his best to slow it down. When MacPhail pushed through the players' pension plan, Rickey scoffed, telling players in his employ it would never amount to anything. They sniped at each other through 1946 and into 1947, when MacPhail unintentionally got Leo Durocher suspended as manager of the Dodgers just when Rickey needed him most—to bring Jackie Robinson into the majors.[35]

Sitting around a conference table in the late summer of 1946, baseball's official hierarchy carefully digested MacPhail's steering committee report—and then mostly destroyed it, taking no action on the race issue. Jackie Robinson was playing for the Montreal club of the International League. MacPhail's conclusions were plainly pointed at the man who had signed Robinson, Brooklyn Dodgers President Branch Rickey. In everyday English, Larry MacPhail was saying that Branch Rickey should think long and hard about the feelings of the other team owners before placing Jackie Robinson on the Dodgers roster. Rickey of course ignored that piece of advice. He waited a year and a half to strike back at MacPhail.

Much happened in 1947. Jackie Robinson achieved "Rookie of the Year" honors in the National League. Rickey's Dodgers lost the World Series to MacPhail's Yankees in seven games, the last straw so far as Rickey was concerned. He told MacPhail never to speak to him again. MacPhail retired from baseball, not without a last round of controversy within the Yankees organization. Rickey and MacPhail had truly grown to hate one another. Itching for one last measure of revenge, Branch Rickey decided to play his trump card. He was, after all, the man who had brought integration to the major leagues.

At a speech delivered at Wilberforce State University in February 1948, Rickey told his audience that at a meeting held in April 1945, 15 of the 16 major league clubs voted to adopt a secret report banning black players. Rickey maintained that Commissioner Happy Chandler had passed out 16 copies of this report, each labeled with the name of the person receiving it. Following the discussion and subsequent vote, Chandler collected the copies, checked off the names against a list, and saw that all were destroyed. "I sat silent while the other fifteen clubs approved it," Rickey claimed. He had no copy of the report to sustain his recollection of the event, but his word was more than sufficient to be taken as truth after the 1947 season.[36]

The speech touched off a media explosion. The wire services seized on Rickey's accusations, splashing lurid headlines in major newspapers across the nation. Portions of the speech were fully and carefully quoted. Happy Chandler and the 15 other baseball owners, Larry MacPhail included, got roasted to the bone.

With no copy of the steering committee report available to the press, Branch Rickey could make his memories as fuzzy as he wished. If he was in fact attempting to recall real actions taken in owners meetings, Rickey had to be referring to the MacPhail report. He recollected the date incorrectly, along with the content of that report. Just one section had considered blacks in the majors. Not a favorable section certainly, but there was no move to ban integration. What made the report dangerous in the eyes of his fellow owners was not "E. Race Question," but the portions dealing with labor relations and monopoly power. Rickey would later back away from at least some of his accusation, admitting that the other owners had voted to approve a report considering several issues apart from the race question. Branch Rickey was using the lack of hard evidence to bash Larry MacPhail one last time.[37]

The owners never took anything resembling a formal vote to ban blacks from the major leagues. As Cleveland Indians owner Alva Bradley observed after hearing of Rickey's remarks, "Major league owners would never be unwise enough to do a thing like that." Bradley and Cubs owner Phil Wrigley both denied such a vote took place, as did Bob Carpenter of the Phillies and George Weiss, General Manager of the Yankees. Interviewed by several reporters regarding the accusations, MacPhail emphatically denied that any such vote had ever taken place, suggesting that Rickey was becoming "muscle-bound from patting himself on the back."[38] Such was the cloak and dagger world of baseball in the late 1940s, when a carefully constructed story, leavened with a careful but limited measure of fact, could make a man a saint. Or a reprobate.

The report Larry MacPhail did issue in 1946 included several recommendations essential to the future of baseball. His committee addressed the labor issue most successfully, recom-mending adjustment to the minimum salary and a maximum allowable cut in salary, the estab-lishment of a player pension plan, and funding of player costs in spring training. Controversial enough, some of theses measures. One section of the report, frankly critical of the Commis-sioner's Office and its function, was deemed offensive and removed before most of the owners received copies for discussion. The whole report was dangerous, not least because Larry MacPhail openly admitted that Organized Baseball *did* function as a monopoly.

The document came to be known as the MacPhail Report, and it is certain that Larry MacPhail wrote the section on blacks in the major leagues, later to become a source of con-siderable controversy. The report was never meant for the general public, and most of the owners later denied that such a document had ever existed. They did try to gather up all the existing copies and burn them at the close of the Chicago meeting, but Commissioner Happy Chandler kept one, which he turned over to a Congressional Investigating Committee in 1952. (Larry MacPhail kept another.) Congress was looking into issues of monopoly power, but it is the report's Section E, entitled "Race Question," that has drawn the greatest attention in the ensuing years.[39]

The majority of the owners probably did not read MacPhail's discussion of the race ques-tion before the summer of 1946, but he wrote much of the section several months earlier. Very possibly, the essay originated as a direct response to the announcement that Branch Rickey's Dodgers organization had signed Jackie Robinson to a minor league contract in late October 1945. MacPhail sent a copy of his thoughts to the Quinn-Ives Commission, charged with ending racial discrimination in New York State, and New York City Mayor Fiorello LaGuardia's commission organized for the same purpose. Neither commission ever published MacPhail's memorandum, though they incorporated portions in their reports. MacPhail did nothing more than add a few sentences regarding Jackie Robinson's progress in Montreal when he submitted the section as part of the steering committee report to the major league own-ers.[40]

MacPhail began his discussion of race positively enough, emphasizing the importance of baseball to all races living in the United States, acknowledging the athletic excellence of black performers in sports including track and field, boxing, and football. Performance counted for more than race, he insisted, and went on to point out the sacrifice black athletes had undertaken in World War II. "Fifty-four Negro players served with the Armed Forces in this war—one player was killed and several wounded in combat."

Next came a paragraph framing the reasons why a discussion of race came to be included in a report on baseball's problems. Blacks were important, MacPhail argued, an essential support to the future of the game, both as players and fans. Plainly they deserved better than the almost non-existent cooperation they had received from Organized Ball through 1946. Neglect had created problems. "Certain groups in this country, including political and social-minded drum-beaters, are conducting pressure campaigns in an attempt to force major league clubs to sign Negro players." The way Larry MacPhail read the situation, outside agitators had seized on baseball's failings to advance their own political and social agendas, using the game as a very visible symbol of segregationist practice. Such people were not interested in baseball and made no effort to understand it, as a game, or more especially, as a business. In short, such people were not at all interested in the welfare of blacks actually employed in the game. For the agi-tators, it was enough to starkly accuse the major leagues of Jim Crow practices, a charge

MacPhail now vigorously denied. (Remember, this was the same Larry MacPhail who had labeled Judge Landis's denial "hypocrisy.")

What the agitators failed to recognize, said MacPhail, was that baseball was a private enterprise, where profit margins spelled survival and ticket sales trumped all other considerations. This was as true for the Negro Leagues as for Organized Baseball. Black baseball represented a very large entrepreneurial investment, one that should not be ignored in the demand for racial justice.

It is at this point that MacPhail's argument takes a very odd turning. Thus far, the reader might fault the report for failing to consider the larger context of racial division in America, and baseball's role in maintaining and promoting that division. His concerns regarding black and white baseball as vulnerable business enterprises do make sense, in a limited way. But having said that, MacPhail—in a section added to his original 1945 memorandum—abruptly turned his attention to the success of Jackie Robinson, who had spent the 1946 season drawing large crowds at AAA venues in the United States and Canada. The report estimated that at games in Newark and Baltimore, more than half the attending fans were black. MacPhail did not see this phenomenon as a business opportunity, a chance to draw new fans to major and minor league ball parks across the land. Instead, it was one more source of worry: "if Negroes participate in major-league games, in which the preponderance of Negro attendance in parks such as Yankee Stadium, the Polo Grounds, and Comiskey Park could conceivably threaten the value of the major league franchises owned by these clubs."

What the ruckus was really all about, according to Larry MacPhail, was property values.

What to do? Again the report sounded a sympathetic note, arguing that blacks deserved better than what they had. But the answer was not to absorb a handful of outstanding black players onto major league teams—MacPhail thought this would do more harm than good. The writer advanced three lines of reasoning to support this point. The first was to doubt the ability of black players to make it in the majors. Not for lack of aptitude, mind, but for lack of proper training in the game. "A major-league baseball player must have something besides great natural ability," the report intones. MacPhail cited a pessimistic summary of Negro Leagues talent from Sam Lacy to support his position—black players just were not ready. White players spent an average of seven years in the minors preparing to play top level ball, MacPhail argued; black players would have to undergo similar apprenticeship.

There were three things wrong with this argument. First of all, the time the average major league player spent in the minors was closer to four years than seven. Second, the black players the major league owners were most likely to consider had spent years playing Negro League ball; they were far from green. And finally, Jackie Robinson had just torn up the International League in 1946, visible proof that at least some black players possessed the kind of ability MacPhail doubted.

The second argument at least carried some validity of a kind. A persistent thread in the report was the value of the Negro Leagues. For whatever reason, MacPhail could not picture a future without them, and he preferred them to be strong rather than weak. Here was the very nub of the integration question, so far as baseball was concerned. To what extent would the mixing of black and white affect the institutions of each? How would such institutions function, to what extent would they cooperate, if integration came to be? The thought of killing the Negro Leagues to profit major league ball was plainly unpalatable to Larry MacPhail, and he advanced some reasons why. The Negro Leagues represented a black business investment amounting to $2 million, he noted. The Kansas City Monarchs had drawn 300,000 fans to their home games. Hosting a Homestead Grays game, Griffith Stadium had posted an attendance record unmatched by the Senators. Fans were flocking to the East-West Game in Chicago more than ever. Black people were spending money to see black baseball; black business men were raking in cash. Would this continue if the majors were to take up most or all of the Negro Leagues stars? It would be like picking the pockets of black owners.

That said, the reader finds a more mercenary consideration that underlies this concern for Negro League survival. MacPhail's third line of argument was that black ball was a very lucrative source of income for major league ballpark owners. For the most part lacking profitable venues of their own, black franchises had come to rely on major league stadium rentals to house the growing Negro Leagues fan base. As president of the Yankees, MacPhail knew first-hand that his club made practically $100,000 a year renting Yankee Stadium to black teams—not a small item in the budget. The White Sox made $6,000 from the East-West Game alone. Who besides Clark Griffith knew how much he made renting their ball park to the Grays—or how much he depended on this infusion of money? Six of the eight American League clubs made serious cash from the Negro Leagues. Did they really want to pursue a course that would bring an end to such a windfall?

The "Race Question" section of the report did not attempt to offer solutions to any aspect of the issue. "There are many factors in this problem," MacPhail suggested, "and many difficulties which will have to be solved before any generally satisfactory solution can be worked out." What the report does object to is the disposition of one ball club to take action on the integration question without coordination with the other 15 franchises. More than anything else, MacPhail's conclusion to "Section E. Race Question" reflected the hesitance expressed by Sam Lacy. Resolution was "going to be a slow and tedious process ... one that should have serious consideration by an executive council."

Larry MacPhail's last paragraph on the subject drove home his point: "Your committee wishes to go on record as feeling that this is an over-all problem which vitally affects each and every one of us—and that effort should be made to arrive at a fair and just solution—compatible with good business judgement and the principles of good sportsmanship."[41]

When MacPhail's report surfaced in 1953, the paragraphs considering the Race Question confirmed what had been only too obvious: that major league baseball had not been anxious to make any positive move on the race issue. Hiding behind the hoary old fairy tale that no black player had the ability to play in the majors, the heart of the issue lay in the second and third of MacPhail's "facts." The Negro Leagues were a profitable and growing concern important to the black community, and several major league owners profited from their existence. What had developed was a strange and ironic ambiguity.

In the diseased mind of Jim Crow, what was supposed to exist was an America where white was white and black was black; no mixing, thank you. But that was not what had taken shape in the world of baseball. Jim Crow was powerful enough to force the creation of racially distinct leagues, but it was unable to keep them completely separated. This was America, where the pursuit of money trumped every other consideration in the end. The Negro Leagues naturally sought to maximize their profits, build their enterprise into a strong and viable institution that would survive. That meant selling lots of tickets. The best way to do that was to play often in the largest venues available, the very same ball parks utilized by the major league teams. Stadium owners were more than happy to take a substantial percentage of the box office. What resulted was not separation, but a symbiotic relationship between black and white at the very top, where money spoke the loudest. In the minds of owners white and black, that relationship was a roadblock in the path of integration.

The implications were not lost on black team owners. Cumberland Posey, owner of the Grays and one of the more influential voices in the Negro Leagues, was braver than most in acknowledging the difficulties. Posey wrote a regular column—"Posey's Points"—for the *Pittsburgh Courier*, and he used this soapbox to argue against efforts to promote integration. In essays written in 1942 and 1943, he worried about the future for black players and black leagues. "To build an every-day major Negro-League," Posey argued, "the Negro league must have star players just as does the National league and the American league." If even a few stars were taken up by the majors, the luster of the Negro Leagues would be irretrievably tarnished, he believed. Gates would fall, teams on the edge of bankruptcy would disband, the Leagues would fail. Whither then the 200 or so players the Negro Leagues employed? More to the point, what about the very large cash investments of owners such as Cumberland Posey? Following the 1943 meeting of the Lacy delegation with the major league owners, Posey really worked up steam:

> A group of men without consulting one person who had their life savings invested in colored base-ball, asked for a meeting presided over by Judge Landis and attended by the owners of the sixteen major league clubs, and at this meeting asked for the privilege of giving away all the stars of the various Negro baseball clubs.... If that is not offering a whole Negro enterprise to white businessmen, then what is it? That would automatically put organized Negro baseball out of business.[42]

Far preferable, in Posey's opinion, to continue the work of constructing "a major Negro baseball league"—one league, eight to ten teams, with a regular schedule of games played in major venues. Negro Leagues team owners such as Effa Manley and J. L. Wilkinson would later concede that they recognized this same dilemma, but felt powerless to do anything about it.[43]

Though self-serving, Larry MacPhail's point regarding the profits white owners derived from black baseball was certainly true. The Comiskey family made considerable amounts of money renting out their park for the East-West All-Star Game, with attendance reaching the 40,000 range by the World War II years. Additional revenue came from the Chicago American Giants, who used Comiskey as their home park. Out east, Yankee Stadium—the largest of all the ballparks—became an especially favored venue, featuring those four-team Sunday doubleheaders. When the Yankees got new uniforms, they gave the Black Yankees their old ones. In Washington, Cum Posey and Clark Griffith had their hands in each other's pockets regularly. Griffith's staff handled all the box office and publicity responsibilities for the Grays, and even supplied the team with a large order of bats every year. The Philadelphia Stars were occasionally using Shibe Park for home games, while the Cleveland Buckeyes played in both League Park and Municipal Stadium, same as the Indians. In 1944, home parks for nine of the major league teams were also home for black counterparts, unassociated but working in parallel.[44]

Satchel Paige recalled the impact of gaining access to major league ballparks on the Negro Leagues. Playing for the Pittsburgh Crawfords in 1933, Paige got a visit from owner Gus Greenlee:

> "Get ready for a big show in Cleveland," he told me.
> "What show?" I asked.
> "We're going to play a team there and we're going to play in the Cleveland Indians' stadium. We won't have to turn away those crowds when you pitch."

I just sat there. They'd opened up the major league parks to the Negro leagues, opened them up
because the parks we played in wouldn't hold the crowds I pulled.
    "That means the money's gonna be rolling in fast now," I said.
    Gus grinned. Man, did he grin.[45]

The arrangement cut in two directions and offered experiences that taught contradictory
lessons. Take Comiskey Park. The East-West Game, along with American Giants rentals, represented money in the till for the White Sox. On the one hand, this was a cash cow very difficult
to sacrifice. But it was also a potential message. If that many black fans were paying to see
black baseball in Chicago, how many more fans might the White Sox draw if there was a black
player or two on the team? Dave Malarcher, for one, believed that the Negro Leagues success
in Chicago really ignited integration. Blacks had proved "to the white man that we can bring
him something.... The East-West games really did it, when the whites saw 50 to 60,000 people
out there."[46]

With black populations in every major league city rising significantly, there was obviously
a new market for the owners to consider. But while some recognized an opportunity, others saw
the opposite—too many black fans would drive away the whites. Joe Greene of the Kansas City
Monarchs recalled that in 1938, "we had 42,000 people up there in Detroit for a Negro game.
But Walter Briggs, the Detroit owner, said we damaged the park and we couldn't play in it
anymore." Briggs was perhaps the most open and notorious racist among major league owners,
one who valued Jim Crow sentiments more than any profit to be made from black ball. Calling
to mind the subsequent history of integration in the American League, it is instructive that the
two organizations least willing to cooperate with the Negro Leagues were Detroit and Boston—
the last two teams to include black players. Walter Briggs spoke to a fear that many owners
shared—the destruction of property values. George Weiss, General Manager of the Yankees
beginning in 1948, was very forthright in admitting his reluctance to open his roster to blacks—
he believed he owed it to his white fan base to discourage blacks from coming to the Stadium.
Griffith Stadium in Washington and Shibe Park in Philadelphia, both built in the fashionable
outskirts of their towns long before the Depression, were by the 1940s firmly imbedded in
black ghetto neighborhoods. "White flight" became a hand-wringing problem in most major
Eastern cities after the war. If blacks came to major league games in increasing numbers, would
whites stay away? Would standing firm on the color line help or hurt, and just how much?[47]

Black players were anxious about their fans, too. The problem was rooted in the effects
of the great migration of black people from the South during the 1930s and 1940s. In the
Northern cities, Negro Leagues baseball had become an important expression of black culture,
a visible symbol of pride. At league games, and especially at such extravaganzas as the East-
West Game or the Yankee Stadium doubleheaders, the traditional black urban fan base turned
out in their Sunday best, dressed to kill and on model behavior. In Washington, middle class
blacks often eschewed Negro Leagues contests altogether, preferring to see and be seen at Senators games. Migration from the south threatened to swamp such displays of urban black triumph in a sea of crude behavior. Integration was not simply about race. There was an element
of class expectation at work as well.[48]

    "Our crowds were unruly quite a few times," Buck Leonard admitted. Men sometimes
wore no shirts at all. Drinking was too public, what with whiskey bottles openly passed around,
and the bad language, the loud and sometimes lewd activity, the gambling followed on that.
It got bad enough in May 1945, that Fay Young chronicled the ugliness in his *Chicago Defender*

column. Two fans attacked an umpire at Wrigley Field, resulting in cancellation of four doubleheaders. Five fights broke out at Comiskey Park, another ten at Briggs Stadium. Somebody stole a gun from a sheriff's deputy in Columbus. Young called for more strenuous police activity, lest the Negro Leagues "be broken up by the rowdies who seek to break up or destroy everything in sight." The more sophisticated urbanites tried their best to educate the "country" folk in proper behavior at a big league ball park, but they worried. Ball park owners worried too. Could black fans keep black players out of major league baseball?[49]

The unease extended to consideration of the players. Negro Leagues stars such as Hilton Smith and Double Duty Radcliffe, along with Wendell Smith, expressed concern that there were few good black players available to achieve integration after the war. There were several reasons for this—the player pool among whites was not very inspiring either—but the real concern among blacks was not ability, but character. With the barnstorming, the uncertain pay, the endless travel, the rugged play, the Negro Leagues had bred a lot of hard-bitten athletes, guys who performed well but never got introduced to anybody's sister. Buck O'Neil felt that his fellow players "didn't know how to eat, they didn't know how to dress, and most of all they didn't know how to act."[50] Thoughtful members of the black baseball community recognized that a black player taken up by a major league team would be held to an exacting standard of behavior. There would be no excuses, no margin for bad judgment. One bad apple could confirm the estimations of too many whites looking for an excuse to restore the color line. Fay Young of the *Chicago Defender* spelled it out in 1947: "The major league owners and managers will stand for 'no stuff' to be pulled. There is no place on any club for the foul-mouthed, uncouth, liquor drinking, huzzy-chasing player. To them he is a plain 'rat' and won't get into the barrel to spoil the rest of the lot. This applies to white as well as Negro players."[51]

In 1946, when Larry MacPhail reported and Branch Rickey planned, 1947 was still the future. It was beginning to look more and more as if some positive resolution of the race issue might possibly come, but no one could say how soon, or in what fashion. The array of challenges looked like a minefield from a lot of different angles—not a good metaphor to use just after World War II. Looking back upon the cloud of ambiguous and interlocking problems Jim Crow had invented for baseball and America, the wonder would seem to be that any resolution ever came. But the news was not all bad. The experiences of World War II forever altered the social chemistry that had made America's experiment in apartheid possible in the first place. More importantly, there were people positioned to press for change when the opportunity presented itself. An unlikely mélange of almost unrelated events would encourage the process.

# IV

# A More Honest Face

## *How Integration Happened*

---

A color line is an imaginary entity, conjured into arbitrary existence by the wishful thinking of tiny minds. There are no walls running through the streets, no chalked barriers insisting that one side belongs to one kind of folks and everyone else needs to stay on the other side. To be sure, there were color lines in America, sometimes invisible, sometimes posted with warning signs. Eating places had them, and hotels. Transportation services. Voting booths. Job opportunities. But it was all very arbitrary, conditional, circumstantial, the product more of habits of mind than physical restraint. Color lines seemingly stood guard everywhere in America, yet there was no absolutely definitive border between black and white. In the place of the absolute barrier racist America so much desired wandered a nebulous, difficult to define frontier, where blacks and whites met, worked together, profited, and enjoyed one another's company. In the 1930s and 1940s, baseball harbored an extensive racial frontier.

Yes, there were no black players in Organized Ball, and blacks had their own leagues, but out on the fringes black regularly met white in meaningful contests. There were outlaw leagues in remote rural places, where racism was too weak to exclude blacks from traditionally white teams, and highly publicized tournaments where blacks got an equal chance to compete. There were barnstorming gigs, exhibitions that grew seriously competitive when black played white. There was Mexico, an aggravation to organized baseball and the Negro Leagues alike, a testing ground where talent could be measured without racial handicapping. The color lines drawn in people's heads pawed at all these opportunities, yet they persisted, suggesting over and over just how arbitrary and false were the assumptions justifying American apartheid. In the end, the lessons learned on baseball's frontiers would do much to overwhelm the hidebound thinking in the corporate offices.

"Outlaw leagues" in North Dakota, Minnesota, and Canada existed in defiance of the Basic Agreement dictated by the big leagues, which officially protected baseball's reserve clause and unofficially the color line. Refusing to acknowledge the agreement, such leagues maintained autonomy and sometimes provided a haven for the baseball refugee. Their locations, remote from large urban influences, were their greatest protection and their deepest flaw. They were independent, but they were tiny, making profits too small for the big guys to be bothered about. They were important because they occasionally fostered interracial competition and fielded integrated teams. Satchel Paige pitched car dealer Neil Churchill's Bismarck, North Dakota, club to league championships in 1933 and 1935, much to the chagrin of Gus Greenlee, who thought he had Paige under contract with the Pittsburgh Crawfords. In one crucial game, Paige squared off against Willie Foster, starting pitcher in the very first East-West All-Star Game. Other refugees from the Negro Leagues included Webster McDonald, Red Haley, Double Duty Radcliffe, and Quincy Trouppe, all chasing better money on the Northern Plains. They encountered some ignorant racism from white players and fans, but they played and played well. The world did not cave in.[1]

For a brief while, the annual *Denver Post* Baseball tournament, the most popular and influential baseball event in the West during the 1930s, provided another frontier haven. In 1934, the *Post* agreed for the first time to allow black participation. J. L. Wilkinson sent a beefed-up Kansas City Monarchs team to compete. Wilkinson also entered a barnstorming team ostensibly comprised of long-bearded Orthodox Jews, the House of David. Satchel Paige pitched for them in Denver (maybe in a false beard, maybe not). The House of David won the tournament, Paige defeating Chet Brewer of the Monarchs in the final, 2–1. The result was widely publicized by national wire services, and white audiences began to hear about the talented black players. The *Post* would ban black players not long after—the Klan's reach was very long in Depression days—but a point was made.[2]

More constant was the barnstorming. Freelance travel and competition with local nines was a way of life for black teams, but it was an attractive moneymaker for white players as well. Skinflint major league owners were not hard to find even during the financial boom of the 1920s; most big leaguers worked elsewhere during the off-season. For a few with enough star attraction, there was money to be made in the late autumn, touring the cities and towns the major leagues never reached. In the days before television, a barnstorming troop provided the only opportunity for many to see the stars in action. The money was very good; players stood to make more from a well-organized barnstorming tour than from a winners' share in the World Series. For some, the opportunity to play against black competition was an added incentive.[3]

Babe Ruth loved to barnstorm, loved the cash that flowed in his direction, loved the chance to mingle with fans all across the country. He savored the opportunity to appear on a diamond with black players, always speaking well of their abilities, and black fans loved him for it. Sometimes he hit towering home runs off black pitchers; sometimes he struck out more than once. It was enough to provoke newly appointed Commissioner Landis to rigorously enforce barnstorming restrictions imposed by the owners. No barnstorming with ineligibles—that is, criminals, convicts, or black people.[4]

Despite a variety of injunctions dictated by the Commissioner to limit play between white and black, the practice continued—a kind of forbidden fascination. Blacks and whites were firmly barred from competing together in any officially sanctioned contest, and this piqued natural curiosity: just how would such a competition shake out? By the time Babe Ruth (later joined by Lou Gehrig) began to fade from the barnstorming scene, new interest focused on an almost-cartoon character from Arkansas, one Dizzy Dean. Dean might be considered the original legend in his own mind, except that he fashioned the numbers to back up his mouth— 18 wins as a rookie for the 1932 St. Louis Cardinals, another 102 over the next four seasons. Dean had the usual prejudices of a young man coming of age in the Depression South, but he wore them lightly. Growing up, he spent plenty of time in the fields with blacks, picking cotton. He saw no harm and plenty of cash sharing a ball field with black players, and was more than ready to concede the considerable talents of Negro Leagues opponents. Dean once told Satchel Paige that if they both could pitch for the Cardinals, they would have the pennant wrapped up by July and could take the rest of the summer off to go fishing. Just as important, Dean was not reluctant or afraid to voice such sentiments to the press. The black guys could play. Dean's "All Star" teams (generally Diz, his brother Paul, and a selection of local semi-pros) barnstormed through much of the 1930s, often playing Negro Leagues teams on the Plains, meeting up with more black stars in the California winter league. Satchel Paige became a nationally-known athlete, a legend, as a result of the barnstorming tours. True, the Ted Shane story about him in the July 27, 1940, issue of The *Saturday Evening Post* indulged in condescending racist imagery, but it did break another barrier by acknowledging the remarkable talent of a black pitcher.[5]

A broken toe suffered in the major league All-Star Game in 1937 brought a premature end to Dizzy Dean's stardom, though he continued to tour off and on through the remainder of the decade. Eventually, the torch would pass to another phenom, the much quieter but equally self-confident Bob Feller, Iowa born and Cleveland Indians raised. Feller pitched his first major league game in 1936, at the age of 17. His star was well-established when war broke out in 1941. Feller was one of the first ballplayers to enlist; he spent most of four years in the Navy, returning to the Indians late in 1945. By then he was the poster boy for America's pastime. New Commissioner Happy Chandler relied on Feller heavily for advice, encouraging him to organize an instructional baseball camp for returning servicemen. Chandler even bent Judge Landis's rules to allow Feller to undertake extensive barnstorming tours over the next three autumns.

For Feller, it was all about the money. He and his father had naively allowed themselves to be cheated out of thousands when he signed with the Indians before he finished high school. Then came the war. He lived four years of what should have been the prime of his career making no more than enlisted sailors' pay. Proceeds from the few exhibitions in which he played went to wartime causes. Released from service, Feller was determined to cash in on his fame. There was not enough time to get things fully organized in 1945, but he did enjoy a successful tour, mainly competing against black teams featuring Satchel Paige. In 1946, Feller and Paige did it up big, piecing together the grandest tour of them all. Refusing to rely on agents, Feller made all the arrangements himself. His All-Stars, for once a team of quality major league players, made a bundle. So did the Satchel Paige All-Stars, a Negro Leagues team selected by J. L. Wilkinson. The two outfits flew from gig to gig on theoretically identical war surplus DC-3s, sometimes playing games in separate cities on the same day. Feller did it again with considerably less panache in 1947, the end of the big-money barnstorming era.[6]

Strangely, one of the voices who persisted in denigrating black talent was none other than Bob Feller. Asked his opinion about Jackie Robinson's chances in 1945, Feller scoffed, saying Robinson was built more for football, that a steady diet of outside fast balls would crush his chances. A year later, after spending the autumn flying back and forth across the country with the Satchel Paige All-Stars, Feller was asked if there were any blacks with major league potential. "Haven't seen one—not one," he replied. "Maybe Paige when he was young. When you name him you're done." Feller was in some ways a strange guy. No one could ever accuse him of crude racism; he went out of his way to be fair to Paige and his All-Stars. Certainly he did his part to encourage integration when his Indians broke the color barrier. But when it came to assessing black talent, he was more than a little blind. His tours, featuring interracial play framed in a national spotlight, did more to advance integration than Feller himself ever did.[7]

For Feller, the golden goose of opportunity was the frontier beyond the fringes of the color line. Ironically enough, his efforts to cash in with tours of competing black and white all-stars did much to kill the goose. The tours broke down some powerful racial preconceptions, visibly demonstrating that black and white could play together—play quality baseball. 1947 saw Jackie Robinson, Larry Doby, and three other black players break into the major leagues. The intrigue of witnessing black play against white disappeared; Jackie Robinson was doing that pretty much every day. Integration, along with television, brought an end to big-time barnstorming.[8]

While Bob Feller's barnstorming tours brought black and white closer together in the United States, events much farther south both accentuated the playing ability of American blacks and made the prospects for integration a little more imperative. Baseball in Mexico gave Negro Leagues players an opportunity to showcase their talents in a multi-racial setting. Just as importantly, the Mexican League, the one outlaw league with enough money to matter, scared the willies out of Organized Baseball, posing a real threat to the long-cherished reserve clause.

Mexican League baseball became attractive to Negro Leagues players late in the 1930s. Stars such as Cool Papa Bell, Chet Brewer, Lou Dials, and, yes, Satchel Paige formally joined Mexican teams in 1938, after several seasons spent following the Caribbean dollar in winter ball. A few Cuban Negro Leagues players blazed the trail: Martin Dihigo, Cristobal Torriente, Jose Mendez. Baseball in Cuba was a pleasant contrast to the racial divide in the United States, but there were still barriers, places blacks found they could not go. Mexico turned out to be far more relaxed, relatively unconcerned about such minor issues as skin color. Mexican players and fans treated American blacks as welcome guests—highly skilled guests who improved their teams. The pay was better, the living conditions were better; the playing fields were no worse than what blacks generally experienced back in the States. Word spread quickly.

In 1940, things began to hop in Mexico. Jorge Pasquel, Vera Cruz businessman and human dynamo, became involved in Mexican League baseball early that season, initially as a part-owner, very soon as president of the League. After a brief interregnum of competing organizations and some nasty competition, Pasquel emerged as the unassailable power in Mexican baseball. He quickly set about to create a league to rival the best in the United States, recruiting several Americans, first black and later white, to play for his teams. Pasquel operated the league as a syndicate, distributing recruited players as teams needed them, employing league funds to keep shaky teams afloat. By the end of 1940, 63 American blacks were playing in the Mexican League. Teams instituted quotas on the number of foreigners allowed on the roster. The limits rose steadily, first four, then five, and soon enough, seven. Jorge Pasquel's own team featured 13 Negro Leagues players, including Willie Wells, Ray Dandridge and Josh Gibson. Quincy Trouppe, veteran Negro Leagues catcher, played nine satisfying seasons in Mexico and even changed the spelling of his name to reflect a more Hispanic pronunciation. Willie Wells, another popular player in Mexico, was very pointed in his reasons for playing there. "I've found freedom and democracy here," he said, "something I never found in the United States. I was branded a Negro in the States and had to act accordingly. Everything I did, including playing ball, was regulated by my color."[9]

In all, at least 103 Negro Leagues players would jump to Mexico between 1938 and 1947. The exodus frightened and shocked the Leagues' owners, who threatened all kinds of sanctions against the jumping stars, with little visible effect. When the Negro American League laid down suspensions, Negro National League teams happily ignored them. One more weakness of the Negro Leagues, exposed to the light of day.

With the end of World War II, Pasquel, working with his brothers, became even more aggressive in his determination to build up the Mexican League. All but seven of his black players returned home for the duration, but several returned to Mexico for 1946. Having already lured most of the leading black stars southward, he now began to offer suitcases of money (literally) to major league players willing to jump. He set his sights very high, speaking to among others, Ted Williams, Joe DiMaggio, Stan Musial, and Phil Rizzuto. All four were seriously tempted, but in the end said no. The biggest star Pasquel actually landed was Junior Stephens, the power-hitting young shortstop who helped the St. Louis Browns reach the World Series in 1944. Pasquel offered Stephens $25,000 a year and a $15,000 signing bonus. Stephens played two very uncomfortable games in Mexico before getting cold feet, returning to the United States in disguise, accompanied by his father.[10]

A handful of lesser lights spent some playing days in Mexico before turning tail for America. By far the most interesting case was Mickey Owen, catcher for the Brooklyn Dodgers, the man most famous for dropping a third strike in the 1941 World Series. Owen signed on as a player-manager with Pasquel's own Vera Cruz team, but quickly lost his nerve when he found so many black players on his roster, to say nothing of opponents. He mishandled and degraded the black pitchers he was supposed to catch, and created palpable tension with his open racism. A sleazy tag of a black baserunner provoked a fistfight he soundly lost, and suddenly Mickey Owen found his home country very inviting.

He could not play in the United States. Panicked by the drain to Mexico when the major leagues were hurting for capable players, Commissioner Happy Chandler had issued an edict: any player jumping to Mexico was suspended from organized baseball for five long years. Junior Stephens had come running back pleading forgiveness soon enough to avoid suspension, but Owen and several others were not so fortunate. Probably they were not valuable enough to keep Happy Chandler from making an example of them.

Chandler was in an unenviable position. Jorge Pasquel's Mexican League was the first serious challenge to Organized Baseball's reserve clause since before the First World War. Pasquel was obviously not a party to the National Agreement worked out in 1921; the only way to combat his suitcases of large bills was the threat of long suspensions. But that opened another door. If returning players sued to regain their rights to play, would the courts continue to uphold baseball's exemption to the anti-trust laws? Chandler was a man beset with problems: Jorge Pasquel and the Mexican League, the ever-growing pressure for integration, declining attendance during the war years, the complicated restoration of service veterans to their old major league jobs. A decision on any of these issues had to be made in the context of the possible effect on the others.[11]

One thing was certain. The major league owners were very, very determined to meet Pasquel's challenge head-on and destroy his league if they could. Clark Griffith of the Washington Senators was especially outraged—for years he had been tapping into Cuba and Mexico for cheap, light-skinned Hispanic ballplayers to fill his roster. Now Jorge Pasquel was offering much larger amounts of money for the same players. Major league owners did everything they could to discourage jumping among their own players, warning them not to risk their careers, painting vivid pictures of the misery awaiting them in Mexico. Rather than attempting any serious negotiation with Pasquel to include his league in the National Agreement, they attempted to undermine him by encouraging formation of a rival Mexican league. (That went nowhere.) The Yankees sued Pasquel for tampering with players under contract in 1946, and won an injunction. Organized baseball even attempted to cut off exports of bats and balls to Mexico, forcing the Pasquels to buy needed equipment from American retail stores.[12]

The Mexican threat persisted through the 1947 season, fading very quickly thereafter. As anyone might have guessed, the problem was money. The Mexican League made a huge splash and drew heady support for tweaking the major leagues in 1946, but they lost more than $400,000 in the process. Attracting American ballplayers was not cheap, and apparently did not pay. 1947 proved another year of big publicity and no profits, and Jorge Pasquel discovered there was a limit to his largesse. His pockets remained very deep, but he was above all else a businessman, naturally reluctant to throw good money after bad. He refused to continue indemnifying the losses suffered by rival teams, and the balloon slowly collapsed. Pasquel quit as League president in 1948.[13]

Mexico was a meteor that flashed across baseball's horizon for a decade, burning brilliantly for the briefest of moments before disappearing. Never the power Jorge Pasquel envisioned, the Mexican League still managed to change the face of American baseball in irreversible ways, exposing again the weaknesses of the Negro Leagues while hitting Organized Baseball at its most vulnerable point: labor relations. Larry MacPhail's steering committee report of 1946, with its discussions of organization, legalities, player relations, public relations, the race question, and operations, was, as much as anything, an acknowledgment of the issues exposed by the Mexican threat. MacPhail argued that Organized Baseball was very vulnerable to charges of monopoly—that in fact, baseball *was* a monopoly. To protect itself, ownership would have to take some drastic steps to improve labor relations, including player representation at meetings, a better minimum salary, and a decent pension plan. They would also have to deal with the integration issue, even if they preferred to ignore the whole thing. Happy Chandler got the point; lawsuits brought against baseball by returning Mexican League players were settled out of court. Suspensions were quietly rescinded.[14]

The Mexican League taught the majors a harsh lesson in reality. Big league arrogance was anchored on a sandy foundation; ownership was vulnerable at several points. Beneath the obvious, yet another lesson rested. Very briefly, Mexico was home to the very best international baseball could offer, a haven where players of all races could play on equal footing. There was no mistaking that American black players had done very well, both on the field and living in a more cosmopolitan society. The major league players jumping to Mexico had not coped nearly so easily. If blacks could more than hold their own in Mexico, what did this imply for their potential in America?

Taken together, the long years of interracial barnstorming competitions and the brief meteor of the Mexican League tended to confirm what some players and officials on both sides of the racial divide had long contended. Black and white could play together, play well together, without serious incident or repercussion. Such advocates were swimming upstream against a heavy current of noxious garbage, but the ball field experiences offered some hope.

Experiences in Mexico and on American exhibition fields proved an effective punctuation to developments that began almost immediately after the shift in American consciousness in December 1941. Black and white had already toured together enough to suggest that the racial divide was in no way "natural." The declaration of war made segregation a construct the nation could no longer justify. Here and there, blacks saw an opportunity to press for greater equality. Baseball was an obvious forum; the direct push for integration was well under way by 1942.

More than one major league owner expressed a wish to hire black players even before the War. Some variation on the theme "If only you were white" came from the mouths of Connie Mack, Clark Griffith, Grace Comiskey, and many, many others. As Judge Landis insisted, there were no injunctions against hiring black players to be found anywhere in the National Agreement. Segregation was an informal, unwritten, but well-policed policy. With war at hand, the time had come to test ownership's resolve. Black players and their spokesmen began to request tryouts, simple auditions intended to demonstrate the talent available and waiting on the far side of the color line.

Rumors of prospective tryouts surfaced as early as 1935, but one of the first actually to take place occurred in Pasadena, California, in March 1942. Chicago White Sox manager Jimmy Dykes agreed to take a look at Negro Leagues pitcher Nate Moreland and his former junior college teammate, Jackie Robinson. The White Sox needed some help. Dykes was a pretty decent manager, taking over in 1934 and getting the team as high as third in 1936, 1937, and again in 1941. But, apart from Luke Appling, Dykes had no horses. He watched Moreland and Robinson apparently with real interest, but his hands were tied. "The matter is out of the hands of us managers," he told reporters. "We are powerless to act and it's strictly up to the club owners and in the first place Judge Landis to start the ball a rolling." Grace Comiskey never blinked.[15]

More tryouts and rumors of tryouts followed, though. The military draft was thinning the ranks of major league rosters; every team needed quality players. Pittsburgh Pirates owner William Benswanger reportedly scheduled a tryout for late August 1942, then backed out. The Cleveland Indians committed to a session with four Negro Leagues stars in early September, but that never happened either. Sporadic tryouts in the Pacific Coast League followed. Black journalists became actively involved in the process, seeking out possibly sympathetic owners, finding black players willing to audition. By 1945, the journalists were growing disgusted. The War ground on, the major leagues cried out for skilled players, and still no breakdown of the color line. Joe Bostic of *The People's Voice* grew desperate enough to bring two over-the-hill Negro players unannounced to the Brooklyn Dodgers spring training camp at Bear Mountain, New York, in April 1945. (A photographer from a Communist newspaper also attended.) The last thing Branch Rickey wanted to do was stir up bad racial publicity, so he watched Bostic's players go through the motions, making no commitment. Dodgers wheels were already in motion. Joe Bostic had unwittingly provided a convenient camouflage.[16]

The most infamous and pointless tryout of them all occurred just a week and a half later, in Boston's Fenway Park. This one took place due to the combined determination of three men: city councilman Isadore Muchnick and journalists Sam Lacy and Wendell Smith. Lacy got the ball rolling, writing letters to the management of both the Boston Braves and the Boston Red Sox, demanding black players be given a chance. Muchnick, a young Jewish politician representing a district with a significant black constituency, began applying political pressure. Both the Braves and the Red Sox had stoutly resisted every previous attempt to crack the race barrier. The Braves held firm, ignoring Muchnick, but the Red Sox blinked. The Sox were a hidebound bunch when it came to race issues, which made them vulnerable to outside pressure. Management was smart enough to understand political threats, and Isadore Muchnick made a good one: if the Boston clubs did not give black players a tryout, Muchnick would

Jackie Robinson tries out. A nationally recognized collegiate athlete, Robinson suffered through a few sham tryouts with major league teams following his honorable discharge from the military. The contact with Branch Rickey was for real. (National Baseball Hall of Fame Library, Cooperstown, N.Y.)

move to discontinue the Red Sox's special permit to play baseball on Sundays. The Councilman got Wendell Smith to round up some ballplayers. The Sox agreed to look.

The whole business quickly assumed the character of a farce played out to satisfy outside political pressures, illustrating the racist leanings of a management on the brink of becoming a grim anachronism. The tryout took place on April 16, 1945, after four days of delay. Two of Boston's coaches supervised as the black players underwent drills in the company of white minor league pitching prospects.

Just two facts are certain. The first is that three blacks tried out for the Red Sox that day. Two were seasoned, highly skilled Negro Leagues players, Sam Jethroe, outfielder for the Cleveland Buckeyes, and Marvin Williams, second baseman for the Philadelphia Stars. Jethroe played four seasons in the National League beginning in 1950; Williams never made it. The third player had not yet played a game in the Negro Leagues, though he was a nationally recognized athlete, recently discharged from the military. He was Jackie Robinson. That is the second certain fact, that the Boston Red Sox had baseball's first black star for the taking, months before he met Branch Rickey. The Red Sox could have been first; 14 years later they were the last major league team to abandon the color barrier. Red Sox general manager Joe Cronin did sit with Wendell Smith that day, watching impassively from the stands. Cronin saw a good athlete in Robinson, but he did not think he saw a major league ballplayer. And almost all of the Red Sox farm teams were in Southern cities, where it would be impossible to send a black man to train. So...

Robinson knew. From the day he arrived in Boston, he knew the Red Sox tryout was a sham, a stunt intended only to silence meddling journalists and politicians. Robinson needed to look no farther than the crew running the Sox operation. They were not going to be first, not by a long stretch. Sam Jethroe knew it too. Returning to Cleveland, Jethroe told teammate Willie Grace that Cronin "didn't even bother to look. He was just up in the stands with his back turned most of the time." The Red Sox never contacted any of the players again.[17]

Despite the disappointments, black journalists sensed an opportunity developing. Newspapers such as the *Chicago Defender, Pittsburgh Courier*, and *Baltimore Afro-American* had spent the better part of 20 years extolling the excitement of Negro Leagues play. Their reward had been to witness and chronicle an almost unpalatable record of events, wherein black baseball's ownership had repeatedly failed to improve the product and had allowed the sport to degenerate into a haven for racketeers. The war provided a chance to shift direction, to abandon separated black enterprise and strike a blow for integration. The journalists did not hesitate.

The fracturing of black solidarity turned out to be crucial, providing black people a conscientious choice of avenues to the future. Columnists such as Wendell Smith, Fay Young, and Sam Lacy recognized very quickly that America's entry into World War II would necessarily change the domestic social equation. The United States was going to have to mobilize every ounce of human power available to fight the war against fascism, both in the Armed Forces and in home production. Blacks would be expected to shoulder their share of the burden. Membership in the NAACP and the Urban League began to grow immediately as both black and white determined that justice was a fair return for war support. As an integral part of the campaign, the black press began to lobby for the integration of baseball.[18]

Journalistic strategy eventually evolved into a three-part approach. The first element was to stress the quality of play among Negro Leagues stars. Since the 1930s at least, writers had been making a habit of favorably comparing black stars with the very best of the major league players. The always excellent Buck Leonard was regularly identified as "the black Lou Gehrig," while feared home run hitter Josh Gibson became "the black Babe Ruth." Satchel Paige got labeled "the black Mathewson." Such treatment would seem self-defeating if the goal was to promote black baseball as a separate enterprise, but declaring that there was another Lou Gehrig waiting out there should make integration look awfully attractive to white owners. Larry MacPhail, for one, agreed that "Negroes are ready for the big leagues." As President of the Dodgers, MacPhail had been scouting Negro Leagues players for years.[19]

The owners would be needing players. By the end of the War, 117 of the players listed on American League rosters in 1941 served in the military, and every one of them needed to be replaced. Black players might never have a better opening. In a column published in March 1942, Joe Bostic of *The People's Voice* dreamed of a parade of major league officials, beating down his door in a search for quality replacements. "First came Joe McCarthy of the New York Yankees, looking for a seasoned third baseman.... So, I sold Ray Dandridge of the Newark Eagles for a paltry $25,000. (Sorry sir, no checks; cash only and in $1 bills.)" A dream was all it turned out to be, as major league owners chose to privilege a one-armed .218 hitter and a bunch of teen-aged kids over veteran black players.[20]

Probably the biggest obstacle to this dream was the cold water reality of Kenesaw Landis, who pulled every lever necessary to keep blacks off Organized Baseball's rosters. Chester L. Washington of the *Pittsburgh Courier* wrote "An Open Letter to Judge Landis" in 1942, pointing out that the United States Navy had recently ended discrimination in onboard duties. "Big-league baseball should take a tip from the U.S. Navy," Washington wrote; "No country or organization should deny a chance to make good."[21]

The third aspect of black journalism's effort to promote integration was a brutal attack on the quality of the Negro Leagues. The *Courier*, the *Defender*, and the others may have been full of supportive coverage and helpful suggestions before Pearl Harbor, but after 1941, the writers made an obvious choice. If black enterprise had to suffer to achieve integration, that was a price the writers were willing to pay. Coverage of Negro Leagues play shrank significantly in 1942, while editorial after editorial celebrated resolutions in support of integration from labor and civic organizations across the country. The next year, Sam Lacy and Wendell Smith were forcing the meeting with Landis and the major league owners, completely ignoring the opinions of Negro Leagues spokesmen. The *Pittsburgh Courier* published Cumberland Posey's protests but did nothing to support him. Thereafter, black owners, despite their unparalleled success at the gates, adopted what historian Brian Carroll has described as a "bunker mentality," desperately shielding themselves from barrages on all sides. Sam Lacy openly stated that he had "little sympathy" for the black owners, who had ignored invitations to participate in the committee organized after the 1943 meeting. White owners had disregarded this same committee, but that did not seem to matter quite so much.[22]

Far more disparaging and damaging material was to come. When Branch Rickey did finally break the color line by signing Jackie Robinson to a minor league contract late in 1945, he pointedly refused to compensate J. L. Wilkinson, owner of Robinson's current team, the Kansas City Monarchs. (Would Rickey have acted differently if Wilkinson was black?) Wilkinson chose not to stand in the way, but Negro Leagues owners could see the danger in the situation—bad enough to lose their stars, but to lose them without compensation would mean bankruptcy. Wendell Smith felt little but contempt. The Negro Leagues, he argued, had no commissioner, no governing structure worthy of the name, no reserve clause, often no written contracts at all. Robinson had every right to jump, and the Negro Leagues owners had no legal justification to expect anything at all, from Branch Rickey or any other white owner. By summer, the *Baltimore Afro-American* was reducing its already sketchy coverage of Negro Leagues play to make room for a feature entitled "Following the Stars," a detailed chronicle of Robinson's play with the Dodgers and Roy Campanella's games in Montreal. To achieve integration, the *Pittsburgh Courier* and the *Baltimore Afro-American* were more than happy to sell black baseball down the river. Wendell Smith would go on to attack black players who failed to cooperate fully with Rickey's integration program in 1947. What had once been viewed as a possible road to integration was now portrayed as a hostile roadblock. It was only after the Negro Leagues began their slow death in the late 1940s that the black press portrayed them more positively, first with amusement, finally with nostalgia.[23]

The black press was by no means alone in their efforts to promote integration. While the mainstream white press for the greatest part ignored Negro Leagues ball and refrained from drawing attention to the color line Organized baseball was so obviously honoring, a few white columnists did join the fray. Dave Egan of the *Boston Record* was a continuous thorn in Red Sox General Manager Eddie Collins' side, demanding to know why black players were not being considered to supply the manpower shortages on Boston rosters caused by the war. Shirley Povich regularly called Clark Griffith's policies to question from his vantage point at the *Washington Post*.

Others included Harold Parrott at the *Brooklyn Eagle*, Stanley Frank with the *New York Post*, and Heywood Broun, Bill Dooly, Hugh Bradley, and Bob Considine of the Hearst Syndicate. Jimmy Powers made a habit of riding Branch Rickey ("El Cheapo") at the *New York Daily News*. Coming at the issue from the other side of the fence, these writers most often deployed a strong sense of moral suasion, aimed at the owners and the Commissioner, as their journalistic weapon of choice. Where was the justice in expecting black men to fight while refusing them the opportunity to play?[24]

Efforts by the black press to spur integration sometimes attracted support they did not especially want. Baseball was a very visible, very tangible expression of the racist practices pervading America's economy, and thus became an inviting target for all manner of social reformers. In 1942, the Greater New York Industrial Council, comprising a half-million members of the Congress of Industrial Organizations belonging to over 250 union locals, resolved to "demand that Judge Landis end jim-crow in the big league baseball now." Eighty thousand members of the United Auto Workers followed suit. Innumerable local chapters of major unions adopted resolutions affirming that "We must continue this good work. Jim Crow has got to go. In base ball and everywhere in our freeland." Black players and newspaper columnists could have little objection to that kind of union activity, but such resolutions represented just one aspect of a multi-faceted effort.[25]

The American Communist Party was nothing if not inventive. And resilient. The repression that froze America after the Great War had targeted two large groups: radical labor and the black population. The Red Scare of 1919 crushed radicalism while strengthening Jim Crow. A decade later, the onset of the Great Depression would give Karl Marx's ideas new footing among a minority of intellectuals and trade unionists, reviving the party. Throughout the 1930s, the communists attempted to harness such advantage as they could through the press, particularly *The Daily Worker*. Their hope lay in promoting the cause of radical labor and creating alliances with downtrodden social groups. They did not have to look very far. The color line was the largest injustice ever invented by a democratic nation, just the kind of institution that cried out for radical reform.

So baseball became an obvious candidate for Marxist action. *The Daily Worker* took up the cause in 1942 with a brilliantly titled campaign, "Can You Read, Judge Landis?" A combination of sharply worded editorials and a petition drive netted more than one million signatures calling for an end to segregation in baseball. *Daily Worker* sports editor Lester Rodney (who ironically was not a communist) sent a long open letter to the Commissioner emphasizing the dangers black soldiers faced all over the world while organized baseball fenced them out. "You are the one who by your alliance is maintaining a relic of the slave market long repudiated in other American sports," Rodney reprimanded the Judge. "You are the one who is refusing to say the word which would do more to justify baseball's existence in this year of war than any other single thing."[26]

The communists were prepared to do more than talk. They tried to arrange tryouts for Negro Leagues players with major league clubs on several occasions, never successfully. Their most influential moment came when they organized a picket line at Yankee Stadium on Opening Day in 1945. William Harridge, President of the American League, received a telegram explaining the action.

> GENTLEMEN YOU ARE HEREWITH ADVISED THAT ON OPENING DAY OF YOUR LEAGUE WE THE NEGRO VETERANS OF WORLD WAR TWO AND BUSINESS MEN OF NEW YORK CITY WILL BOYCOTT YOUR GAMES. YOUR FAILURE TO EMPLOY COMPETENT NEGRO PLAYERS MOTIVATES THIS ACTION. BASEBALL IS THE GREAT AMERICAN SPORT. BLACK AMERICANS CONTRIBUTE HUNDREDS OF THOUSANDS OF DOLLARS ANNUALLY TO ITS SUPPORT YET WE ARE DENIED THE OPPORTUNITY THAT IS RIGHTFULLY OURS TO PARTICIPATE AS PLAYERS IN THE GAME. OUR SACRIFICES IN THIS AND OTHER WARS IN DEFENSE OF OUR COUNTRY FOR DEMOCRACIES CAUSE ENTITLES U.S. TO EQUAL OPPORTUNITIES IN ALL PHASES OF AMERICAN DEMOCRATIC ENDEAVOR. YOUR DISCRIMINATORY PRACTICES ARE ALIEN UNDEMOCRATIC AND AT VARIANCE WITH THE DEMOCRACY FOR WHICH WE FIGHT.[27]

The picket line drew considerable publicity, especially in city newspapers, and inspired repeated demonstrations in years to come. The organizers tried hard to get Negro Leagues players to picket or sign petitions, but no player was willing to go that far. "We're not signing anything," Buck Leonard recalled telling them, "We're not making a statement. Any writing you want done, go ahead and do it. We're out here to play ball, we're not out here to demonstrate or anything like that."[28]

The thread of Communist activism was very visible in the years leading up to 1947. Major league owners certainly recalled Paul Robeson, one of the most highly visible members of the American Communist Party, speaking at the owners' meeting in 1943. (At Branch Rickey's urging, Jackie Robinson would repudiate Robeson's views before Congress in 1949.) The Communists were there, they did their best to forward the integration of baseball, and they took some effective measures. These were some of the "social-minded drum-beaters" Larry MacPhail railed against in his 1945 memorandum. Their persistence created an awkwardness.[29]

The black population could in no way reject the principles of the Communist campaign; the editorials and the demonstrations demanded no more than what most blacks wanted to see: social justice, symbolized by black players in major league uniforms. But it was a fine line. The Communists were stronger, more politically acceptable in 1945 than they had been in

1920, but they were still feared and loathed by much of American society. More than one government official was already looking past Germany to confront what they saw as an inescapable fact: the Soviet Union would prove an even more dangerous enemy. An open affiliation with the Communists could only hurt blacks in the long run. With the beginnings of integration so palpably close, blacks found themselves having to choose their friends carefully. Buck Leonard was okay with the Communists demonstrating on his behalf; he wanted no part of joining in.

By 1947, Wendell Smith was actually disparaging the Communist effort to support baseball's integration. In late August, after three major league teams had broken the color line, Smith attacked a *Daily Worker* essay on Satchel Paige, branding the piece a propaganda fiction intended to credit the Communists with getting blacks into the big leagues. "The truth of the matter is," Smith wrote, "that the Communists did more to delay the entrance of Negroes in big league baseball than any other single factor." In his estimation, the fear of Communist associations held the owners back throughout the war years. Jackie Robinson "had to take it on the lam" when reporters from the Communist newspapers sought an interview. Smith in 1947 was very firm. The Communists had hurt, not helped, and he was not about to let them steal the credit for breaking baseball's color line.[30]

A fair assessment, perhaps. The Communists agitated as Communists are wont to do, stirring up anger over issues of social justice, creating new fears over their proposed solutions to life's problems. Probably fear eventually did much to achieve integration. Not so much the fear of the American Communists, but terror inspired by the emerging cold war with the Soviet Union. If American Communists were agitating for racial justice, the Soviets could use the issue as an effective propaganda weapon, challenging America's claim to liberty and justice for all. It is very hard to be a bastion of democracy and practice apartheid at the same time. In the end, integration came to baseball and America in some measure not because of the Communist effort, but because of the dread of Communism.

The advocates of integration in the press and the labor unions may have had more friends than they wanted, but still the chorus grew in volume as World War II came to an end. New York State, home to three of the 16 major league ball clubs, passed the Quinn-Ives Law, designed to eliminate racial discrimination in the state, in March 1945. The law established a commission to study the race problem. Soon after, New York Mayor Fiorello LaGuardia, facing growing racial tensions, organized yet another committee to consider race relations in baseball. The mayor naturally tapped Branch Rickey and Larry MacPhail to serve, along with several more whites and just two blacks: famed entertainer Bojangles Robinson (part owner of New York's Black Yankees), and an Episcopalian minister. By the time their work was finished, LaGuardia's committee had become just one more element in the ongoing chess match between Rickey and MacPhail. The final report was a strange amalgam of the two operators' views.

The thing began rather differently. The impetus came from Dan W. Dodson, Executive Director of the Mayor's Committee on Unity of New York City. Dodson, a sociologist, had set about interviewing the executives of the city's three major league teams, searching for ways to promote integration. MacPhail blew him off, but Rickey saw an opportunity. The last thing Branch Rickey wanted was some gathering of politicians interfering with his own elaborate plan to sign a black player to his organization. A smokescreen, however, could be a very useful thing, and Dodson agreed to supply just that—a committee that would organize and debate, absorbing heat that might otherwise be directed at the Dodgers. While the committee hashed out the issues, Rickey quietly went about the business of tapping Jackie Robinson for his great experiment. Rickey, not wanting to be tied to committee decisions, would resign before the group issued any report.[31]

LaGuardia's committee, directed by Dodson, took on a life separate from the intentions of its creators. On the surface, it seemed Larry MacPhail blew off this particular assignment as well, but he did participate, sending the LaGuardia group a copy of "The Negro in Baseball" memorandum he wrote in response to the announcement of the Jackie Robinson signing. This was, of course, substantially the same essay he would submit to baseball's owners as part of the steering committee report ten months later. When Dodson's commission published a report in November 1945, they chose to embody much of Larry MacPhail's thinking, to the discomfiture of Branch Rickey.[32]

The commission determined that black and white youths demonstrated equal ability on the baseball field and in the name of democracy deserved an equal chance in organized ball. Blacks had done well in sports where the color line was less firmly drawn—boxing, track and field, football. Baseball—America's game—lagged behind the others because of the institutional discrimination practiced on both sides. The Negro Leagues, with their hectic scheduling and poor discipline, could only hinder the full development of player skills. This state of affairs was hardly the fault of blacks—the Negro Leagues had taken shape as a logical response to white discrimination. But now the Leagues had become entrenched, expecting their considerable investment to be honored while they failed to develop players to their full potential. "If the equity of Negro professional baseball clubs were never to be disturbed, the reform could never be accomplished and the onus of present Jim Crow practices would be placed on Negroes themselves." Of all things, the Committee had chosen to lay much of the blame for baseball's failure to integrate on the Negro Leagues.

The solution? Simple, really. The "contractual relationship" between black players and management "is a loose one at best," what with contract jumping, failure to discipline unruly players, and bizarre pay arrangements. Without coming out and saying so, the commission was plainly suggesting that Negro Leagues owners had established no contractual bond that white owners should feel obligated to respect. Black youth was ready to play baseball, and needed better training than the Negro Leagues could possibly offer. To achieve racial equality, organized baseball would have to intercept black players bound for the Negro Leagues and find places for them on proper teams. The money issue was not worth worrying about. Precisely what Branch Rickey was determining for himself.

Boiled down, the Mayor's commission seemed determined to fight racism with racism.

The commission's words may have provided a useful camouflage for Branch Rickey, but the report in many ways anticipated the infamous "Race Question" section of the report Larry MacPhail presented to major league baseball a year later. Each report cites essentially the same statistics to evaluate the financial condition of the Negro Leagues and their relationship with major league clubs. Each draws a distinction between the native athletic ability of black players and the training they received. Each recognizes the potential impact of integration on black enterprise. What differs is the conclusion. MacPhail's own report emphasizes careful and coordinated study, a gradualist approach defying ever-increasing pressure from the black community. The Mayor's commission made no overt recommendations, but it did open the door to drastic action. Branch Rickey was preparing to oblige.[33]

What Branch Rickey did was not so much to address the problems of bringing blacks into organized ball, but to short-circuit them. The existence of the Negro Leagues, the large amounts of cash invested in them, their ties of obligation with the best black players available; these could be serious stumbling blocks. Like Alexander cutting the Gordian knot with his sword, Rickey simply chose to deny any legitimacy to their existence, just as the Mayor's commission suggested. The Negro Leagues were outside organized ball; they possessed no command structure worthy of the name. The teams were owned by crooks, confidence men who preyed on the poorest members of their communities. The owners stipulated no reserve clause in their contracts; more often than not, they had no contracts. Black players could and did jump such contracts as existed with impunity, as Josh Gibson, Chet Brewer, Willie Wells, Cool Papa Bell, Satchel Paige and several others demonstrated time and again. Black players were there for the taking.[34]

Branch Rickey was the most moral man Branch Rickey knew, so there is no surprise that he found the Negro Leagues wanting in character. No legal foundation, run by crooks, populated by bad sorts—what choice could he have but to exercise his moral duty, begin the process of extending the protections of organized ball to young black players? That it was convenient to his goals as President of the Dodgers was no more than a happy coincidence. Rickey wanted to improve his team, and what better way was available than to grab a very good player without having to pay anything to a previous employer? And Robinson would pay dividends. Attendance at Ebbets Field during the war was not all that Rickey might have hoped. Add a good black player to the mix, the likelihood was that a whole new legion of fans—black fans—would come out to see him. Branch Rickey was not one of those owners worried about property values. He was staring at the other side of the balance sheet, the one recording the numbers of paid admissions.[35]

Buck O'Neil, a teammate of Robinson's with the Kansas City Monarchs, saw it all perfectly:

> What had most to do with it was this: When we played in Yankee Stadium for 40,000 people, Branch Rickey was playing over there in his ballpark, 20,000 people the same day. You understand? And 99 percent of those 40,000 we got in Yankee Stadium, black. That's a brand-new clientele. And Rickey was an astute businessman. He saw this. He saw this. And this is a capitalistic society. Money talks.[36]

It is always comforting when your moral convictions square so perfectly with your financial interests.

Branch Rickey announced the signing of Jackie Robinson to a minor league contract on October 23, 1945, after a careful search for just the right player. Robinson was born in Georgia, but grew up in California, where he excelled in interracial competition in football, basketball, and track and field, eventually starring at UCLA. Honorably discharged from the Army early in 1945, he was well known enough to find work in the Negro Leagues. Baseball was his fourth-best sport, but the only one with real paying job opportunities for black athletes. That summer, Robinson played for J. L. Wilkinson's Kansas City Monarchs. Rickey's minions scouted him; Rickey determined he was the man he wanted. Rickey never gave Wilkinson, probably the most scrupulously fair and honest of the Negro Leagues owners, so much as a dime in compensation. Neither Rickey nor Robinson ever acknowledged anything resembling remorse.[37]

The next two years of Jackie Robinson's life comprise an oft-told story. As with all heroic stories, there are some contradictions in the telling. Very few wanted to be the villain as it became obvious that Robinson's advent was as much as anything a morality play. First was the year in the International League at Montreal, where he overcame initial doubts to prove that a black player belonged, hitting .349, scoring 113 runs and, most importantly, establishing himself as a very intelligent player. He had his challenges, particularly in the more Southern towns such as Baltimore and Louisville, where Jim Crow could not believe what was happening. Even after Robinson ripped apart a AAA league, the nay-sayers hovered. Surely Rickey would never entertain the notion of bringing Robinson to the Brooklyn Dodgers. The Dodgers themselves—so many of them Southerners—would not stand his presence in the locker room. Opposing teams would ride him unmercifully, while fans would make his life a living hell and perhaps kill him.

It all came to pass. Dodgers manager Leo Durocher had to quell a threatened player strike against Robinson before the season even started. (Durocher himself would be suspended before the season began.) Philadelphia Phillies manager Ben Chapman led his players in a torrent of racial abuse that sickened Robinson's teammates. National League President Ford Frick aborted a possible player strike purportedly organized by St. Louis Cardinals players to protest Robinson's presence. There were death threats in Cincinnati, investigated by the FBI. Robinson, swallowing hard and adhering to Branch Rickey's injunctions, turned the other cheek and played ball. Hard, Negro League ball, inside ball laced with timely hitting and unbelievably daring base running. Again he triumphed, hitting .297, scoring 125 runs, and leading his team to the World Series. He was the very first recipient of the Rookie of the Year Award.[38]

The measure of Jackie Robinson's impact is not in his statistics, nor in his awards, impressive though they are. The true import of Jackie Robinson as a Brooklyn Dodger was that he played, he played well, and he faced down the adversity thrown at him. There were indeed black men who could make it in the major leagues. There were no tragic catastrophes stemming from the fact he did play. So many cherished assumptions got smashed by Robinson, it became very difficult to find excuses anymore. How integration would continue to unfold remained very much an open question in 1947. That it would continue and grow was no longer in doubt.

There are pitfalls for the unwary when it comes to examining the history of baseball's integration. A very important one, rising at just this point, is the temptation to adopt a "heroes and villains" kind of narration, where anyone who forwards the cause becomes a saint, and anyone appearing to create obstacles becomes necessarily evil. Branch Rickey and Larry MacPhail have become obvious candidates for the respective roles. An inspiring morality play perhaps, but not much as history. Neither man was a cartoon cutout.

Certainly Rickey deserves enormous credit for being the first to sign a black player, but he was no saint. Lots of people thoroughly disliked him, for reasons having nothing to do with integration. Nor were his motivations for signing Robinson completely high-minded and pure; Rickey made certain money would be migrating to his pocket on the deal, even as it cost others their livelihoods. Branch Rickey was a man of complex and multiple motives, as was his nemesis, that roaring redhead, Larry MacPhail. Just what was MacPhail trying to say, in 1945, when he wrote his "Negro in Baseball" memorandum, or in 1946, when he included the little-revised version in his steering committee report? Was he simply the voice of Jim Crow? The thing to remember is that MacPhail offered his report to the major league owners in the middle of the 1946 season, when Jackie Robinson was playing for Montreal. Branch Rickey, MacPhail's arch enemy, was responsible for that. But Robinson had yet to break the major league color line, and MacPhail was doing what he could to stall that happening. He did not like Rickey, and legitimately complained of Rickey's failure to pay J. L. Wilkinson for the rights to Robinson. Was MacPhail opposed to blacks playing in the majors? Perhaps personally he was, but he was no fool. His reputation as an innovator rested on his ability to sense the direction of inevitable change, and get there first. Was he upset that Branch Rickey was going to get the credit for putting the first black player on a major league ball field? Absolutely. Red Barber's memory of MacPhail says it best. "Was it that he was thinking about being first with a black player? And Rickey had trumped his secret ace?" Very possibly. When Jackie Robinson excelled in 1947, and Larry Doby signed with the Cleveland Indians, Larry MacPhail's chance to create one more chapter of baseball history was gone. He would not be the pioneer on the most challenging of frontiers. At the end of the 1947 season, his only championship in hand, the roaring redhead quit baseball for good.[39]

Branch Rickey s maneuvering naturally provoked some interesting responses from competing club owners. As Bill McKechnie, Casey Stengel, and the other National League managers told Wendell Smith back in 1939, the decision on integration was solely the province of the club owners; the managers would play whoever was assigned to the roster. Now an owner had acted unilaterally, leaving the other 15 with very visible choices to make. Very few were anxious to tip their hands immediately. Horace Stoneham of the New York Giants said he would begin scouting the Negro Leagues in 1946, although he was more concerned with finding roster spots for veterans returning from the War. Connie Mack of the Philadelphia Athletics made no public statement, but privately expressed extreme disappointment with Branch Rickey, believing the issue should have been left alone. Another long-entrenched team owner, Clark Griffith of the Washington Senators, took up a defense of Negro Leagues owners. "The only question that occurs to me is whether organized ball has the right to sign a player from the Negro League," he said publicly. "That is a well-established league and organized baseball shouldn't take their players. The Negro League is entitled to full recognition as a full-fledged baseball organization."[40] Griffith wrote privately to Commissioner Happy Chandler to state his case even more firmly:

> The Negro National League is going to send you a protest on the taking of their players and they say that all their players were under contract but no reservation was in that contract until this year. However, according to *custom* and custom is *law* both of the Negro National Leagues are entitled to every consideration and fair dealing from organized baseball. We have helped them to grow, cooperated with them in every way, shape and manner in giving them the use of our ball parks. They have established the Negro National and American League that has the support and respect of the colored people all over this country. They are not *pirates* and have not stolen anything from organized baseball and we have no moral right to take anything from them without their consent.[41]

Griffith subsequently decried Rickey for behaving as an outlaw, stealing players from legitimate Negro League organizations. Whether this was a case of crocodile tears is a question to ponder quietly.

Larry MacPhail worked behind the scenes, in what turned out to be a mostly unhelpful fashion, a man attempting to slow an onrushing train. Clark Griffith made his feelings known publicly, but he was compromised by his own considerable investment in the success of Negro Leagues ball. A more pertinent response to Branch Rickey's action came from a man unconnected to organized baseball throughout much of World War II, a maverick with a heart fashioned by P. T. Barnum. Bill Veeck was an outsider to the comfortable little club that was American League ownership in 1947. The newly arrived owner of the Cleveland franchise firmly believed Branch Rickey was right; also, that the "Mahatma" was very much wrong.[42]

# V

# The American League Tries

## *The Pioneer Experiments*

---

Race was a laughing matter in the late 1940s, if you happened to be white. In November 1945, Dan Daniel, writing in *The Sporting News*, reacted to the Dodgers organization's signing of Jackie Robinson in 1945 with a satire that he felt conveyed the essence of the situation. "First thing you know, we'll have Old Black Joe McCarthy managing the Yankees ... and the club turned into a minstrel show." A few months later, Daniel reported that a skit performed at the Baseball Writers' Association annual dinner was "the best yet." Fellow reporter Arthur Daley recorded the skit, a skewering of baseball's new commissioner, Happy Chandler. Midway through the palaver came some heady dialogue: "Jackie, you old woolly-headed rascal. How long yo' been in the family?" The pseudo–Robinson supposedly responds, "Long time, Kunl, mighty long time. Ebber since Massa Rickey bote me from da Kansas City Monarchs." There is nothing like some crude stereotyping to diffuse a delicate racial situation. Daniel and Daley were so obviously proud of their handiwork. Both were highly respected reporters for New York City newspapers.[1]

The war years would witness the beginnings of a profound sea change in American race relations, but not without incident. In some ways, the emotional hatred intensified as the course altered. The racism that Daniel and Daley played for laughs was the same racism that provoked race riots in several American cities and on military bases—all hushed up by the national government as part of the war effort. There were 12 lynchings during the war, another nine in 1946; several of the victims were black servicemen. Racism was not going to go away quietly. Baseball was one of the more prominent national private institutions to challenge Jim Crow's hold on American society. It was not going to be easy, for a lot of different reasons. There was the politics of power, the economic struggle. There was housing. Transportation. Labor issues. And underlying all of these, there was the most explosive, the most irrational issue of them all.

The deep-seated faith in white supremacy was never more firmly expressed than in matters of sex. Say what you want about politics or economics, sexual relations were society's loco-spot; the least suggestion of racial mixing was, to Jim Crow, the greatest, most horrific threat of all. Baseball, with its obvious emphasis on physical performance, was far from immune. Mostly the dread was a thought left unspoken. One of the few to speak openly to the issue was Effa Manley, never a person to mince words over issues of race. In 1948, as she was leaving baseball, she recounted her exchange with an unnamed major league team owner, apprehensive over the prospect of integration. "I would like to sign Negro players," the owner confessed. "But, you know how fans idolize ball players. Many of our fans are white women. It might cause unpleasantness if these women became 'attached' to a Negro home run hitter."

Here was the primal fear that launched hundreds of lynchings north and south over the past century, lynchings that would continue through 1955. This was the unspoken yet deeply raw emotion that dictated that the first black men in Organized Ball be of honorable, upright character. The vast majority of the states rigidly enforced miscegenation laws, providing a legal framework to guarantee white supremacy at its most fundamental. No mixing of the races. Whatever the prospects for baseball's integration, whatever the attractions, this blind fear rippled through the backs of club owners' cautious and conservative mindsets. They would be responsible if some black player's heroics set (white) female hearts a-flutter. Black players on the field was one thing...

Effa Manley later indicated that the owner expressing such concerns was none other than Larry MacPhail. How best to protect the womenfolk? The supreme prejudice of Jim Crow was at the uttermost zenith of his power. Baseball's owners trembled. They would tread cautiously, and above all, they would move exquisitely slowly.[2]

At least there was some movement. Despite the pitfalls, despite the snags.

Bob Feller was not afraid to say it. For once, Jackie Robinson agreed with him completely. Branch Rickey reached much the same conclusion. Bill Veeck and his scouts concurred. Whisperings among several key Negro Leagues players amounted to much the same thing, the same sobering news. In the year 1947, there was not a lot of black talent ready for major league baseball. The search for the right players to break the color line was going to require care and patience.[3]

The dearth of talent had a little to do with race—though not in the way America's apartheid race mongers would have argued it—and a great deal more to do with circumstance. The race part of the equation was that despite the unparalleled success of the Negro Leagues during and just after the War, leading players still found the pay very low and the working conditions nearly intolerable in Jim Crow America. They took themselves off to Mexico, where they were treated like human beings and saw little incentive to return stateside. This significantly reduced the talent pool that Rickey, Veeck, or anyone else would have to choose from.[4]

The circumstances were more complex. First, there was the fact of World War II. In 1944, the *Negro Baseball Pictorial Yearbook* included a feature article highlighting the participation of Negro Leagues players in the armed forces. At that date, 54 players were in service, including 45 in the Army and seven in the Navy. One player, Philadelphia Stars pitcher Ralph Johnson, had died in the Pacific. The war decimated most Negro Leagues teams; 13 members of the Stars were gone, along with six players from the Homestead Grays, five from the Kansas City Monarchs, and 12 from the Newark Eagles. The damage to the careers of major league stars such as Ted Williams and Joe DiMaggio is well known and often cited; the impact on Negro Leagues players was precisely the same. They lost time, and their baseball skills gathered rust. 1946 became a year of excitement when the big boys returned to the diamonds, but the baseball was less than outstanding. Players had been wearing different uniforms and putting their lives at risk for three and four years. This was bound to show. If nothing else, key players were older, with reduced reflexes. The major leagues would see at least five years of uneven play before skill levels reached the levels of the pre–War era.[5]

The time lost to service by established players in both the major leagues and the Negro

Leagues was not the most critical aspect of the problem by far. The fates of established stars may be easy to trace, but the real impact was on the very young, the men who reached 18 years of age during the War and immediately got drafted. A great many young baseball prospects found themselves in the military, where they too lost time, lost their health, sometimes lost their lives. At the very least, they came out of the armed forces in 1945 and 1946 with no serious baseball training or conditioning at all—professional baseball had for the moment lost many of the young men who would normally be finishing their apprenticeships and preparing to assume the places of aging players. Between 1946 and 1950, baseball would have to make do with elder statesmen, military veterans with eroded skills, or very green youngsters. The situation was not as bad as it had been during the war, but rosters comprised odd assemblages for quite some time. This was as true for the Negro Leagues as it was for the majors and the high minors. The ongoing bankruptcy of talent in the majors would help to open the door for black players, but the opportunity beckoned as the Negro Leagues themselves were hurting for fully developed talent.[6]

A second circumstance further contracted the potential number of Negro Leagues players available to the majors. The pioneers—Branch Rickey and Bill Veeck—had pretty much independently reached the same conclusion. Apart from the very obvious social significance, breaking the color line represented a risky business investment that would run up some bills in the short run. To lessen the risk, it made sense to both men to choose not an aging star such as Josh Gibson (34 at the end of 1945), Hilton Smith (33), or Satchel Paige (older than God), but a younger man who could deliver quality play over a substantial career. With the war severely limiting the opportunities for young blacks to develop their skills, this decision alone shrank the potential pool. And still a second, unspoken but very real attribute would have to be present: any black player coming to the majors would have to be a military veteran. In 1946, several major league teams divided into two clearly defined camps—those who had worn a military uniform, and those who had not. Players such as Joe DiMaggio were especially sensitive on this issue. Any player crossing the racial divide would face discrimination because of his color; adding a second divisive factor would not be practical politics.[7]

So it was true, what Bob Feller and Jackie Robinson and so many others observed. Unpalatable though the truth was for so many right reasons, the search for black players to fracture the color line was not going to be an easy one. Any observer with the slightest sense of the situation understood that any black man joining a major league roster would have to be something more than just another player; he would have be someone of more than ordinary potential, a player with star qualities. He would have to demonstrate beyond quibble just why blacks should be included, why fans should want to come and see them. That perspective profoundly influenced the integration of American League baseball from the very beginning, and remained essentially unchanged for a very long time. As Larry Doby later observed, "for a black man to play in the majors he had to be much better than a white player."[8]

Bill Veeck had baseball in his blood, growing up in the confines of Wrigley Field, where his father was General Manager of the Cubs. Veeck learned the business from every angle: selling tickets, arranging promotions, working with the grounds crew, planting ivy. By 1941 he was club treasurer, but knew he could rise no farther in an organization owned by the Wrigley family. He bought his own club, the lowly, run-down Milwaukee Brewers of the American Association, establishing a pattern that would persist throughout his varied career. Veeck had no money to speak of, certainly not enough to buy a baseball franchise, however close to bankruptcy. What he did have was an ability to put together teams of investors, coupled to an enthusiastic charm that sat well with loan-making banks. His operations invariably began on a shoestring, relying totally on his ability to build up a team and draw attendance. It worked in Milwaukee; it would work in Cleveland, in Miami, in Chicago—it almost worked even in St. Louis.

Veeck set the pattern immediately in Milwaukee, wooing the press, sprucing up the ball park (paint was always one of his initial expenditures), and inventing crazy promotions that actually worked. Bill Veeck was a nationally known figure before he ever owned a major league team, appearing in theatre newsreels when he hosted morning ball games, aimed (successfully) at swing shift workers in local defense plants. He quickly turned the Milwaukee operation into a moneymaker, and left to serve in the Marines. He sold the team while convalescing from leg wounds in the South Pacific (not before an embarrassing run-in with Casey Stengel).

The wounds were serious enough to require eventual amputation, but if anything, this fueled Veeck's enthusiasm. He became very anxious to rejoin the baseball fray even as the war wound down. In his autobiography, *Veeck—as in Wreck*, he maintains that in 1942 he hatched a plan to purchase the woebegone Philadelphia Phillies, rebuild the team with Negro Leagues stars, and take the pennant in the war-depleted National League. Veeck said his mistake was apprising Commissioner Landis of his intentions. The Judge made sure the franchise got sold elsewhere. The story has become standard text in the mythology of baseball's integration. Skeptical historians have cast considerable doubt on Veeck's tale, which would make him a racial trailblazer in advance of Branch Rickey. Others have risen to Veeck's defense, pointing out that there is nothing to disprove his version of events. (Arguing from negative evidence is invariably a hazardous enterprise.)[9]

Bill Veeck. A showman with a conscience, Veeck saw several reasons to pursue black players, not least because he saw the racial barrier as ugly. He also enjoyed tweaking the stolid fellowship of American League owners. (National Baseball Hall of Fame Library, Cooperstown, N.Y.)

There is no denying that Bill Veeck took over as owner and president of the Cleveland Indians on June 22, 1946, purchasing the team from Alva Bradley. Most of the funding came from quiet investing partners and trusting banks; what Veeck had to do was put enough fans in the seats to make the expenditure worthwhile. He began immediately and on a grand scale, providing fans not just a ball game but a multi-varied entertainment package. There were bands, fireworks, promotions, giveaways, recognitions, media broadsides, and whatever else occurred to the owner's fruitful imagination. Veeck may have been a skillful baseball operator with a shrewd eye for talent, but above all he was P. T. Barnum in a ball park. Just why people came to Indians games—be it the bands, the fireworks, or the players—did not matter, so long as they came. "The whole of it, in Cleveland," Doc Young wrote, "was like a prolonged day at the circus. Ringmaster Veeck was in his glory."[10]

Veeck probably had it in his mind to recruit a black player for the Indians even as he bought the team. There were lots of good reasons to do so. If his Philadelphia story was even partly true, he had incentive to make good on a design that had eluded him. More to the point, Veeck wanted his team to win. The Indians had finished fifth in 1945, just one game over .500; in 1946 they placed sixth, winning just 68 games. The club needed an infusion of talent, but Veeck, as always, suffered from a lack of cash. Where could you get fully developed players more cheaply than from the Negro Leagues? A black player on the Indians would very possibly draw considerable numbers of new, black fans to the ball park, too. If there was one thing Bill Veeck clearly understood, it was that whatever their color, every fan's money was green.

There were other benefits, less tangible. Buying the Indians, Veeck had joined a very exclusive and clannish club of baseball executives, men who, with rare exceptions, resented change and were unable to imagine any. They were already appalled by his circus approach to baseball promotion; breaking the color line would irritate many of them almost beyond endurance. Bill Veeck liked that idea.[11]

Above all, there was the most intangible, most materially unrewarding factor of them all: adding a black player, dissolving the color line, defying Jim Crow—it was very simply the right thing to do. Veeck looked hard at segregation—in baseball, in American life—and decided, "This is ugly." He continued:

> Thinking about it, it seems to me that all my life I have been fighting against the status quo, against the tyranny of the fossilized majority rule. I would suppose that whatever impels me to battle the old fossils of baseball also draws me to the side of the underdog. I would prefer to think of it as an essential decency.[12]

A rare sentiment for 1962, when Veeck wrote his autobiography, to describe an advocacy for racial equality as "essential decency." Even more rare, and perhaps dangerous, in 1947. Veeck's organization reported receiving 20,000 pieces of hate mail when they signed Larry Doby to an Indians contract.

An elusive concept, essential decency. Even as Veeck began his search for a black player, he adopted a new logo for his team's uniforms, a cartoon caricature of a grinning American Indian face, with yellow skin, a giant nose, and a single feather. Before long, sports reporters were referring to the logo as "Chief Wahoo," a clear example of the racial insensitivities all too common in 1947 America. Bill Veeck worked to diffuse racial discrimination with one hand, but promoted racial imagery with the other.

If Veeck was sure in his own mind, he was uneasy about the reception in Cleveland. The city was a tough industrial town, much hurt by the Depression, and the black population (148,000 in 1950) had largely developed within the previous 15 years. Certainly Cleveland had done little to suggest there was much in the way of racial inclusiveness at work. Veeck laid his groundwork carefully, hoping "to force the critics to make their attacks on the basis of pure prejudice—if they dared—and not on other grounds." One of his first moves was to hire a black man, Lou Jones, to assist with public relations. The Indians established a solid working relationship with members of the black press, who quickly sensed what Veeck had in mind.

Thoughts and suggestions rolled in, confirming what Veeck's own scouts were telling him. The second baseman for the Newark Eagles, 22-year-old Larry Doby, looked to fit the bill in all respects.[13]

There were some critical parallels in the early lives of Larry Doby and Jackie Robinson that in small ways prepared them for their ordeals in 1947 and later. Both were born in the Deep South—Doby in Camden, South Carolina. The fathers of both men disappeared early in their lives, after which their mothers moved them to more racially tolerant surroundings. Larry Doby played his high school sports at Eastside High in Paterson, New Jersey—football, basketball, track and field, and baseball. He was one of about 25 black students in the school, meaning he learned early the parameters of mixed race team play, just as Robinson learned in California. And both attended college, though Doby was able to stay just four months before being drafted in 1942. All around, the two were psychologically more prepared than the large majority of their Negro Leagues teammates. Throughout their careers, each would exhibit a tremendous will to endure, a determination to maintain dignity in the face of enormous stupidity—from fans and opponents, from teammates and management.

Yet they were very different individuals. Jackie Robinson fed off the abuse that visited his presence, channeling his anger into productive energy that spelled key hits, dazzling defense, and defiant base running. Robinson's competitive fire engulfed everyone he encountered on the playing field.

Larry Doby simply did not have that kind of presence.[14] He was talented, God, he was talented. Major league players and owners were aware of that long before 1947. Serving in the Navy throughout World War II, Doby found himself stationed on the island of Ulithi in the Central Pacific, a supply depot. A makeshift ball diamond gave Doby the opportunity to play with Mickey Vernon, already a star with the Washington Senators, and Billy Goodman, a hot prospect for the Red Sox. Both were very impressed, Vernon enough that he called Clark Griffith's attention to Doby's skills. It would be another ten years before Griffith could bring himself to break the color line in Washington. So Doby returned to Newark in 1946. He had played one promising season (under an alias) with the Eagles before the war intervened. Now he tore it up, hitting .348, raising his average 25 points in the last weeks of the season. Larry Doby established himself as a coming star.[15]

Not everyone was sold. Willie Wells, Doby's manager, found him difficult to manage. Newt Allen thought he was a decent double play man at second base, "but his weight and his size kept him from staying loose like he could be in the outfield." Hilton Smith was very skeptical. It wasn't just that he struck Doby out three times in the 1946 East-West Game, it was that he started "jawing with the umpire." Doby was a player of some promise, but he was by no means a finished product. He was young, he was a war veteran, he had experience in interracial athletics, he had spent some time in college and read Shakespeare, he could play—he was the kind of man Bill Veeck wanted.[16] Or so he thought. Long after 1947, Veeck would admit that selecting Doby to become a race pioneer hurt the young man's career.

> Speaking purely about his career as a ballplayer, it was too much on his mind. Not that he wasn't a very good player. He led the league in home runs twice. In 1954, when the Indians won the pennant, he led in both home runs and runs batted in. With all that, his inner turmoil was such a constant drain on him that he was never able to realize his full potential. Not to my mind, at any rate. If Larry had come up just a little later, when things were just a little better, he might very well have become one of the greatest players of all time.[17]

The lives of a great many people intersected on July 5, 1947, the day Larry Doby first took the field in a Cleveland Indians uniform. On the Negro Leagues side of the equation stood Abe and Effa Manley, owners of the Newark Eagles and the contractual rights (such as they were) to Doby. Both were anxious to see black players in the big leagues, though they were considerably less anxious to lose their stars, and probably their livelihood into the bargain. Effa Manley was one of several Negro Leagues owners to be shocked and disgusted by Branch Rickey's refusal to pay the Kansas City Monarchs anything for Jackie Robinson.[18]

Within organized ball, several groups of people would be tested. Lou Boudreau, Cleveland's player-manager, ran interference as Doby shyly met his new teammates, the press, the fans, and the opposing Chicago White Sox. Bill McKechnie, formerly manager of the Reds, now Boudreau's right-hand man, would be a considerable influence. Some of the Indians players would help, others pointedly refuse. Doby's appearance was in many ways a shock to the system, a challenge to the rhythms of baseball life. Orchestrating it all was Bill Veeck, the ringmaster.

Veeck thought the thing through very carefully before signing Doby; it only appeared he had not. Soon after buying the Indians, he sought advice from Branch Rickey, who was already experiencing the challenges raised by Jackie Robinson's year in the International League. The two men shared a less than positive history. Veeck preferred Larry MacPhail's brand of inventiveness to Rickey's, and like so many operators, he had gotten the short end of the stick in some player deals. But Veeck understood that Rickey's experience could help him in this unique situation. The two men agreed that it was wise for more than one franchise to break the color line as soon as possible. Rickey was well aware of Doby's promise, but deferred to Veeck. For integration to gain ground, Veeck needed a good player. And it was the other league, after all.[19]

Despite the rapprochement, Veeck determined to do his integrating in quite the opposite fashion of Branch Rickey. Foremost was the issue of obtaining rights to the selected player. Rickey claimed the moral high ground while signing Robinson, arguing that the Negro Leagues were "in the zone of a racket"; Robinson, Wendell Smith, and Negro Leagues president Doc Martin went along. Veeck vehemently disagreed, recognizing Negro Leagues franchises as legitimate business concerns, even if their player contracts included no reserve clause. Once he settled on Larry Doby, he entered into careful negotiations with Effa Manley. Both sides knew that the $10,000 the Indians were offering was considerably below Doby's market value (if he were white), but at least it was something. When Manley hesitated, Veeck kicked in an additional $5,000, contingent on Doby sticking with Cleveland. Manley countered by offering a package deal: Larry Doby and Monte Irvin. Veeck would live to regret deeply refusing that offer, but refuse it he did, and Effa Manley reluctantly accepted the offer for Doby alone. She did manage to extract two additional promises: that Doby would be paid no less than $5,000 for the year with the Indians, and that he not be sent to the minors during the 1947 season. Veeck was as good as his word; Doby was well paid for spending much of the 1947 season on the Cleveland bench. The Manleys got the full $15,000.[20]

Veeck tried very hard to keep the signing a complete secret. Again, his aversion to Branch Rickey's methods played a large role—this time with a more negative outcome. Jackie Robinson's appearance in a Dodgers uniform in 1947 was just one aspect of Rickey's master plan to integrate his franchise. The process, begun in a flourish of publicity back in 1945, involved not just Robinson, but Roy Campanella, Don Newcombe, and two additional black players, all in the minors. The glare of this much exposure seemed to Veeck a large mistake. Better to do the thing quietly, draw no special attention to it, let it happen naturally. One day the Indians would take the field, and one of the players would be black.

So Veeck ordered his scouts to find him one black player, figuring that if the attempt went horribly wrong, he could back away without too much damage. When the scouts found Larry Doby, Veeck signed his man in utmost secrecy, not even telling his manager, Lou Boudreau, much less his players. In retrospect, Veeck recognized that in this case, Rickey's approach had proven more effective. In an America where Jim Crow lurked everywhere, better to at least accustom your players to the idea of sharing the locker room with a black teammate. Certainly the haste to put Doby in a Cleveland uniform was no help to the young man; all the enormous pressure burst on him at once.

There is circumstantial evidence to suggest that Veeck did make some effort to make the Indians' clubhouse more receptive to the presence of a black player, in a back-handed way. After the 1946 season, Veeck cleaned house, rebuilding a team that had finished a poor sixth. In the back of his mind may have been the Jim Crow refrain that you could not integrate a major league team because the Southern players would not stand for it. A silly argument on its face—the North was full of its own racism, while several Southerners had no objection at all to black players, so long as they could play. But the contention was there, and Veeck seems to have acted on it. Of the 13 players Bill Veeck chose to move after the 1946 season, seven were Southerners, leaving just three on the team. True, many of the replacements were Southerners, but they were generally younger men with military experience, perhaps more open-minded. The majority of the 1947 Indians came from the Midwest or California.[21]

These Indians were in Chicago, playing the White Sox, when word escaped that the Indians had signed Larry Doby. The plan was to bring Doby to Cleveland, sign him to a contract, and put him on the field at home on July 10. Between the Cleveland organization and the Newark Eagles, too many people were in the know. Bob Whiting of the *Newark Morning Call* sniffed out the story, and very soon the wire services were publicizing what the Cleveland Indians players and manager had not heard. The scoop forced Veeck's hand. He finally got around to telling Lou Boudreau, less than 24 hours before Doby would join the team on the field. The strategy, such as it was, could not have been more opposite the machinations of Branch Rickey. The entire Dodgers organization had a year and a half to smooth the way for Jackie Robinson. The Indians must have felt as if they had ten minutes.[22]

At least Veeck had a manager better equipped to cooperate than most. Lou Boudreau was one of the last great player-managers, and one of the youngest, possessing the nerve to apply for the job at age 24. In 1947 he was in his sixth season at the helm and it was one of his best as a player—he hit .307 and led his position in fielding. As a manager he was so-so, as the Indians rose to fourth place, 17 games back. Veeck didn't want Boudreau as his manager, probably preferring Jimmy Dykes, the man who had tried out Jackie Robinson and two other black players while managing the White Sox in 1941. Boudreau became an integral part of the Cleveland integration story simply because the fans would not stand to see him fired, and said as much in every way possible. Veeck relented, and Lou Boudreau, the boy manager, became the first Cleveland Indian to shake Larry Doby's hand.[23]

Boudreau was a college graduate and nobody's fool; he handled a nearly impossible situation as well as anyone could. Doby signed his major league contract just three hours before game time in Chicago on July 5. Boudreau had to go through the usual exercises of acclimating a player to a new team, and he also had to diffuse the unavoidable awkwardness of the whole situation. No one had ever so much as asked the coaches and players how they would react to a black player joining the team—the first black player in the history of the American League. Boudreau met the issue squarely, getting Doby into uniform, enthusiastically introducing him to each Indian as opportunity presented. The majority welcomed Doby, with varying degrees of acceptance. The story of that first day changed some in the long years of retelling between 1947 and Doby's death in 2003. The earliest accounts had three players refusing to shake his hand; by the 1990s the tale was six who pointedly refused to acknowledge his presence. By any stretch it was an unusual moment, and the numbers don't mean a thing. Veeck had let it be known that Doby possessed more potential than any player on the team, and anyone not caring to share the field could have his ticket punched elsewhere. "This boy can really tag the ball," Veeck advised. Set that opinion against the oft-spoken fear that blacks were going to take white people's jobs; there was enough social confusion for anyone. It is quite possible that most of the players welcomed Larry Doby; it is also possible that most of them wished this bit of history had occurred somewhere else.

Larry Doby never wrote an autobiography, but he did sit down for a number of interviews and oral histories through the years. Reading them, it is very difficult to gauge the degree of animosity he felt in the Cleveland locker room, but animosity there certainly was. Doby consistently singled out just two Indians players who strongly supported and helped him that first season: manager-shortstop Lou Boudreau and second baseman Joe Gordon. These were the two best players on the team and, oddly enough, the two with whom Doby would have to compete if he wished to remain a middle infielder. No one, least of all Boudreau, was taking that possibility seriously. In the one game Larry Doby started for the Indians that summer, he played first base. That was another travail.[24]

A brief digression here. Just why was Larry Doby playing second base for the Newark Eagles in the first place? At 6'1" and 180 pounds, he was built more on the lines of a defensive halfback than, say, Nellie Fox. But this was not entirely unusual in the Negro Leagues; several of their star middle infielders were big guys—major league scouts grasped this fact straightaway. Apart from pitchers and catchers, very nearly all the earliest Negro Leagues recruits were middle infielders who did not fit the major league image of their positions. Jackie Robinson played shortstop for the Monarchs, Larry Doby second base for the Eagles. Hank Thompson was a second baseman, and Willard Brown played shortstop in his younger days. Monte Irvin was the Newark Eagles' shortstop. Al Smith played shortstop for the Cleveland Buckeyes. Minnie Minoso played third base for the Cubans. Even Henry Aaron started as a shortstop. All were signed by big league teams, and all were moved to less demanding positions. Robinson spent a year at first base before moving back to the middle; the others became outfielders. Probably there was some stereotyping going on, but the shifts may also have had to do with the differences between black and white baseball. Unlike the majors, where slow-moving thumpers were all the fashion, the Negro Leagues continued to play small ball, or inside baseball, emphasizing speed and agility. Inside baseball dictated the corner infielders—first and third—had to be the smaller, more agile ones, to handle all those bunts and rapid-fire situations. Bigger athletes got pushed to the middle—perfectly sensible for Negro Leagues play, but not at all what the majors expected or wanted.

The first day, Doby met his teammates, and he met the press, two heart-pounding moments. By his own admission then and later, he was very, very nervous, nearly terrified of the sudden attention. The press was largely positive and sympathetic, coming away with the impression

**Larry Doby masters the outfield. A second baseman with the Newark Eagles, Doby was deemed too big for the middle infield in major league baseball. At the suggestion of Bill McKechnie, Doby studied out-field play, eventually becoming an All-Star center fielder. (National Baseball Hall of Fame Library, Cooperstown, N.Y.)**

of a very shy and polite young man with a voice so low he almost could not be heard. The day following Larry Doby's first game in Municipal Stadium, *Cleveland Plain Dealer* sportswriter Gordon Cobbledick made the issue very simple: Doby would be accepted if he could play. Bill Veeck to the contrary, race was not an issue in Cleveland; fans were well accustomed to black stars playing for the pro football Cleveland Browns. What Cobbledick saw as Doby made his first appearance on the field confirmed his expectations.

> As Doby emerged and started across the field to the Cleveland bench a few spectators saw him and applauded. With each step the chorus swelled until, as he approached the first base dugout, it had attained the proportions of an ovation. An uncommonly large proportion of the spectators were colored, but it was noticed that Negroes and whites alike joined in the greeting.

Cobbledick went on to assess Doby's potential with a clear-eyed cold-bloodedness: "The boy showed promise, that he might hit, might be an outfielder, that he definitely was not a shortstop or a second baseman and equally definitely was not ready for the big leagues."

Cleveland's black community was less than pleased with that description.[25]

Unfortunately, Lou Boudreau leaned very much to the same conclusions. That first day in Chicago, the manager warmed Doby up, observed him in batting practice, and had to make a very quick decision on how to use a green rookie with just two and a half years of professional experience, a kid with enormous expectations, good and bad, weighing on him. The boss had already made it clear that Doby was on the team to stay. Boudreau did the only thing that made sense: he went with his baseball instincts, employing Doby in spots where he could not hurt his team or his own confidence too much, trying his best to utilize his new player's obvious skills. Doby sat at the far end of the bench for most of his first major league game, accompanied by two plainclothes police officers provided by Bill Veeck, presumably not to help the kid's nerves. Boudreau called on Doby to pinch-hit in the seventh against Chicago's Earl Harrist. He stood up to the plate (Chief Wahoo grinning on his arm), shook like a leaf, and managed to hit a wicked line drive foul before striking out. American League play was integrated at last, a little more than 12 weeks after the National.

When Boudreau decided to start Doby in the second game of the following day's doubleheader, the organization's failure to prepare the way created more problems. Boudreau was not about to take Gordon or himself out of the lineup, leaving first base the only possible place for Doby to play. He had no experience there, and he had no glove. The Indians' regular first sacker, rookie Eddie Robinson, was not about to lend his—not because of race, he would later contend, but because he did not want to risk losing his job to any prospect. It was a potentially explosive moment, diffused when Robinson tossed his glove to a team official, who gave it to Doby. To many, Robinson came to represent the other side of the racial equation, a young man from Texas possessing a modicum of talent and perhaps some doubts about blacks playing on his team, certainly playing ahead of him. The incident could easily have spiraled out of control, but the clubhouse—Doby, Robinson, Boudreau, and everyone else—chose to let it die an unheralded death. Jim Crow found no wedge among the Cleveland Indians.[26]

The second game on July 6 turned out to be Larry Doby's only start of the entire 1947 season. He made no mistakes, handling eight putouts and managing a single through the infield in four tries, but he demonstrated no real aptitude for the position, either. As the season progressed, Boudreau had Doby work out at second base and at short, but he never tried him at first base again. Nor did he start him in another game. Doby made four late-inning appearances at second base and one at shortstop. He made no errors, but he made no impression on his man-ager. The Indians were trying to sneak into the first division for the first time since 1943; Lou Boudreau clearly was taking no unnecessary chances. He used Doby in a few spots as a pinch-hitter—he hit just four singles and one double in 28 at-bats—and employed him once as a pinch-runner, taking advantage of his considerable speed. Doby showed flashes of potential, especially in pre-game workouts, but the overall conclusion was that considerable work lay ahead to make him a true major league ballplayer. As the season wound down, Bill McKechnie, the wise old man of the Cleveland coaching staff, gave Doby some encouragement. He had the talent, McKechnie told him; he could make it in the big leagues. But not as an infielder, not with his fielding skills and his size, not with Boudreau and Gordon and even Eddie Robin-son in front of him. First chance, get to the library, get your hands on a book on how to play the outfield. Your future is there.[27]

That was about as encouraging as it got.

Looking back over the experience of the season, it was clear that the Branch Rickey approach to integration held considerable advantage over the Bill Veeck route. Placing Jackie Robinson in the minors at Montreal for a year had given everyone in the Dodgers organization ample opportunity to discover the practical problems integration posed, and time to learn how to deal with them. By the time Robinson took the field with the Dodgers in April 1947, the players were conditioned to the idea, the media had covered it thoroughly, and the fans had already exhausted every argument, pro and con. The sailing was by no means smooth, but the time allowed for considered reflection did much to reduce the potential difficulties. Jackie Robinson was adequately prepared, mentally and physically, to be a full-time major league player.

Larry Doby was spared much of the vitriol aimed at Robinson as he slowly but surely made his way to the majors. But the price was very high. By throwing Doby directly into the fray, Veeck denied himself any opportunity to learn about the abilities and the psychology of his young player. No one else in the Indians organization had a clue. Lou Boudreau undertook a most careful balancing act, doing his best to make Doby welcome while doing nothing to rankle his 23 other players. The marginal ballplayers offered the most resistance, fearing tal-ented blacks such as Doby would replace them. Larry Doby endured a soul-wrenching first season because Bill Veeck sprang him on the club. No one knew what to do; everyone did what they thought might ease the situation. At season's end, Larry Doby remained a question mark, just as he was in July. Veeck would later allow that "he was not the best man we could have picked for the first Negro player in the league. I don't say that from the club's point of view, but from his."[28]

Watching from the sidelines at mid-season in 1947, the majority of the club owners were witnessing an uphill battle that looked to promise little reward. True, Jackie Robinson was tearing it up, but Larry Doby looked like he was more trouble to Bill Veeck than he was worth. Much of the critical reaction was pure venom. *The Sporting News* took on the subject once more in July 1947, nine days after Larry Doby joined the Indians. This time the headline read "Once Again, That Negro Question." J. G. Taylor Spink and his editorial staff were not happy with the recent signings. After making the obligatory observation that "there has never been a major league regulation barring Negro players," the piece outlined the injustice of it all (inso-far as white players were concerned), the readily understandable resistance. A "vast percentage of the white players in the majors" remained opposed, the staff contended. How the staff arrived at this estimate was anyone's guess, but they could cite some complaints. Foremost, the influx of black players threatened the economic well-being of whites by taking away jobs. Then there was the fact that Jackie Robinson had spent just one season in AAA ball, while Larry Doby never played a game in the minors. After speaking with one unidentified white All-Star at the game in Chicago, *The Sporting News* quoted:

> "I fought my way through the minors for five years. I rode buses all night for three of those five years, so that I could get a chance in the majors.
>
> If we are to have Negroes in the majors, let them go through the long preparation the white player is forced to undergo. Let us not discriminate against the white player because he is white."
>
> THE SPORTING NEWS believes that this summarization is worthy of consideration.

*The Sporting News* apparently thought that the grind of the Negro Leagues, where riding antiquated buses and sleeping in Jim Crow hotels was a way of life, did not count. The editors were too worried about two white guys losing major league jobs. So worried that they allowed one voice to stand for the majority opinion among the white players.[29]

At least Bill Veeck had evolved something of a plan before bringing Larry Doby into the fold. That was more than anyone in the St. Louis Browns organization could claim, even if they were the third team in the majors—the second in the American League—to have a go at integration. The Browns made no bones about what they were doing, or why. The franchise was in greater financial trouble than ever; the decision to sign two players from the Kansas City Monarchs was little more than a cynical attempt to draw black fans. This by an organization that had abolished Jim Crow seating at Sportsman's Park just three years before.

Dick Muckerman, a wealthy ice manufacturer, was essentially conned into buying the perennial doormat St. Louis franchise in 1946, believing the pennant won by the Browns in 1944 was the sign of a real turn-around, rather than a wartime fluke. Reality came hard and quickly. The team finished a poor seventh in 1946, and was running dead last in July of 1947. Team stock values dropped to a record low. Muckerman had fully swallowed the half-truth that the Browns fielded several promising players in the farm system. Turned out that the honest-to-God prospects were all in the low minors, several years away. Muckerman needed a quick fix, for his team, for his gate. Eyeing the runaway train that was Jackie Robinson, the Browns owner and president concluded that the Negro Leagues provided the answer to both his problems. He quickly bargained with Kansas City Monarchs owner J. L. Wilkinson, coming away with a veteran talent in Willard "Home Run" Brown, and a very promising youngster, Hank Thompson. Brown and Thompson were immediately assigned to the big club, where they were expected to assume starting positions. The team also purchased a 30-day option on Birmingham Barons second baseman Piper Davis, but made no move to bring him to St. Louis. They added a fourth black player to the farm system later in the season, signing Charley Harmon straight out of college. On the surface, the Browns appeared to have made a commitment.[30]

The signings may have been hasty and almost thoughtless, but at least they were honest. The black players were briefly observed by Browns senior scout Jack Fournier, who reported to Bill DeWitt, the team's General Manager. DeWitt sent his scout to Kansas City not to look at Brown or Thompson, but to check out catcher Earl Taborn. The Browns needed catching help desperately, but Fournier concluded that Taborn was not the answer. Brown and Thompson, however, looked like the real thing. DeWitt negotiated directly with Wilkinson, promising $5,000 each for the two players, half to be paid immediately, with the balance due at the close of the season, should the players stick. What ensued was mostly a disaster, but still this was an important moment. Muckerman and Dewitt chose to follow Bill Veeck's lead and pay J. L.

Wilkinson, rather than simply take the players from the Monarchs in the fashion of Branch Rickey's signing of Jackie Robinson. Wilkinson, they felt, was running a legitimate ball club, and not "something in the zone of a racket."[31]

Thereafter, owners in both the National and American Leagues generally followed Veeck's lead rather than Rickey's, negotiating for the rights to players on Negro Leagues rosters and paying the owners. Major league franchises paid bargain basement prices, to be sure—nothing like the true value of the players involved—but they did pay. Negro Leagues owners understood that they could not stand in the way of black players going to the majors; that would be a race betrayal that would net them nothing but horrendous publicity. When the Negro National League folded after the 1947 season, the bargaining position grew that much weaker. Black team owners protested mildly, some of them, and swallowed hard, accepting perhaps a quarter of the real value for some of their most promising players. It was a buyers' market, but the money derived cushioned the blow just a little as the Negro Leagues faded down the stream of time. Apart from selling their entire franchises (usually at a loss), selling players was the only form of compensation Negro Leagues owners ever saw. Veeck had set a precedent; Dick Muckerman and Bill DeWitt honored it.

The Browns signed Hank Thompson on July 17, just 12 days after Larry Doby debuted in Chicago. Two days later, they signed Willard Brown and Piper Davis. For the moment, the pace of integration appeared to be quickening. If St. Louis, a border town with a lot of Confederate ancestry, could see the light, how long before the entire edifice came tumbling down? St. Louis taught some harsh lessons.

The two players joining the Browns were not wisely chosen. The marquee star was Willard Brown, a strapping 200-pound outfielder who could hit the ball a very long way. Seven times he led the Negro Leagues in home runs. None other than Josh Gibson hung the nickname "Home Run" on Brown, after losing a home run derby to the Monarchs center fielder. Brown went on to star in the Mexican League, hitting .354 for Nuevo Laredo in 1940. World War II found him in Europe, where he grew his legend by hitting long home runs for armed services teams. Returning to Kansas City in 1946, Brown became one of the brightest attractions in the Negro Leagues. In all, he participated in the East-West Game five times.

That was the up side. More ominous was the fact that Home Run Brown had just turned 36 years old (he claimed to be 34). His best years were irretrievably behind him. He had begun as a shortstop, then shifted to center field, staying there ten years. His throwing arm was weak, the result of being hit in the shoulder with a bat. His teammates and Negro Leagues opponents had mixed emotions regarding his abilities. Some would remember him as a player of surpassing skills, an outfielder who made the hardest plays look easy. Buck O'Neil compared him to Henry Aaron, another player who performed the most difficult maneuvers so smoothly no one ever noticed. Others were not so sure. Othello Renfroe recalled that "Willard Brown, who played for us, could hit the ball and outrun anybody in the league. But he'd only play hard on Sunday; he'd loaf the rest of the time." Brown was anxious to test his skills in the major leagues. How he would do was anyone's guess.[32]

At the opposite end of the spectrum was the Kansas City second baseman, Hank Thompson, who would not turn 22 until that December. He had joined the Monarchs at age 17, playing one season in right field, hitting around .285. Then came his draft notice, followed by three years in the Army lasting to June 1946. He rejoined Kansas City in time to help them win the Negro Leagues championship, and in the next season truly came into his own. In July of 1947, Thompson was playing a solid second base and hitting .354. Small wonder Browns scout Jack Fournier was impressed.

But again there was a downside, in this case a very large one. Thompson was young, he was green, and he had already found his way into serious trouble. Othello Renfroe remembered. "Hank Thompson of the Monarchs was another one who was a real fine ballplayer, but Hank always had trouble drinking, plus he was mean as hell, a mean, mean guy. Kept some kind of weapon on him all the time." Thompson later explained that he was copying several veterans on the club who carried guns. The fact was, Hank Thompson had begun drinking heavily by age 15, and he had already done a stint in a Texas reform school. Military service did not straighten him out; it instead gave him a taste for rotgut whiskey. In 1948, just a few months after the Browns dropped him, Thompson shot an old acquaintance in a Texas bar, killing him. Officials ruled self-defense. Hank Thompson was a talented, troubled kid.[33]

The St. Louis Browns expended the absolute minimum of time and effort to sign two question marks—an aging star with a questionable work ethic and a promising prospect with some personal demons. The team, with both eyes on a rapidly plunging bottom line, simply did not care. The point was to build attendance, so they signed some black players, not quite at random, but very, very close. They did nothing to prepare the few fans they had, and nothing to inform the team. Browns manager Muddy Ruel was taken completely by surprise when Hank Thompson showed up on July 17. The team was for the most part openly hostile. Almost half the players on this last-place team in the baseball's southernmost city were Southerners; they and most of their fellow players froze the newcomers out. Just a few Browns made any effort to welcome Brown and Thompson. Junior Stephens, the team's only star, had learned enough playing briefly in Mexico to display some essential human values. Thompson remembered Stephens being especially helpful. Johnny Berardino, Walt Judnich, and Bob Dillinger all came from California, Jeff Heath from Canada. They were the helpful guys.[34]

To his credit, Muddy Ruel did his best with an impossible situation. He started Thompson in a night game against the Philadelphia Athletics on the day he reported. Understandably terrified, Thompson went hitless and made an error. Two days later, when Brown joined the team, Ruel started "Home Run" in center field, batting him fifth. Again no luck; Brown went 0-for-3, hitting into two double plays. Four days later, Ruel started both Thompson and Brown, the first time two black players appeared in the same major league starting lineup. Thompson did manage a hit in that one. (Brown had one of his few good days in the majors, hitting four for five, driving home three runs.) Some days later, Brown became the first black player in the American League to hit a home run, an inside-the-park rip off Detroit's Hal Newhouser. He also managed a four-hit game against the Yankees, but that was about it for highlights. Thirty-four days after joining the Browns, Willard Brown was hitting just .179. In 21 games, he hit just the one home run and drove in six runs. Hank Thompson was doing a little better job of adjusting, his averaging rising to .256 after a very slow start. Ruel had him leading off at times. Thompson's problems came in the field; he was slow on the pivot, and demonstrated little range to his right.[35]

Five weeks was not much to measure by. Whatever their performance on the field, Brown and Thompson failed in the one critical area that brought them to St. Louis in the first place. People did not come out to see them. There was a spark of initial interest in St. Louis when the two first appeared, but that quickly died out. No one could say for sure, but many analysts claimed that the black population of St. Louis saw the signings for the cynical shams they were, and chose to stay away in protest. More likely, they were just disappointed. Fans black and white flocked to see Jackie Robinson not simply because he was black, but because he was so good, so exciting. Larry Doby never got enough exposure in 1947 for fans to get his measure. But Brown and Thompson did get to play just enough for fans to be very disappointed with them. Black fans, so the explanation went, would not pay to see mediocre black performance.

The Browns did draw better on the road, as black and white fans in other cities came out to see Thompson and Brown. This helped the bottom line a touch, as the visiting team received a portion of the gate. The Browns quickly evolved a strategy that demonstrated just how cynical the business was. As the team moved from town to town, Ruel would insert one and sometimes both his black players into the opening game lineup, bringing out the crowds. More often than not, the two would sit the remaining games in the series. Hank Thompson played a bit more than Brown, probably because regular second baseman Johnny Berardino got hurt, giving Thompson a fuller opportunity.[36]

The grim farce came to end on August 23, having lasted a whole five weeks. In a press release, the Browns said, "the two men had failed to reach major league standards," an observation that left baseball people and black sportswriters shaking their heads. What could you tell in just five weeks? In those circumstances, playing for a terrible team, receiving no help at all from management, Muddy Ruel was honest and sympathetic, telling the *Baltimore Afro-American* in early August, "I can truthfully say that they've done nothing spectacular, yet neither have they done anything wrong. I can't say that they've had a fair trial as yet, but I also find it rather hard to determine just what is a 'fair trial.'" Ruel thought that Thompson was a fine fielder, and that Brown was an excellent long-ball hitter who had yet to deliver. Two weeks later they were gone.[37]

The truth of their leaving, or at least some element of the truth, was more difficult for the Browns to acknowledge. Had they been anxious to make their experiment work, the obvious solution was to send Brown, and more especially the young Hank Thompson, to the minors for seasoning, just as the Indians were obviously planning to do with Larry Doby. The thing was, the Browns could not afford the option. They had brought the two to St. Louis in the hope of attracting a large infusion of cash. The experiment had produced hardly a trickle, and to keep Brown and Thompson, the Browns would be liable to pay the Monarchs another $5,000 they simply felt they could not afford. One more evidence, at least, that most major league organizations felt obligated to deal honorably with their Negro Leagues counterparts. Both players immediately returned to Kansas City, finishing out the season. The Browns dropped their option on Piper Davis for the same reason.

Willard Brown would later claim that it was not true that the Browns released him, maintaining that he quit of his own accord. Whichever way it went, he must have seen the writing on the wall. At 36, his one chance was gone. Home Run Brown played one more season for the Monarchs, then bumped around, eventually becoming the first black everyday player in the Texas League, hitting 23 home runs for Dallas in 1953. He retired three years later.[38]

Hank Thompson was a different story. Even the Browns could see he possessed real major league potential, well worth harvesting, as he was just 22. After another season with the Monarchs, Alex Pompez recruited Thompson to play the outfield in the New York Giants organization. He was back in the big show by 1949, becoming an important cog in a Giants team that won a pennant in 1951 and a World Series in 1954. His only real limitation was himself. Hard drink, by his own admission the one thing more important than baseball, fueled his journey down a dark road ending in a Texas penitentiary. More troubles followed.[39]

Thompson recalled his last days playing for the Browns with mixed emotions. No one treated him badly, he recalled; the fans, the players, the management were all supportive. Still, things were not right. When Muddy Ruel gave him the news of his release, he paid a visit to the front office. "I went to Bill DeWitt and I said, 'I'm doing as good as lots of other guys on this club.' And Mr. DeWitt looked uncomfortable and finally he said, 'There are some things I can't discuss with you, Hank.'

That ended the conversation. We both knew what those things were."[40]

So ended a mordant experiment. If anything positive came out of the St. Louis lack of effort, it was a lesson for the 13 franchises yet to integrate. An ordeal compounded of desperation, lack of cash, complete lack of preparation, and the resultant indifferent play demonstrated a harsh and sobering reality. There was more to breaking the color line than grabbing what looked like a skillful black player and adding him to the roster. Integration required groundwork and attention to detail—attention to the needs of the black man suffering culture shock, attention to his fellow players and their mixed reactions, attention to the ability of the manager, the coaches, and the front office to set things right. There was the press to persuade and cajole, there were the fans to educate and entertain. Integration was a serious business. The Browns did not take it seriously.

As the 1947 season drew to a close, the friends of integration, particularly in the American League, had to be scanning the landscape with a nervous eye. Decades later, knowing that they all lived happily ever after (sort of), it is easy to forget just how precarious the cause of integration seemed as winter descended. Jackie Robinson had triumphed, leading the Dodgers to the pennant and earning the Rookie of the Year Award, but that was the other league, and Robinson was the only one. The Dodgers had tried Dan Bankhead at the end of the season, but that was a disaster. They had more promising players on the farm, but the lesson there seemed to be that a franchise had to go to the time and trouble of seasoning black players before they could make any possible impact in the majors. The experiences of Larry Doby, Willard Brown, and Hank Thompson appeared to confirm such an assessment. Lou Boudreau was pretty sure Larry Doby needed some time in the minors, and the St. Louis Browns' experiment was an embarrassing waste of time for all concerned. Meanwhile, none of the other six American League franchises—nor most of the National League clubs, for that matter—demonstrated any interest in signing black players. Real integration—blacks playing day in and day out with American League teams—could be years away.

The outfield picture for the Cleveland Indians entering spring training in 1948 was a crowd of confusion. Larry Doby followed through on Bill McKechnie's suggestion, studying a book on playing the outfield, pondering the instructions carefully. In camp, he would train with former Cleveland center fielder and player-manager Tris Speaker. Speaker was no great supporter of integration, but he did what Bill Veeck paid him to do, and he did it well. Still, it was going to be an uphill struggle just to make the club. The Indians also had Thurman Tucker, Dale Mitchell, Allie Clark, Hal Peck, Pat Seerey, and Hank Edwards vying for outfield spots. And Larry Doby was laboring under a handicap none of his teammates much thought about.[41]

In 1949, Lou Boudreau brought out *Player-Manager*, a chronicle of Cleveland's 1948 World Championship season, their last of the 20th century. Boudreau duly recorded the confidence he felt going into the season, the enthusiastic reaction "most of the men" expressed to shifting camp from Florida to Tucson, Arizona. According to Boudreau, the only player to express any reservation was Bob Feller, who could not work up a sweat in the arid climate. The boy manager apparently chose to forget Larry Doby's situation.

Bill Veeck had chosen to move the Indians camp to Tucson in part because of his decision to break the color line. He was very familiar with Tucson, owning a horse ranch in the area and living there much of the off-season. It is something of a puzzle, then, that neither Veeck nor Lou Boudreau tumbled to the fact that while the ball fields might accept integration, the City of Tucson would not. Larry Doby, to his shock and anger, discovered that he was barred from staying in the Santa Rita Hotel with the rest of his team. He wound up staying in the private home of Chester Willis, a service contractor with the hotel. Away from the field, Doby had almost no contact with his teammates, an awkwardness they all felt. The arrangement continued through another six spring training seasons, as Veeck and his successors made no effort to challenge Jim Crow in Tucson. There is next to nothing even to suggest that Veeck or Boudreau attached any importance to the issue. Larry Doby certainly felt it—one more set of insults to add to a long and growing list.[42]

With what he had seen in 1947, Lou Boudreau went to Tucson reasonably sure that the answer to the Larry Doby dilemma was a trip to the minors. Doby had the talent, but he lacked confidence and had some trouble dealing with the unique challenges major league baseball dealt him. Plus, he was learning an entirely new position. Doby did little in the early weeks of camp to dispel this perception, hitting well sporadically, showing no real consistency. There were distractions. When Doby accidentally spiked Washington's (white) shortstop sliding into second during a Los Angeles exhibition game, the event got coverage in *The Sporting News*— because nothing happened. No riot. Boudreau did see enough to promote Doby to the "A" team, but worried about his tendency to go after bad balls. The minors still looked like a good idea.

Doby's anger and frustration came to a boil when the Indians went to Houston for an exhibition game. Jim Crow almost kept him from getting to the ballpark at all, and the crowd booed him long and loud. It was a kind of visceral hatred Doby had not faced before, not in Paterson, not in the Navy, not in Cleveland or the other American League cities, though those places were hard enough. Doby channeled his anger like Jackie Robinson playing in Philadelphia, hitting the longest home run ever seen in Houston. He hit another home run, two doubles, and a triple that day. The crowd cheered and Doby resented them for it. Determination had overwhelmed intimidation.[43]

Opening Day in Cleveland found more than 73,000 fans in Municipal Stadium. Doby had their full support—a rousing cheer greeted his first plate appearance—but that was the highlight of his day. He went 0-for-4, and played a shaky right field. Three days later in Detroit he was impressive, slashing a long home run and two more hits. So it went in the first months of the season, flashes of real brilliance alternating with pedestrian play. Lou Boudreau agonized, not least because the Indians got out of the gate well, contending for the league lead. The Indians could not afford to provide Larry Doby a leisurely interval to find his stroke; they needed an outfielder they could count on. Boudreau focused on the positives: Doby's bursts of power, his superb base running, and his improving outfield play, and stayed with him.

On June 27, with the Indians clinging to a slender first-place lead over the Philadelphia Athletics, Larry Doby sprained his right foot sliding into second base against Washington. The injury kept him out of action for more than a week. When he returned, he was a man renewed, more aggressive, more confident. Boudreau, recognizing the subtle change, installed Doby in center field and kept him there. As the pennant raced quickened, Doby grew steadily more

**Satchel Paige, off duty. Paige would carry the history of the Negro Leagues on his shoulders when he joined the Cleveland Indians in 1948. Sometimes the burden was lighter than at other times. (National Baseball Hall of Fame Library, Cooperstown, N.Y.)**

productive, slugging key home runs to win games down the stretch and putting together a 21-game hitting streak through August and early September.[44]

Inconsistencies remained. Playing the Athletics in late July, Doby misjudged a fly ball so badly it caromed off his head, allowing two runs to score. "Doby was brokenhearted," Boudreau recalled. "He might easily have cracked right there and never been any good again." Bill McKechnie challenged Doby, telling him starkly this was the kind of incident that could prove or disprove his ability to play major league baseball. Doby saw the point, shook off the humiliation, and became a key player down the stretch. The pennant race ended in a tie, with Cleveland contesting the first one-game playoff in the history of the American League against the Red Sox in Boston. Larry Doby hit two doubles in that game, helping the Indians to their first pennant since 1920. It was nearly the year's most significant event in the ongoing process of baseball's integration.[45]

In Cleveland, on July 9, 1948, in the fifth inning of a night game the Indians were losing, 4–1, to the St. Louis Browns, a long-limbed and ancient pitcher began a slow, very slow walk from the bullpen to the pitcher's mound. He had never been one to move quickly; a graceful conservation of energy had always been his style. But on this night, his slow and purposeful stride was a matter of nerves and history. Satchel Paige was carrying on his shoulders the skill, the legends, the joy, the pain of every Negro Leagues veteran who ever played, a burden that Jackie Robinson or Larry Doby could never understand. The crowd of nearly 35,000 recognized just what his presence represented. They cheered every step.[46]

Satchel Paige's biography is a reader in the history of Jim Crow America. Born to grinding poverty in Mobile, Alabama, he learned to throw with deadly accuracy, aiming rocks at posts, tin cans, small birds, large flying birds, and white boys who wanted to beat him up. He learned the craft of pitching at a reform school in Mount Meigs, Alabama, and in 1925 embarked on a long, almost mythical journey that took him back and forth across America, down into the Caribbean, and on to Mexico. He had a fastball hitters couldn't see, and after recovering from an arm injury, a bewildering array of speed balls, curves and changeups that left batters in knots. Paige intimidated hitters, but more importantly, he outwitted them.

From the very beginning, he understood his own worth. Very few pitchers could even approach his skill; his arm was money, and he was determined to get his share. In a game where most athletes surrendered to the exploitation of owners and scheduling agents, Satchel Paige heeded no rules but his own. He jumped from one lucrative offer to the next, displaying no loyalty save to his own wallet, fully comprehending that baseball was business, that owners were loyal to him only if he continued to draw. When his arm went dead, the only man interested in his fate was J. L. Wilkinson, who signed him to a secondary Monarchs travelling team, hoping to make them both a little cash off his name recognition. When the arm returned to life, Paige, for one of the few times in his life, felt some real gratitude, and stuck by Wilkinson, helping to make the Monarchs the dominant team in the Negro Leagues. Pitching the Monarchs to greatness, barnstorming with Babe Ruth, Dizzy Dean, Bob Feller, and so many others, Paige's unbelievably long career embodied the essence of the Negro Leagues experience, a constant quest for livelihood against long odds and the constant echoes of racial hatred. Paige had lived it all.[47]

In 1948, Satchel Paige had been pitching professionally for 24 seasons, an unbelievably long career by any standard. No one knew how old he was; Paige found it profitable to be vague about that, another part of the legend. Bill Veeck tried to find out and came to the conclusion that the pitcher was at least 48 years old. Recent research claims to peg his birth year as 1906. Whatever the math, Paige was, and still remains, the oldest rookie ever to pull on a major league uniform. Probably the word "rookie" could use a little definition.

*The Sporting News* was all over this story, too, righteously accusing Bill Veeck of more sideshow antics in the middle of a pennant race. At least the editors had the decency not to run the story as "That Negro Question Yet Again," opting to object to the Paige signing on the grounds of extreme age, on the surface at least. "Further complicating the issue," the editorial intoned, "is the suspicion that if Satchel were white, he would not have drawn a second thought from Veeck." As Veeck later pointed out, if Satchel were white he already would have been pitching in the majors for 24 years.[48]

Tom Meany of the *New York Post* intimated a vastly superior understanding of what was at work, contending that "It was inevitable that the bigotry which kept Negroes out of Organized Ball would be beaten back, but I'd never heard of Robinson at that time. With Paige, it's different. The Satchmo has been a baseball legend for a long time, a Paul Bunyan in technicolor." Paige, for one, fully appreciated Meany's sense of the moment, quoting the lines in full in his autobiography, *Maybe I'll Pitch Forever*. Satchel Paige on the mound in Cleveland was a culmination, a melding of two very long traditions of baseball brought together at last.[49]

Not that the relief appearance was intended wholly as some kind of symbolic gesture. Cleveland was trying to win a pennant; Satchel Paige was there because Bill Veeck was sure he could provide the middle relief and spot starting the pitching corps desperately needed. Paige, Veeck, and Lou Boudreau all tell the story of the pitcher's tryout with the Indians; how Veeck found Paige with the help of Wilkinson and Abe Saperstein; how Boudreau was called to the ballpark early one morning to test a mysterious new pitching prospect; how a travel-stiffened Paige threw a few warm-ups before Boudreau stepped into the batter's box. Paige threw 20 pitches; 19 were strikes. His trademark was unbelievable pinpoint control, no matter what he threw. Boudreau, hitting close to .400 against the American League, could not manage a decent hit off the old man. Paige signed a contract for a full season's pay the next day.[50]

He delivered. The first man to face him stroked a sharp single, but that was it. Paige set the Browns down for two innings before being lifted for a pinch-hitter—appropriately enough, Larry Doby. That was just the beginning. If somebody made a fairy tale of Paige's 1948 season, no one would believe it. At least 42 years old, Paige, six foot five, took the mound and stared down at each hitter's knees, searching out his weakness. Then came the old fashioned windup, the right arm wheeling once, twice, maybe three times before the left foot kicked over his head and the ball came suddenly out of nowhere. Paige showed them everything, his "be" ball, his "bat dodger," his "hesitation pitch" the American League would declare illegal. No matter. He was a force, pitching in 21 games, winning six, losing one, and saving another. He started seven games, completing three, including two legendary shutouts. His ERA for 72⅓ innings pitched was 2.48. And the Indians won the pennant by a hair's breadth.[51]

Paige was far more valuable to Cleveland than what met the casual (or hostile) eye. One of the key elements in the Indians' stretch run was the performance of Larry Doby, more relaxed and living up to his potential at last. For a year following his initial signing, Doby lugged around the hope of the black race, the sole black in the American League, save for the five weeks of the Browns fiasco. Paige, the living emblem of black baseball's past, took that weight off Larry Doby's shoulders. Doby faded into the background as far as the race thing went; Paige naturally commanded center stage, a larger-than-life personality commanding attention. While Doby concentrated on hitting and fielding, Paige "held court," entertaining teammates and the press with endless stories of baseball in the wilds of America. The tragedy was that Doby never fully appreciated Paige for who and what he was.

Through his first year; Doby had roomed alone; sharing with a white player was unthinkable in 1948 America. Paige softened Larry Doby's burden at a practical level, becoming his roommate on the road. But Doby avoided association with Paige as much as he could, seeing in Satchel too much of the stereotypical "Amos and Andy" character he felt at all costs he needed to bury. Doby was more militant. In his youth, he encountered some of the radical thinking propounded in the "New Negro" philosophy as taught by Wendell Williams, his recreational baseball coach in Paterson, New Jersey. Doby did not much understand the talk about Marcus Garvey or W. E. B. Dubois back then, but by 1948 he had decided one of the determining attributes of the black pioneer was a quiet dignity. Satchel Paige seemed the antithesis of that.

Which was too bad. Had Doby been able to peer beneath the surface of Paige's public persona, he would have found a most intelligent individual, perceptive and knowledgeable in the ways of the world, a shrewd judge of character. Paige could be a very funny man, but at bottom he was his own man—not an easy thing to be in a Jim Crow world. Those who knew him well invariably described him as a loner, a description Paige himself confirmed. On the surface, it seemed Larry Doby was emblematic of the young black man in baseball—serious, no-nonsense, sensitive, a little enraged—while Satchel Paige was a representative of the Jim Crow days—a combination of Ol' Mose and Amos and Andy. That perception of Paige could not have been more wrong.[52]

Whatever their differences, Larry Doby and Satchel Paige were essential cogs on a Cleveland team that made it to the World Series, and won that, too. The two became the first black players to achieve championship rings, though Doby's was by far the more satisfying experience. Cleveland beat the Boston Braves in six games. Lou Boudreau called on Paige just once, to pitch two-thirds of an inning late in a 6–0 loss. Larry Doby made a much deeper impression, leading the regulars in hitting at .318 and smashing a home run to win the fourth game of the Series.[53] From a baseball point of view, from a Cleveland Indians point of view, Doby enjoyed a breakout season, capped by a solid World Series. From an integrationist point of view, Doby managed a blow the equal of Jackie Robinson.

A photograph can say so much. Not long before he died, Doby recalled the moment.

> When I hit that home run that won game 4 in the '48 World Series, there was a fellow by the name of Steve Gromek. He pitched and I hit the home run to win the game, and we embraced each other. And it wasn't an embrace where it was orchestrated or planned, it was just two happy people; and if you look at the smile of the two people, there was no such thing as a planned thing, or there's no such thing as a Hollywood thing; it's a thing of a joy of a happy moment in our lives that we had been able to accomplish.[54]

A photograph of that embrace went out over the wire services; the next day the image of an overjoyed white man facing the camera cheek to cheek with an overjoyed black man appeared in newspapers all over the country. Jim Crow was knocked back on his heels by that one. Steve Gromek listened to people bemoan that picture for years afterward, how it should have been more than enough just to shake the black man's hand. Gromek could only shake his head. The photograph showed two teammates sharing a triumphant moment at the pinnacle of the game. Others would have to supply the racial implications in that moment.[55]

The 1948 title augured the beginning of something special in Cleveland, but the magic—the unusual good luck, some would have it—faded quickly. The Indians stayed a very good team—the second best in the American League over the next ten years—but they won just one more pennant, in 1954. The Yankees won the other nine. Most of the key figures in the drama of 1947–1948 scattered quickly. Bill Veeck was the first to go, selling the Indians after the 1949 season, supposedly for reasons of health, but mainly because he needed as much cash as possible to settle a nasty divorce. Among the projects he left unfinished was the search for a female professional ballplayer. Very soon after Veeck departed, Satchel Paige got a letter from Lou Boudreau, notifying him of his release. Paige's chronic stomach problems had become acute in 1949, limiting his effectiveness. Reading between the lines of Lou Boudreau's autobiography, it would seem Boudreau was less than crushed to see Paige out the door—he helped the team to victory in 1948, but he remained a very independent soul. The boy manager spoke of a youth movement. Little did he know that he would be next to leave. The new ownership dared do what Bill Veeck could not, relieving Boudreau of his managing duties after 1950 and trading him to Boston. Bill McKechnie went with him.[56]

Larry Doby played on. In 1949, he became the first black player to join the American League All-Star team, where he remained a fixture through 1955, the last year of his first stint in Cleveland. An All-Star he was, though a maddeningly inconsistent one. He won the home run title in 1952, and led the league in homers and RBI in 1954, the season Cleveland won the pennant and he nearly received the American League MVP Award. There were no poor seasons over the nine years, though as Bill Veeck observed, Doby's anger and frustration often seemed to limit his accomplishments. The Cleveland papers, disappointed with a team that perennially finished second, rode him hard for not producing more, very nearly suggesting that he alone should have beaten those Yankees. Surely that did not help.[57]

The Indians remained the only American League team to include black players through 1950. A few clubs, including the Yankees, signed Negro Leagues players to minor league contracts, but this was a maneuver intended to deflect criticism without making a commitment; almost none of these players ever joined the parent club. The National League was little better. The Dodgers under Branch Rickey continued to improve by adding players such as Roy Campanella and Don Newcombe, but the New York Giants were the only other team to add a black player. Integration was effectively stalled, and would remain stalled—especially in the hidebound American League—for quite some time.

Cleveland at least maintained its commitment to fielding black players after Bill Veeck's departure, for much the same reasons. The younger Indians prospects, their careers postponed by the war, were not yet ready; the Negro Leagues remained a relatively cheap source of mature talent. The Indians, with Hank Greenberg now the General Manager, established a working agreement with the San Diego Padres of the Pacific Coast League, using the connection to develop the black players they signed. (Several PCL teams signed black players in the late 1940s, making the west coast league a far more active proving ground for integration than either the National or the American circuit.)

The Indians became especially fascinated with a promising slugger named Luke Easter, who seemed to come out of nowhere to hit baseballs farther than anyone could imagine possible. *The Sporting News* became fascinated, too, running several features throughout 1949 extolling his power and promise, and his cheerful good nature. As matters turned out, Easter had good reason to be cheerful. He convinced the Indians he was 28 when he was really at least 34. The main reason no one had heard much about him was that he had spent years recovering from fracturing both feet in a car accident. Certainly he was exciting to watch, and the fans loved him, but as a prospect, he was a chimera. The Indians brought Easter to Cleveland late in 1949, but he suffered a knee injury and could not deliver. He did have three productive seasons in him, but faded very quickly after 1952.

As much as anything, what Luke Easter did was to create a situation where the Cleveland Indians had more black major league prospects than they could use. No one in Cleveland management ever said as much, but the black players in the organization were certain that the Indians—along with the Dodgers and the Giants—were establishing a quota. Two or at the most three blacks on the major league roster, and no more. Cleveland newspapers grumbled that the Indians failed to repeat as champions because there were too many black players on the team, a charge they would repeat every year until 1954. The press also complained of a "Negro corner" in the Indians clubhouse, where the blacks would isolate themselves from their fellow players, destroying team cohesion. This created a dilemma for Hank Greenberg and the rest of Indians management. They released Satchel Paige, but they still had Larry Doby, Luke Easter, and two more very promising prospects, Harry Simpson and Orestes Minoso. One too many, so the thinking went.[58]

Searching the Negro Leagues for promising talent, major league scouts concentrated their efforts on young players on the way up, the analogues of Robinson, Doby, and Thompson. Despite some mediocre numbers in three seasons with the Philadelphia Stars, Harry Simpson looked the ideal. The Georgia-born Simpson, 25 years old in 1951, had the kind of pop in his bat to remind people of Ted Williams. But he was faster than Williams, and much better in the outfield. Signed by the Indians in 1949, "Suitcase Harry" spent the next two years in the minors, batting over .300 each season. The time had come, so it seemed.

Orestes Minoso looked less promising. Three years older than Simpson, Minoso had been recruited from Cuba to play for the New York Cubans in 1945. Cubans owner Alex Pompez sold him to the Indians four years later. Minoso hit just .188 in a nine-game trial with Cleveland in 1949, and played the next two seasons with San Diego, hitting .297 and .339. Minoso and Simpson were teammates in the Pacific Coast League in 1950, and both joined the Indians to begin the 1950 season.[59]

Some time during their brief years playing for the same teams, Harry Simpson and Minnie Minoso found themselves in an ambiguous yet revealing conversation. Simpson informed Minoso that he (Minoso) was not black. This was certainly news to Minoso. Decades later, the "Cuban Comet" could find some amusement in the pronouncement. "What nonsense!" Minoso wrote.

> I told these players to look at me and then tell me I am not black. Cuba was not the racial paradise some might want them to believe. Just as in the United States, there were many sections of Cuba, and many neighborhoods, where you saw only white people.... And here in this country, the signs in restaurants and buses prohibiting blacks applied as much to me as it did to them.[60]

As a black man, Minoso was subject to the same kinds of Jim Crow discrimination as Harry Simpson wherever he went in the United States. But the issue was not simply color. Simpson grasped a fact of life that Minoso, coming from Cuba, would understand differently. For more than half a century, American blacks had been systematically shut out of organized American baseball, forced to form their own separate and unequal leagues, just as blacks were forced into separate but unequal schools, houses, hotels, restaurants, buses, and railroad cars. The struggle to integrate major league baseball was emblematic of the American struggle to diminish and eliminate Jim Crow. Fielding a Cuban black man was an end run around that fundamental issue, an integration that did little or nothing for American blacks.

**Harry Simpson. One of the more militant American black players, Simpson maintained that black players from the Caribbean were not black, at least not in the same sense as players born in the United States. (National Baseball Hall of Fame Library, Cooperstown, N.Y.)**

The division between them ran deeper even than that. Simpson and Minoso were representatives of vastly different cultures. What they held in common was the ugly discrimination they faced from whites. What divided them were there root experiences, and the cultural expressions that wrought identity. Harry Simpson was of the American South, bearing the racial memories of slavery, reconstruction, systematic exclusion—a sorrow and an embrace of life reflected in speech, in music, in religion, in character itself. The souls of black folk W. E. B. Dubois captured so brilliantly a half century before. Orestes Minoso was Cuban, rising from a background of sugar plantations heavily influenced by Spanish colonialism and hoodoo. Minoso was most comfortable in a language completely foreign to Harry Simpson. He heard the world differently. Minoso came to professional baseball in a country where race was not so much a stumbling block. Racial attitudes affected him differently. "I didn't let nothing bother me," he recalled. "They can call me any kind of name you want to call—black, nigger, or whatever. It didn't bother me. They never found out the secret word that bothered me. You know what would have bothered me if they would've called me? If they called me 'whitey,' I'm not white. They call, 'Hey, blackie!' I say, 'Yes sir. That's my color.'"

Minoso and Simpson may have come to share a challenged minority status in the world of white American professional baseball, but they did not share much else. Harry Simpson and other American-born black players often resented the presence of Latino blacks, one more ethnic group keeping them out of the majors. In the coming decade, this conflict would complicate the efforts to integrate several American League franchises.[61]

The Cleveland Indians guessed wrong, keeping Simpson and trading away Minoso. Harry Simpson was not the next Ted Williams. Burdened with this forecast of his potential, he never got comfortable at the plate, hitting just .229 in 122 games in 1951. Shuttled between the outfield and first base (to fill in for the oft-injured Luke Easter), Simpson's fielding suffered as well. He played two more ineffective years in Cleveland before a trade salvaged his career. Over the next decade, the Indians would remain the American League team most committed to integration, though they found few players of star quality. After 1954, the fortunes of the Indians franchise began to fade.[62]

Orestes Minoso went to Chicago, site of the 1919 riot, one of the worst in America's racial history. Chicago, where Jim Crow flourished, where a vital black

**Minnie Minoso. Recruited for the Negro Leagues from Cuba, Minoso saw the world differently from Harry Simpson, though both would suffer discrimination playing in the United States. (National Baseball Hall of Fame Library, Cooperstown, N.Y.)**

population amounting to almost 14 percent of the total was shoehorned into substandard neighborhoods on the South Side, what sociologists would later consider "hypersegregation."[63] Chicago, where the integration of the White Sox proceeded more easily than in most places, because Minnie Minoso was foreign and likable, and his manager wanted him.

Chicago's White Sox were a cornerstone in the founding of the American League, though they had fallen on hard times in the half-century since. If Ban Johnson was the architect of the League's founding, Charlie Comiskey, owner of the White Sox, was his chief lieutenant. Their visions diverged over the next two decades; the Black Sox scandal was the last nail in the coffin of their relationship. The betting scandal proved the downfall of a flagship franchise. In the 30 years following lifetime suspensions of the eight accused players, the White Sox finished in the first division just five times, never higher than third. In 1942, Chicago's Jimmy Dykes became the first major league manager to entertain seriously a tryout of black players for a very practical reason. He needed help he would not get. Signing no black players, the White Sox drifted from mediocre to poor as the world war progressed. In the hopeful years just after, the team seemed to worsen still, finishing fifth in 1946, achieving three sixths and a last place in the next four years. The White Sox were a moribund franchise.[64]

The problem was not the market. Chicago was the nation's second-largest city in 1910; it would remain so in 1950. While all the other cities providing homes for two teams would see a franchise depart during the 1950s, Chicago would hang on to both their Cubs and their White Sox. The money was there. The problem was management and perception. The reputation the White Sox wore as the house of scandal persisted for years, making the team unattractive to young players. More important was the image attached to Charles Comiskey in the scandal's aftermath—he was close-fisted, unforgivably cheap. Run like a second-rate operation, the White Sox continued to play like one, for three long decades.[65]

Charles Comiskey died in October 1931—of a broken heart, so his supporters say. His family held on to the team. Son Louis held the reins until his own death nine years later; his widow, Grace Comiskey, then assumed control. As mediocrity followed mediocrity she grew tired, and in 1948 determined to shake things up. Mrs. Comiskey, by now firmly encouraged by son Chuck Comiskey, hired Frank Lane as the General Manager, impressing on him the need to build a winner in Chicago.

Trader Lane came with an impressive pedigree. After a very brief career in professional football, Lane in 1937 landed a position with the Cincinnati Reds, where he moved up the organizational ladder until enlisting at the outbreak of World War II. Leaving the Navy in 1945, Lane served one year as president of the Yankees' top farm club in Kansas City, then spent two years as president of the American Association. Landing the job of White Sox general manager was his gold-plated opportunity. Shake things up he would. Over the next seven years, Frank Lane involved the White Sox in 241 trades, relentlessly searching for the right combination, unable to stop himself. He was an astute trader at times, landing White Sox stalwarts Nellie Fox, Billy Pierce, Sherman Lollar, and Jim Rivera. And Orestes "Minnie" Minoso.[66]

Despite all the moves, Chicago continued to play second-division baseball in 1949 and 1950. After going through two managers in those two seasons, Lane made what proved to be a fundamentally important move, hiring Paul Richards from Seattle to manage in 1951. Richards was a tough but patient catcher for four major league teams in an eight-year playing career. Four years managing in the minors demonstrated the same patience and a good command of strategy. In his first year with Chicago, Richards saw the White Sox improve by 21 games, moving from sixth place into the first division. Over the next three seasons, Lane and Richards meshed reasonably well, shaping a dynamic and exciting baseball club fitted to the players they found and the park they played in. While most American League clubs were constructing teams around slow-footed sluggers, Chicago became the "Go-Go-Sox," far more committed to inside baseball than any of their competitors.[67]

The critical consideration in creating such a team was to find players familiar with the inside game. Not unnaturally, Paul Richards turned his sights to veterans of the Negro Leagues, where small ball flourished long after Babe Ruth altered the equation in the majors. Managing at Buffalo of the International League, Richards witnessed first-hand the havoc wrought by Sam Jethroe, one of the three players who participated in the sham tryout perpetrated by the Red Sox in 1945. Eventually signed by the Brooklyn Dodgers, Jethroe was sent to Montreal, where he stole 89 bases in 1949. As a young manager faced with the task of slowing Jethroe down, Richards hit on the strategy of intentionally walking the pitcher ahead of him, clogging up the base paths. If Jethroe did get a hit, "he can't hurt us with his speed because he's got the pitcher in front of him," Richards explained. "We tried it, and it worked." The strategy brought Richards some notice. The experience also left Richards the impression it might be good to have a guy like Jethroe on his side.[68]

Sam Jethroe was not available in 1951, but Richards, managing in the Pacific Coast League in 1950, did get an eyeful of Orestes Minoso. Upon joining the White Sox, Paul Richards told his general manager that Minoso was the player he needed. Trader Lane engineered a three-way trade with Cleveland and the Philadelphia Athletics on April 30, 1951, acquiring Minoso and Paul Lehner. In his debut in Chicago against the Yankees the next day, Minoso made an immediate impression, hitting the first pitch he saw into the bleachers. He would also make an error at third base in a losing effort, but Richards was more than pleased with the potential his team now promised. "Nuts to fourth place," he told a sportswriter. "Minoso is the kind of player you need to win pennants. He's the guy we wanted. He'll show them something." Paul Richards was the first manager in the American League to request a black player be added to his team.[69]

Minoso more than fulfilled expecta-

Paul Richards, manager of the Chicago White Sox. Richards was the first American League manager to request a black player be added to his roster. He continued to seek out black players as manager and general manager of the Baltimore Orioles. (National Baseball Hall of Fame Library, Cooperstown, N.Y.)

tions, hitting .324 with 14 triples and 31 stolen bases. The Sox did finish fourth in 1951, but the club grew as a contender, finishing a strong third behind New York and Cleveland in the three remaining seasons Richards headed the team. Permanently moved to left field in 1952, Minoso became the team's anchor, a solid hitter who was always among the league leaders in runs, doubles, triples, stolen bases, and hit by pitches.

Hit by pitches. Every season the debate raged. Did pitchers purposely throw at Minnie Minoso because he was black? Or was he hit because of his batting stance, crowding the plate, head hanging over the dish? Minoso suffered a fractured skull in 1955, hit by a pitch thrown by the Yankees' Bob Grim. Grim came to the hospital to say he was sorry, that the pitch was an accident. Minoso believed and forgave him, but the White Sox remained convinced that the Yankees played dirty, and that pitchers throughout the league threw purposely at black players. Larry Doby suffered the same problem, as did black stars in the National League. There would be an ugly fight in Chicago in 1957, when Yankees pitcher Art Ditmar hit Doby with a pitch.[70]

Paul Richards was long gone by then. Richards lasted just four years in Chicago before the partnership with Frank Lane soured. Richards would later explain that he could not pass up the opportunity to rebuild the Orioles from scratch as manager and general manager, but there does seem to have been a falling out with Lane. One trade too many perhaps. Paul Richards left a powerful legacy in Chicago, laying the foundation for a team that became a perennial contender and, in 1959, a pennant winner. Ironically, Minoso too was gone by then, traded to Cleveland in 1958.[71]

What happened between Chicago and Cleveland during the 1950s provides a particular window into the whole issue of race relations. The White Sox and the Indians, the only competitors to offer the least threat to the Yankees during the decade, formed a symbiotic bond of sorts, trading often, sharing management personnel. Frank Lane, the White Sox general manager in the early 1950s, would have the same job in Cleveland at the decade's end. (His trading was, if anything, more frantic there.) Al Lopez served as Cleveland's manager from 1951 to 1956, winning one pennant; he would move on to Chicago, where he won a single pennant. The White Sox and the Indians were the two American League teams most firmly committed to integrating their franchises during the period. And black players had decidedly mixed feelings about the managers they played for.[72]

In Chicago, Paul Richards determined to obtain Orestes Minoso. A few additional black players contributed to the White Sox turn-around: Sam Hairston (very briefly), Hector Rodriguez, Connie Johnson, and Bob Boyd. Yet Boyd was certain Richards did not like black players. "He was prejudiced," Boyd recalled. "I was in enough team meetings where he would talk about the black players who were on the team coming in and he wouldn't say very nice things about them." But Paul Richards traded to acquire Bob Boyd soon after he took over the Orioles.[73]

Minnie Minoso remembered differently. "Paul treated everyone the same," he claimed, wishing "I could have played my entire career with Richards." Minoso also had kind words for Frank Lane, his "second daddy"—a sentiment not shared by many. The manager Orestes Minoso thought was prejudiced was Al Lopez—a suspicion shared by other black players. Lopez did see to it Minoso was traded away from his teams three separate times. But Al Smith, former Negro American League star, a key player for Lopez with the Indians since 1953, followed his manager to the White Sox in 1958. "Al Lopez had gone over there," Smith explained, "and he wanted me." Lopez had Minoso traded to Cleveland to get Smith. Perhaps it was race. Perhaps it was personality. Probably it was baseball.[74]

The long song of the White Sox and the Indians during the 1950s raises all the essential questions. There was race, there was ethnicity; there was the personal equation. What seems on the surface such a plain and simple problem—the very expression of a "black and white issue"—becomes so complicated, so intertwined, very, very quickly. Was Orestes Minoso a black man? Certainly yes, and absolutely not, depending on the social context. Did Al Lopez dislike Minoso and want him off his teams? The answer to that seems a safe yes. But why? Was it race? Ethnicity? Too much enthusiasm? Whatever reasons lay behind the distaste suggest complicated questions rather than stock answers. Was Paul Richards, a man who actively sought out black players, prejudiced against them? As Minoso once suggested, if you are looking for prejudice, you will find it, whether it is there or not.

Race is never a simple equation. Not in America.

# Interlude

# The End of the Road

## *The Negro Leagues Wither*

There was very little ambiguity in the minds of black people. Presented a choice between a continued loyalty to Negro Leagues ball or the exploits of Robinson, Doby, Minoso, and the growing ranks of black stars in the major leagues, black fans voted freely with their wallets and their feet. Attendance at Negro Leagues games dropped immediately in 1947, like a stone. The boom created by wartime abundance vanished utterly, never to return. Negro Leagues owners were hard put to salvage anything from long years of investment as their financial houses crumbled. Worst of all, apart from themselves, no one seemed to care.

The abrupt collapse of the leagues themselves tells a stark story. In 1947, the Negro National League fielded six franchises, including two teams in New York City, another in nearby Newark, and clubs in Baltimore, Philadelphia, and Washington—where the Homestead Grays played. A year later, there was no Negro National League. Three of the six teams simply ceased to exist, and the circuit folded. The Negro American League took in the survivors, but that too proved a brief halt on the road to oblivion. The Cleveland team was gone by 1951, Chicago by 1953. The last of the Negro Leagues boasted ten teams divided into two divisions in 1950, reduced to eight teams in 1951, six in 1952, four in 1953. Six teams committed to the league in 1954, all but one located in cities where major league teams did not play. (Detroit was the exception—the next to last major league franchise to integrate, in 1957.) That turned out to be the last year. Hemorrhaging cash, Negro Leagues teams simply could not compete. "Like General Custer at the Battle of the Little Big Horn, the men who carry on in Negro League ball today are making a gallant last stand against forces they cannot control," Doc Young advised.[1]

Even if a city's major league teams dragged their feet on integration (Philadelphia and Washington come to mind) black fans turned their back on Negro Leagues franchises, paying instead to see the Indians or the White Sox come to town. When the Philadelphia Athletics moved to Kansas City after the 1954 season, the move finished the Kansas City Monarchs and the Negro American League. A few black teams struggled to live on, barnstorming, some of them clowning their way across rural America. Aging black stars gathered in Yankee Stadium in 1961 to stage one last East-West Game, attended by just 7,245 nostalgic fans. The curtain closed; the show was over.

The message was crystal clear. Black fans much preferred seeing one or two black players competing in major league uniforms to watching poorly funded, entirely black teams square off against one another. Attendance at NNL games played at Yankee Stadium dropped by 60 percent in 1947, when Jackie Robinson began playing across town. That was the writing on the wall—Negro Leagues doubleheaders at the stadium had long been the most lucrative of all venues. Negro Leagues owners had no choice but to cut salaries, and that was an expedient on the path to bankruptcy. James Semler's Black Yankees lost $20,000 and tried to move to Rochester, New York. Alex Pompez took to barnstorming with his Cubans. Abe and Effa Manley lost $25,000 and sold the Newark Eagles to a Houston investor at a very large loss. The Houston Eagles dissolved by 1951. Cumberland Posey, irascible owner of the Homestead Grays, did not live to see the collapse of his enterprise, dying in 1946. His heirs watched the shaky empire crumble, folding the Grays for good in 1950. J. L. Wilkinson, 70 years old, saw what was coming and sold the Monarchs to assistant Tom Baird in 1948 for $27,000. Sixteen years later, Wilkinson died in poverty. His Monarchs left the field forever in 1960, after seven years of barnstorming.[2]

About the only recourse open to Negro Leagues owners bleeding money was to sell their best players to major league franchises. Branch Rickey went a long way toward killing even that unenviable alternative, refusing to pay Wilkinson for Jackie Robinson's services, painting Negro Leagues teams as rackets rather than legitimate businesses. John P. Joy, president of a Chicago-based organization called The Negro Major American and National League Base Ball Teams, Inc., wrote to Happy Chandler, the new commissioner of baseball, to express agreement with Rickey that the Negro Leagues were "in the zone of a racket." He wanted to do away with "wild cat ball playing," put a Negro team in every major league ball park, and generally build up the organization.[3] The actual owners of Negro League franchises were not nearly as supportive of Rickey's position.

Owners such as Bill Veeck and Dick Muckerman, and general managers including Bill DeWitt were more scrupulous, but Rickey's pronouncements certainly depressed the market. Abe and Effa Manley got about half what Larry Doby was worth; Alex Pompez received $5,000 for Orestes Minoso. Five thousand quickly became the standard in these transactions. Yet even that market, brisk as it was for about five years, dried up quickly. The more committed major league teams had their own scouts out scouring the country almost immediately, signing future stars including Maury Wills and Frank Robinson directly out of high school, bypassing the Negro Leagues completely.[4]

Possible roles for the Negro Leagues in the newly integrated universe of professional baseball naturally generated considerable discussion, and even a little action. Prodded after long years of controversy, the Negro Leagues owners finally adopted a written constitution.[5] The Negro National League finally elected a president, John H. Johnson, who was not one of themselves. Johnson, an Episcopal minister and community leader in Harlem, proved somewhat independent in judgment, though not terribly effective in the face of the coming crisis. Probably the task was too much to ask of anyone. To survive, the Negro Leagues had to gain entry into Organized Baseball's National Agreement—after more than a quarter century of exclusion. The Agreement was black baseball's only hope of protecting contractual rights to their players.

In January 1946, a few months before Jackie Robinson began his season in Montreal, the Negro Leagues owners gathered in Cincinnati to meet with Happy Chandler, the commissioner of Organized Baseball. Chandler encouraged the black owners to continue and grow. They would need to build their own stadiums and develop a standard player contract with a reserve clause. At the same time, Chandler refused even to discuss the issue of compensation—or the lack of such—in Robinson's move from the Monarchs to the Dodgers. The road ahead was not clear to anyone. Here was the commissioner advocating (with sympathy and complete sincerity) an enormous capital outlay, while at the same time laying the ground for Negro Leagues dissolution. When the Leagues did frame the standard contract Chandler suggested, organized baseball still found excuses to continue their exclusion from the National Agreement. In rejecting their application, baseball's Executive Committee observed "that it would be impossible to do anything with these applications at this time, other than to express a sympathy for your problems and to offer you our aid in helping you set up an organization that would meet your needs."[6] Cold comfort, that. Major league owners wanted black players, not black enterprises. Still the Negro Leagues owners appealed to Chandler, asking his advice on how to deal with Cum Posey, who had gone rogue, refusing to honor the new standard contracts. Chandler had no real advice to give them. Nor did he want to be Negro Leagues commissioner.[7]

Ideas got floated, kicked around. America had been so profoundly Jim Crow such a few years before, it was difficult for people, black and white, to wrap their minds around the idea of major league teams seeking out American black prospects on their own. Back in the 1930s, blacks imagining integration did not often picture black players playing for the major league teams already in existence. When the change came, so the thought went, the Negro Leagues would organize two teams of their best players. One would join the National League, the other the American—one all-black team and eight all-white teams in each circuit. (Such arrangements did occasionally flicker into existence in the lower minors during the 1920s. Oscar Charleston very briefly played with an all-black team in an Interstate League centered in Pennsylvania in 1926.[8]) As the Negro League owners had no suitable ball parks, the black clubs would have to be traveling teams, endlessly on the road from city to city. A difficult world, and not really an integrated one. Black and white would play against each other, maintaining separate identities and relying on completely separate sources of manpower. The color line would not be dissolved, but relocated, creating an abyss in each major league.[9]

By the late 1940s, with the beginnings of integration at hand, segregated thinking persisted. Most people assumed the Negro Leagues would continue to function, finding the young black players, training them up in their own leagues, and selling the best of the lot to the majors. This was the habit of mind instilled by Jim Crow, still hard at work. Even if baseball were to have integration, it would presumably do so in a segregated fashion. The actual mixing of black and white would be confined and minimal—a black player or two on the major league teams that wanted them, nowhere else. Jim Crow would continue to govern small town America. After all, most major league farm organizations operated one or more franchises in Southern minor leagues; that alone would preclude blacks playing at Organized Baseball's entry levels. The Negro Leagues would continue, of necessity.[10]

Idle dreams. A clutching at straws, insofar as the Negro Leagues were concerned. The reality was vastly more simple. Once the major league teams committed to fielding black players, they would seek to control every step of the process. The Indians, the Yankees, and other big league teams began signing Negro Leagues players to minor league contracts very quickly after 1947. Integration in practice meant blacks would play in Organized Baseball's minor leagues just as much or more than the majors. The Negro Leagues would be entirely peripheral. Negro

Leagues owners were building false hopes on a baseball world 20 or 30 years in the past. Powerful independent minor league franchises dominated the landscape back then, making serious money selling their best players to major league teams. By 1947, that way of doing business was mostly dead, giving way to farm systems owned and operated from top to bottom by the big guys (another device initiated by Branch Rickey). Alex Pompez's Cuban Giants became a farm team for the New York Giants during the 1948 season, but that was the one exception that drove home the harsh reality. Once the majors got serious about signing black prospects straight out of high school, the Negro Leagues were finished.[11]

Jackie Robinson was not one to lament their passing. His brief article in the June 1948, edition of *Ebony*, "What's Wrong with Negro Baseball," was not as brutal as its reputation might suggest, but it was very honest. Most tellingly, Robinson depicted the poor business practices of even a franchise as well run as the Kansas City Monarchs. He expected to sign a contract when he joined the team for spring training, only to discover that his correspondence with the club was considered sufficient. "This was my first taste of Negro baseball and this was the first of many things I found to be wrong with the game." That eye opener was followed by several others. Robinson discovered that the Monarchs exercised little control over their players, that several drank heavily, and some never went to sleep at all. Bus travel from game to game was a grueling ordeal, while the pay scarcely made the life worthwhile. Hardly the profession the clean-cut Robinson envisioned for himself. When he signed with the Dodgers, he was committing to more than a mere playing career with a major league team. He was seeking a professional life. His experience with the Monarchs convinced him that it was far better for black youths to play in organized minor league ball than to join a Negro Leagues team. "I only hope that the other owners will give more Negro players similar breaks," he lamented.[12]

To Robinson and to Branch Rickey, the Negro Leagues represented some kind of poison hovering on the outer edges of baseball, preying on unsuspecting black youth. Robinson's response was understandable. Certainly there was discrimination in his pre–War California, but nothing like the color line frozen on the Midwest, the Northeast, and the South. He starred on interracial teams as an amateur in high school and college, and stood up to Jim Crow during his military service. Completely unfamiliar with the conditions Negro Leagues baseball had endured for years on years, he could never see that the black ball life was not a product of shady character or loose morals, but a shape dictated by segregationist institutions that left black enterprise scrambling on the edge. Robinson arrived just in time to witness what Jim Crow could inflict, and just as quickly escape. He may never have had it made, but he was very fortunate compared to Josh Gibson, Buck Leonard, and hundreds of other victims of the color line.[13]

Robinson's attack was harsh, a swipe at the hand that had nurtured as well as it could. Several Negro Leagues veterans lost respect for Robinson. Even Wendell Smith backed away, assuring his readers he had played no part in writing the piece. But black journalists did pile on as the Negro Leagues began to sputter and die. The *Pittsburgh Courier*, the *Chicago Defender*, and other black newspapers virtually ceased their coverage of Negro Leagues games to follow the performance of black players in the majors. By 1949, Smith was characterizing the Negro Leagues game as a "burlesque," the owners attempting to save "their shaky, littered, infested segregated baseball domicile." The integration of Organized Baseball was just half the battle; the utter destruction and burial of the Negro Leagues was the other half. To kill Jim Crow, black enterprise had to die as well.[14]

For the most part, Negro League owners accepted their fate quietly—there was little

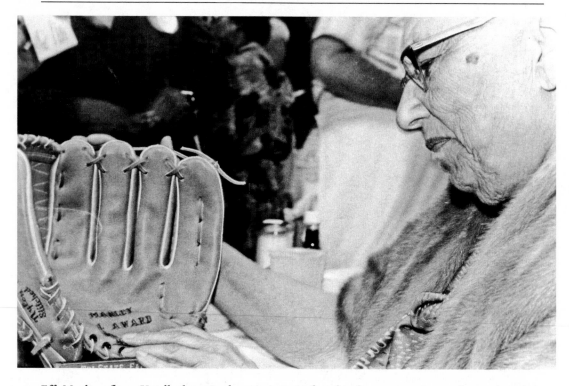

**Effa Manley reflects. Usually shown in glamour portraits from her days as part-owner and general manager of the Newark Eagles, Manley looks back at a world that abruptly held no place for her baseball acumen. (National Baseball Hall of Fame Library, Cooperstown, N.Y.)**

choice. But Robinson's criticisms in *Ebony*, surely an echo of Branch Rickey's sentiments, did provoke Newark Eagles co-owner Effa Manley enough to speak out. Ironically, it was Manley who had pushed for many of the reforms the Negro Leagues were now belatedly adopting—the written constitution, the tighter governance, the independent commissioner, the standard contract. The fact that she was the only woman at the table had not helped her. But she was also the only one brave enough to speak her mind as black baseball unraveled. "Negroes have to develop some race consciousness and stop ramming themselves down white people's throats," she told the *Defender*'s Frank Young. Railing against Rickey's refusal to acknowledge the Negro Leagues as legitimate business concerns at every opportunity, Manley did her best to defend her investment and her position in baseball. In responding, the black press was not kind. "Do you think that Mrs. Effa Manley, who says she is giving up the Newark Eagles, is really serious about being Negro baseball's unofficial ambassador," Wendell Smith wrote, "or is she just a publicity hound? ... Wouldn't it be nice if owners of Negro ball clubs would quit blaming the press for their stupendous failures and took a look into a mirror?" Crueler still was an editorial from the black weekly newspaper *Kansas City Call*, warning her "the day of loyalty to Jim Crow anything is fast passing away. Sister, haven't you heard the news, democracy is coming fast."[15]

Effa and Abe Manley sold their Eagles in 1948, and faded rapidly from the world of baseball. When Jim Crow ruled, she was an ardent spokesperson for civil rights, serving as a volunteer on several commissions. Among the special events held at Newark's Ruppert Stadium was a collection taken up to support an anti-lynching campaign—not a typical ball park promotion (one that Bill Veeck never considered). But once the color line was breached, Effa

Manley's protests in defense of black enterprise left her painted a defender of the old, segregated order.[16]

The simple and obvious interpretation of this unhappy episode would be to portray Effa Manley as a woman caught in the crossfire, bravely defending her life's investment as rapid change overtook her team and her league. But there was a larger, more subtle issue brewing, one Manley seems to have glimpsed, at least in part. What was happening all around her was the slow, sporadic, and complete breakdown of baseball's old order, a cracking of the color line that most blacks and many whites plainly desired. But it was a surrender negotiated completely on the terms of Organized Baseball—white people's baseball. Black and white baseball were not integrated in any but a superficial sense—there was no melding of black and white institutions. Beginning in 1947, white baseball granted a very few black players the right to play their game, a right they should have possessed from the beginning a century before. While surrendering this right, Organized Baseball doomed the Negro Leagues, their black counterpart. It was an inevitability the white owners saw and desired—in exchange for putting blacks on major league playing fields, competing black enterprise would cease. The black community fully supported this bargain, abandoning the Negro Leagues, emblematic of the hated Jim Crow, in favor of the new beginning in Brooklyn, in Manhattan, in Cleveland, in Chicago. Most probably, this was the only way integration could have proceeded in the America of the 1940s and 1950s. With so many deeply entrenched racial barriers to challenge, baby steps were all that could happen.

So Organized Baseball gradually and painfully began the process of adding black players to their teams, while the institutions of black baseball diminished and soon vanished. This is what Effa Manley perceived, in a veiled and hazy fashion. The major leagues accepted some of the best young players from the Negro Leagues, and nothing else at all. Manley understood that professional baseball was much more than a bunch of guys dressed in uniforms playing a game. Baseball is structure, organization, a vast number of people working behind the scenes to make the game on the field happen. A few of the players on major league fields came to be black beginning in 1947, but no one in the front office would be black for a very long time. Apart from the one or two positions on the playing roster, blacks would continue to be a minuscule and virtually powerless voice in the evolution of baseball's regime. Here and there, a black scout was hired, mainly to scour the failing Negro Leagues and the high schools for more black talent. Sometimes there might be a black spring training instructor to assist the new black arrivals. Or a black publicity agent, to hawk season tickets in the black community. But a black coach during a regular season game? Not in the 1940s, nor the 1950s. Elston Howard was the first in the American League, in 1969. A black manager? Not before 1975. Some black person in the front office, making meaningful decisions? A black owner? Please.[17]

This deeply ingrained resistance to placing blacks in positions of authority was justified by any number of excuses, but the genuine reason lay in the bigoted pattern of the nation's invented social structure. For centuries, Americans sought for cultural and scientific corroborations for the belief that black people belonged at the very bottom of society's pyramid. Our pioneer anthropologists—Samuel George Morton, Josiah Nott, S. A. Cartwright—expended considerable effort attempting to "prove" the intellectual inferiority of blacks, employing dubious methodologies and fudging the figures to verify a pre-determined idea. As late as 1906, Robert Bennett Bean, a Virginia medical doctor, was publishing both technical and popular articles claiming to demonstrate the inferiority of black brains (and women's brains as well). Bean's own mentor, Johns Hopkins professor Franklin P. Mall, exposed the inescapable flaws in Bean's research, showing that there were in fact no measurable differences at all. But the damage was done, a common and evil perception promoted. Such efforts, invariably demolished by analysts employing truly value-neutral procedures, persisted well into the 20th century, and still occasionally appear in journals that should know better. Though the science has been proven groundless time and again, the perception continued well into the Civil Rights Era. Baseball's executives were not only not immune; they were by and large preconditioned to accept the notion. Al Campanis, interviewed on ABC television's "Nightline" in 1987, voiced a belief obviously shared by a vast majority of baseball's movers and shakers. Blacks "lack the necessities" to be managers, Campanis explained. Organized Baseball's executives believed that in 1947, and for the most part still believed it 40 years later. Blacks could play, but they would not be making any critical decisions.[18]

From beginning to end, organized baseball dictated the conditions of integration. Social conventions demanded they integrate visibly, meaning black players had to appear on the field. This they did, at times with enthusiastic support, more often with great reluctance (especially in the American League). Most major league teams would eventually undertake the minimum they felt was needed to tap into the black community, draw these newer residents of the cities to the ball park. There was money to be made. And that was about as far as integration went. Like the older black players who saw integration on the field come too late, the people who organized and ran black baseball were shut out. The Negro Leagues did not die of old age. Effa Manley was just 47 the year Robinson and Doby broke the color line. Alex Pompez was 54. Gus Greenlee, who came out of retirement to assist Branch Rickey in his new Negro Leagues subterfuge, was also 54, a full 12 years younger than Rickey. At 59, Larry MacPhail was also older than many of his Negro Leagues protégés. Certainly the executives operating creatively on a shoestring in the Negro Leagues were much younger than Clark Griffith or Connie Mack. An awful lot of good baseball knowledge was forced into early retirement with the death of black baseball. Organized ball may have flourished with the addition of young and promising Negro Leagues stars, but no one contemplated integrating the decision-making process. A few black laborers were entering a white-operated universe.

So black baseball became—amazingly rapidly—an unwelcome anachronism, a too visible relic of Jim Crow. The black community abandoned the Negro Leagues, black sportswriters mocked them, and the owners watched their money disappear. Organized Baseball took what little they wanted, showed no interest or sympathy for the rest. In little more than a decade, the last vestiges of this black enterprise were gone, willfully forgotten. All that remained would be the eventual romanticizing of a grim reminder of America's vicious racial past.[19]

# VI

# Reluctant Realists

## *A Change Gathers Momentum*

---

The world was changing by 1953—both the limited world of American society and the exceedingly limited world of American League baseball. The initial efforts to integrate the game had emerged in a confused and tentative atmosphere; the entire nation was troubled, becoming by unwanted default the leader and symbol of western democracy. New obligations presented themselves. For reasons of justice, for reasons of image, the United States had no choice but to undertake some fundamental change in race relations. That much was obvious. Less clear was the direction of the change, or how change might be achieved. Baseball played an emblematic role in the immediate postwar world, providing a highly visible standard of peaceable yet determined integration, a change embraced by most of the black community and supported by many whites.

What the actions of Branch Rickey, Bill Veeck, Horace Stoneham, Frank Lane, and another small handful of baseball officials did was to point up the implausibility, the inherent injustice, the unacceptability of the "separate but equal" concept. The impermeable divide between organized baseball and the Negro Leagues was a painfully obvious separation, with no chance of achieving equality. When Jackie Robinson and Larry Doby moved from the Negro Leagues to the majors, the black community moved with them, abandoning the institutions of baseball separation to seek acceptance in the larger society. Realistically, there could be just one baseball enterprise, one in which blacks and whites could work together.

The United States Supreme Court embraced the principle of separate but equal in 1896; black people, largely through the aegis of the NAACP, fought the doctrine for half a century. Much of the fight was uphill; the reaction to American participation in the Great War, followed by the Great Depression, created fertile ground for Jim Crow. The beginnings of Cold War slowly but perceptibly shifted the odds. By 1953, the NAACP was pursuing several highly publicized legal cases intended to end public school segregation and demolish forever the cruel fantasy called separate but equal. The Executive Branch of the United States government was squarely behind the effort now. Secretary of State Dean Acheson told the Court in 1952 that "The continuation of racial discrimination in the United States remains a source of constant embarrassment to this government in the day-to-day conduct of its foreign relations; and it jeopardizes the effective maintenance of our moral leadership of the free and democratic nations of the world." Not precisely a call for justice, but recognition of a need for change. The Civil Rights movement was assuming a definite shape, mounting a frontal attack on separate but equal.[1]

As the course of national integration crystallized, major league baseball became one more industry facing enormous pressure to fall into line. The first wave of baseball's own integration, daring as it was, proved a limited victory for civil rights. In the American League, blacks gained entry to just three of the eight rosters, one of these (the pathetic Browns) abortively. In what sounded suspiciously like a celebratory article, Dan Daniel informed his readers in an August 1947, issue of *The Sporting News* that the Negro issue was "fizzling out." "The complete letdown in conversation about the Negro issue is a good thing," Daniel observed. "It means the Negro in the major leagues is no longer a talking topic, because he no longer is that rarity he was when Robinson was the only non–Caucasian in the major company."[2]

Apart from Cleveland and Chicago, the American League teams held aloof, clinging to the grim traditions that characterized the circuit since its beginnings in 1901—poor labor relations, weak infrastructure, competitive inequality, racial discrimination. Publishing an essay in *Ebony* in 1953, Wendell Smith detailed the very limited success of integration, judging Detroit to be the most prejudiced team in the American League, followed by Boston, Philadelphia, Washington, and New York.[3] Rather than pointing the path for the nation, the remaining six American League teams would share the burden of intense public criticism as they wrestled with the issue. Four of the six would integrate (or re-integrate) in a two-year period between 1953 and 1955, very much in the midst of the fundamental developments altering the struggle for civil rights. By the end of 1955, the Supreme Court abolished separate but equal in *Brown v. the School Board of Topeka, Kansas* (1954), the last victim of open lynching was dead, and Rosa Parks had refused to give up her seat on a bus in Montgomery, Alabama. Integrating a ball club was no longer a pioneering step, but an expected surrender to reality.[4]

For three American League teams—Philadelphia, Washington, and St. Louis—integration would be addressed in the context of economic chaos. The St. Louis Browns lost tons of money for two sets of ownership before departing for Baltimore, after integrating unsuccessfully not once but twice. The two remaining doormats, the Athletics and the Senators, shared strikingly similar problems: their owners were battle-scarred veterans of the first days of the League, lone men clinging to the past, ill-equipped to face the coming changes in professional baseball and society. Reactionaries such as Connie Mack and Clark Griffith were not about to listen to any subversives, even if they were having trouble just trying to make ends meet. Dragging their heels on integration, their responses at first glance seem sadly similar. The differences that emerged shed a little light on the nuances of the process.

In 1950, Connie Mack, owner, operator, and field manager of the Philadelphia Athletics, was one of the most revered men in professional baseball. A key figure in the establishment of the American League, Mack was there from the very beginning, eventually becoming the living embodiment of the circuit's half-century history. When the National Baseball Hall of Fame opened in Cooperstown in 1939, the "Tall Tactition" was there, one of the group of original inductees. Eighty-seven years old and plainly failing by 1950, Mack was beloved throughout the baseball world, honored and respected wherever he went.

Except in Philadelphia.[5]

The Athletics were a powerful force in the earliest days of the upstart American League, winning pennants in 1902 and 1905, and established one of baseball's first modern dynasties by winning the World Series in 1910, 1911, and again in 1913, winning one last pennant in 1914. Supported by the very deep pockets of sporting goods magnate Ben Shibe, Mack played an aggressive role in building the League, successfully competing in the bidding war for National League stars. The Athletics quickly outgrew the new wooden ballpark Shibe and Mack built in downtown Philadelphia, inspiring the partners to construct a new and vastly upscaled structure on the city's edge, soon known as "North City." The area they chose was largely vacant grassland, gridded for streets not yet constructed, connected to the population centers by trolley, shunned because of the proximity of a smallpox hospital. Shibe quietly purchased a block of this land on the cheap, and proceeded to build the gaudy wonder of the baseball world— Shibe Park, the first concrete and steel girder ballpark in America. Opened for the 1909 season, Shibe Park was an enormous success, an architectural stroke that quickly proved home to world championship teams.[6]

The good times lasted until 1915. The short-lived Federal League, employing strategies very similar to those employed by Connie Mack and his American League companions less than 20 years before, inflated player salaries beyond the squeezing point. Mack blew up his team, watched some of his stars walk, sold or traded others. The defending American League champions fell all the way to the basement one year after capturing the pennant, winning just 43 games.

The A's stayed a hapless second-division team for ten seasons, generally finishing dead last. Ben Shibe died in 1922, but his sons, Tom and Jack, assumed the partnership, sustaining Mack as he slowly built another winner. By 1925, Philadelphia was challenging the juggernaut New York Yankees. They broke through in 1929, winning the American League pennant by 16 games, claiming the world championship for two consecutive seasons, and one last pennant in 1931. This second dynasty coincided with the onset of the Great Depression; Connie Mack discovered he had a great team too expensive to keep. Again he began to sell off his stars. By 1935, the club was back in the cellar.

When Tom Shibe died the next year, Connie Mack made what turned out to be the biggest mistake of his already long life. Rather than looking for another investor, Mack began looking to find enough money to become majority owner himself. After 1940, the Philadelphia Athletics were Connie Mack's very own money-starved show. As president, general manager, and manager of the franchise, the only man with the power to fire Connie Mack was Connie Mack.[7]

The Depression hit all of professional baseball hard—there was just not much recreational cash in easy reach. With a team once again devoid of stars, Mack experienced more trouble than most owners in attracting patrons, a situation that led to two alienating decisions. Since Shibe Park's inauguration in 1909, the northern Philadelphia neighborhood had grown considerably, becoming an ethnic neighborhood peopled by Irish, Italian, and Jewish enclaves. (The smallpox hospital closed.) Now a row of houses across the street commanded views of the action inside the ballpark. Fans began paying to watch from neighboring roofs, funneling away cash the Athletics desperately needed to feed a precarious balance sheet. Though it was Jack Shibe who ordered the outfield wall raised 50 feet, blocking the view, it was Connie Mack the neighbors blamed for the "spite fence." The next year, Mack compounded the ill feelings by installing lights to hold night games at Shibe Park—the first American League franchise to do so. Neighbors could no longer see into the park, and they could not go to sleep either; the hugely powerful lights made the vicinity as bright as day.[8]

While relations with his neighbors soured, Connie Mack's teams floundered—right on through and past World War II. In 1938, the National League Phillies moved from the Baker

Bowl to become tenants at Shibe Park, providing Mack some welcome income. But not very much—the Phillies were awful, too.

As the 1950s rolled in, what had once been the American League's flagship franchise was a crippled and decrepit shadow of its own glory. Shibe Park, flawed and outdated, was deteriorating badly; the franchise possessed no funds to make repairs. The surrounding neighborhood was deteriorating and crime-ridden, a prospect that kept many fans away. There was no place to park an automobile, either. The entire city was uneasy with change. When Connie Mack unveiled his team in 1901, Philadelphia was the fourth largest city in the nation, home to more than 575,000 people, 6.2 percent of them black. By 1950, the population stood at more than two million, third largest in the United States. Nearly one resident in five was black—the second highest percentage among towns hosting major league ball clubs. The black migration now extended into the North City area, close to the ball park—one more factor making white fans uneasy in a racially charged community. By the early 1960s, the area was one of Philadelphia's poorest ghettos. (Precisely the "real estate values" issue Larry MacPhail posited so crudely in his 1946 report to the major league owners.)[9]

The Athletics showed some small signs of resurrection in the postwar years, but Connie Mack was out of touch, unable to recall the names of his own players. His sons from two marriages assumed greater control of the team, feuding between themselves, persuading the old man to quit the dugout after the 1950 season. The move exposed yet another layer of problems for the A's—management was now top-heavy with semi-competent relatives who possessed no other source of income, no means to keep the team from stumbling toward bankruptcy. By 1950, it was obvious to just about everyone that most cities could no longer support two increasingly expensive major league franchises. Philadelphia was not showing much interest in keeping even one. But then the Phillies had the nerve to win the National League Pennant in 1950, leaving the Athletics more deserted than ever. Survival would require a miracle. Not a promising context for the first black player to join the ball club.[10]

In 50 years, Connie Mack never made the least move toward integrating his franchise. He had dealt with racial issues before, playing Luis Castro, a light-skinned Latino from Columbia, as his second baseman in 1902; relying heavily on Albert Bender, an Ojibway Indian, to pitch him to the World Series four times beginning in 1910. He was not a pioneer in either case, but the moves remained daring in many quarters. Later, he would use Roberto Estalella, one of Clark Griffith's more controversial Cuban discoveries, in his infield. In his heyday, Mack could handle the skeptics of such controversial moves with intelligence and tact. And Mack was certainly aware of good Negro Leagues ball players—the Philadelphia Stars occasionally rented Shibe Park for marquee games. Yet he declared himself disappointed when Branch Rickey signed Jackie Robinson. As Robinson and Larry Doby completed their first season in the majors, *The Sporting News* described Mack as "wary on the subject of Negroes in baseball." Off the record, his comments were far more ugly. Black journalists felt certain the Athletics would prove one of the toughest nuts to crack. Even as his franchise collapsed around him, Connie Mack refused to budge on the prospect of black integration.[11]

Very soon after Mack stepped down from day-to-day operations, the club made their first tentative move toward integration, hiring Judy Johnson, Negro Leagues star of the 1920s and 1930s, as a scout ("ivory hunter" is how *The Sporting News* put it, in their usual sensitive way). Johnson, a third baseman, played several seasons for the Hilldale club of Darby, Pennsylvania, the Philadelphia entry in the early Negro Leagues. Back then, Mack openly wished Johnson was white, so he could sign him up. Now an employee of the Athletics, Johnson took the opportunity to ask the old warrior why he never signed a black player. "There were too many of you to go in," Mack told him. "It would have taken too many jobs away from the white boys." When Johnson recommended that the Athletics purchase the contract of one Henry Aaron from the Indianapolis Clowns for $3,500, he was informed the money was "too much for a man like that."[12]

The scouting organization—a new innovation for the Athletics—turned up a former Negro Leagues pitcher, Bob Trice, who played for three seasons with the Homestead Grays before moving on to Canada's Provincial League, pitching for Farnham in 1950 and 1951. Signing him, the Athletics assigned Trice to St. Hyacinthe, another Provincial League team, where he did well enough to earn promotion to Ottawa of the International League. There he exploded, pitching in 38 games, winning 21 with an ERA of 3.10, earning both Rookie of the Year and Most Valuable Pitcher honors. The A's purchased his contract at the end of the summer, starting him for the first time against the St. Louis Browns on September 13, 1953. The Athletics became the fourth American League team to break the color line.

The club at least tried to do the right things. Faced with mounting public pressure, located in a neighborhood made predominantly black by the Great Migration, the Athletics could be accused of following the cynical path of the St. Louis Browns, integrating merely in the hope of saving the box office. But at least the Athletics allowed Bob Trice to nurture slowly, signing him in 1951, keeping him in Canada where the racial heat was considerably lessened, bringing him to the big show at the close of the 1953 season. They gave him his first start against the Browns, the A's chief competitor for most pathetic team in the League. And Trice was an American black, born in Georgia, raised in West Virginia. The move made every kind of sense, in both the social marketing and the baseball context.[13]

Bob Trice stood 6'3" tall. Strong and athletic, his teammates found him to be easygoing, a fun-loving guy. The one ominous note came at the end of a brief article printed in the Pittsburgh *Courier*, underscoring that although Trice loved the game of baseball, "I would rather do anything than pitch." A pitcher he was, and slowly but surely, the thing unraveled.[14]

Beleaguered Athletics manager Jimmy Dykes did his best to play down the larger significance of Trice's debut, telling

Bob Trice. He looked so promising, but pioneering for Philadelphia's Athletics in 1954 was a lot to ask. Trice was the best starting pitcher the Athletics had at Kansas City in 1955, but the game was no longer fun. (National Baseball Hall of Fame Library, Cooperstown, N.Y.)

his pitcher, "this is just another game.... You don't have a thing to worry about." Trice heeded this advice pretty well, pitching at a quick pace, mixing in the occasional slider with his fastball, displaying sharp control over eight innings. But the Browns ripped enough big hits, including a home run by opposing hurler Don Larsen, to beat Trice, 5–2. More inauspicious was the game's attendance figure: just 8,477—for a Sunday doubleheader.[15]

Trice earned his first American League victory a week later, defeating the lowly Washington Senators despite giving up seven runs and striking out just two batters. His control continued sharp at least; he issued just two walks. He won again in his third and final start, to finish the season 2–1, though with an ERA of 5.48. The Athletics were high on his chances, penciling him into the rotation for 1954.

Philadelphia won just 59 games in that 1953 season, finishing seventh. Changes were inevitable, and the Athletics made two critically important to Bob Trice. The team hired Judy Johnson as a spring training instructor, giving the future Hall of Famer the task of working with Trice and newly acquired Vic Power—the A's doubled the number of blacks on their roster. The team also had a new player-manager, shortstop Eddie Joost, a man who once remarked that he had not learned a thing listening to Casey Stengel. He was right. The Athletics lost 103 games in 1954, finishing dead last in the American League, crushing the last hope for the Macks in Philadelphia. As Joost later recalled, "the Athletics disintegrated because several families were living off the franchise and they put nothing back into the team."[16]

The fortunes of Bob Trice unfortunately mirrored the clubs. Mentored by Judy Johnson in the spring (Johnson did not accompany the team north), Trice got off to a solid start in the rotation, winning his first four games and posting a shutout against the Yankees. But he was pitching for a very bad team, and by midseason his record stood at 7–8, still close to .500, for a club that was losing two games out of every three. (Trice's seven wins were second highest on the club for the entire season.) But his ERA was once again very high, 5.60, and on July 11, Bob Trice requested a return to Ottawa. "I figure that in the long run, this is what's best for me," he told reporters. "And since I cannot seem to win in my present frame of mind, the team shouldn't miss me." Baseball in Philadelphia was not fun for Bob Trice. "Things are different here." Trice was speaking of baseball things, though the racial atmosphere in Philadelphia was not much fun either. (Jackie Robinson was more brutally abused in the Quaker City than anywhere else.) What Trice cited was the inability to play in the field, to work on his hitting, to fool around. Concentrating wholly on pitching was not his idea of enjoying the game. "Maybe I am crazy," Trice allowed, "but to me it seems logical enough. I think everything will work out better this way."[17]

Things did not work out. Trice fully expected to come back to the Athletics a better and happier pitcher, but another stint in the International League brought little improvement. The following season, Trice pitched just ten innings for the A's, earning no decisions and posting an ERA of 9.00. Then he was gone for good, another brief stop in the minors, followed by three years in the Mexican League. A tentative experiment ventured in the midst of chaos, Bob Trice was caught in the crossfire of too many kinds of pressure. The first black player in a racially nervous town, attempting to bolster a weak and crippled pitching staff amidst terminal financial crisis for the club, was a lot to ask of a good-natured young man long sheltered in Canada.

One more black player joined the team for the doomed September of 1954. Joe Taylor, a notorious streak hitter, hit a bad streak in his one try with the Athletics, batting .224 in 18 games before disappearing back to the minors.[18] The Athletics' experiment in integration was reduced to just one person as the team straggled to the end of their last year in Philadelphia. They still had Vic Power. They just could not figure out what to do with him.

Power was an intriguing personality, almost a lightning rod for many of the controversies surrounding the American League's integration. First was the fact that he was born and raised in Puerto Rico, where the color of a man's skin raised few issues. He began his professional career in Canada, playing with refugees from Jorge Pasquel's Mexican League. He did very well, hitting .339, attracting the attention of the New York Yankees, the most important of the major league teams yet to integrate. Power spent two seasons playing first base for Kansas City, the only black on the Yankees' top farm club until Elston Howard joined him. Power was impressive, an aggressive line-drive hitter capable of batting .360, and a dazzling fielder. So dazzling, in fact, that he routinely caught baseballs one-handed, a skill outlandish enough to earn him a reputation as a "showboat"—not the tag the press would have placed on a white fielder. Yankees owner Dan Topping heard reports that Power was "a poor fielder." Still, Vic Power

Vic Power tries to catch two-handed. The Yankees traded Power to the Athletics for several bad reasons, including their belief that he was a poor fielder. Roundly criticized for his one-handed style, Power would win seven Gold Glove Awards once he was settled at first base. (National Baseball Hall of Fame Library, Cooperstown, N.Y.)

was very much the leading candidate to break the color line in the Bronx, though he drew attention to himself in manners disturbing to the ultra-stuffy Yankees brass. Voicing aloud his displeasure at remaining in the minors too long, Power also publicly chastised the team for paying less money to black players. More disturbingly, he openly challenged the most dangerously irrational of racial taboos, dating white women. This did not go down well in racially sensitive Kansas City. Vic Power was not what the Yankees had in mind when General Manager George Weiss stated that "the first Negro to appear in a Yankee uniform must be worth having been waited for."[19]

The Yankees had to promote Vic Power after the 1953 season or leave him exposed to the Rule V draft. After the World Series, they added Power to the 40-man roster, along with Elston Howard. Then they traded Power to Philadelphia.[20]

Both the Yankees and the Athletics insisted Vic Power was the key figure in a 13-player trade. The Yankees were looking for pinch-hitting and pitching help in their quest for a sixth straight World Series title; the A's were looking for any help at all. "We did not want to lose Power," George Weiss insisted. "But the Athletics would not make the deal without him being included. He was the first player they asked for." Whether this was true or not, the trade worked out far better for Philadelphia than New York. The handful of players the Yankees acquired added essentially nothing to a team that finally fell from the top in 1954. Power, 26 years old, hit just .255 with 30 extra-base hits for a dispirited and nearly moribund team, but there was plainly a well of potential.[21]

He still insisted on catching those hot liners one-handed. "With one hand I catch the ball better, stretch better," he would explain. "If I catch with one hand and make no error I don't see why I should catch with two hand because a lot of sportswriter want me to." But the image was cast. Following the script written for him by the Yankees, Athletics manager Eddie Joost could not see anything more than stubborn persistence in bad play. He started the season with Power in left field, the first base job belonging to .231 hitting Lou Limmer. Over the season, Joost tried Power in all the outfield positions, at shortstop, at third base, even 21 games at first. Small wonder he hit just .255—which was still better than all but two regulars on the team. The following season in Kansas City, new A's manager Lou Boudreau played Power at first base exclusively. Power hit .319 and led the team in RBI. But Boudreau could not resist tinkering either, positioning his best player at second base and shortstop for nearly half the next season. The complaints droned on. "No one else caught the ball with one hand in those days," Power recalled. "Little League coaches complained about me, and writers and other players accused me of showing off." "Hot dog" was the usual expression. This for a man who would eventually earn seven Gold Glove Awards as a first baseman.[22]

Kansas City. The new home of the Athletics. Connie Mack's semi-competent sons twisted every way they could through the 1954 season, desperately trying to attract some new investment, watching a newspaper campaign determined to keep the team in Philadelphia fail dismally. Despite some last-minute shenanigans, the only real choice was to sell the team or declare bankruptcy. The Macks sold out to construction millionaire Arnold Johnson, a man long interested in baseball but with no real experience in the game. All would be well—Johnson was a close associate of Dan Topping and Del Webb, owners of the New York Yankees. They would point him in the right direction, give him valuable advice on players and such. Johnson did know something about construction; he immediately reached agreement with officials in Kansas City to refurbish and enlarge the town's Municipal Stadium, creating a fit home for what would now be major league baseball's westernmost franchise. Philadelphia and the Athletics had endured more than enough of one another. Connie Mack died during the winter of 1956, one season after the move. He was 92.[23]

Arnold Johnson may have been determined to begin a new era in A's history in Kansas City, but he owned a roster full of Philadelphia players. Refusing to retain any of the Macks in the front office, Johnson brought in new people—many of them former New York Yankees executives—and hired Boudreau as his manager. Miraculously, the team did demonstrate some minor improvement in Kansas City, finishing the season in sixth place and winning 63 games, 12 more than the last season in Philadelphia.

Vic Power could do nothing but shake his head. Of all the places to land, Kansas City was not at the top of his list. He got married in 1956, which should have ended at least one of his problems. But his Puerto Rican wife, Idalia, was fair-skinned, and the Kansas City cops kept pulling him over anyway. (Sportswriter Leonard Shecter observed that "Kansas City, which doesn't quite know where it stands in the matter of integration, is more self-conscious than, say, Biloxi, Mississippi, which does.") The charges of showboating and failure to hustle kept on, too. The Athletics management took to giving automobiles to players they appreciated, Enos Slaughter (who had been with the team a month) among them. But they never gave a car to Vic Power, their best hitter. "I don't care" became his mantra.[24]

Power did find friends on the team. Bonus baby Clete Boyer sought him out; they went out on the town together. And very soon, Power had black teammates. Hector Lopez, a Panamanian who played an interesting form of third base, became a regular in 1955. In May of that season, the Cleveland Indians shipped Harry Simpson to Kansas City, where he enjoyed his best season, driving in 105 runs, hitting .293, playing nearly every game. "The important thing as I see it," Simpson observed, "is that I, as a Negro, have been given a great privilege and I just wish all members of my race felt the same deep gratitude that I do." Lopez and Simpson both pressured Power to stop befriending white guys "because they thought we blacks should stick together." Simpson actually called Vic Power an "Uncle Tom" and wanted to fight him over the issue. Another episode in the struggle to establish identity for a small minority.[25]

One year later, the A's purchased Jose Santiago, a Puerto Rican pitcher, from the Indians, their fourth black player. During their first three years in Kansas City, the Athletics showed every sign of whole-hearted commitment to integration. Then strange things began to happen.

In retrospect, the most noteworthy and troubling aspect of the early Kansas City years was the symbiotic relationship that the team apparently developed with the Yankees. A regular pipeline grew between Yankee Stadium and the Athletics' diamond; trade after trade shuttled developing stars to the Bronx in exchange for aging veterans. This was not entirely accidental, and it was not entirely new, either. The Yankees, the Indians, and the Red Sox were lifting promising players from their weaker competitors long before the Second World War. In this case, an added impetus seems to have been at work. Jose Santiago was released to the minors after the 1956 season, never to return. Harry Simpson went next, shipped in 1957 to New York in the Billy Martin trade. Sources maintained that Casey Stengel specifically wanted Simpson, but Stengel wanted no part of this trade at all. Martin was the son Stengel never had; Stengel was so angry with George Weiss he refused even to use Simpson for a while. "I'll play who I want."[26]

Simpson came back to Kansas City in the middle of 1958, only to be traded again, this time to the White Sox, in 1959. While the Simpson odyssey played out, the Athletics traded Vic Power to the Cleveland Indians and Hector Lopez to the Yankees. The club brought in no additional black players. Whatever commitment there was to integration came to a full stop. The 1960 team picture of the Kansas City Athletics, a team that finished dead last again, is completely, shockingly white. Just before the season began, Arnold Johnson died suddenly of a cerebral hemorrhage. Team ownership remained in limbo until 1961, when Charley Finley took over. Baseball changed after that, Athletics baseball especially. Finley eventually moved the team to Oakland, where his black stars were instrumental in winning three consecutive championships.[27]

The wobbly, half-hearted, grudging, cynical, self-serving approach to integration exhibited by the Philadelphia/Kansas City Athletics found its parallel in the saga of the Washington Senators, or Nationals. This was no accident. Like the Philadelphia A's, the Washington franchise was at the very heart of the origins of the American League. Connie Mack and Clark Griffith were the most ardent of Kenesaw Mountain Landis's supporters, and remained determined defenders of the traditional status quo, even as their competitive fortunes shrank and eventually vanished. Clark Griffith's Washington team in many ways mirrored the Philadelphia franchise, though the two cases are not entirely analogous. Griffith was his own man, determined to spite himself in his own fashion. That he, like Connie Mack, stalled on integration until the mid–1950s was reflective of the American League at its core. What once was revolutionary, exciting and new was now frozen in the past, unwilling to embrace changes promising a competitive edge, on the field or at the box office.

Like Connie Mack, Clark Griffith was no patrician. Baseball was his escape from a youth so poverty-ridden he nearly starved to death. He became a pitcher, and a crafty one, beginning his major league career with the American Association in 1891 and rising to the top of his profession with the National League's Chicago franchise from 1893 to 1900. (Cap Anson, that vocal leader in keeping blacks off the field, served as Chicago's player-manager until 1897.) At 1.88, Griffith led the National League in ERA in 1898.[28]

With the National League's owners collaborating to control and severely limit baseball salaries, Clark Griffith jumped at the chance to participate in the establishment of the American League. While Ban Johnson, Charlie Comiskey, and Connie Mack saw to the administrative end of the uprising, Griffith's job was to persuade National League stars to jump to the new circuit. He succeeded in 39 tries out of 40. (Hans Wagner supposedly hid from him.) Griffith was rewarded with a plum role on Comiskey's Chicago White Sox, and then agreed to become player-manager when the new league determined they needed a franchise in New York to guarantee success. Griffith stayed with the Highlanders (soon the Yankees) for five seasons. Thirty-eight by this time, "the Old Fox" wandered back to the National League, hanging on as a coach until Ban Johnson realized he needed him again. Brought in to manage the Washington franchise, Griffith was able to buy ten percent of the team's ownership. Over the next eight seasons, as Connie Mack managed his first dynasty and the dead ball era reached its end, Griffith brought the Nationals home in the first division five times, twice finishing second.[29]

The picture changed radically in 1919, when Griffith persuaded Philadelphia grain merchant William Richardson to purchase 40 percent of the club. Additional purchases by Griffith himself gave him 19 percent of the team. Richardson agreed to allow Clark Griffith to vote his shares, giving Griffith controlling interest in the club. The Old Fox immediately voted himself president, and soon after resigned as field manager to devote himself to the front office. Clark Griffith had himself a ball club. One of the first moves he and Richardson made was to rename the Washington ball diamond, originally called American League Park. The park was another of the pioneering steel and concrete stadiums, built poorly on the fly in 1911, just two years after Shibe Park opened. Expanded piecemeal over the following decades, the park assumed a peculiar shape and reputation. It became Griffith Stadium.

The stadium saw a few triumphs and a lot of sorrow over the next 35 years. Defying enormous odds, Washington won the pennant in 1924 and 1925, even winning the World Series in 1924. They won another pennant in 1933, and were generally respectable for the first 15 years of Griffith's presidency. But the team finished seventh in 1934 and struggled to remain competitive thereafter. Like Connie Mack, Clark Griffith suffered with the Great Depression, unable to find the funds to invest in player development or stadium upkeep. Baseball was Griffith's sole source of income; he had no way of laying hands on any money except to attract fans to his deteriorating stadium to watch inferior teams. Like Connie Mack, he had a seemingly endless list of dependents holding positions with the club. None of them brought in any extra income either.[30]

The one aspect of the game where Clark Griffith differed from Connie Mack was in his relations with black people. Mack always held aloof, demonstrating severe indifference to black fans attending his games, refusing to countenance black players playing on his teams, renting out Shibe Park to Negro League clubs very occasionally, and only through the aegis of Abe Saperstein, the notorious white booking agent.[31]

Clark Griffith was different. He was so different, he is by far the most difficult of the American League owners to assess, in action or intent. How to characterize the man? He was comfortable among black people, comfortable enough to accept willingly an honorary deaconship at the black working class Church of God, located across the street from Griffith Stadium. The church held baptismal ceremonies in the ballpark (presumably on off-days). Griffith hosted all manner of black events—football games, drill-marching competitions, religious revivals. Clark Griffith was actively helpful and considerate of the black community, comfortable in the black and white world of the Depression era—the Jim Crow world.[32]

The District of Columbia harbored an awkward relationship with Jim Crow. By statutes passed by Congress during reconstruction, all forms of public discrimination were outlawed. But segregation certainly existed in Washington—in housing, in public accommodations, in restaurants, in schools. Griffith Park stood squarely in the midst of one of the city's more prominent black neighborhoods, one that took shape after 1911. Between 1910 and 1950, the number of blacks living in the District grew from 28.5 percent of the population to 35 percent, by far the largest percentage of blacks to live in any major league city. Here was a population to be considered when planning market strategies. One way or another, Clark Griffith needed to serve this essential element of the community. That he apparently took pleasure in so doing long made him a favorite among the city's black residents.

As the nation's capital and a city with a large black population, Washington had a large and influential black middle class. Ironically, these professional people and their families generally eschewed efforts to bring Negro Leagues baseball to Washington. Teams came, drew poorly, and left, while the black population flocked to see the lowly Washington Senators at segregated Griffith Stadium. The park was not officially segregated—that was against the law—but everyone understood the black section to be the right field bleachers. Through the 1920s and early 1930s, the most popular attraction by far was Babe Ruth, a colossus known to be sympathetic to black players. The right field bleachers were the best vantage spot to see him up close.[33]

The dynamic did not change until 1940, when the Homestead Grays, one of the most talented teams in Negro Leagues history, announced that they would begin playing home games at Griffith Stadium. The Old Fox was behind the move, shrewdly noting that the Grays lacked a suitable ballpark in Homestead or nearby Pittsburgh. Washington's black population initially greeted this latest incarnation of Negro Leagues play with more indifference. Then Satchel Paige came to town a couple of times, pitching for the Kansas City Monarchs, facing off against the Grays. Already a legend, Paige drew crowds wherever he performed, even in indifferent Washington. Black baseball became more acceptable. In 1942, the Grays outdrew the Nationals. Black baseball had arrived. "The atmosphere inside Griffith Stadium was like a rock concert," a Grays fan recalled. And Clark Griffith made money he desperately needed.[34]

Griffith was a model of cooperation with the Grays operation. His office took care of booking arrangements, tickets sales, and cleanup, and helped with publicity. Able to make a home in a full-fledged major league ballpark without having to pay one of those greedy white booking agents, the Grays flourished, garnering a marked profit every season through 1946 (no small triumph in the financially strapped Negro Leagues) and winning eight championships (or maybe nine). Clark Griffith basked in the sunshine of his perceived goodwill—a man willing to work with black enterprise in a friendly and productive manner.

Most observers simply did not realize how much needed cash Griffith was making from the operation. He charged a 20 percent fee from admissions for each game the Grays played at his ballpark, and required his guests to pay the cost of cleanup, as well as a fee for operating the lights. Most importantly, Griffith kept all the money earned from concessions—by far the most lucrative source of income at any ball game. In 1943, Clark Griffith raked in more than $100,000 renting his park to the Homestead Grays, no small item in the year's final accounting.[35]

He needed every cent. Barely surviving the Depression, Griffith was willing to try anything to feed the wolf at his door. Firmly believing that baseball played at night was "just a step above dog racing,"[36] he was appalled when Larry MacPhail put up lights at Crosley Field in 1935. Before long, Griffith Stadium was equipped, and when the war came, Clark petitioned the American League for more night games, to provide entertainment for all those people working long days in the defense effort.[37] By some miracle, the Senators were actually worth seeing in 1943 and 1945, somehow finishing second, to the Yankees, and then the Tigers. The war years, with lots of people making money and few recreational opportunities to spend it, with the Senators and the Grays drawing reasonably well—this was as close as Clark Griffith would come to the gravy train. Reality soon beckoned—the Senators finished out of the first division every season from 1947 through 1960. People do not come in large numbers to watch a last-place team.

If Griffith sought to attract extra money by cooperating with Negro Leagues owners, he needed still to shave costs wherever he could. He had relatives to feed. The Senators became a penny-wise, pound foolish operation, failing to organize any kind of farm system, employing very few scouts, relying primarily on word of mouth to find ball players. Remember, Griffith had players such as Buck Leonard, Josh Gibson, and Satchel Paige under his eye every summer. They were great players, and they would come cheap for the opportunity. They were just the wrong color. But Griffith was willing to skirt even that issue, in his own classless way, if the price was right.[38]

About the only scout the Senators had worth mentioning was Joe Cambria, former minor league player, Negro Leagues team owner, exploiter of minor league clubs, and bane of Judge Landis. Griffith once rescued Cambria from the Commissioner's wrath, and the scout repaid the Senators by finding some legitimate stars, including Early Wynn, Mickey Vernon, and Eddie Yost. Most importantly, Cambria spent much of his time in Cuba, where ballplayers were abundant and, above all, cheap.

Beginning in 1941, Griffith and Cambria set up a regular shuttle operation, moving cheap players from Cuba to the United States and eventually to Griffith Stadium. Finances being what they were, the Cubans received virtually no preparation for the cultural shock of the American mainland, where Spanish was a foreign language, the locals mistrustful, and the customs strange. What Cambria was supposed to monitor carefully was the color of his chosen Cubans' skin. Judge Landis and every sports journalist in America would be scrutinizing carefully, making sure that each Cuban was wholly of Castilian descent. Whatever that might mean.[39]

As the War absorbed able-bodied ballplayers and most major league teams made do with gray-whiskered veterans and beardless youths, the Senators answered with Cubans. Despite the watchful eye of Landis and the horde of scribblers beholden to Jim Crow, Clark Griffith may have been the first owner to break the color line. More than anything, the Washington owner's desperate subterfuge unmasked the bizarre nightmare that was America's vision of race.

Major league baseball was an organization restricted to whites; the Negro Leagues were the black remedy. Players from Cuba could play in either set of leagues, depending wholly on their shade of skin color. Light enough, you could play for the Senators; a shade too dark consigned you to the Cuban Giants. Who arbitrated? Who decided which players belonged where? According to Jim Crow, the least drop of black blood made a person black. In the much more elastic boundaries of race operating in Cuba, questions of racial mixing were farcical. Virtually no one could say precisely what percentages of black and white flowed through anyone's arteries, claims of pure "Castilian" heritage to the contrary. Because they were Cubans rather than Americans, because Clark Griffith was financially strapped, players survived the suspicions of journalists, teammates, and fans to play major league baseball. The Washington Senators ignored the color line while steadfastly defending segregation. That line's true function was to separate American blacks from white institutions.[40]

In the early 1940s, names such as Carrasquel, Ortiz, Gomez, Torres, and Estalella began to appear on Washington rosters. Catcher Mike Guerra stuck with the team despite hitting just .210 in 1945; the Cuban pitchers needed a Spanish-speaking battery mate. But Roberto Estalella was the puzzle. Born in Cardenas, Cuba, in 1911, Estalella began playing for Clark Griffith as early as 1935. Officials took to calling him "Bobby Estalella" to Americanize the young man for American audiences, journalists especially. His Washington teammates were certain Clark Griffith had crossed the line, that Estalella was a black man by American standards, and hazed him accordingly. But Estalella was a decent hitter who came cheap, and the poverty-stricken American League franchises passed him around. After three seasons with the Senators, Estalella spent a year with the Browns, another season with Washington, and the last three war years with Connie Mack's Athletics. Severe need could bend the color line— American blacks could not play for Philadelphia or Washington even in the desperate years of the war, but puzzling Cubans could. The real function of the color line was obvious. All those years

**Roberto Estalella. One of Clark Griffith's many Cuban discoveries, Estalella began playing for Washington in 1936. Players and journalists alike suspected Griffith was hedging on the color line. (National Baseball Hall of Fame Library, Cooperstown, N.Y.)**

before, when the first black professional team called themselves the Cuban Giants, they knew what they were about.[41]

The strange juxtaposition of Clark Griffith's supportive relationship with Negro Leagues baseball and his pipeline to Cuban players led many to believe the Old Fox would be the first to defy the color line openly. He certainly had access to black players, observing the best at his own ballpark year after year. And he certainly had reason, always looking for dimes on the pavement, operating in a city one-third black, his stadium in the middle of a prominent black neighborhood. But Griffith remained coy about integration, constantly arguing that the Negro Leagues needed to tighten their own organization, place themselves on a firm business footing to better compete against the majors. Griffith was happy with the segregation of black and white baseball, more than willing to assist the black community in an entirely paternalistic way.[42]

During the early 1940s, when the Negro Leagues were flourishing and the Homestead Grays were making him a lot of money, this was an attitude that made sense, so far as business went. But the arrival of Jackie Robinson, followed soon after by Larry Doby, killed that goose. The Grays stopped making money in 1947; by 1950, the team had disappeared for good. And still Clark Griffith needed money, needed to appeal to a fan base one-third black. Branch Rickey understood the situation perfectly. "Don't let Mr. Griffith fool you," he told *The Courier*'s Wendell Smith back in 1945. "He's not interested in Negro baseball other than from the standpoint of financial gain. He's afraid he won't make a big chunk of money next year that he got this year from the Homestead Grays. Griffith's thinking more about his pocketbook than he is about the right and wrong in the thing."[43]

For years, members of the press favoring integration, black and white, treated Clark Griffith with gentle good favor, appealing to his obviously human side, anticipating the break they expected any day. As the disappointments mounted, as Griffith chose to sign a known racist such as Jake Powell while ignoring Buck Leonard and Josh Gibson, the hope turned to bitterness. By the late 1940s, Wendell Smith, Sam Lacy, and other leading black sportswriters became openly hostile. Shirley Povich of the *Washington Post* also maintained a steady drumbeat, repeatedly questioning the justice of segregated baseball and football operations in the nation's capital.[44]

The Old Fox never wavered. "I will not sign a Negro for the Washington club merely to satisfy subversive persons," he told *The Sporting News*. "I would welcome a Negro on the Senators if he rated the distinction, if he belonged among major league players." Subversive persons—that ugly contention that the civil rights movement was some kind of communistic plot. The voice of Paul Robeson was still echoing in Griffith's reactionary ear. The Old Fox at least claimed to lament not signing Minnie Minoso, one Cuban Joe Cambria apparently missed.[45]

If anything, Clark Griffith grew more defiant with advancing age. By 1954, he had seven Cubans lined up to play in a minor league camp at Winter Garden, Florida, including Angel Scull, slated to become the first indisputably black player on the Nats. The plan soured when a Winter Garden town official allegedly told the Nationals' farm director "to get his Cuban Negroes out of town." Pleading ignorance, the mayor of Winter Garden, along with several other government types, denied responsibility and expressed their desire to have the Cubans stay. By then, the Cubans were afraid to return, concerned about "what 'some fanatic' might do." Lost in the controversy, Angel Scull was optioned to the International League's Havana, Cuba, franchise, never again figuring in Clark Griffith's plans. There were more Cubans out there.[46]

In standard texts, Washington is listed as the fifth American League team to integrate, bringing up outfielder Carlos Paula in September 1954. Paula was plainly black, and he was born in Havana, the latest in the line of Cubans stretching back to the 1930s. Griffith was growing a little bolder, but the strategy remained entirely the same—cheap Cubans, no American blacks. "Mr. Griffith would give Washington fans dark players from other lands, but never an American Negro," Shirley Povich pointed out in 1954. Clark Griffith died one year later, still refusing to cross the line that mattered to him, the one that kept American black players from appearing with his Senators. Jackie Robinson referred to Griffith as "that unreconstructed Virginian."[47]

Whatever his homeland, Carlos Paula made a very small impression in Washington in 1954, hitting just .167 with two RBI in 24 at bats. There was promise; he was quick on the basepaths. If only his coaches could persuade him to stop moving his front foot in the middle of his swing. He did impress with the bat in 1955, playing in 115 games, hitting .299, showing some punch, though not much for a guy who stood 6'3". Regrettably, he had to play in the field, where he was "something of a crudity," as Shirley Povich put it. Patrolling right field, he made ten errors in 155 chances. By 1956, opposing pitchers had caught on to the fact Paula could not hit a curve ball to save his life. Hitting just .183 in 33 games, he was shipped to the minors, eventually landing in the Pacific Coast League.[48]

The Cuban experiment was far from over. With the death of the Old Fox, nephew Calvin Griffith assumed control of the team. Making a complete mockery of the integration question, Calvin added four more black Latino players to the roster in 1955. Cuban League "Rookie of the Year" Juan Delis played in 54 games for Washington, batting just .189 while the Nats tried to figure out where to play him. Experiments at second base, third base, and the outfield mercifully ended with his release. Twenty-nine-year-old Wenseslao Gonzalez, veteran of the Mexican League and the Arizona-Texas League, pitched in just one game for the Senators, giving up six earned runs on six hits in two innings. Vibert Ernesto Clarke of Panama reached the team in September, making seven relief appearances, walking more than he struck out, and building an ERA of 4.64. He too was gone at season's end.[49]

The one true major leaguer of the five was Julio Becquer, a first baseman from Havana. One more black player who found his way to the American League through Canada, Becquer impressed enough in the minors to earn a September call-up in 1955. Not given much opportunity, he managed just three hits—none for extra bases—in 14 tries. But, unlike his four Latin American compatriots, Becquer stuck. He spent all of the next four seasons in Washington before moving to the Los Angeles Angels in the 1960 expansion draft. After playing in just 11 games in California, Becquer rejoined his old team, now moved to Minnesota. He was released after a single appearance in 1962.

Becquer was used almost exclusively as a pinch-hitter, appearing in 488 games over seven seasons but batting just 974 times. 1959 proved his best season, when he hit .268 and drove in 26 runs. More often than not, he was below .250, the product of too much time on the bench. Becquer was almost certainly correct in believing he could have hit better playing regularly, but he had no complaints. "I love the game," Becquer said, "and I believe that is true of most major league players."[50]

Washington's fans had considerably more to complain about. Under Calvin Griffith's direction, the Senators finished seventh in 1956 and last the next three seasons, averaging 59 wins a year before finally rising to fifth in 1960. Calvin did finally get around to addressing the integration issue a little more honestly, signing pitcher Joe Black of New Jersey in August 1957.

Black had known stardom as the National League's "Rookie of the Year" in 1952 and starring for the Dodgers in the World Series that year. But the Dodgers tried to expand his pitching repertoire, and he lost the strike zone instead. Five seasons of frustration with Brooklyn and Cincinnati followed. Washington was his last chance, and it was not much of a chance, 12⅔ innings spread over seven games. Black's ERA amounted to 7.11. No one could quarrel with his release.

Almost two years passed before the Senators acquired another American black, trading starting center fielder Albie Pearson to the Baltimore Orioles for speedster Lenny Green on May 26, 1959—less than two months before Boston became the last major league team to add a black player. Green, born in Detroit, showed flashes of genuine promise. He covered a lot more ground than Pearson in center field, and made few errors. His hitting was indifferent during his first season with Washington, but he blossomed in 1960, hitting .294, scoring 62 runs in 127 games, and leading the team in stolen bases. With Cubans Jose Valdivielso at short-stop and Julio Becquer actually playing some first base, the Senators finally looked to have a truly integrated team. And then they moved to Minnesota for 1961.[51]

Calvin Griffith explained the move in a speech delivered at Waseca, Minnesota, 17 years later, when he thought no reporters were around. "It was when I found out you only had 15,000 black people here," he told Minnesota. "We came here because you've got good, hardworking white people here." Perhaps the most honest statement concerning integration the Griffiths, uncle or nephew, ever offered. Clark Griffith was far more comfortable operating in the Jim Crow 1930s, a paternalistic friend of black people, with no intent of becoming anything like an equal partner. Calvin was not much different. The seedling did not fall very far from the foster parent's tree.[52]

While Connie Mack and Clark Griffith made a hollow mockery of their integration efforts, the third of the American League's bottom feeders continued to wrestle with integration in its own twisted fashion. If the Philadelphia and Washington franchises were in deep trouble by 1953, the St. Louis Browns were terminal. Not even the efforts of Bill Veeck could save them.

Veeck sold his ownership of the Cleveland Indians in 1949, mostly to pay for that messy divorce. Itching to get back into baseball, he shaped a precarious and money-starved partnership to purchase the Browns, believing that sound and innovative management could save the team and drive the Cardinals out of town. Innovation of course meant providing a broader range of entertainment than a mere baseball game, and Sportsman's Park in St. Louis soon became the site for some of Veeck's more inventive promotions and stunts. Attendance did improve a bit, but the ingredient that drove success in Cleveland was conspicuously absent—the Browns could not possibly win half their games, much less a pennant.[53]

Hard pressed for cash, and with most of the promising Negro Leagues players signed elsewhere, Veeck could not do as much to address integration as he would have liked. He inherited an all-white team—the Browns made absolutely no move to place another black player on the roster after the Hank Thompson/Willard Brown debacle. So Veeck ordered such scouts as he had to begin looking out for promising young black players, and he signed Satchel Paige to fill the immediate need. Again he faced heavy criticism for the move, and again Paige proved him right. Released by Cleveland after Veeck sold out in 1949, Satchel Paige, somewhere between 48 years old and infinity, was still master. Indifferent in 1951, Paige became a force the next year, pitching in 46 games, tying the team lead by winning 12, and fashioning a 3.07 ERA.

Casey Stengel named him to the All-Star team. More importantly, Satchel Paige drew fans, doing his part to increase attendance by more than 150,000 (still not nearly enough). Paige was not quite so effective the following season, despite a 3.57 ERA, but neither was the team. The Browns fetched up against the bottom, losing 100 games. Worse yet, Augie Busch of the deep-pocketed Busch Brewing Company purchased the rival St. Louis Cardinals. The Browns would be the team to leave town.[54]

This is where Bill Veeck encountered the full animosity the remaining American League owners felt for the maverick in their midst. Joining ranks, the deeply conservative majority refused to permit the Browns to move to another venue without Veeck selling his interest. Facing bankruptcy, Bill Veeck had no choice. Some dubious horse-trading left the team in the hands of a partnership centered in Baltimore, where they would welcome the team for the 1954 season. One of the first moves the new ownership made was to release Satchel Paige.[55]

So the St. Louis Browns became the Baltimore Orioles, the latest incarnation of a name that had previously appeared in the lists of the National League, the American League, the Federal League, and the International League. Full of pathetic optimism, the new ownership envisioned a tripling of attendance over the last year in St. Louis, and an accompanying climb up the American League ladder. Apparently they forgot that while the city and the name were new, the franchise was still loaded with Browns. The team lost 100 games again in 1954.

So far as integration was concerned, the transfer from St. Louis to Baltimore was at best a move sideways. By the standards of major league baseball, both were Southern towns. If anything, Baltimore carried the grimmer reputation. In 1946, playing his one year of International League ball, Jackie Robinson suffered more ugly abuse in Baltimore than anywhere else. Two years later, Bill Veeck cut the Cleveland Indians' ties to the Baltimore franchise rather than face the prospect of sending Larry Doby there for seasoning. Hagerstown, Maryland, a half-hour from Baltimore, was especially dreaded by minor league black players. "Hagerstown was the worst team in the whole damn league," Joe Durham recalled. "They were really bad. I used to hate going there." Willie Tasby, another eventual Oriole, echoed the sentiment.[56]

Baltimore was a fully segregated metropolis. The vast majority of the 166,000 black residents were confined to "Old West," an area including both quiet upper-class neighborhoods and dangerously sub-standard slums. Transportation, schools, housing, public accommodations, baseball, everything was segregated in Baltimore. The city was so firmly entrenched behind Jim Crow that the NAACP mounted a protest against the very notion of moving an American League team to Maryland. When the League ignored the complaint, Roy Wilkins, NAACP administrator, tried to persuade officials at least to work to integrate facilities for the ball players. Will Harridge, president of the American League, apparently failed to respond to that relatively innocuous request as well. Baltimore wanted a ball club, the American League wanted Baltimore, and racial concerns counted for nothing in the calculation.[57]

Bill Veeck's well-intended efforts to turn up black players for the franchise had borne some success by the time the team left for Baltimore without him. Satchel Paige was gone, but Willie Tasby (signed in 1950, before Veeck's arrival), Joe Durham, and Lenny Green were available in the minors. Veeck had signed or at least tried out several Negro Leagues veterans as their teams collapsed, but they were mostly gone by the time the franchise shifted to Baltimore. The one survivor to appear with the Orioles was Jehosie Heard, who pitched for Birmingham, Houston, and New Orleans of the Negro American League between 1946 and 1951. Veeck assigned him to Class A ball. Heard won 20 games, earning promotion to the Pacific Coast

League, where he won 16 in 1953. Invited to the first training camp of the shiny new Orioles, Heard fascinated journalists with his ability to throw such a hard fastball despite weighing just 147 pounds. Jay Heard became the one black player on the go north with the team. Not too far north—this was Baltimore. Between April and June, manager Jimmy Dykes found situations to use Heard twice, once in late April, and again at the end of May. He pitched a total of 3⅓ innings. Rumors of heavy drinking made the rounds.

After Heard rusted in the bullpen for half a season and posted an ERA of 13.50, the Orioles sent him back to the PCL. He joined the Orioles' expanded roster in September, but never pitched again in the major leagues. Joe Durham, another September call-up, actually got into ten games, batting 40 times, hitting .225. Durham spent the next two seasons in a military uniform, setting back whatever plans the Orioles may have had in mind for him.[58]

The Orioles changed ownership again after the horrific inaugural season in Baltimore. New management determined that Jimmy Dykes, with a resume that included 96 losses in Philadelphia to go with the 100 in Baltimore, was not the answer to their problems. They entered into negotiations with the White Sox' Paul Richards before the 1954 season was over, hoping to acquire a firm hand to reshape Baltimore's bleak future. What followed was one of the most complete makeovers a major league baseball team ever encountered.

Assuming control in 1955, Richards watched his Orioles lose 97 games his first year, finishing seventh. The next year, they lost 85, climbing to sixth. More importantly, during that two-year period, Richards, acting as field manager and general manager, traded, released, consigned to the minors, or saw into retirement every last one of the players figuring in the first Orioles season. Holding on only to a couple of fringe players (including Joe Durham), Richards reconstructed the entire team. In the two-year period, he would acquire 41 new players by trade or purchase, primarily from the Yankees (one trade involved 16 players), the Cleveland Indians, and his former employer, the White Sox. Promoting a few young players from the minors and signing no fewer than eight bonus babies, Richards set out to remake the Orioles in his own image.[59]

Paul Richards was remarkable for two reasons. One, very obviously important considering his commitments, was his patience and attendance to training, especially with young players. The "baby birds," as the press labeled them, would require considerable patience—baseball is a game so often learned through mistakes. The second quality was the trust he placed in black players, despite the prejudice those players saw in him. Richards was an essential element in the relatively painless integration of the Chicago White Sox; now he would bring that determination to bear in Baltimore.

Paul Richards would have liked to acquire Minnie Minoso from the White Sox, "the most colorful player of his era."[60] With Chicago unlikely to give him up, Richards searched a little more deeply into memories of his old organization, eventually securing former Negro Leagues players Bob Boyd and Connie Johnson. Though neither had flourished with the White Sox, each would make the most of the opportunity offered in Baltimore.

Boyd, a ferocious line-drive hitter from Mississippi, played five years with Memphis of the Negro American League, generally hitting well above .350. Signed by Chicago, Boyd spent part of one season in the Western League before moving to Sacramento of the Pacific Coast League in 1951. A solid performance out west earned him a September call-up with the White Sox, but he managed just three hits in 18 at-bats. The next three seasons became an exercise in frustration. Assigned to various minor league stops, he consistently hit over .300 but never made enough of an impression to stick with Chicago. His best chance came in 1953, when Richards played him in 55 games. Boyd hit .297, drove in 23 runs in 165 at-bats, and earned another trip to the minors. Doc Young, writing in *Jet* magazine, observed that "Boyd's case is typical of Negro players who linger in organizations unwilling to give them a chance." Boyd did not linger much longer; the St. Louis Cardinals purchased his contract after the 1954 season, in which he came to bat just 56 times. His impressions of Paul Richards were decidedly ambivalent. "Strangely enough, one of the men who didn't like black players was Paul Richards," Boyd recalled. "Yet in some ways he was the greatest man I ever played for and the smartest manager. But he was prejudiced.... Yet he wanted me playing for him when he went to the Orioles."[61]

Apparently Paul Richards thought highly of Bob Boyd, at least as a player. When the Cardinals failed to protect him, Richards drafted Boyd under Rule V and installed him at first base. Boyd missed over half the 1956 season with a broken hand, but hit .311. The following year he truly took off, batting second in the order, scoring 73 runs, and hitting .318. Baltimore's win-loss record reached .500 for the first time. Boyd's consistent line-drive slashes amazed the baby birds, reinforcing his nickname, "The Rope."[62] As the Orioles hovered at the brink of respectability, Boyd put in three more excellent seasons before time caught up with him. Reduced to a pinch-hitting role in 1960, he watched his team rise to second place. That winter, the Orioles traded him to Kansas City, where he lasted just 26 games before finishing his career with the Braves.

Connie Johnson played a very similar role for Paul Richards in Baltimore. Johnson, a native of Georgia, pitched for eight seasons in the Negro Leagues, primarily with the Kansas City Monarchs, before choosing, like so many Negro Leagues veterans, to head to Canada in 1951. Picked up by Chicago, Johnson joined the White Sox in 1953, starting ten games and winning four. Like Bob Boyd, Johnson spent the next few years bouncing between Chicago and a couple of minor league cities, never quite able to establish himself in the White Sox rotation. Roughly as good as several Sox starters, Johnson was one more black man who was not better enough. But Paul Richards remembered him, saw Johnson as the kind of pitcher he wanted as he shaped his needs. Connie Johnson could eat up innings, buy time for the fledgling birds. Richards traded for Johnson in May 1956, as part of a six-player deal with White Sox. Observers saw Johnson as a throw-in, but Richards later indicated that the pitcher was the man he wanted. "The deal was for a couple of other guys," Johnson recalled, "but Richards wanted me and I was sort of throwed in. In Baltimore they said, 'We was really after you but we had to make this trade with them others and they got 'em to throw you in.'"[63]

Finding opportunity at last, Johnson started 25 games for the Orioles, finishing second on the team in wins and leading the rotation with a 3.43 ERA. He was the workhorse in 1957, pitching 242 innings, leading the team with 14 wins, and reducing his ERA to 3.20. It may have been too much. Johnson, who relied on sharp control and a wicked fastball, was 35 years old at the beginning of 1958, his last year in the majors. He pitched just 118⅓ innings and suffered a rise in ERA of more than half a run. The baby birds were nearly ready; Connie Johnson's time was past.[64]

Apart from buying time with Bob Boyd and Connie Johnson, Paul Richards's efforts to add black players to the roster came to very little. A 1955 trade with the Cleveland Indians for Dave Pope proved disappointing. Joe Durham returned from the Army in 1957, but his skills had diminished; he hit .183 in 27 games and was released. Charley Beamon, a fireballer with a fascinating array of breaking pitches who signed straight out of high school, raised hopes that September and the next season, but arm troubles ended his major league career before age 25. Lenny Green came out of the minors that September of 1957, impressing more with his speed and his glove than with his bat. When he began the season batting .292 in 1959, the Orioles took the opportunity to trade him to Washington. By that time, Richards had settled on another speedster, Louisiana-born Willie Tasby, as his center fielder. Tasby's range and arm drew comparisons to Willie Mays, though no one confused their bats. Tasby did show a bit more power than Green, though apparently not enough; Baltimore traded him to the Red Sox early in 1960. Two more outfielders, Joe Taylor and Fred Valentine (one of Richards's few black amateur signings), made minimal impressions. By 1960, Bob Boyd was the sole black player on the Orioles, and he would be gone by the end of the year.[65]

It could have been worse. Most civil rights advocates expected worse. Inheriting a bad team with a very weak history of integration, the Orioles raised no real ruckus over the integration question, maintaining a barely noticeable black presence on the team in 1954, committing themselves more fully when Paul Richards took over. But looks could be deceiving. Black players on the Orioles assumed one of two roles, neither integral to the long-term goals of their manager. Needing to buy time, Paul Richards sought out a few older, stop-gap players who could provide needed skills while the baby birds learned the game. Thirty-six-year-old Bob Boyd and 33-year-old Connie Johnson fit the profile; they were the two black players to settle into full-time roles with the team. Younger black players—Durham, Tasby—products of the seat-of-the-pants scouting system of the St. Louis days, experienced limited opportunity (Durham played in 87 games over two seasons, Tasby 199 games in three) before disappearing. The highly efficient scouting system Richards rapidly developed in Baltimore turned up eight bonus babies and several more promising young players—nearly all of them white. The few black prospects the system did identify—Lenny Green, Charlie Beamon, Fred Valentine, Chuck Hinton—were not offered any lucrative bonus baby contracts. Nor did they stay long. It was hard to be young, black, and remain an Oriole. The first black player to be signed by the Orioles and remain with Baltimore over several seasons was Sam Bowens, signed in 1960. Paul Blair signed in 1962.

The Baltimore Orioles did not resist integration as Connie Mack and the Philadelphia Athletics had, nor make a mockery of its goals in the manner of Clark Griffith and the Senators. Paul Richards made good use of two aging veterans of the Negro Leagues, and he sought out a few promising young black players. The Orioles brought them along, gave them tries with the big show. Then they quickly sent them elsewhere. The minors, the trading block, the waiver wire. There were a lot of options.

In his book *The Integration of Major League Baseball*, Rick Swaine lays much of the blame for Baltimore's sketchy integration record at the feet of Lee MacPhail. MacPhail, son of "Roaring Redhead" Larry MacPhail, took over as the Orioles' General Manager in 1959. Two seasons later, nearly all the black personnel with the Orioles were gone. One more case, perhaps, of the seed falling close to the parent tree. But the actions of Paul Richards are difficult to understand as well. His respect for black players was obvious, his reliance on Bob Boyd and Connie Johnson a real commitment. His impatience with the younger black players is far more puzzling.[66]

For the fourth and last of the teams to grudgingly integrate in the mid–1950s, a most telling incident would underscore the urgency they faced. In the spring of 1956, Elston Howard, the first black man to take the field with the New York Yankees, was dreading the annual horror story of training in the South. Howard's godfather, thinking to soften the experience just a little, arranged for the family to stay one night at the home of a minister he knew in Alabama. On the appointed night, Howard called from the road to ask specific directions to the house. They couldn't stay after all. Martin Luther King's house in Montgomery had just been fire-bombed. "The police are there now," Howard told his wife. The screws were tightening by 1956.[67]

From the perspective of more than half a century later, society tends to interpret the integration of baseball primarily as a social process, a search for justice, an attack on a Jim Crow world. More elusive is the fact that in the beginning, integration occurred in large part because a few owners sought a competitive edge, and understood that many of the players they saw in the Negro Leagues could improve their clubs. Signing Jackie Robinson and Larry Doby created social waves, but they proved their value by improving their respective teams enough to win pennants. Enhancing the gate did not hurt either.

The one team that saw little need to upgrade their competitive performance at the time was the New York Yankees. By far the wealthiest, the most independent of the 16 major league franchises, the deep pockets of Yankees ownership maintained a steady supply of All-Star caliber players the team would deploy to win pennant after pennant—14 out of 25 from 1921 to the end of World War II. The club would win another pennant and the World Series in 1947, defeating Jackie Robinson's Dodgers. Beginning in 1949, the Yankees would reel off five championships in a row, a record never matched. If ever a club had the right to be confident of its competitive abilities, not to say arrogant, that club was the New York Yankees. As integration got under way, the Bronx Bombers did not feel any pressing need to go out looking for new sources of competitive players.[68]

There was more to the team's resistance than that, of course. In the face of mounting pressure from the press—black and white—from the state and city governments of New York, from other franchises, from opposing players, Yankees management maintained a stubborn opposition to integration that grew more ugly with each passing year. Larry MacPhail, co-owner in 1947, boxed himself into a narrow corner on the integration issue. He told *The Sporting News* his scouts "checked both Negro Leagues and didn't find a player worth signing." Dan Topping and Del Webb ousted MacPhail at the close of the season, but continued down the restricted path the Roaring Redhead laid out for them, growing very defensive over the issue by 1953. Defending his team against charges of racism, Topping proclaimed, "Jim Crow, my eye. Who brought the first Negro football player into the All-American Conference? I did. I signed Buddy Young. How can anybody accuse any organization of which I am the head of Jim Crowism?" (The All-American Conference was football, Yankees of an entirely different sort.) Topping went on to repeat the oft-expressed organizational position. "We are not going to bring up a Negro just to meet the demands of pressure groups. We will be glad to place on the Yankees any Negro player who can make that place for himself on his ability." Sentiments fully echoing the platitudes of Connie Mack or Clark Griffith.[69]

The franchise did begin a half-hearted search for a potential black Yankee very soon after Branch Rickey and Bill Veeck made their moves, acquiring Negro Leagues stars Artie Wilson and Luis Marquez, signing them to suspect contracts that led ultimately to arbitration by the Commissioner's Office. Neither player came remotely close to wearing a Yankees uniform, though each eventually appeared on National League rosters. A handful of additional signings took place over the next four years, none of them very serious. The Yankees were the fifth major league organization to sign black players, the 13th to place a black man on a major league field.[70]

A far more accurate gauge of the team's scouting efforts saw the light of day in 1974, when extensive renovation work at Yankee Stadium unearthed a letter written 25 years earlier. Joe Press, a Brooklyn cog in New York's vast scouting network, wrote a frustrated complaint to Paul Krichell, the team's chief scout. "It is quite hard for me to understand your complete turn-around as far as the Negro baseball players are concerned," Press wrote. "Within the past two years I have given you reports on practically every player, with the exception of a very few, who have since signed with other teams. You could have had practically all of them, just for the asking. A few of those I mentioned to you were Art Wilson and Orestes Minoso and there are still more of these whom, in my opinion, would fit in Organized Baseball without any trouble. They are Piper Davis, infielder, and Mays, outfielder, both of the Birmingham Black Barons."

Imagine Willie Mays and Mickey Mantle in the same outfield. The Yankees also passed on Ernie Banks, who would have been ready just as Phil Rizzuto was coming to the end.[71]

The essential architect of Yankees integration policy was their sadly flawed genius of a General Manager, George Weiss. Director of the team's scouting operations since 1932, Weiss succeeded as GM with the removal of Larry MacPhail. It was Weiss who hired Casey Stengel to manage the Yankees, defying the advice of the many who saw Stengel as a buffoon. It was Weiss who provided Stengel with the seemingly endless supply of ballplayers capable of winning pennants. "There is less wrong with the Yankees than with any club I've ever had," Stengel enthused. And it was George Weiss who said in 1952 that "I will never allow a black man to wear a Yankee uniform. It would offend boxholders from Westchester."[72]

Weiss spent a good deal of time backing away from that and similar unguarded observations over the years. More importantly, he softened his stance somewhat as the seasons rolled by—not because his feelings for blacks warmed at all, but because of the competition thing. Other teams were catching up, threatening the Yankees' dominance. The Indians were closing, led by Larry Doby; the White Sox were rising behind Minnie Minoso. The World Series showcased the talents of Jackie Robinson, Roy Campanella, Don Newcombe, and the eye-popping Willie Mays. Weiss, sitting in his box, saw this in person. Finally he gave orders to his scouts: find a "suitable" black player. That meant finding someone with a reserved personality who could fit into a lineup featuring Mickey Mantle, Yogi Berra, Hank Bauer, Gil McDougald, and the other stars. There would be some pressure.

On Opening Day of 1952, the American Labor Party picketed Yankee Stadium, ramping up the pressure on the one New York City team yet to integrate. The following November, Jackie Robinson appeared on a local television show, "Youth Wants to Know," where he was asked, "do you think the Yankees are prejudiced against Negro players?" Robinson baldly replied, "Yes, I think they are. I don't mean the players are—they are a fine bunch of fellows and sportsmen and I really had a good time talking to those fellows when they got on base and at other times. But I think the Yankee management is prejudiced. They haven't a single Negro on the team and very few in the Yankee organization." *The Sporting News* editorialized in its usual insipid fashion, berating Robinson for singling out the Yankees among the eight teams yet to add black players. "Robinson should be player, not crusader," the headline read. Sighing over the inequities faced by American blacks, the journal intoned that "the full solution of the problem is a matter of social evolution which cannot be accomplished overnight."[73]

As *The Sporting News* undoubtedly recognized, there was more to Robinson's response than mere loathing for a team that had just beat him in the World Series for the third time. Robinson understood, as the American Labor Party understood, as anyone with real knowledge of baseball understood—the New York Yankees were the gold standard. If a baseball team could give social evolution a shove, the Yankees were that team.

The Yankees were Babe Ruth, Lou Gehrig, Joe DiMaggio; they were all those pennants, all those championships. They were loved; more often they were hated; above all, they were expected to win. The Yankees went about the business of winning in no uncertain fashion, drawing on by far the largest fan base in baseball to finance a continuous rebuilding, exchanging one star for the next. The Yankees were inevitable. That was why they mattered. Brooklyn could integrate, Cleveland, Chicago; that was a good thing. The Athletics could surrender with bad grace, and Calvin Griffith ruled in Washington. Every team that broke the color line was important, but in part because each integration put that much more pressure on the Yankees. When the Bronx Bombers finally put a black man on the field, the color line would be truly broken for good.

The Yankees took their sweet time, perhaps in part to re-emphasize their own importance—they would be deliberate, they would find the right guy for the right reasons, reasons defined by the Yankees. Even loyal fans grew impatient; a supporter from Texas wrote *The Sporting News* to say she was "convinced that they don't want a Negro player; they want a Negro superman." Two players with sufficient promise emerged once the team got serious. It did not help that one of them, Elston Howard, got drafted into the military as soon as the team signed him. The other was Vic Power, with his hot bat, his "showboat" glove, and his irrepressible personality. They reached a decision. The troublesome Power went to Philadelphia—the Athletics wanted him so badly!—leaving Howard.[74]

Elston Howard played three seasons with the Kansas City Monarchs before signing a minor league contract with New York. He showed considerable versatility, playing first base, the outfield, and catching. Equally important, Yankees management found him "a clean-cut religious young man." (Just the words they used to describe Mickey Mantle and Whitey Ford.) When Howard returned from the Army in 1953, the Yankees decided to put him behind the plate. Critics saw this as one more stall—it would take years for Howard to master the skills necessary to become a big league catcher, and the Yankees already had Yogi Berra, the American League's Most Valuable Player in 1953. But the move made sense. Berra had been catching more than 140 games just about every year since 1949; he would be 30 years old in 1955. Few catchers lasted too long past that, not with that kind of work load. Just as importantly, the Yankees, a team that paid more attention to baseball's fundamentals than anyone, saw real promise in Howard's catching skills, especially his arm. Bill Dickey, the former Yankees great who taught Yogi Berra "all of his experience," set to work. Howard eventually emerged as the best defensive catcher in the American League.[75]

The call finally came in 1955. The Yankees put their first black player on the field without fanfare, substituting him in the late innings in Boston when Irv Noren got thrown out. Howard played in the outfield, as he would for much of the season. Yogi Berra was still going strong, would catch the bulk of the games for another four seasons. Casey Stengel introduced Howard to New York and the world on the *Ed Sullivan Show*, saying, "This is my three-way man here. He's the best I ever got at a lotta positions and he can do a number of things a lot of them can't." Stengel knew perfectly well that Elston Howard would not see much action behind the plate in his first season. Berra was Stengel's field general, the man he relied on to make the team click. Not for nothing was Berra named MVP again in 1955.[76]

Charles Dillon Stengel was known to one and all as Casey since he hailed from Kansas City, born there in 1890. So he grew up in a town well-versed in racial antipathies, to put it kindly. In one sense, he was a man of his time and upbringing. Racial and ethnic slurs came easily—he referred to Joe DiMaggio, the greatest player he ever managed, as "the Dago." Combine that with his well-earned reputation as a clown, both as a player and as a manager in the National League, what emerges is the picture of an unthinking bigot, one of hundreds populating organized baseball. But Stengel was no fool, and he wasn't much of a racist, either. When Wendell Smith did his series of interviews with National League managers back in 1939, it was Stengel who provided the most thoughtful and nuanced answers. And it was Stengel who saw a group of black soldiers playing baseball at Camp Stephen D. Little in Arizona, and called their attention to J. L. Wilkinson, who made them the foundation for his Monarchs. Stengel understood baseball talent as well as anyone alive, and he was completely color-blind when it came to that. If a man could play, color did not matter. This was the attitude he brought to the pressure-filled atmosphere of 1955. The Yankees had provided him a new catcher he did not immediately need, but a man who could hit. He found Elston Howard

**Elston Howard. The New York Yankees stalled until 1955 before adding a black player to the roster. Howard met their expectations—a quiet family man with pop in his bat and the ability to play several positions in Casey Stengel's platoon system. (National Baseball Hall of Fame Library, Cooperstown, N.Y.)**

places to play in 97 games that first season. He also called him "eight ball." Casey did try to cure himself of the nastier racial slurs, but he had to catch himself a lot.[77]

Though he never publicly referred to the pressures facing Howard, Stengel did his level best to make him a welcome part of the club. At team celebrations—there were a lot of them—Stengel always made a point of dancing with Howard's wife Arlene, while Elston danced with Edna Stengel. And Stengel became very angry when he was told Howard had to stay in separate hotels in Chicago, Kansas City and Baltimore. Confronting Yankees traveling secretary Bill McCorry—one more team official not overwarm to civil rights—Stengel demanded to know, "Is he on this team or not?" George Weiss heard it, too. "Howard's one of my players, ain't he? If he don't stay there, we don't stay there." Phone calls were made. Howard began staying in the same hotels (except in Chicago), though he had no roommate until the Yankees acquired another black player. Bill Skowron did room with Howard during a trip to Japan after the 1955 season. "Me and Ellie were probably the first interracial teammates in baseball history," Skowron observed. No one in Tokyo said anything.

If Yankees management was hesitant and uncommitted, the team's players were more than ready for integration. Skowron, a former minor league teammate, met Howard at the train station when he came to Florida for his first spring training. Mickey Mantle stayed on the team bus with Howard when he was barred from entering Southern restaurants. Yogi Berra was effusive in his support for the man slated to replace him. Phil Rizzuto became Howard's "great white father." "I got pretty lonesome at times," Howard recalled, "and Phil would sense when I hit the real blues." Hank Bauer would come out of the dugout to confront opponents riding Howard. A square-jawed ex–Marine, Bauer was not a man to cross.

When Howard got his first game-winning hit, "he found a carpet of clean white towels leading from his locker to the showers," and an honor guard, led by Mickey Mantle and Joe Collins. It was a Yankees tradition. Elston Howard belonged. Unlike the rosters of most major league teams, the New York Yankees were a supremely confident bunch. Howard represented not a threat, but one more weapon to extend their string of championships. A long line of player oral histories relates just one poor racial episode in Howard's first years. Whitey Ford took care of that one. If anything, installing Howard on the Yankees was more an education for the team than their first black player. Gil McDougald and his wife adopted mixed-race children.[78]

Stengel understood the player he had, stood by him as Howard waited patiently for the opportunity that seemingly would never come. Yogi Berra was made of iron. Howard did not begin to catch significantly until 1958, even if Stengel maintained, "He's got one of the greatest arms I ever saw, and he's gonna be a great catcher." Howard caught more games than Berra beginning in 1960, Stengel's last season as the Yankees manager.[79]

The success with Elston Howard aside, the Yankees were less than rich when it came to black players. The farm system was largely empty, and most major league teams were no longer trading with George Weiss; he was too smart, too successful. That left the conduit to the Kansas City Athletics as just about their only outside source for major league players. For whatever reason, the Athletics became especially anxious to move their black players. The Yankees found two roommates for Elston Howard.

The first was Harry Simpson. Suitcase Harry found a measure of contentment in Kansas City, at last finding the stroke that made him such a promising prospect back in the Cleveland days. He was hitting .296 for Kansas City when the Yankees traded to get him. The thought was that his left-handed power would be perfect for the short fence in Yankee Stadium's right field. But there were too many factors working against him. Stengel, very unhappy that George Weiss traded Billy Martin to acquire Simpson, used him grudgingly. Playing left field and first base, Simpson appeared in 75 games, but hit just seven home runs. Turned out Simpson was not a pull hitter, could not take advantage of the short track down the line. Hitting the ball over the right-center fence required Babe Ruth's approach. Simpson did not have that kind of power. And Simpson was in many ways a sensitive soul, not responsive to pressure. Pressure was what the Yankees were all about. Stengel worked with him as much as he could (Simpson led off in the first World Series game ever played in Milwaukee), but it was no go. Harry Simpson found himself traded back to Kansas City in 1958, and then on to Chicago.

The revolving door brought Panamanian Hector Lopez to New York in 1959, the Yankees' first black Latino player. Lopez was much the same for Stengel as he had been for manager

Harry Craft in Kansas City, a solid right-handed hitter with some power, and a liability in the field wherever you put him. Third base, second base, left field; it made no difference. He was a threat to lead the league in errors wherever he was positioned. But the Yankees stuck with him. Lopez became a critical role player for a team that won five straight pennants between 1960 and 1964.[80]

That was it. Between 1956 and 1960, the New York Yankees put just three black players in uniform. The early 1960s saw little more commitment. New York City papers such as *The Daily News* went tabloid insane when the Yankees actually promoted Al Downing, their first black pitcher, for a very brief stay in 1961. Black Yankees remained a rarity, right through to the end of the dynasty in 1965.

Certainly the Yankees chose their own path when it came to integration, slow, stubborn, and thorough. They were at least honest when they claimed they wanted players who could genuinely help the team, rather than break the color line for token political reasons. The team placed just three black players on the roster during the 1950s, but Stengel did play them; each man was an important cog on his ball clubs, used regularly. The Yankees also acknowledged that their responsibility extended beyond the simple act of putting a black man on the club. They fought to provide Elston Howard equal treatment on the road, though spring training remained a grim challenge. Unlike most of the American League teams, where the integration process was a revolving door and a sham, the Yankees found a very few players they wanted and played them. But they did take their time doing it.

In the space of just 20 months between September 1953, and April 1955, three additional American League teams placed black players on the field, while a fourth continued sporadic explorations. None of these commitments was entirely satisfactory from an equal rights perspective. In the midst of disastrous collapse, the Philadelphia Athletics gave integration something of an honest try before surrendering to the consequences of extreme mismanagement. Moving to Kansas City, the team seemed determined to continue the experiment, only to back away completely by 1960. Clark Griffith's Washington franchise was worse, holding out false hopes, dawdling interminably before making a mockery of integration with the Cuban players. The Browns became the Orioles, hoping very much to shape an entirely new identity and leave their sordid past behind. One aspect that persisted was the team's ambivalence toward black players. Several came and went; just two stuck for any length of time. In the end, the Orioles too backed away.

Philadelphia/Kansas City, Washington/Minnesota, St. Louis/Baltimore. These were the three weak teams in the pyramid of the American League, competitively and financially—the three teams forced to leave for more hopeful climes. Their efforts to integrate were in large part cynical—small steps taken to stave off ruin. Given the managerial ineptitude of all three clubs, it is not difficult to understand why the efforts to add black players came to so little. These were three franchises hanging by their fingernails—they could not do much of anything right.

The fourth team was very much at the opposite end of the pyramid. The very top, in fact. The New York Yankees did not go about integration in any way ineptly; they were careful, desiring a player who would fit well on a powerhouse team. But they were arrogant. Yankees management failed to comprehend the larger issues at stake or recognize that their maneuvers would be emblematic of baseball's integration as a whole. Or worse, perhaps they did understand their position entirely too well; several key figures in Yankees management proved themselves ill-disposed to equal rights. Their reluctance mirrored the stubborn reluctance of America as a nation.

But it was no accident that all this movement in team integration came when it did. Two or three American League teams adding black players by 1951, that was one thing. A handful of blacks among the two hundred players in the American League was not really much pressure. But when the newspapers began to report a steadily increasing drumbeat of court decisions, bus boycotts, and house bombings, the issues surrounding integration amplified. The question was no longer simply who could play in the major leagues. That was settled. By 1955, the issue was which America baseball would reflect—the Jim Crow segregation of the past, or the era of equal rights dimly beckoning. Much more than baseball hinged on the outcome.

# VII

## Ungracious Surrender

### *The Ongoing Resistance of the Final Two*

---

By 1958, the struggle for civil rights in America was gathering inexorable strength and momentum. The bus boycott in Montgomery, Alabama—the one that got Martin Luther King's house fire-bombed—achieved its goals. Buses were desegregated. Boycotts spread to other Southern cities. School integration began to take shape in several Southern states, punctuated by cruel incidents in Kentucky and Tennessee. President Eisenhower reluctantly decided to send Federal troops to Arkansas to enforce the integration of public schools in Little Rock. Congress passed the Civil Rights Act of 1957, establishing a Civil Rights Commission and creating a new civil rights division in the Department of Justice. The City of New York outlawed discrimination in housing. Civil rights leaders organized the Southern Christian Leadership Conference, with Martin L. King as first president.

Althea Gibson in 1957 became the first black woman to win at Wimbledon. Two months later, she added the U.S. tennis championship at Forest Hills, New York.[1]

Yet there were still two American League baseball teams refusing to integrate. The last two in all of major league baseball.

Refusal is the correct word. Despite the fact that the other 14 teams managed to reach conscientious decisions over an eight-year period, despite the plain fact that several teams had demonstrably improved their play by adding black players, the front offices in Detroit and Boston, the two northernmost American League cities, refused to budge. The Tigers and the Red Sox did not merely fail to place a black player on the field; they did almost nothing in the way of laying groundwork. No amateur free agent signings, no real scouting of what was left of the Negro Leagues. When these two teams did capitulate, their efforts were breathtakingly minimal, as if they wished to underscore their unwillingness. Certainly they were not trying to make their teams more competitive, nor satisfy their fans, black or white. The closing of the first phase of baseball's integration can only be treated as one more ugly episode.

The intransigence of the Detroit franchise was very much a reflection of the city's strained and difficult history of race relations. In 1910, as the American League closed its first decade and the automobile industry waxed, Detroit was the nation's ninth largest city, at not quite a half million people. Just 1.2 percent of these people were black. Henry Ford, the city's prime mover, encouraged a black migration to Michigan, promising steady work at good wages. Ford kept his promise—not because he harbored any warm feelings for the newly-arrived blacks, but because he could pay them less. The new black workers also posed a difficult problem for the one group of people Ford truly did despise: union organizers. By 1940, Detroit's population had tripled and was now 9.2 percent black. The black population was largely confined to an area east of downtown, known as Paradise Valley—or Black Bottom.[2]

World War II brought critical importance to Detroit's heavy industrial capacity, and Ford put out the call for more workers. Fifty thousand black and 300,000 white people descended on the city, mostly from the rural South. Here was a recipe for trouble in a city already burdened by a strong and growing chapter of the Ku Klux Klan. Incidents multiplied as white refused to work with black on several factory floors, while a lack of adequate housing created mounting pressures. Paradise Valley was grown too crowded and substandard; white Detroit was determined to confine blacks to those neighborhoods. A brawl between black and white youths at a public park ignited a conflagration in June 1943. The usual atrocity rumors aggravated the tension, and mobs spun out of control, attacking property, looting businesses, starting fires, and beating pedestrians. Detroit's police did their predictable part, arresting blacks at every chance while ignoring white violence. The rioting ended after three days when Federal troops intervened. Thirty-four people were dead, 25 of them black, killed mostly by police. The city, state, and national governments did everything they could to hush up the violence—not at all a good thing in war time. But people remembered.[3]

The end of the war saw an escalation of racial division, even as tensions seemed to ease. The housing covenants that had confined blacks to Paradise Valley were outlawed. The United Auto Workers fought hard for equal pay and equal rights in the factories. A substantial black middle class soon emerged, rivaling the wealth and influence of the black community in the District of Columbia. Standards of living plainly improved, but the police remained hostile and the white population began to melt away. White flight to the suburbs, a growing concern in several northern cities, was especially pronounced in Detroit. Between 1950 and 1960, the metropolis lost almost 200,000 people to surrounding areas, though remaining the fifth largest city in the country. The black population grew from 16.2 percent to 28.9. Even as income improved and expectations rose, blacks were made to understand they remained second-class citizens in Detroit. Baseball was simply one more expression of the separation.[4]

Baseball was very popular in Detroit, had been since the 19th century. Blacks and whites played the game at various amateur levels, sometimes on the same fields. Wendell Smith saw his chance of a major league career vanish in Detroit; professional baseball was Jim Crow there as much as anywhere. Various Negro Leagues teams came and went in the city, including the Stars of the 1920s, owned by none other than Rube Foster. Black teams played at their own field, Mack Park, seldom appearing on the diamond established for Detroit's Tigers.[5]

The Tigers, one of the eight original teams in the American League, proved a consistently successful franchise, profitable and competitive. Probably that success dampened any potential interest in integration once the question took serious shape. Leaving aside the social justice issue—which inspired very little sympathy among Detroit's powerful—the motivations for change on most clubs were profit and competitive performance. The Tigers felt pressured in neither sense. The franchise maintained a strong and steady profit margin, and was often near the top of the standings (though with just two championships to their credit). The team finished a close second as late as 1950.[6]

Certainly the social fabric of Detroit was no great encouragement to integration. Henry

Ford taught people how to hate coldly and effectively with his vicious anti–Semitic campaign of the 1920s. Memories of the race riot of 1943 lingered, while the run-down, growing ghettoes remained a living reminder of the latent hostility between black and white. One third of the city's blacks lived below the poverty line. The Tigers themselves lived with the legacy of Ty Cobb, perhaps the greatest player in modern baseball history, certainly one of the more determined haters. Cobb's refusal to play against blacks was well known, though tales of his near-psychotic violence would not emerge until after his death.[7]

Balancing the memories of Cobb's hatreds in a small degree was the more recent example of Hank Greenberg, twice an MVP for Detroit, the nation's first Jewish star. Greenberg faced down overwhelming prejudice with courage and grace, a telling counterpoint to Cobb. But it was not nearly enough.[8]

The heart of the problem was the Tigers managerial organization—meaning, from 1919 past 1952, Walter Owen Briggs. Briggs was a self-made man. The son of a skilled railroad worker, Briggs worked at several jobs in the railroad industry and elsewhere before joining the B. F. Everitt Company in 1904, at age 23. Everitt had managed to get in on the ground floor of the burgeoning automobile business, finishing carriage interiors. With his widespread experience and undeniable organizational ability, Briggs was soon in charge of the shops, while Everitt sought to expand and build his own autos. Everitt sold out to Briggs in 1910. Briggs Manufacturing immediately landed a huge contract with Henry Ford, agreeing to supply the interiors for 10,000 Model T's. Innovation and expansion followed rapidly, and in 1924, as the 1920s roared loudest, Walter Briggs took his company public. Very soon he was a millionaire, with contracts to supply not only Ford, but Chrysler, Packard, and Hudson.[9]

Briggs was generous with his newfound well of money, sponsoring programs at Wayne State University, the local symphony, and the Detroit Zoo. He also loved baseball, and welcomed the opportunity to become the moneyed partner in ownership of the Tigers.

Since 1909, the Detroit Tigers had been the property of Frank Navin, who began his career as the team's bookkeeper. Buying out co-owner William Yawkey (oddly enough, the uncle of eventual Red Sox owner Tom Yawkey), Navin ran the club alone for ten precarious years, relying on team profits as his sole source of income. Struggling to remain competitive despite the presence of Cobb, Navin sought out a partner with real money, landing Walter Briggs in 1919. Despite owning half the club, Briggs remained in the background, giving Navin room to make all the baseball decisions. Briggs's most important contribution was to lend the team $100,000 in 1934, with the expressed condition the money be used to purchase the contract of Mickey Cochrane from the Philadelphia Athletics. Serving as player-manager, Cochrane led the team to a pennant in 1934, and Detroit's first world championship the next season. A champion at last, Frank Navin died almost immediately after, suffering a heart attack following a fall from a horse. Walter Briggs bought out Navin's heirs, making himself sole owner of his beloved Tigers.[10]

Briggs's first move as owner was to remake the Detroit ballpark. Double-decking the entire park, roofing all but the deepest center field bleachers, he spent $1 million to shape the space into an enormous bowl, very much a quirky hitters' park, with a seating capacity of around 56,000. No longer a mere field, the facility acquired a new name: Briggs Stadium.[11]

Among the policies Briggs enforced at his new stadium was a rule barring black patrons from the box seats. Perhaps because of Briggs's reputation, the Tigers were not overly popular with Detroit's black community anyway. There was no overt Jim Crow seating, but the few black fans attending tended to congregate in the right field bleachers. Briggs occasionally rented out the stadium for important Negro Leagues games, using isolated incidents of violence in the stands as an excuse to bar more. Too much damage, so he said. Briggs placed armed guards at the concession stands during Negro Leagues contests.[12]

Certainly Walter Briggs felt no compunction in obeying the unwritten rule against black players in major league baseball in place before World War II. He preferred arrangements that way. As the integration issue grew after 1946, an expression supposedly heard often in the front office was "no jiggs with Briggs." The Tigers were the last major league team to sign a black player to a minor league contract—and that was after Walter Briggs was safely dead.[13]

Attempting to defend Briggs against charges of racism, a few sources point to the fact that he employed black workers in his factories. A dubious proposition. The auto body plant where blacks labored was known as the "Briggs Slaughterhouse,"

**Walter Owen Briggs. The owner of the Detroit Tigers proudly displayed a picture of Kenesaw Mountain Landis on the wall of his office, years after the commissioner's death. (National Baseball Hall of Fame Library, Cooperstown, N.Y.)**

one of the most dangerous workplaces in Detroit. The place actually blew up in April 1927, burning for two days. Twenty-one workers died. Ironically, 13 members of the Detroit Stars had left jobs at the factory the day before, headed for spring training in Louisiana.[14]

By the 1950s, "the Briggs name was synonymous with racism" among Detroit's black citizens. Certainly he never took the least step to discourage the image. Detroit was a racially charged community; the city's white newspapers brought little pressure to bear, portraying Cleveland's signing of Larry Doby as either a carnival gimmick or some kind of red radical plot. Connie Mack and Clark Griffith would have agreed whole-heartedly. Initially, not even the *Michigan Chronicle*, the city's black newspaper, took much of a stand. The black community felt little stake in the Tigers.[15]

Perhaps the saddest aspect of the whole sordid business was the fact that Walter Briggs was a victim of polio, contracted in Florida in 1940. Confined to a wheelchair, his condition gradually worsened until he became a paraplegic, completely dependent on others.[16] The bitter luck never softened him, at least on the issue of race and humanity. If anything, Walter Briggs hardened his stance as death approached. In the 1930s, his attitude made him one of the crowd; by 1952 that same position was growing increasingly wrong.

Briggs got his fancy new stadium built in time to witness one of Detroit's more successful eras—the team won championships in 1935 and 1945 and contended with varying degrees of success through 1951. Briggs loved his players, protected them, paid them well. If anything, he treated them too well. By the early 1950s, the remnants of the 1945 championship were complacent and very old. Walter Briggs died in January 1952. The next season, the Tigers lost 104 games, finishing last.

Confusion ensued. In the short term, Walter Briggs Junior, better known to all as Spike, became owner. Tigers great Charlie Gehringer was named general manager, enduring a difficult time as Spike tried to reshape the team to his image. Regrettably, Spike was overly fond of alcohol (he was a well-known reveler at some of Black Bottom's faster nightclubs), and this did not aid his judgment. Gehringer did his best to keep the younger Briggs away from Bill Veeck once Spike got to drinking at winter meetings. But Gehringer turned out to be no shrewd judge of talent himself. Panicked by their descent into the basement—the first in the team's history—the Tigers embarked on a series of disastrous trades that left them floundering for a decade.[17]

If ever there was an opportunity to address the integration question logically and cleanly, this was it. The Tigers desperately needed young men who could play; quality players were still coming out of the Negro Leagues. Spike Briggs did depart from his father's blanket racism enough to sign a few black players at the minor league level, beginning in 1953. Just two of his signings ever reached the majors, neither in a great hurry. Jim Proctor, a pitcher, could have been the first black Tiger, but he received his draft notice in 1957. He managed to escape that, only to suffer a sore arm. Proctor joined the Tigers in 1959 for a major league career consisting of two appearances. The other signee, Bubba Morton, was a reserve outfielder who did get the chance to make some noise, though not before 1961. Spike also hired four blacks for the grounds crew. While undertaking this very minimal effort, the younger Briggs spent a quarter of a million dollars signing bonus babies. Al Kaline worked out pretty well; the rest was money poorly spent.[18]

Spike Briggs was able to call the team his own for four seasons. The provisions of his father's will made his siblings equal beneficiaries in a trust that included the ball club, and in 1956 a judge ruled the franchise was not a sufficiently stable investment to guarantee an income for the other heirs. Forced to divest, Spike tried to form an investment group to purchase the team himself, but drinking buddy Henry Ford II dropped out on him. A bidding war ensued, with a group of 11 investors headed by local media magnates Fred Knorr and John Fetzer beating out Bill Veeck. Spike Briggs was supposed to remain as general manager, but he was gone by 1957. Just as well. The team had gone through four managers and a virtually complete player turnover since 1952, getting no farther than the middle of the pack. A proud team was in turmoil, unstable from the top down to the end of the bench. New ownership continued along the same path, jockeying for position among themselves, extending the management turnover. The horrible accidental death of Fred Knorr left Fetzer in charge in 1961, ushering in a very long period of self-satisfied, conservative complacency.[19]

When Walter Briggs Senior died in 1952, his defiance of integration was still typical of American League ownership. Black players took the field at Briggs Stadium only when the Indians, the White Sox, or the Browns came to town. Detroit's black community, disgusted with Briggs, showed little interest. By the time Spike quit the office four years later, conditions had changed fundamentally. Every American League opponent except the Red Sox fielded black players, and community contempt was transformed into increasingly forceful demands for action.

In the spring of 1958, the Briggs Stadium Boycott Committee, a pressure group "headed by the Rev. George Hill, Jr., dean of United Theological Seminary in Detroit," announced plans to sponsor an attendance boycott should the Tigers fail to add a black player. Needless to say, Tigers management condemned the effort, attacking the committee's "immature leadership and potentially dangerous program." The protest group did have its problems, eventually dividing into two organizations squabbling over tactics. But the message was clear. Civil rights was now an imperative national issue; an organization as public as a baseball team could not expect immunity from severe criticism and economic threat. Tigers officialdom sounded two familiar refrains, suggesting that the pressure groups were led by dangerously subversive radicals and promising the Tigers to "have a Negro player if we can find a good one." A page borrowed from Clark Griffith or George Weiss.[20]

Seventeen black players toiled in Detroit's minor league organization at the end of 1957. Not one of them was deemed suitable to join the parent club the next season. Boycotts planned for early May and early June did not materialize, but the pressure mounted. Jim Campbell, the club's executive vice president and eventual general manager, recalled, "They were after my ass to bring up a black man but there was no one available that we liked."[21]

The end was anti-climactic in every sense. In a city wrought with racial tensions, faced with a large and increasingly angry black community, the Tigers chose to integrate with a light-skinned, 25-year-old Dominican who played a solid utility infield and insisted he was not black. Certainly Ozzie Virgil was not an American black, which was very much the point to the people who cared in Detroit.

The Tigers had acquired Ozzie Virgil in a trade with the New York Giants the previous winter. Born in the Dominican Republic, Virgil moved to the Bronx with his parents at age 13—he did go to high school in the United States. He also served in the United States Marines during the Korean War, signing with the Giants after his discharge. He made his major league debut with New York in 1956, becoming the first of a great many Dominicans to play in the major leagues. Virgil appeared in 96 games for the Giants in 1957, hitting just .235 in 226 at-bats. His value was his versatility—Virgil could catch, play any infield position, and patrol the outfield. The Tigers naturally sent their seasoned acquisition to Charleston to begin 1958.[22]

A threatened picket of Briggs Stadium set for May 31 did not come off, but Tigers management heard the voices. Six days later, Ozzie Virgil stood in the Tigers dugout, reportedly telling anyone who would listen, "I'm not Negro; I'm Dominican; I'm Spanish." It was not an unusual position to take. Roberto Clemente, Puerto Rican-born and very limited in his English, told teammates, "I no black." Years later, Frank Robinson described Virgil as a man "regarded as black in this country, though not in [his] native land." One more retelling of the Orestes Minoso–Harry Simpson dispute. Much of Detroit's black community was prepared to agree that Ozzie Virgil was not black, at least not in the sense that mattered, even if he did live as a black man. What the charged situation in Detroit demanded was an American black. The Tigers were not disposed to go that far.[23]

The announcement of Virgil's arrival came from a visitor's dugout—the team was in Washington, playing the fourth game of a two-week road trip. Tigers management could not bring themselves to introduce the man they considered their first black player at a home game. They did at least wait until after a three-game series in Jim Crow Baltimore to introduce him. Virgil played third base—the Tigers were desperate at the hot corner—demonstrating solid

**Ozzie Virgil. After acquiring him from the New York Giants, the Detroit Tigers introduced Virgil as their first black player in 1958. Detroit's black community remained skeptical. Virgil, born in the Dominican Republic, graduated from a New York City high school. (National Baseball Hall of Fame Library, Cooperstown, N.Y.)**

defense and managing one hit in five tries, batting sixth. Before the game, Jack Tighe, Tigers manager of the moment, told Virgil, "We brought you up here to play ball. All this extra attention is a compliment to you. Don't let it bother you." The attention was considerable. The Tigers dared not leave their first black player rusting on the bench. By the third game in Washington, Tighe had Virgil batting second.[24]

The honeymoon lasted until late July. Batting second in his first home game on June 17, Virgil went 5-for-5—a great day, a day that raised expectations far too much. By mid-month, he was dropped back to sixth in the order, and then lower. By the end of June, Billy Martin was playing third, spelled by Reno Bertoia. They were not hitting much either, but the Tigers had come to recognize a hard fact—Ozzie Virgil was not an everyday player. Played exclusively at third, he fielded well, but hit just .244. After July, Ozzie Virgil never started another game. The Tigers sent him back to the minors for 1959.

Virgil spent 1960 and a portion of 1961 as a utility player for Detroit. Traded to Kansas City, he would play for three more teams before coming to the end in 1966. His status as a pioneering black player is in some ways mirrors the career of another light-skinned Latino player—Cuban-born Roberto Estalella. The difference was their situations. Clark Griffith, trying to do his darnedest under the watchful eye of Judge Landis, insisted in 1935 his man was white, playing him despite widespread suspicions to the contrary. Twenty-three years later, the Tigers, desperately needing a black player, settled on a similarly light-skinned Latino, this time insisting he fit the necessities of a much-altered social situation. Color was not so much complexion as context and definition. Take so much as a single step down the road to classifying people by color, the result very quickly becomes confusing, contrary, and hurtful. Like Minnie Minoso, Vic Power, Carlos Paula, and so many others, Ozzie Virgil was a Latino caught up in an American racial struggle. In Detroit in 1958, the real issue was not simply skin color, but whether American blacks were ever going to play with the Tigers.[25]

Employing Ozzie Virgil to break the color line in some ways placed the Tigers organization in a more awkward situation. Having bowed to community pressure, they could not very easily claim integration a success while fielding an all-white team again in 1959. But Tigers management remained woefully unprepared to enter a world where black players were recruited, trained, and brought to the majors on the same footing with white prospects. Their loudest mistake of 1959 was allowing shortstop Maury Wills to slip through their grasp. After purchasing Wills from Spokane and including him on the winter roster, the Tigers decided at the end of spring training to let him go. Wills caught on with the Dodgers that same season. Three years later, he was the MVP of the National League.[26]

Detroit's second mistake was almost as egregious. In the middle of spring training, the club traded Tito Francona, one of their most promising young players, to Cleveland for none other than Larry Doby. "I am definitely looking forward to playing in Detroit," Doby enthused. "I wish I could have gotten this break a few years ago. I consider this move to Detroit as the second biggest break of my entire career." Briggs Stadium was very much a hitters' park, a prospect Doby found heartening. That is what he told the *Michigan Chronicle*, anyway. He probably came closer to the truth when he told Willie Horton many years later that he was ready to retire in 1959, but requested the trade to Detroit as one last laugh at Walter Briggs. The previous two seasons had been tough for the 34-year-old outfielder, his RBI and home run totals falling considerably. He was also beginning to move from team to team quite a bit, which should have been a warning to the Tigers brass. Larry Doby was no longer the All-Star of the early Cleveland days.[27]

The experiment in Detroit lasted just 18 games. Aged beyond his years by far too much undeserved abuse, Doby was slow and unsure in the field. In his first games with the Tigers, played in near-freezing conditions, the man could not buy a hit, and a grim fielding error let in three runs and cost the Tigers a game. The fans booed that. Doby found himself competing against younger and stronger hitters, Harvey Kuenn (who would win the batting title) and Charley Maxwell, for playing time. After Doby hit just .218 with four RBI in 64 at-bats, the Tigers mercifully sold him to the White Sox on May 13. He may have had a laugh at the memory of Walter Briggs; whether he did anything to further the cause of integration in Detroit is another question. Injuries caught up with him in Chicago; he played in just 21 games for a pennant-winning club. The end had come: 1959—the year the last major league team integrated—was the last for the American League's pioneer black player.[28]

Twelve years down the line, the situation for black players was certainly better than the conditions Larry Doby faced in 1947, but still matters were not entirely settled. The Tigers fielded another marginal Latino infielder in a continued lip service to integration. Cuban Ossie Alvarez played in just eight games, coming to bat twice and managing a hit. Then he was gone, too. The next year, Cuban shortstop Chico Fernandez joined the team from Philadelphia, becoming the first black player to win a regular starting position in the Tigers lineup. Ozzie Virgil rejoined the team that same season, playing four positions and batting .227. The Tigers would add a third black player in May 1960, trading for Cuban outfielder Sandy Amoros, remembered for one moment of World Series glory with the Dodgers. Amoros played in 65 games in 1960, coming to bat 67 times and hitting .149. Detroit was trying, in a manner too reminiscent of the Griffiths—Clark and Calvin. Black people in Detroit still hold that the Tigers did not really integrate until the 1960s, when Billy Bruton, Jake Wood, Gates Brown, and Willie Horton established themselves. "Racism pervaded that organization," Gates Brown recalled. "They'd tell you jokes with the N-word in them while they were instructing you. You never opened your mouth." Billy Bruton, acquired in a trade with the Milwaukee Braves, would be the one to force the Tigers to address the hard-line discrimination at their Lakeland, Florida, training site. "I went through this early in my career with the Braves," Bruton warned, "and I am not going to do it again."[29]

Integration remained a shaky proposition in Baltimore and Kansas City as well. On top of that, there was the horror story of the Boston Red Sox.

The saga of the Red Sox in the 20th century—their rise to glory in the first two decades of the American League, followed by their hubristic fall, their desperate seeking, their self-inflicted mistakes, their so-near misses—could be portrayed as the stuff of legend. And it has, of course. Two supreme moments shape the mythology: the sale of Babe Ruth to the Yankees, and the phantom tryout of Jackie Robinson. Weaving these moments into the stuff of tragedy, the history of the Red Sox can assume the qualities of doom. Larger than life stuff. And this is silly. The Red Sox were what they were because they were poorly led, blind, stubborn, and divided. The ongoing mess was entirely self-inflicted, the profound antipathy to integration an integral part of the picture.[30]

Leaving aside Babe Ruth and his curse, what remains is the performance of the Sox between 1933, the year Tom Yawkey purchased the franchise, and 1959, the year a black man finally joined the club. The problems plainly persisted long after this period, but the point is to analyze the Red Sox's approach to integration. Or, more honestly, their lack of approach.

Begin at the top, with Tom Yawkey, the man who owned the franchise for 43 years until his death in 1976. Yawkey was a multi-millionaire who got his money the old-fashioned way—by inheritance. The nephew of William Yawkey, half-owner of the Detroit Tigers early in the century, Tom was adopted by his uncle, becoming heir to a vast fortune rooted in the timber business. Not very interested in business and in no way prepared for the entrepreneurial life, Tom Yawkey bought the Red Sox at the age of 30, aiming to emulate or exceed his uncle's success on the diamond. (The Tigers won three pennants in William Yawkey's time, but no World Series.) Money and enthusiasm posed no problems for the young man; know-how was harder to come by. Over the next four decades, Yawkey would employ varying strategies to bring a winner to Fenway Park, first acquiring banks of big stars who somehow could not play together, then jettisoning that bunch in favor of building through the farm system. Always he was too impatient, moving on to the next strategy before giving the previous idea proper time to work. Like Walter Briggs, Tom Yawkey treated his minions well, pampering the players, overpaying them by the standards of the day.[31]

The jury remains out on the question of Tom Yawkey and racism. Historians of the Red Sox are able to cobble together long lists of quotations and incidents supporting either side of the question. Certainly there was an element of racism in his upbringing; after all, he came of age in Detroit just after World War I. In his youth, he went on hunting expeditions in South

**Eddie Collins (left) and Tom Yawkey. The brain trust of the Boston Red Sox passed on Jackie Robinson after a sham tryout in the spring of 1945. (National Baseball Hall of Fame Library, Cooperstown, N.Y.)**

Carolina with his uncle's good friend, Ty Cobb—probably not a constructive influence on the young man's racial perceptions. Yawkey also inherited an honest-to-God plantation in South Carolina from his uncle, 31 square miles of forest and marshland, operated by more than 100 laborers, mostly black. The new owner eventually had a ball field built, well away from the big house, for his "colored boys" (as his chief mechanic referred to them).

In his first ten years of ownership, Yawkey's position on the matter could hardly have mattered. He was one of the boys in the closed shop of the American League. Tom Yawkey felt the pressure to integrate even less than his fellows. In 1940, just 3.1 percent of Boston's population was black. The city never hosted a Negro Leagues team. The black community in Boston would grow, but 20 years later, it remained the smallest of all the cities fielding American League franchises. Tom Yawkey was wealthy; there existed no market reason to change his ways. His approach to integration would be governed by attitudes, not economics. Even in the late 1950s, there was not a black person to be found anywhere at Fenway Park, from the playing field through the front office down through the maintenance crews.[32]

Tom Yawkey has to be considered by the actions of the team he owned, and the company he kept. Begin with Eddie Collins. Hall of Fame great with the Athletics and the White Sox, Collins became General Manager of the Red Sox when Yawkey bought the club, moving over from the Athletics' front office. There he remained, implementing Tom Yawkey's strategies and whims, until illness slowed him in 1947.[33]

In January 1943, Collins sent a note to William Harridge, president of the American League. "Here is another from our friend again," Eddie Collins wrote. "The Judge [Landis] called me about this writer the other day, so I take it you must have shown him one of the clippings I sent you. Maybe you will 'enjoy' reading this one." Enclosed was a column from the *Boston Record* dated January 26, 1943, written by Dave Egan.[34]

If Dave Egan ("the Colonel") is at all remembered now, it is for his vicious attacks on two of baseball's most beloved figures, Ted Williams and Casey Stengel. But Egan was a far more complex individual than that, a Yale graduate with a law degree, a prodigious drinker with a social conscience. The column drawing Collins's ire was a plea to resolve the wartime manpower shortage on Boston's two ball clubs by hiring "colored ballplayers." Egan pulled no punches. "Nothing except dark and ancient prejudices will keep them from giving the black man an opportunity with the white." The column included a photograph of Eddie Collins.[35]

Then there was Joe Cronin, Clark Griffith's son-in-law. Collins hired Cronin to play shortstop and serve as player-manager for the Red Sox in 1934. Cronin hung on as manager through 1947, though he stopped embarrassing himself and his team in the infield after 1941. Cronin managed the Sox to a pennant in 1946, a few second-place finishes, and a great deal of mediocrity, deploying the teams Collins was forced to provide him. Tom Yawkey was a very loyal man.[36]

Here then, was the cast for the debacle that took place in the spring of 1945, a year the Red Sox finished seventh. Dave Egan was about the only Boston journalist to take note of the tryout of the three Negro Leagues players arranged by Sam Lacy. Egan, in his usual abrasive fashion, took on Eddie Collins directly. He said on April 16, 1945, "Here are two believe-it-or-not items, exclusively for the personal enlightenment of Mr. Edward Trowbridge Collins, general manager of the Boston Red Sox. He is living in anno domini 1945, and not in the dust-covered year 1865. He is residing in the city of Boston, Massachusetts, and not in the city of Mobile, Alabama."[37]

Collins hid consistently behind the position that no black player ever applied to try out with the team. Now there were three black prospects, one of them Jackie Robinson. The Red Sox had no choice; City Councilor Isadore Muchnick possessed the power to shut down Sunday baseball in Boston if the Sox failed to carry through with the trial. (Muchnick was naturally accused of playing politics, which is true if you define politics as the exercise of responsibility to represent the desires of a significant constituency.) So the charade went ahead. After being stalled a couple of days, Robinson, Sam Jethroe, and Marvin Williams took the field at Fenway for about an hour and a half. There are so many conflicting stories of what transpired, the truth is anyone's guess. Cronin supposedly kept his back turned much of the time, though he observed that Robinson was "good and fast." Many years later, a Boston sportswriter claimed he heard someone cry out, "Get those niggers off the field!" as the session ended. Some claimed that Collins yelled, or Yawkey himself. Others say the incident never happened.

What is indisputable is that some Red Sox official thanked the players for their time, saying the team would be in contact. No contact ever came. Newspapers in Boston made virtually no mention of the tryout. Sam Jethroe knew straight away he was not going to be offered any contract. A decision was made, a tone set. One sportswriter maintained, "Yawkey wanted no part of it. He didn't want to be the one to break the color line." Six months later, Robinson signed his contract with Branch Rickey. The Red Sox were at the wrong end of a legend in the making. They did their best to stay there.[38]

The Red Sox won a pennant in 1946—the first for Tom Yawkey. They stumbled to third in 1947, Joe Cronin's last season as manager. Cronin moved upstairs to the General Manager's office when Eddie Collins unexpectedly sickened. With Joe McCarthy as the new field manager, the Sox came so close the next two years, losing a one-game playoff to Cleveland in 1948, and losing out to the Yankees on the last game of the 1949 season. Then came two lackluster seasons, followed by implosion under newly hired manager Lou Boudreau.

Yawkey and Cronin panicked, making a series of ill-advised trades as the club settled into mediocrity. Ted Williams, the only genuine impact player on the team, spent most of two years flying fighter jets in Korea while the Red Sox reconfigured their roster. Williams, 35 years old in his first full season back, hit unbelievably for the next five years and spent much of his time frustrated. After the near misses of the 1940s, the Red Sox settled into a lackadaisical pattern, never challenging the Yankees nor even the Indians or the White Sox, apparently satisfied in their pedestrian ways. The one obvious maneuver they might have taken to improve—seriously scouting the black players available—never came close to occurring. Lou Boudreau, a manager who knew as much as anyone about the experience of meshing black and white to create a competitive team, was fired in 1954 after winning just 69 games.[39]

The man who replaced Boudreau was a much better fit to the Yawkey pattern. Pinky Higgins, who played 14 seasons for the Tigers, Athletics, and Red Sox, was a racist front and center. "There will never be any niggers on this team as long as I have anything to say about it," he informed a Boston reporter. How right he was, for his first tour of duty, at least.[40]

The Red Sox were drawn into the early search for black players very nearly without their knowledge, failing to take advantage of an exclusive window into the faltering Negro Leagues. In 1948, the Sox changed their affiliation in the Southern Association, a double-A league, dropping the New Orleans Pelicans in favor of the Birmingham Barons. As part of this agreement, the Barons maintained communication with the Birmingham Black Barons of the Negro American League. Piper Davis, player-manager of the Black Barons, acted as a scout for their white counterpart. Sure enough, in 1949, Davis passed the word that a teenage kid named

Mays looked awfully good. The stories vary at this point—one more legend of opportunity arrogantly neglected. One scout or another supposedly made the trip from Boston to Birmingham, but never took the trouble to evaluate the young man. Couldn't hurt a curve ball, according to one version of the story. No need for him at this time, maintained another. Somehow, the New York Giants found room for Willie Mays.

In 1950, the cross-town rival Boston Braves traded for their first black player, Sam Jethroe—one of the three Negro Leagues representatives who participated in the sham tryout with the Red Sox back in 1945. Jethroe proved his worth, becoming the National League "Rookie of the Year." Perhaps Red Sox management heard faint footsteps, as they now made their first limp effort to find a black player of their own. They signed Piper Davis. Having passed on Mays, they now signed his 32-year-old manager. Davis was a good player, a sure-handed infielder with speed, but the Sox were not serious. They bought Davis's contract with a 30-day option and returned him to Birmingham when the month was up, even though he was leading his Class A team in hitting and home runs. " I had to pay my own fare back home," Davis recalled. Whatever interest there was evaporated as the Braves' experiment produced mixed results. Sam Jethroe was very fast but fragile, and he did not boost attendance as the Braves had hoped. Jethroe left for Pittsburgh in 1953, and the Braves departed for Milwaukee. Whatever small pressure the Red Sox management may have sensed was gone. Covering their tracks, the Red Sox signed two black players that year, burying each in the low minors. The team maintained no scouting apparatus anywhere in Latin America. No black player would be appearing at Fenway anytime soon.[41]

So the Red Sox settled into self-satisfied mediocrity. With the Braves gone, the team had no market competition; the Sox became a take-it-or-leave-it proposition. They were exciting, sometimes—they could score runs in bunches, but the pitching was overmatched, defense a foreign concept. Tom Yawkey, by this time the top man more than 20 years, had settled into the comfortable role of owner. He had his team; he had his drinking buddies—Joe Cronin and Pinky Higgins among them. Not for nothing was the Red Sox front office known as "the Plantation." Build a team that might win? That was hard, very hard. Over 20 years, Yawkey had tried nearly every strategy known to baseball, and failed at them all, usually through lack of patience. The one obvious path was to pursue black players. That door remained firmly closed and bolted.[42]

In 1953, the approach was still not all that atypical. Just three American League teams included black players, and one of those (the Browns) was nearly moribund. That set of conditions changed radically over the next five years. The civil rights movement caught fire, and three more American League teams bowed to the changes taking place around them, including the New York Yankees. Then came 1958, and two events that placed Boston directly in a harsh, uncompromising light.

The first was the appearance of Ozzie Virgil with the Detroit Tigers. Half-hearted though the effort was, the integration of the Tigers left Boston the last city on the far side of the color line. Tom Yawkey had not wanted to be first; he certainly accomplished that. The second event was the naming of Yawkey's confederate and drinking pal, Joe Cronin, to be the new president of the American League, effective on the first of January 1959. Cronin was a very political man, always careful to appear thoughtful, to say the right things when that vexing question of integration came up. The fact remains that the Sox finally caved seven months after he left the front office.[43]

The new general manager was Bucky Harris, the boy-manager of the Washington Senators back in the 1920s, the veteran of innumerable stops as player, coach, manager, and team official over the next three decades. Harris was Boston's field manager for one season (1934) before Eddie Collins contrived to get rid of him in favor of Cronin; Yawkey was always one to turn to old friends. As matters turned out, Harris was made of braver stuff than Collins or Cronin. He defied the long traditions of the Plantation, engineering the inclusion of the first black player on the Red Sox roster.[44]

There were not a lot of choices available. Just seven black prospects toiled in the Red Sox farm organization in the spring of 1959, two with any immediate chances. One was Earl Wilson, signed as a catcher in 1953, soon converted to pitcher. Wilson had a strong arm and he could wield a bat, too, eventually becoming one of the most feared hitting pitchers in baseball. Two years of military service interrupted his path to the majors; he returned from the Marines for spring training in 1959, not quite ready. Would the Red Sox have integrated sooner had Wilson been available? Not likely, with Yawkey, Cronin, and Pinky Higgins making the decisions.[45]

The second possible prospect held no great promise. His name was Elijah Green, nicknamed "Pumpsie" for no reason the young man cared to explain. In a color-blind world, Pumpsie Green would have been a respectable utility infielder, a .250 hitter with a little speed. Instead, he became one more ill-suited Red Sox legend, the man who broke the color barrier in the last bunker of the major leagues.[46]

Green was signed in 1953, showing enough promise over the next six years to move from franchise to franchise in the minor leagues, but never enough to stir anyone's dreams. Such focus as there was came because of his color, because he was one of the very few blacks playing anywhere in the Red Sox organization. Interest quickened in 1959. As the larger world looked on impatiently, the Red Sox, training in Scottsdale, Arizona, sent Green to separate housing 15 miles away. Scottsdale was Jim Crow. Not the kind of national publicity the Sox desired. Nor was Green's performance. In peak condition after playing winter ball in Panama, Green went wild, hitting .444, impressing as the strongest rookie in camp. At least one sportswriter was certain he had made the team. Could it be?[47]

The answer was no. Pinky Higgins was still the field manager. Pumpsie Green was sent to the Minneapolis Millers for more seasoning—at 28 years old, after six full seasons playing in the Red Sox farm system. That was one straw too many. Herbert Tucker, president of the Boston chapter of the NAACP, expressed himself to be "quite surprised and disappointed." As the 1959 season began, Tucker, along with the Ministerial Alliance and the American Veterans Committee, filed an official complaint with the Massachusetts Commission Against Discrimination, a state agency.[48]

It was awfully hard to understand how things could come to such a pass in Boston, of all places. As Dave Egan noted, "It is especially shocking in this city, where the old cobbles still ring with the inspired words of William Lloyd Garrison and John Greenleaf Whittier and Wendell Phillips; where Faneuil Hall, the Cradle of Liberty, still stands as a monument to the proposition that all men are created equal." Egan wrote those words in 1943. Fifteen years down the line, Boston's Red Sox still had not taken more than the barest step to end segregation. Boston had changed since Garrison's time, becoming a city of sullen divisions, intense hatreds. The baseball team was a reflection of the community, complacent in its discrimination.[49]

The Massachusetts Commission Against Discrimination deliberated for a week over the complaint, taking testimony from Bucky Harris and Red Sox vice-president Richard O'Connell, holding public hearings. A Tufts University student picketed Fenway Park, carrying placards that read "Race Hate is Killing Baseball" and "We Want a Pennant, Not a White Team." (That there was just the single picket may say something about the city's attitude.) In a letter to the Commission, Harris fell back on the usual platitudes, denying bias and contending "when capable players are available they will be used, regardless of race, color, or creed." (The mention of creed was not simply formulaic—harsh divisions between Protestants and Catholics on the Red Sox reached back to Babe Ruth's time.) Dick O'Connell was a little more open in his frustration, expressing his wish that the team already fielded a black player. "If we had, I wouldn't be sitting here this morning." After listening to the hard facts and the twisting evasions, the Commission decided against any drastic measures. The Red Sox organization did have to sign a letter promising "every effort to end segregation." Soon.[50]

The opportunity to remove the last major stumbling block came at mid-season. Ted Williams, suffering from a stiff neck, was in the midst of his poorest campaign, and the rest of the team was measuring up to their usual standard. On July 3, the Sox languished in last

**Elijah Green. The pioneer on the last major league ball club to integrate, Pumpsie Green never felt comfortable during the four years he played with the Red Sox. (National Baseball Hall of Fame Library, Cooperstown, N.Y.)**

place, 11 games under .500. Bucky Harris seized his opportunity, firing Pinky Higgins. (Yawkey gave him a job in the front office.) Eighteen days later, Pumpsie Green joined the Red Sox.[51]

Green had sustained the promise he demonstrated in spring training, opening his season at Minneapolis with a ten-game hitting streak. His average remained high, and he demonstrated his value and versatility by playing well at the different infield positions. Millers manager Gene Mauch was very high on Green, saying, "the kid is just an athlete; that's all there is to it." And the Red Sox needed a shortstop. Given a three-year trial, Boston's regular, Don Buddin, had been christened "Bootin' Buddin" by the Boston press.[52]

Like the Detroit Tigers the season before, the Red Sox chose not to introduce their first black player at home. Pumpsie Green made his major league debut at Chicago's Comiskey Park, pinch-running and filling in at shortstop. There was more than a little irony in the choice. It was in July of 1947, a full 12 years before, that Larry Doby appeared at the same Comiskey Park, becoming the first black player in the American League. A circle had closed at long last.

Like Ozzie Virgil, Elijah Green was

a reluctant pioneer. In a color-blind world, Green would have endured a struggle to succeed. He was very good defensively, and valuable for his versatility, but he was a marginal hitter at the major league level, even if he could switch-hit. A utility role was the logical spot; instead, he had to make good as a starter in the harsh glare of unwanted publicity. "To me, baseball was a tough enough game to play itself," he later said. "I can't think about racial things and try to get a jump on a curveball." Jackie Robinson was concerned Green needed more time in the minors, even as he lashed out at Red Sox management for their continued discrimination.[53]

New manager Billy Jurges decided to retain Don Buddin at shortstop. He started Green at second base in his second game with the team, and was soon trying him as the leadoff hitter. Green made a big impact in his first game at Fenway, lining a triple off the Green Monster. Twenty thousand extra fans showed up that day, many of them black. They had to rope off center field to accommodate the crowd. Green was a regular until August 10, when he broke a bone in his hand trying to tag Mickey Mantle. Out for two weeks, he returned to assume the leadoff spot until the last five days of the season, when he did not start at all.[54]

Pumpsie Green had his supporters. Ted Williams made it a point to warm up with Green before every game, neutralizing any danger of animosity from teammates. No one on the Sox dared cross the Splinter. Green recalled warm memories of other teammates, including All-Stars Jackie Jensen and Frank Malzone. Soon, the Red Sox brought up pitcher Earl Wilson from Minneapolis to provide Green a roommate (and a very tough pitcher the team definitely needed). But it was a lot to ask of a young man who just wanted to play baseball. "Almost every game I played, I felt like I was trying out," he recalled. "I *never* felt comfortable.... When I was playing, being the first black on the Red Sox wasn't nearly as big a source of pride as it would be once I was out of the game." When all was said and done, Pumpsie Green hit just .233 in 172 at-bats, scoring 30 runs and driving in ten. He played three more seasons for the Red Sox, never making enough of an impression to hold down a regular job. Which would have been all right, in more usual circumstances.[55]

Earl Wilson made more of an impression in the majors. Wild in his early seasons with the Sox, he still managed to win more than 56 games over six-plus seasons, pitching for horrendously bad teams in the definition of a hitter's park. As anyone might expect, race issues would eventually end his years in Boston. The Red Sox failed to support him after a nasty incident during spring training in Florida in 1966. Traded to Detroit two months into the season, Wilson led the league with 22 wins the next year. The Sox of the Tom Yawkey era were never a team to sacrifice their social preferences for on-the-field performance.[56]

The team did stay the course on integration. When it became obvious that Earl Wilson needed to work out his control problems in the minors in 1960, the Red Sox traded for Baltimore's Willie Tasby to provide Pumpsie Green another roommate. Installed in center field, Tasby led off or batted second for much of the season's remainder, hitting .281 and scoring 68 runs. Boston left him unprotected in the off-season expansion draft; Tasby became the center fielder for the new edition of the Washington Senators in 1961.[57] The Red Sox acquired former Cleveland infielder Billy Harrell from the St. Louis Cardinals in the Rule V draft, maintaining the expected equation of two black players on the team in 1961. Probably hoping to diffuse more unwanted criticism, Boston did just enough to placate Jackie Robinson, the Massachusetts Commission Against Discrimination, and that student picket from Tufts University. But a reputation was established. Boston would be viewed as the worst place for a black man to play professional baseball for decades to come.

The Boston Red Sox were, infamously, the last. When Elijah "Pumpsie" Green took the field in July 1959, a milestone was achieved. Jackie Robinson exulted in the title of his 1964 book, *Baseball Has Done It*. Twelve years was an awfully long time to do it in; looking back, the road seems long and unnecessarily torturous. The capitulation of the Red Sox left the appearance of an arduous task finally completed. But a milestone is nothing more than a marker along the path, a distance achieved thus far. The road in front of the now retired Robinson stretched onward into a distance unknown. The 16 major league teams now more or less included two black players each, but that was just the rosters on the field. Major League baseball was a much larger edifice than that, one that was not integrated very much at all. Jim Crow was on the defensive, but he was still breathing.

# VIII

# Looking Back—and
# Looking Ahead

Not to be outdone by a leading competitor, in March 1960, the upstart journal *Sports Illustrated* published an essay on blacks in baseball, just weeks after "The Negro in American Sport" appeared in *Sport* magazine. The editors of *Sport* had interviewed an array of black athletes to attempt some assessment of the integration of professional sports in America—the milestones achieved since World War II, the challenges still to be faced. Recognizing a further aspect to the story, *Sports Illustrated* chose to focus on the culture developing among black baseball players, their response to a narrow and limited inclusion in what was viewed as the national sport. "The Private World of the Negro Ballplayer," written by Robert Boyle following interviews with several black major league players, offered a cogent portrayal of the social conditions black players had come to share after 13 years of integration drama.[1]

Integration came about on terms orchestrated by the colossus known as Organized Baseball, an enterprise willing to open its doors, but only a tiny bit. A limited number of blacks were contracted to join the whites on major league fields, but there was no true amalgamation of the separated currents of baseball experience operated under Jim Crow. Negro Leagues baseball disappeared, along with most of their players and all their management people, leaving a small minority of black players struggling to compete in organized ball—white man's ball. Faced with this kind of pressure, black players defiantly created their own bonds, a system of mutual support that extended across team lines, across leagues. As Robert Boyle described the newly arrived world of black men in professional baseball, "in the minors and the majors the American Negro players 'hang kind of close.'"[2]

Note the qualifying adjective—*American* Negro players. The division Harry Simpson understood to exist between himself and Minnie Minoso was generally acknowledged among American blacks in 1960. "The reason is simple and painful," Boyle wrote. "To be a Negro in the United States is to be socially inferior." Jim Crow flourished still, dug in like grim death throughout much of the South, bubbling near the surface in most northern towns. Discrimination was a hard fact of life for American black people. Blacks from Cuba, the Dominican Republic, and Puerto Rico were unaccustomed to such blatant bias, and often held themselves apart from their American counterparts. The animosity was not universal, but it was very common, and it was mutual. American blacks expressed resentment from the fact they helped Latinos with language problems and other social barriers, only to be shunned down the road.

179

Latinos tended to keep their distance, not wanting to be seen as American blacks were seen and treated—as second-class citizens. The Americans saw themselves as tougher and wiser than their Caribbean counterparts when it came to confronting Jim Crow—they were born to segregation. Boyle's essay made almost no attempt to provide any Latino perspective on the issue— perhaps the language barrier defeated him. Alex Pompez, once owner of the New York Cubans, tried to explain their particular problems. "When they first come here they don't like it," he told Boyle. "Some boys cry and want to go home. But after they stay and make big money, they accept things as they are." Black Latinos saw themselves as separate, "at least as far as they themselves are concerned," Boyle concluded. "They are Cubans, Dominicans, Puerto Ricans." Boyle, accepting the perceived division, sought out none of them for comment. First-person assessments of the black Latino experience in the major leagues were a long time coming.[3]

So the black culture Robert Boyle encountered in Florida in 1960 was a construction nurtured almost exclusively by American blacks. Their social cohesion was at once a defense against an overweaning white world surrounding and threatening them, and a bold statement of their own unique worth. "The most interesting group in sports," Boyle found.[4]

"Negroes aren't supposed to stick together," Reds pitcher Brooks Lawrence pointed out, "but the closest kind of adhesion I've ever known has been among Negro players." It was a purposeful self-identity that commanded respect in America's black community. E. Franklin Frazier, sociologist at Howard University, portrayed the players as "an important part of the bourgeoisie elite." One wonders how W. E. B. DuBois would have felt about that assessment.[5]

The black players did stick together, helping one another, establishing a code that defined proper behavior, developing a slanging language that allowed them a private commentary on conditions shared and endured. White players were not excluded completely, but they were viewed with suspicion if they intruded too deeply. Black players knew all too well that Organized Baseball had been an all-white dominion until a mere 13 years before, that black inclusion had been reluctant and painful, that black participation was still very limited and probably subject to unwritten quotas, that many whites still preferred exclusion. "I'm not up here to make friends," Harry Simpson explained. "I'm here to play baseball. Any team I've been on, I've made friends. But maybe a guy doesn't want to be friends. Well, it's a free country, and that's his privilege." Blacks tended to become suspicious if a white player was too overt in extending friendship, fearing he was out to get something.[6]

By Robert Boyle's count, 57 of the more than 400 players on the major league rosters in 1960 were black. A long step from the five who first cracked the color barrier back in 1947 (three of them very temporarily), but still a small and all too definable minority. And some of these blacks were Latinos, yet another subset. That the tiny group of American black players, representatives of the most persecuted minority in American life, should find strength in one another's support made perfect sense. The code of conduct they evolved produced an identity. They were black men, professional men. No hair-straightening. That was for entertainers, black people who had to make even more compromise with the white world. (Think being a black man on a major league ball club was exclusionary? Try singing on national television.) No mentioning the name of any woman you're dating. The social circle was too small. No fighting with other black players, even when opposing teams scuffle. And always share with your fellows. Pay attention to the younger guys, help them out. Don't leave anyone sitting alone in a hotel room, staring at the wall.

Language created another sense of common identity. Advised that there were 57 black players in major league baseball in 1960, one informant agreed that there were 57 "hog-cutters" of varying kinds—diplomatic, sneaking, quiet, king-size. "Hog-cutter should not be confused with hot dog, another baseball term. A hot dog is a showboat, a player who calls attention to himself…. While only Negroes are hog-cutters, anyone can be a hot dog, though Latin players have a sort of monopoly in the field." The brass on the Yankees and the Athletics could consider Vic Power a hot dog, but only another black player could say what kind of hog-cutter or berry or road his teammate might be. An inside understanding was further conveyed by the nicknames blacks conferred on one another. Elston Howard may have been "Ellie" to most of his Yankee teammates, but to teammate Hector Lopez and the few black competitors they faced on the other American League clubs, Howard was "Steelie."[7]

Every sub-culture has its leaders. Teams with a fair number of black players, such as the Giants, the Reds, or the Dodgers, might have a leader in their own clubhouse, but the coterie was so small—especially in the American League—most black players looked for fellowship and support across team lines. Race could be more important than team affiliation in some circumstances, though racial identity did not influence competition on the field. But living and travelling in a world governed by white choices, black players did their best to help one another out—sharing knowledge of what to look for, what to watch out for in a strange city, how to handle unexpected discriminations, how to deal with vicious segregation at spring training facilities, where to find suitable living quarters following a trade. George Crowe, who entered the major leagues as a 31-year-old first baseman with the Braves in 1952, played for nine seasons with three National League teams, mostly as a part-time player. His importance to fellow blacks was immense. If a player encountered problems, needed advice, needed help, George Crowe was the man to see, no matter your team, or even your league. When Elston Howard joined the Yankees in 1955, George Crowe arranged for Howard's family to stay at his house in Queens. Crowe was playing for Milwaukee at the time.[8]

Crowe, along with most of the American blacks in baseball, saw themselves as "race men," individuals committed to furthering the fortunes of black people throughout the nation. Several were lifetime members of the NAACP, and contributed extra funds to support the black struggle in the courts. Their role as major league ballplayers made them a highly visible element of American society. Most saw this as an opportunity to win respect for blacks everywhere. Militancy grew, encouraged by the black press, welcomed more readily by some. As E. Franklin Frazier expressed the position, "baseball is an American sport with American respectability." A black ballplayer willing to make common cause with all his race could be a powerful voice. Most players were prepared to embrace the opportunity, whether *The Sporting News* liked it or not.[9]

Integration had come to baseball in a left-handed kind of way. Every team listed at least one black player on the roster by 1959, but in too many cases—especially in the American League—the effort was half-hearted and narrow, done for the wrong reasons. What was worse, many teams felt that simply adding a black man or two was enough. The color line was broken; that proved the team fostered no exclusive racial policies. The fact that the black players, so few in number, were left virtually defenseless against ongoing discriminations made little matter. There was no one to mitigate the hostility—there might be one or two blacks in the dugout; there were none in management positions, none in the front office.

When Robert Boyle set out to write his article on the private world of the Negro ballplayer, very nearly all his informants came from National League teams. This was no accident. Of the

57 black players Boyle counted in the spring of 1960, he must have calculated that 40 played in the National League. (Boyle's math was approximate at best; there were 55 black players in the National League alone.) The Giants played nine blacks during the 1959 season, the Reds eight, the Dodgers, Pirates, and Cardinals seven each. The Braves and the Cubs fielded six black players; the Phillies—the last and most reluctant National League team to integrate—played five blacks in 1959. The pace of integration in the League can be expressed in a simple table.

**Table 8.1[10]**

### Integration in the National League, 1947–1959

| Year | Integrated Teams | Total # of Black Players |
|------|------------------|--------------------------|
| 1947 | 1 | 2 |
| 1948 | 1 | 2 |
| 1949 | 2 | 5 |
| 1950 | 3 | 7 |
| 1951 | 3 | 11 |
| 1952 | 3 | 12 |
| 1953 | 5 | 15 |
| 1954 | 7 | 25 |
| 1955 | 7 | 30 |
| 1956 | 7 | 37 |
| 1957 | 8 | 37 |
| 1958 | 8 | 44 |
| 1959 | 8 | 55 |

Sheer numbers tell less than half the story. Black players had not merely become a commanding presence in the National League—an average of almost seven per team by 1959—they had also come to dominate. The first black players named to the National League All-Star Team appeared in 1949. There were three—Robinson, Campanella, and Newcombe—all from the Dodgers. By 1955, there were seven black All-Stars; by 1960, ten out of the 30 players picked. In all, 16 different black players were named All-Stars during the era. A black player was chosen National League "Rookie of the Year" in nine of the 14 years after 1946; and Most Valuable Player in nine of 19 years as well. The first Cy Young Award ever was voted to Don Newcombe in 1956. Black players won four batting titles (in 1959, six of the top ten hitters were black), three home run titles, and five RBI titles (generally considered the most important offensive category at the time). Black pitchers won one ERA title, twice led the league in wins, twice in strikeouts. The National League was not without prejudices; there were a lot more black sluggers in the league than black pitchers. But the essential importance of black players to the circuit's play is exceedingly plain. An hour spent looking at the appropriate section of *Baseball Reference.com* provides an almost incomprehensible number of further examples of black leadership, in both the traditional statistical categories and the more modern additions, such as Wins Above Replacement or Runs Created. The mere names resonate. Jackie Robinson. Campanella. Irvin. Mays. Aaron. Banks. Frank Robinson. Clemente. McCovey. Gibson. Cepeda. Billy Williams. Ten black players competing in the National League during the era made the Hall of Fame, many of them on the first ballot.

From the American League, there were just two Hall of Famers. Satchel Paige was elected in 1971, not for his work with the Indians and the Browns between 1948 and 1953 (when he was well past 40), but as the first representative of the Negro Leagues. Larry Doby was selected by the Veterans Committee in 1998, 39 years after he stopped playing. He did not produce the usual Hall of Fame numbers; as Bill Veeck contended, the grief he encountered as the pioneer black man in the American League prevented him from reaching his full potential. He was the only black player to lead the American League in any Triple Crown category, capturing home run titles in 1952 and 1954, and the RBI title in 1954. Doby finished second in the MVP voting in 1954, when the Indians won the pennant. Voters split among three Cleveland players, and Yogi Berra won the award. There would not be a black MVP in the American League until Elston Howard won recognition in 1963.

In 1949, the year the first three black players joined the National League All-Stars, Larry Doby was the first and only black chosen to represent the Junior Circuit. He was the only black again the next year; in 1951 Orestes Minoso joined him. Over the next nine years, one to three black players would be named to the team, never more than that. The reality was that there were just not many black players to choose among. Each season, a name or two would appear among the top ten in the key offensive categories, and very occasionally in the pitching statistics. Larry Doby was in the top ten in the MVP voting twice, Minoso four times, Al Smith and Vic Power once each. That was it. To understand the paucity, consider the impact, or, to be honest, the lack of impact suggested by a table documenting the pace of integration in the American League.[11]

**Table 8.2[12]**

**Black Players in the American League, 1947–1960**

| Team | Categories | Year | | | | | | | | | | | | | |
|---|---|---|---|---|---|---|---|---|---|---|---|---|---|---|---|
| | | 47 | 48 | 49 | 50 | 51 | 52 | 53 | 54 | 55 | 56 | 57 | 58 | 59 | 60 |
| Cleveland | Full | 1 | 2 | 2 | 0 | 3 | 4 | 5 | 4 | 4 | 1 | 3 | 5 | 3 | 3 |
| | Tr1 | 0 | 0 | 0 | 0 | 1 | 0 | 0 | 0 | 1 | 0 | 0 | 0 | 1 | 0 |
| | Tr2 | 0 | 0 | 0 | 0 | 0 | 0 | 0 | 0 | 0 | 1 | 0 | 0 | 0 | 1 |
| | Fringe | 0 | 0 | 2 | 0 | 1 | 2 | 0 | 2 | 1 | 1 | 1 | 1 | 0 | 0 |
| | Total | 1 | 2 | 4 | 2 | 5 | 6 | 5 | 6 | 6 | 3 | 4 | 6 | 4 | 4 |
| St. Louis/ Baltimore | Full | 0 | 0 | 0 | 0 | 1 | 1 | 1 | 0 | 0 | 1 | 2 | 4 | 2 | 1 |
| | Tr1 | 0 | 0 | 0 | 0 | 0 | 0 | 0 | 0 | 0 | 1 | 0 | 0 | 1 | 1 |
| | Tr2 | 0 | 0 | 0 | 0 | 0 | 0 | 0 | 0 | 1 | 1 | 0 | 0 | 0 | 0 |
| | Fringe | 2 | 0 | 0 | 0 | 0 | 0 | 0 | 2 | 0 | 1 | 2 | 2 | 2 | 1 |
| | Total | 2 | 0 | 0 | 0 | 1 | 1 | 1 | 2 | 1 | 4 | 4 | 6 | 5 | 3 |
| Chicago | Full | 0 | 0 | 0 | 0 | 0 | 2 | 3 | 1 | 2 | 2 | 3 | 2 | 2 | 2 |
| | Tr1 | 0 | 0 | 0 | 0 | 0 | 0 | 0 | 0 | 0 | 1 | 0 | 0 | 1 | 0 |
| | Tr2 | 0 | 0 | 0 | 0 | 1 | 0 | 0 | 0 | 0 | 0 | 0 | 0 | 2 | 0 |
| | Fringe | 0 | 0 | 0 | 0 | 2 | 0 | 0 | 1 | 1 | 1 | 0 | 0 | 0 | 1 |
| | Total | 0 | 0 | 0 | 0 | 3 | 2 | 3 | 2 | 3 | 4 | 3 | 2 | 4 | 3 |
| Philadelphia/ Kansas City | Full | 0 | 0 | 0 | 0 | 0 | 0 | 0 | 2 | 3 | 4 | 2 | 2 | 0 | 0 |
| | Tr1 | 0 | 0 | 0 | 0 | 0 | 0 | 0 | 0 | 0 | 0 | 1 | 0 | 2 | 0 |
| | Tr2 | 0 | 0 | 0 | 0 | 0 | 0 | 0 | 0 | 0 | 0 | 0 | 1 | 0 | 0 |

| Team | Categories | Year | | | | | | | | | | | | | |
|---|---|---|---|---|---|---|---|---|---|---|---|---|---|---|---|
| | | 47 | 48 | 49 | 50 | 51 | 52 | 53 | 54 | 55 | 56 | 57 | 58 | 59 | 60 |
| | Fringe | 0 | 0 | 0 | 0 | 0 | 0 | 1 | 1 | 1 | 0 | 0 | 0 | 0 | 0 |
| | Total | 0 | 0 | 0 | 0 | 0 | 0 | 1 | 3 | 4 | 4 | 3 | 3 | 2 | 0 |
| Washington | Full | 0 | 0 | 0 | 0 | 0 | 0 | 0 | 0 | 3 | 0 | 1 | 2 | 2 | 3 |
| | Tr1 | 0 | 0 | 0 | 0 | 0 | 0 | 0 | 0 | 0 | 0 | 0 | 0 | 0 | 0 |
| | Tr2 | 0 | 0 | 0 | 0 | 0 | 0 | 0 | 0 | 0 | 0 | 0 | 0 | 1 | 0 |
| | Fringe | 0 | 0 | 0 | 0 | 0 | 0 | 0 | 1 | 2 | 1 | 1 | 0 | 0 | 1 |
| | Total | 0 | 0 | 0 | 0 | 0 | 0 | 0 | 1 | 5 | 1 | 2 | 2 | 3 | 4 |
| New York | Full | 0 | 0 | 0 | 0 | 0 | 0 | 0 | 0 | 1 | 1 | 1 | 1 | 1 | 2 |
| | Tr1 | 0 | 0 | 0 | 0 | 0 | 0 | 0 | 0 | 0 | 0 | 0 | 1 | 0 | 0 |
| | Tr2 | 0 | 0 | 0 | 0 | 0 | 0 | 0 | 0 | 0 | 0 | 0 | 0 | 1 | 0 |
| | Fringe | 0 | 0 | 0 | 0 | 0 | 0 | 0 | 0 | 0 | 0 | 1 | 0 | 0 | 1 |
| | Total | 0 | 0 | 0 | 0 | 0 | 0 | 0 | 0 | 1 | 1 | 2 | 2 | 2 | 3 |
| Detroit | Full | 0 | 0 | 0 | 0 | 0 | 0 | 0 | 0 | 0 | 0 | 0 | 1 | 0 | 2 |
| | Tr1 | 0 | 0 | 0 | 0 | 0 | 0 | 0 | 0 | 0 | 0 | 0 | 0 | 1 | 0 |
| | Tr2 | 0 | 0 | 0 | 0 | 0 | 0 | 0 | 0 | 0 | 0 | 0 | 0 | 0 | 1 |
| | Fringe | 0 | 0 | 0 | 0 | 0 | 0 | 0 | 0 | 0 | 0 | 0 | 0 | 1 | 0 |
| | Total | 0 | 0 | 0 | 0 | 0 | 0 | 0 | 0 | 0 | 0 | 0 | 1 | 2 | 3 |
| Boston | Full | 0 | 0 | 0 | 0 | 0 | 0 | 0 | 0 | 0 | 0 | 0 | 0 | 2 | 2 |
| | Tr1 | 0 | 0 | 0 | 0 | 0 | 0 | 0 | 0 | 0 | 0 | 0 | 0 | 0 | 0 |
| | Tr2 | 0 | 0 | 0 | 0 | 0 | 0 | 0 | 0 | 0 | 0 | 0 | 0 | 0 | 1 |
| | Fringe | 0 | 0 | 0 | 0 | 0 | 0 | 0 | 0 | 0 | 0 | 0 | 0 | 0 | 0 |
| | Total | 0 | 0 | 0 | 0 | 0 | 0 | 0 | 0 | 0 | 0 | 0 | 0 | 2 | 3 |
| Summary | Teams | 2 | 1 | 1 | 1 | 3 | 3 | 4 | 5 | 6 | 6 | 6 | 7 | 8 | 7 |
| | Full | 1 | 2 | 2 | 2 | 4 | 7 | 9 | 7 | 13 | 9 | 12 | 17 | 12 | 15 |
| | Traded | 0 | 0 | 0 | 0 | 1 | 0 | 0 | 0 | 1 | 2 | 1 | 1 | 4 | 2 |
| | Fringe | 2 | 0 | 2 | 0 | 3 | 2 | 1 | 7 | 5 | 4 | 4 | 3 | 3 | 4 |
| | Total | 3 | 2 | 4 | 2 | 8 | 9 | 10 | 14 | 19 | 15 | 17 | 21 | 19 | 21 |

CATEGORIES: FULL provides the number of players playing a more or less entire season with the team. The category is a bit arbitrary in some cases. Larry Doby joined the Indians in July of 1947, playing in just 29 games. The intention was for him to be a full member of the team, and he is so listed.

Tr1 lists players who started the year as full member of the team, but were traded at some point during the season.

Tr2 lists players who were acquired by trade after the beginning of the season. In every case but one (where a player was traded twice, the second time to the National League), the number of Tr1 and Tr2 cases each season balance perfectly. In the summary, trades are listed the once.

FRINGE counts the "cup of coffee" players, generally players called up briefly, receiving little attention or playing time.

TOTAL is the sum of the numbers in the Full, Tr1, Tr2, and Fringe categories.

The most superficial analysis captures the elements of the story. In the first years of integration, most major league teams shied away from what they saw as radical change. Just three teams in each league were integrated by 1952; 12 blacks played in the National League, nine in the American. A step forward perhaps, but a very small and cautious step. Then came the mid–1950s, when issues in the society at large ratcheted up the pressure on the remaining major league teams—highly visible symbols of the national culture. Teams in both leagues responded with varying degrees of willingness, and in another seven years the process was complete—each of the 16 teams fielded at least two black players. But the disparity in the numbers became very large. The American League acquiesced; the Nationals grasped the opportunity. In 1953, black players in the National League outnumbered their counterparts in the American by a ratio of three to two. In six years, that ratio grew to roughly three to one—55 to 19. The National League was plainly more aggressive than the American when it came to recruiting black players; they not only found more, they found far greater players. The Hall of Fame ratio is ten to two, and that needs an asterisk.

What it comes to is this: in 14 seasons, the eight American League franchises found a total of ten black players who made any significant impact on play during the 1950s. Ten. They do not require much space to list. There were Larry Doby, Satchel Paige, Orestes Minoso, Harry Simpson, Al Smith, Vic Power, Elston Howard, Hector Lopez, Bob Boyd, and Connie Johnson. A few more names popped up at the end of the decade, players who would not receive much notice in the 1950s, but did make some noise later on—Earl Wilson, Mudcat Grant, Lenny Green, Zoilo Versalles, Earl Battey. These were some very good ball players, but it is not much of a list to stack up against Jackie Robinson, Willie Mays, Ernie Banks (three players who could easily have landed with American League teams), and all the other National League stars. The black presence in the American League was spread very thin.

There has been considerable discussion of the glaring difference between the two leagues, the reasons behind the dominance of the Nationals. There was of course, the fact that the Dodgers were the first and more successful experiment, Jackie Robinson becoming a powerful and very popular star in New York while Larry Doby took time to develop in more media-remote Cleveland. Several of the black pioneers succeeded quickly in the National League, where there was perhaps more opportunity, more room for highly qualified players who happened to be black. The National was the inferior league going into the 1950s, and vastly superior a decade later. There was also the perception among young black players that they needed or wanted to follow Jackie, the fiery and much-respected pioneer. Robinson certainly went out of his way to aid and support young black players. Larry Doby tried, but his was a vastly different personality.[13]

If young black players were attracted to the National League for positive reasons, the other side of the coin was also true. The American League, dripping with reactionary skepticism and plain arrogance, was the more repellant. For all the speculation, the real reason the American League so noticeably botched integration was the series of historical contingencies that made the leadership such an ossified structure by the 1940s. Once upon a time, the American had been the radical newcomer, the upstart that took hold of organized baseball and gave it a good hard shaking. There were daring men running the League in those days—Ban Johnson, Charlie Comiskey, Connie Mack, Clark Griffith. Fifty years later, their ghosts still lingered—in two cases, the actual persons hovered still. What was radical in 1900 had become conservative, cautious, and self-centered half a century down the line. The memories of two world wars, the Great Depression, and a revolution in baseball strategy that had occurred 30 years before left too many influential figures living in the past, unwilling to change what they saw as a very fragile, almost defenseless structure. Shifting populations in the major league cities, new populations clamoring for recognition out west, aging stadiums, labor issues, integration issues; the old guard in the American League wanted to face none of it. Connie Mack and Clark Griffith were Kenesaw Mountain Landis's most loyal supporters. They thought they understood Larry MacPhail perfectly.

Born 50 years earlier, Bill Veeck might have fit into Ban Johnson's radical band pretty well. But in 1947, Veeck was a radical in a bear garden of arch-reactionaries; he was hated for his inventive approach. The entertainments, the special events, the giveaways; it was much too much. Then Veeck had the audacity to fracture the color line without seeking the support of anyone. The National League brass may have fervently disliked Branch Rickey, but they respected him, even feared him. If Rickey wanted a black player, there had to be reasons the others would need to consider. No maneuver of Bill Veeck's was going to command that kind of respect.

When the St. Louis Browns followed Veeck, the move was immediately perceived for what it was, another ineptly planned, ill-considered, and cynical attempt to bolster the fortunes of a dying franchise. And it did not work—in a month's time, the experiment was lamely ended. Not a positive beginning to the integration process, when the pioneers are Bill Veeck and Bill DeWitt. Not to the minds of the other American League owners.

Over the next six years, the only addition to the American League ranks came of the determination of three individuals who wanted to win. Charles Comiskey's daughter-in-law did not openly encourage integration, but she did hire Frank Lane to run the White Sox, with the firm instruction to do what was necessary to improve the team. Lane hired Paul Richards, and listened when Richards told him he wanted black players—Minnie Minoso specifically—on his team. Richards was one of the very few managers in the American League who made the inclusion of black players—and the construction of a strategy around their skills—an essential part of his rebuilding. It was a model no one else in the American League was prepared to follow.

Veeck left Cleveland, reappearing soon after as owner of the Browns, much to the dismay of his fellow American League owners. He re-integrated the team, employing Satchel Paige in the short run while facing the challenge of finding young black players employing a much-diminished scouting system. The money ran dry; a majority of the league's owners forced the maverick to leave the table. The franchise moved to Baltimore, where Paul Richards soon assumed control. In a rigidly Jim Crow town, integration continued.

That was as far as the process could go for a good while. Taking the remaining teams as a group, it is not difficult to see why integration stalled. These five were the entrenched old guard, stubborn, set, and unwilling to embrace change. The reasons varied from club to club, but the resistance to integration was very much a shared quality. These five were the staunch defenders of the status quo. First came the truly old guard, Connie Mack and Clark Griffith. Each built a stadium in what became extensively black neighborhoods; each could have attracted new fans by integrating their teams. They certainly needed new fans—both franchises knew trouble with the balance sheet. But they were very old men, museum pieces who refused to comprehend the changing world around them. Both identified with the flatly pernicious doctrine equating civil rights with communist subversion. Neither looked past the injustice, the inherent racism in the claim. And neither would place a black man on the field. At least not an American black. Mack's semi-competent sons integrated the Athletics as part of a futile effort to save the franchise, while Griffith's nephew Calvin continued his father's practice of hiring Cubans on the cheap while ignoring the Josh Gibsons and Buck Leonards of American baseball.

The Yankees ownership was not the old guard variety. The original owners were long gone, and their successors as well. The new ownership, assuming control just as integration got under way, included Larry MacPhail, the most enigmatic figure in the history of baseball's integration. Most scholars simply interpret his words and actions as those of a racist, but MacPhail was not so simple as that. Nor were the men who got rid of him, Dan Topping and Del Webb. There was certainly racism in the front office, but the real reason behind the failure to integrate was simple arrogance. The New York Yankees were winners, they had been winners for over 30 years, and they were not about to listen to anyone else telling them what to do, no matter the right or wrong. The Yankees stalled, they avoided, they ignored. When they did finally begin to hear other voices—voices from the United States Supreme Court, voices from Montgomery, Alabama—their decision to integrate, even in the most cautious and conservative manner possible, sealed the issue. If the most self-possessed franchise in American sports was prepared to break down, however arrogantly, change was truly coming.

What remained after 1955 were two hidebound franchises, their roots not running all the way back to the origins of the league, but deep into the past, deep enough to promote a lackluster satisfaction with conditions as they had been, back when much of the country was Jim Crow, when racism was government policy.

Despite signing a black player or two to distant minor league franchises, neither the Tigers nor the Red Sox showed the slightest disposition to bend. Walter Briggs never budged in a town known for intolerance; the timid maneuvers that followed his death suggest his lasting impact on the Detroit club. Tom Yawkey was too comfortable for his own good or anyone else's, building an organization grounded in cronyism, an alcohol-fueled "plantation" where change was seen as unnecessary and unwanted. Detroit and Boston capitulated in the most minimal ways imaginable, only in the face of public pressure, bad publicity, and, in the case of the Red Sox, the threat of government intervention.

To paraphrase Jackie Robinson, baseball had done it, but the American League did so in a painfully superficial fashion.[14] The fact that a token addition of one or two black part-time players to a team was enough to touch off a nationwide congratulatory celebration suggests just how poor race relations were as America slowly backed away from Jim Crow. The reality was that a handful of new laborers were recruited to join organizations operating much as they had 20 years before. This was the only change—except that Negro League baseball disappeared. The black press and the black community agreed that the loss was good riddance, but the dissolution came at a price they could not see. Blacks could now play in organized baseball, but they had no voice in the operation. The addition of black players to all 16 teams was nothing more than a baby step, dictated as much by economics as social conscience.

More than a quarter century after Elijah Green joined the Red Sox, a Dodgers executive—a man known to be friendly to blacks—stated that blacks "lack the necessities" to be managers or general managers in Organized Baseball. "In other words," Frank Robinson interpreted, "blacks were not smart enough to manage in the big leagues, even though there had been a host of white managers who were never confused with college professors, let alone brain surgeons." Robinson went on to document the discrimination that still ruled baseball. In the 40 years since Jackie Robinson took the field for the Dodgers, just three black men had managed in the majors. The first was Frank Robinson himself, with Cleveland in 1975. Jackie did not live to see that happen, dying in 1972. In all that time, there had been just two black managers in all the *minor* leagues. Robinson lasted just two and a half years in Cleveland, and three and a half years in a second gig before being undermined in San Francisco. Larry Doby managed the White Sox for 87 games in 1978, and Maury Wills held the job in Seattle at the end of 1980 and the beginning of 1981. That was the list, over four decades. There was just one black general manager during the period, Bill Lucas, who was hired by the Atlanta Braves in 1976, serving until his death in 1979. Bob Watson would be the second, appointed by Houston in 1993. A few well-remembered black players, such as Henry Aaron, served in various executive front offices. They made for good publicity but were never in powerful decision-making roles. Al Campanis of the Dodgers voiced what the 28 white owners of major league teams privately thought: blacks should not be given executive authority. Blacks played baseball—in significantly large numbers in 1988. They had essentially no part in running baseball.[15]

By that time, the re-interpretation of Negro Leagues baseball was well under way. Celebrated, romanticized, the leagues had become the stuff of tragic nostalgia—the black stars who toiled in unjust obscurity, waiting for the chance that never came. Buck Leonard, Josh Gibson, Judy Johnson. So many. In a sense, the story was true. But it was also misleading. In the reinterpretation, Rube Foster became the patient entrepreneur, building up Negro Leagues against the day the color line would dissolve. And that was not true. Foster was a race man, or at least became one. Looking at the ruins of black Chicago in 1919, he saw Jim Crow for the entrenched monster that it was. If blacks wanted to participate in organized competition, they would have to operate on their own, separate from whites. Any compromise would be a surrender to white institutions, white booking agents especially. Foster did not even want J. L. Wilkinson in his league, even if that white man ran the most financially sound black team anywhere. Rube Foster was a race man, forcefully heading a league by and for black people, intended to be separate.

As the nostalgia-ridden books of the 1970s captured so well, the Negro Leagues had skillful players and an exciting brand of serious professional baseball, despite the shady financing and the hard conditions. But happy stories require happy endings. The Negro Leagues accomplished their task, producing Jackie Robinson and Larry Doby. And Satchel Paige. Having done their supposed job—preparing a few black stars for the organized game—the Negro Leagues gently faded away. The investment, the spirit, the play—none of that mattered, except for the pity that the organized leagues held aloof for so long. Twenty years down the line, black people and white certainly wanted to remember the past in this fairy tale fashion. To recall that the Negro Leagues were a determined expression of race enterprise in a bigoted era of Jim Crow apartheid was too harsh a pill. To acknowledge that Organized Baseball killed that enterprise, refusing to accept any of its participants save a handful of hired laborers—that dulls the luster of integration's story. The real story had no ending; certainly not a happy one. Faced with enormous social pressure, white baseball decided they needed a few of black baseball's more skillful players. What they did not want was any real breakdown of the color line, black and white joined together at all levels to cooperate in providing the best baseball experience possible. Forty years later, organized baseball still did not want that.

The modern civil rights movement began during World War II, slowly becoming a critical agenda for a nation caught up in cold war. The struggle accelerated through the 1950s, slowly but surely becoming more impassioned, more violent. White resistance hardened. Even as baseball succeeded in becoming a visible symbol of integration's potential, perception among elements of the black community began to change. More than a few black leaders became understandably frustrated as basic human rights continued to be systematically denied. The answer seemed to lie in greater independence from white authority and white enterprise. As early as 1961, Malcolm X (who had rooted for Jackie Robinson from a prison cell) came to advocate black segregation from whites, a separate economy seeded by financial reparations for the centuries of slavery. The nickel-and-dime achievements of sit-ins and court cases were not getting black people anywhere. "To beg a white man to let you into his restaurant feeds his ego," Malcolm X told the *New York Times*. Change the wording to fit the situation in organized baseball—begging a white owner for a place on his roster—the militancy black players fostered among themselves in 1960 was a necessity.[16] The players, a small minority in an enterprise governed exclusively by whites, came to define themselves as race men in the image of Rube Foster, black professionals holding hard to a self-developed culture. They would play, but they would not capitulate, maintaining independence in behavior, in language, in their style of play. Even Jackie Robinson came to be seen as too closely affiliated with a white organization. When told by Robert Boyle that blacks had developed their own slanging language, Robinson refused to believe it was so.[17]

Would the race men of the 1950s have wished to hark back to Rube Foster, the race man of the 1920s? Negro Leagues baseball was about as successful an independent enterprise as the black community could create. The leagues survived on a shoestring, barely making payroll through much of their existence, operating in tawdry conditions. Remaking the leagues into a stable and profitable black enterprise would have required an awful lot of cash, and it would have required the support of much the entire black community, two very doubtful propositions. The reality was that integration, growing as it did from the strange, strange atmosphere so long generated by Jim Crow, was going to be a long, agonizing, frustrating process, in baseball and in American life. The plans the Negro Leagues offered to secure their survival—organizing two all-black teams to join the majors, or serving as a farm circuit for black prospects—were the unreal products of desperation. Integration would happen only on the dominant society's terms. Organized Baseball would skim off the most promising young black players, leaving the rest to scatter. They would take no black coaches, managers, general managers, or senior executives. They would very publicly undertake the absolute minimum to demonstrate integration was under way. Justice and equality would continue to come in dribs and drabs as white structures took half a century to acknowledge the right and ability of blacks to participate as full partners in American baseball.

Two-thirds of a century after Jackie Robinson and Larry Doby braved the field, change slowly continues. The appointment of a black manager is no longer news of social import. Blacks have slowly worked their way into executive positions, serving as general managers and in ownership roles. But racism is far from dead—locker room incidents seem to multiply, the Jackie Robinson statue in New York has been vandalized, and players remain the target of the meanest racial slurs from unreconstructed fans. Forty years after exceeding Babe Ruth's home run record, Henry Aaron began receiving hate mail all over again. Most ironically, for two decades, the numbers of American blacks playing in the major leagues has steadily declined. Segregation is not the culprit now. Exercising the freedom Robinson and Doby struggled to achieve, young black athletes now choose to pursue other sports, perceiving baseball as a white man's game. America remains a landscape molded by racial perceptions.

Americans live in a society historically defined by racial boundaries of our own invention. Race: the struggle to understand what the idea means, how the notion limits us; race is the essential thread woven into our national character. In the 1940s, the nation embarked on a long, much-begrudged effort to alter the weave, create a more honestly balanced society. Baseball was a highly visible symbol of that process. The integration of the American League is as good a parable as any when discussing the weakening of systematic prejudice. Faced with the absolute necessity of ending racial segregation, the American League spent 13 long years accomplishing astonishingly little. What this tells us is a truth of American life we would as soon ignore, if not forget. We have defined ourselves by race. Whites divided their own perceived race into half a dozen or more ranked categories, shoved all others to the outside, and spent 500 years building American institutions on stranger and stranger assumptions. Racial discrimination was, and still remains, a fiber so deeply woven into the fabric of American history—socially, culturally, economically, politically—that racial issues *are* the fabric of ourselves. Major league baseball reluctantly made a tiny dent in a vast ugliness, a dent we continue to celebrate as a triumph more than half a century later. This is how deeply race is etched into our lives.

# Chapter Notes

## Introduction

1. The Editors, "The Negro in American Sport: Round Table Discussion," *Sport*, March 1960, 28–35.

2. Po Bronson and Ashley Merryman, "See Baby Discriminate," *Newsweek*, September 14, 2009, 52–60.

3. Edmund S. Morgan, *American Slavery, American Freedom: The Ordeal of Colonial Virginia* (New York: W. W. Norton, 1975).

4. Buck O'Neil, *I Was Right on Time: My Journey from the Negro Leagues to the Majors* (New York: Simon & Schuster, 1998), 100–01.

5. C. Vann Woodward, *The Strange Career of Jim Crow*, 2d ed. (London: Oxford University Press, 1966), 11–31; August Meier and Elliot Rudwick, *From Plantation to Ghetto*, 3d ed. (New York: Hill and Wang, 1976), 87–193; John Hope Franklin, *From Slavery to Freedom: A History of Negro Americans*, 3d ed. (New York: Alfred A. Knopf, 1967), 271–323; Nell Irvin Painter, *Creating Black Americans: African–American History and Its Meanings, 1619 to the Present* (New York: Oxford University Press, 2007), 115–60.

6. Ibid.; Eric Foner, *Reconstruction: America's Unfinished Revolution, 1863–1877* (New York: HarperCollins, 2002); C. Vann Woodward, *Reunion and Reaction: The Compromise of 1877 and the End of Reconstruction* (Boston: Little, Brown, 1966); Lawrence Goodwyn, *The Populist Moment: A Short History of the Agrarian Revolt in America* (Oxford: Oxford University Press, 1978).

7. Stephen Jay Gould, *The Mismeasure of Man*, 2d ed. (New York: W. W. Norton, 1996), 62–104; Nell Irvin Painter, *The History of White People*, (New York: W. W. Norton, 2010), 104–200.

8. Painter, *History of White People*, 190–255.

9. David Block, *Baseball Before We Knew It: A Search for the Roots of the Game* (Lincoln: University of Nebraska Press, 2005); Schwarz; Frederick Ivor-Campbell, "The Many Fathers of Baseball: Anglo-Americans and the Early Game," Richard F. Peterson, "Slide, Kelly, Slide: The Irish in American Baseball," *The American Game: Baseball and Ethnicity*, Lawrence Baldassaro and Richard A. Johnson, eds. (Carbondale: Southern Illinois University Press, 2002), 6–26, 55–67; Alan Schwarz, *The Numbers Game: Baseball's Lifelong Fascination with Statistics* (New York: St. Martins Griffin, 2004), 1–21.

10. Noel Ignatiev, *How The Irish Became White* (New York: Routledge, 1995).

11. Benjamin G. Rader, *Baseball: A History of America's Game* 3d ed. (Champaign: University of Illinois Press, 2008), 1–59; Painter, *History of White People*, 212–27.

12. Rader, *Baseball*, 42–90; Mark Lamster, *Spalding's World Tour: The Epic Adventure That Took Baseball Around the Globe* (New York: Public Affairs, 2006); Warren N. Wilbert, *The Arrival of the American League: Ban Johnson and the 1901 Challenge to National League Monopoly* (Jefferson, NC: McFarland, 2007).

13. Jerry Malloy, ed. *Sol White's History of Colored Base Ball: With Other Documents of the Early Black Game. 1886–1936* (Lincoln: University of Nebraska Press, 1995).

14. Painter, *History of White People*, 201–55; Dennis DeValeria and Jeanne Burke DeValeria, *Honus Wagner: A Biography* (Pittsburgh: University of Pittsburgh Press, 1998); Baldassaro and Johnson, *The American Game*; Byron Farwell, *Over There: The United States in the Great War, 1917–1918* (New York: W. W. Norton, 1999), 60-65.

15. Woodward, *Strange Career of Jim Crow*; Meier and Rudwick, *From Plantation to Ghetto*, 153–231; Franklin, *From Slavery to Freedom*, 324–43; Painter, *Creating Black Americans*, 141–88.

16. William M. Tuttle, Jr., *Race Riot: Chicago in the Red Summer of 1919* (New York: Atheneum, 1970), 89–90.

17. Booker T. Washington, *Up from Slavery* (New York: Barnes and Noble, 2003; originally published in 1901).

18. W. E. B. DuBois, *The Souls of Black Folk* (New York: Barnes and Noble, 2003; originally published in 1903).

19. Meier and Rudwick, *From Plantation to Ghetto*, 220–31; Tuttle, *Race Riot*, 211–13.

20. Meier and Rudwick, *From Plantation to Ghetto*, 232–70; Joe William Trotter, ed., *The Great Migration in Historical Perspective: New Dimensions of Race, Class, and Gender* (Bloomington: Indiana University Press, 1991); Tuttle, *Race Riot*, 74–155.

21. Woodward, *The Strange Career of Jim Crow.*

22. Compiled from Campbell Gibson and Kay Young, "Historical Census Statistics on Population Totals by Race, 1790 to 1990..." United States Census, Working Paper No. 76 (Washington, D.C.: U.S. Census Bureau, 2005).

23. Thomas J. Sugrue, *Sweet Land of Liberty: The Forgotten Struggle for Civil Rights in the North* (New York: Random House, 2008).

24. Tuttle, *Race Riot,* 32–73; Painter, *History of White People,* 245–55; Cameron McWhirter, *Red Summer: The Summer of 1919 and the Awakening of Black America* (New York: Henry Holt, 2011).

25. Meier and Rudwick, *From Plantation to Ghetto,* 236–42; Tuttle, *Race Riot,* 32–73.

26. Woodward, *Strange Career of Jim Crow,* Meier and Rudwick, *From Plantation to Ghetto,* 232–70; Painter, *History of White People,* 201–342; Gould, *Mismeasure of Man,* 176–263.

27. G. Edward White, *Creating the National Pastime: Baseball Transforms Itself, 1903–1953* (Princeton: Princeton University Press, 1998), 10–83.

28. DuBois, *Souls of Black Folk,* 9.

29. Lawrence D. Hogan, *Shades of Glory: The Negro Leagues and the Story of African-American Baseball* (Washington D.C.: National Geographic, 2006); Leslie A. Heaphy, *The Negro Leagues, 1869–1960* (Jefferson, NC: McFarland, 2003); Neil Lanctot, *Negro League Baseball: The Rise and Ruin of a Black Institution* (Philadelphia: University of Pennsylvania Press, 2004); Rob Ruck, *Raceball: How the Major Leagues Colonized the Black and Latin Game* (Boston: Beacon Press, 2011).

30. Sugrue, *Sweet Land of Liberty,* xiii–xxviii.

## Chapter I

1. "William 'Sug' Cornelius," *Voices from the Great Black Baseball Leagues,* ed. John Holway (New York: Dodd, Mead, 1975), 249; "Ted Page," *Voices,* 166.

2. "Webster McDonald," *Voices,* 86; "Cool Papa Bell," *Voices,* 133; "Crush Holloway," *Voices,* 69.

3. "The Exclusion of African Americans from the NABBP," *Ball Player's Chronicle,* December 19, 1867, quoted in Dean A. Sullivan, ed., *Early Innings: A Documentary History of Baseball, 1825–1908* (Lincoln: University of Nebraska Press, 1995), 68–69; "The New York State Baseball Association Bans African Americans," *New York Clipper,* November 19, 1870, quoted in *Early Innings,* 80–81.

4. Sol White, *Official Baseball Guide,* ed. H. Walter Schlichter (Philadelphia: H. Walter Schlichter, 1907), reprinted in *Sol White's History of Colored Baseball,* ed. Jerry Malloy, 10, 74, 110; Jeffrey Michael Laing, *Bud Fowler: Baseball's First Black Professional* (Jefferson, NC: McFarland, 2013). For a discussion of blacks in early baseball, see Hogan, *Shades of Glory,* 4–125.

5. Brian Carroll, *When to Stop the Cheering? The Black Press, the Black Community, and the Integration of Professional Baseball* (New York: Routledge, 2007), 12. Walker's book was entitled *Our Home Colony: A Treatise on the Past, Present and Future of the Negro Race in America* (1898).

6. *Sol White's History of Colored Baseball,* 76–77;

see also Leslie A. Heaphy, *The Negro Leagues: 1869–1960* (Jefferson, NC: McFarland, 2003), 14–27.

7. *Sol White's History of Colored Baseball,* 76–77; Robert Peterson, *Only the Ball Was White: A History of Legendary Black Players and All-Black Professional Teams* (New York: Oxford University Press, 1970), 28–30.

8. *Sol White's History of Colored Baseball,* 5–12.

9. Ibid., Jerry Malloy, "The Birth of the Cuban Giants: The Origins of Black Professional Baseball," *Out of the Shadows: African American Baseball from the Cuban Giants to Jackie Robinson,* ed. Bill Kirwin (Lincoln: University of Nebraska Press, 2005), 1–14.

10. Hogan, *Shades of Glory,* 66–125; "World Champion St. Louis Browns Refuse to Play Cuban Giants," *St. Louis Post-Dispatch,* September 13, 1887, in Sullivan Ed.), *Early Innings,* 150–52.

11. *Sol White's History of Colored Baseball,* 24; Hogan, *Shades of Glory,* 51–53, 73–75.

12. *Sol White's History of Colored Baseball,* 31; Hogan, *Shades of Glory,* 66–125.

13. *Sol White's History of Colored Baseball,* 65.

14. Rader, *Baseball: A History of America's Game,* 1–90; Leonard Koppett, *Koppett's Concise History of Major League Baseball* (New York: Carroll and Graf, 2004), 3–84; Lamster, *Spalding's World Tour.*

15. Bill Felber, *A Game of Brawl: The Orioles, the Beaneaters, and the Battle for the 1897 Pennant* (Lincoln: University of Nebraska Press, 2007).

16. Ibid.; Wilbert, *Arrival of the American League;* Frank DeFord, *The Old Ball Game: How John McGraw, Christy Mathewson, and the New York Giants Created Modern Baseball* (New York: Grove Press, 2006).

17. For a penetrating analysis of black baseball's long litany of institutional problems, see Lanctot, *Negro League Baseball,* 3–203.

18. Carroll, *When to Stop the Cheering?,* 36–37; Robert Charles Cottrell, *The Best Pitcher in Baseball: The Life of Rube Foster, Negro League Giant* (New York: New York University Press, 2001), 62–157; Phil S. Dixon, *A Harvest on Freedom's Fields: Andrew "Rube" Foster* (Xlibris, 2010), 103–74; Hogan, *Shades of Glory,* 126–193.

19. Lanctot, *Negro League Baseball,* 21.

20. Hogan, *Shades of Glory,* 66–125; Heaphy, *The Negro Leagues,* 9–22.

21. Cottrell, *The Best Pitcher in Baseball,* 1–119; Dixon, *Harvest on Freedom's Fields,* 1–102; Andrew (Rube) Foster, "Negro Base Ball," *The Freeman* (Indianapolis), December 23, 1911, 18.

22. Cottrell, *The Best Pitcher in Baseball,* 1–119; Dixon, *Harvest on Freedom's Fields,* 1–102; Carroll, *When to Stop the Cheering?,* 31; David Wyatt, "The Annual Chestnut": Negro Base Ball League," *The Freeman,* January 27, 1917, 7; Billy Lewis, "Negro Baseball Players and the Big Leagues—Rube Foster Says the Door Is Nearly Open," *The Freeman,* May 2, 1914, 8.

23. Tuttle, Jr., *Race Riot;* Meier and Rudwick, *From Plantation to Ghetto,* 246–59; Sugrue, *Sweet Land of Liberty,* 14–16.

24. Tuttle, *Race Riot,* 54–55; "Historically Speaking: Rube Foster," *Black Sports,* February 1972, 44–45.

25. Ruck, *Raceball,* 31.

26. Jules Tygiel, *Past Time: Baseball As History* (Oxford: Oxford University Press, 2008), 116–17; John

B. Holway, *Blackball Stars: Negro League Pioneers* (Westport, CT: Meckler, 1988), 8.

27. John B. Holway, "Rube Foster: Father of the Black Game," *The Sporting News*, August 8, 1981.

28. Rube Foster, "Pitfalls of Baseball," *Chicago Defender*, weekly series, November 29, 1919, to January 17, 1920. Quotations from December 27, 1919.

29. Ibid., January 3 to January 17, 1920. Quotations from January 10 and January 17.

30. Foster quotations found in Donn Rogosin, *Invisible Men: Life in Baseball's Negro Leagues* (Lincoln: University of Nebraska Press, 1983), 33; Cottrell, *The Best Pitcher in Baseball*, 147; Michael Harkness-Roberto and Leslie A. Heaphy, "The Monarchs: A Brief History of the Franchise," *Satchel Paige and Company: Essays on the Kansas City Monarchs, Their Greatest Star, and the Negro Leagues* ed. Leslie A. Heaphy (Jefferson, NC: McFarland, 2007), 99–109.

31. Larry Lester, "J. L. Wilkinson: 'Only the Stars Come Out at Night'"; Tim Rives, "Tom Baird: A Challenge to the Modern Memory of the Kansas City Monarchs," *Satchel Paige and Company*, 110–143, 144–56.

32. Al Monroe, "What Is the Matter with Baseball?" 26–29, 60–61; Peterson, *Only the Ball Was White*, 88–90; Hogan, *Shades of Glory*, 160–65; Heaphy, *The Negro Leagues*, 47–48. Quotation in Cottrell, *The Best Pitcher in Baseball*, 163.

33. Carroll, *When to Stop the Cheering?*, 55–57; Hogan, *Shades of Glory*, 165–67.

34. Ibid.; Heaphy, *The Negro Leagues*, 65–66.

35. Cottrell, *The Best Pitcher in Baseball*, 168–73; Dixon, *Harvest on Freedom's Fields*, 209–16.

36. Hogan, *Shades of Glory*, 222–265; Heaphy, *The Negro Leagues*, 67–70; Larry Tye, *Satchel: The Life and Times of an American Legend* (New York: Random House, 2009); Rogosin, *Invisible Men*, 120, 141; Carroll, *When to Stop the Cheering?*, 128.

37. Larry Lester, "J. L. Wilkinson: 'Only the Stars Come Out At Night,'" *Satchel Paige and Company*, 110–143; Hogan, *Shades of Glory*, 254–57; "Buck Leonard," *Voices from the Great Black Baseball Leagues*, 258.

38. "Willie Wells," *Voices*, 224; "Newt Allen," *Voices*, 95; "George Sweatt," *Voices*, 90; Rogosin, *Invisible Men*, 74.

39. "Ted Page," *Voices*, 149; "Buck Leonard," *Voices*, 263, 269; "Willie Wells," *Voices*, 224; "Pee Wee Butts," *Voices*, 328; Rogoson, *Invisible Men*, 101–02.

40. Rogosin, *Invisible Men*, 100–01.

41. Ibid., 152–177; Hogan, *Shades of Glory*, 115–17; John Virtue, *South of the Colored Barrier: How Jorge Pasquel and the Mexican League Pushed Baseball Toward Racial Integration* (Jefferson, NC: McFarland, 2008), 37–47.

42. Ibid.; "Othello Renfroe," *Voices*, 349; "Cool Papa Bell," *Voices*, 122; Virtue, *South of the Colored Barrier*, 92–93.

43. "Ted Page," *Voices*, 153; "Bill Drake," *Voices*, 33.

44. Rogosin, *Invisible Men*, 152–77; Virtue, *South of the Color Barrier*, 56–59; Tye, *Satchel*, 108–35; Larry Lester, *Black Baseball's National Showcase: The East-West All Star Game, 1933–1953* (Lincoln: University of Nebraska Press, 2001), 97–101.

45. Rogosin, *Invisible Men*, 152–177; Heaphy, *The Negro Leagues*, 167–79.

46. Hogan, *Shades of Glory*, 266–323; Lanctot, *Negro League Baseball*, 153–166; Dick Clark and Larry Lester, (eds.) *The Negro Leagues Book* (Cleveland: Society for American Baseball Research, 1994). I have found the *Negro Leagues Book* chapter entitled "Standings, 1920–1953" to be the most reliable source for tracking the permutations of the various black leagues that appeared and vanished during the period. All subsequent discussion of league memberships derives from this source.

47. Clark and Lester, *The Negro Leagues Book*, 159–66; Lanctot, *Negro League Baseball*, 96–204; Lester, *Black Baseball's National Showcase*, 81.

48. Lester, *Black Baseball's National Showcase*, 9–19; Lanctot, *Negro League Baseball*, 3–204; Peterson, *Only the Ball Was White*, 92–94; Hogan, *Shades of Glory*, 250–70. Essentially every book addressing the Negro Leagues discusses Greenlee at some length. No one is neutral regarding his character and influence.

49. Lester, *Black Baseball National Showcase*, 1–29.

50. Ibid., 21–397.

51. Lanctot, *Negro League Baseball*, 3–204; Hogan, *Shades of Glory*, 208–212; Brad Snyder, *Beyond the Shadow of the Senators: The Untold Story of the Homestead Grays and the Integration of Baseball* (New York: McGraw-Hill, 2003), 33–53.

52. Snyder, *Beyond the Shadow of the Senators*.

53. Rogosin, *Invisible Men*, 105–08; Hogan, *Shades of Glory*, 261–62; Lanctot, *Negro League Baseball*, 59–61.

54. Rogosin, *Invisible Men*, 110–113; Virtue, *South of the Color Barrier*, 56–57.

55. Rogosin, *Invisible Men*, 108–110; Lanctot, *Negro League Baseball*, 79–122; Effa Manley and Leon Herbert Hardwick, *Negro Baseball ... Before Integration* (Haworth, NJ: St. Johann Press, 1976); "Effa Manley," *Voices from the Great Black Baseball Leagues*, 315–26; Bob Luke, *The Most Famous Woman in Baseball: Effa Manley and the Negro Leagues* (Washington, D.C.: Potomac Books, 2011) .

56. Lanctot, *Negro League Baseball*, 40–204; Rogosin, *Invisible Men*, 17–18; Lester, *Black Baseball's National Showcase*, 96; Hogan, *Shades of Glory*, 284.

57. Lester, *Black Baseball's National Showcase*; quotation, p. 3; Carroll, *When to Stop the Cheering?*, 81–85.

58. Attendance data compiled from box scores included in yearly synopses of East-West Games in Lester, *Black Baseball's National Showcase*.

59. Sugrue, *Sweet Land of Liberty*, xxv, 8; Lester, *Black Baseball's National Showcase*, 1–8.

60. Lloyd Lewis, "How Good is Negro Baseball?" *Chicago Daily News*, August 22, 1938, quoted in full, Lester, *Black Baseball's National Showcase*, 114–15.

61. "Cool Papa Bell," *Voices from the Great Black Baseball Leagues*, 111, 119; Rogosin, *Invisible Men*, 79.

62. Bill James, *The New Bill James Historical Baseball Abstract* (New York: Free Press, 2001), 121–22; Rader, *Baseball*, 124–28; Rogosin, *Invisible Men*, 56, 72–73; "Buck Leonard," *Voices*, 251.

63. Lanctot, *Negro League Baseball*, 40–66; 128–32; Carroll, *When to Stop the Cheering?*, 69–124; Hogan, *Shades of Glory*, 266–323; Rogosin, *Invisible Men*, 6.

64. Lester, *Black Baseball's National Showcase*, 120–21; Lanctot, *Negro League Baseball*, 153–204.

65. Lester, *Black Baseball's National Showcase*, 153–54; Virtue, *South of the Color Barrier*, 94–99; Lanctot, *Negro League Baseball*, 142.

66. Rogosin, *Invisible Men*, 26–27; Carroll, *When to Stop the Cheering?*, 165–82.

67. Hogan, *Shades of Glory*, 266–349; Peterson, *Only the Ball Was White*, 158–193.

68. DuBois, *The Soul of Black Folk*, 9.

## Chapter II

1. Wilbert, *Arrival of the American League*; Tygiel, *Past Time*, 35–86; Eliot Asinof, *Eight Men Out* (New York: Holt, Rinehart, 1963); Mike Sowell, *The Pitch That Killed: The Story of Carl Mays, Ray Chapman, and the Pennant Race of 1920* (New York: Ivan R. Dee, 2004); Jim Reisler, *Babe Ruth: Launching the Legend* (New York: McGraw-Hill, 2004); Robert W. Creamer, *Babe: The Legend Comes to Life* (New York: Simon & Schuster, 1974), 217–36.

2. White, *Creating the National Pastime*, 10–83; Jules Tygiel, *Past Time: Baseball as History* (New York: Oxford University Press, 2001), 87–88.

3. William Marshall, *Baseball's Pivotal Era: 1945–1951* (Lexington: University Press of Kentucky, 1999).

4. Tygiel, *Past Time*, 35–63; David Pietrusza, *Judge and Jury: The Life and Times of Judge Kenesaw Mountain Landis* (South Bend, IN: Diamond Communications, 1998), 254–84; Norman L. Macht, *Connie Mack and the Early Years of Baseball* (Lincoln: University of Nebraska Press, 2007); Shirley Povich, *The Washington Senators: An Informal History* (New York: G. P. Putnam's Sons, 1954).

5. Franklin Lewis, *The Cleveland Indians* (Kent, OH: Kent State University Press, 2006; reprint, original (New York: G. P. Putnam's Sons, 1949), 153–55; Jerry M. Gutlon, *It Was Never About the Babe: The Red Sox, Racism, Mismanagement, and the Curse of the Bambino* (New York: Skyhorse, 2009), 67–78; Joe Falls, *The Detroit Tigers: An Illustrated History* (New York: Walker, 1989), 55–122; Patrick Harrigan, *The Detroit Tigers: Club and Community* (Toronto: University of Toronto Press, 1997), 9–65.

6. Frederick J. Lieb, *The Baltimore Orioles: The History of a Colorful Team in Baltimore and St. Louis,* (New York: G. P. Putnam's Sons, 1955), 209–14; Glenn Stout, *Yankees Century: 100 Years of New York Yankees Baseball* (Boston: Houghton Mifflin, 2002), 65–204; Daniel R. Levitt, *Ed Barrow: The Bulldog Who Built the Yankees' First Dynasty* (Lincoln: University of Nebraska Press, 2008), 177–338; Don Warfield, *The Roaring Redhead: Larry MacPhail—Baseball's Great Innovator* (South Bend, IN: Diamond Communications, 1987), 146–201.

7. Bill Veeck, with Ed Linn, *Veeck—as in Wreck: The Autobiography of Bill Veeck* (Chicago: University of Chicago Press, 1962), 100.

8. Marshall, *Baseball's Pivotal Era*; Virtue, *South of the Color Barrier*, 125–61; Lee Lowenfish, *The Imperfect Diamond: A History of Baseball's Labor Wars* (Lincoln: University of Nebraska Press, 1991), 27–168.

9. This and all subsequent statistical material pertaining to on-field performance was compiled from John Thorn, Pete Palmer, Michael Gershman, and David Pietrusza, *Total Baseball: The Official Encyclopedia of Major League Baseball*, 5th ed. (New York: Viking, 1997); David S. Neft, Richard M. Cohen, and Michael L. Neft, *The Sport Encyclopedia: Baseball 2006* (New York: St. Martin's Griffin, 2006); and materials provided by Baseball-Referencewww.

10. Wilbert, *Arrival of the American League*, 185–93.

11. "Organized Baseball—American League: Statements of profit and loss for year ending in 1952," Eighty-Second Congress, *Study of Monopoly Power, Serial No. 1, Part 6: Organized Baseball* (Washington, D.C.: United States Government Printing Office, 1952), 359.

12. For further discussions of team finances, see Marshall, *Baseball's Pivotal Era*; and David G. Surdam, *The Postwar Yankees: Baseball's Golden Age Revisited* (Lincoln: University of Nebraska Press, 2008).

13. See Note 9.

14. Marshall, *Baseball's Pivotal Era*; Stout, *Yankees Century*, 205–62; Surdam, *Postwar Yankees*, 59–277; Lewis, *Cleveland Indians*; Veeck, *Veeck—as in Wreck*, 81–195; Gutlon, *It Was Never About the Babe*, 67–78; Harrigan, *Detroit Tigers*, 9–65; Povich, *Washington Senators*; Tom Deveaux, *The Washington Senators: 1901–1971* (Jefferson NC: McFarland, 2001), 148–209; Lieb, *Baltimore Orioles*, 204–46; Jeff Katz, *The Kansas City A's and the Wrong Half of the Yankees* (Hingham, MA: Maple Street Press, 2007).

15. Marshall, *Baseball's Pivotal Era*, 250–69; Leonard Koppett, *Koppett's Concise History of Major League Baseball* (New York: Carroll and Graf, 2004), 220–251; White, *Creating the National Pastime*, 275–315; Pietrusza, *Judge and Jury*, 328–404.

16. Marshall, *Baseball's Pivotal Era,* ; amateur free agent signings compiled from www.Baseball-Reference.com.

17. Marshall, *Baseball's Pivotal Era*, 250–69; Pietrusza, *Judge and Jury*, 347–70; Lee Lowenfish, *Branch Rickey: Baseball's Ferocious Gentleman* (Lincoln: University of Nebraska Press, 2007), 109–28.

18. Compiled from *Spalding's Baseball Guide and Record Book* (New York: American Sports Publishing, 1947–1954).

19. Brent P. Kelley, *Baseball's Bonus Babies: Conversations with 24 High-priced Ballplayers Signed from 1953 to 1957* (Jefferson NC: McFarland, 2006).

20. Percentages compiled from the *Baseball Register*, 1946. See also Baldassaro and Johnson, *The American Game: Baseball and Ethnicity*; Painter, *History of White People*.

21. See Note 9.

22. Tom Clavin and Danny Peary, *Roger Maris: Baseball's Reluctant Hero* (New York: Simon & Schuster, 2010), 93–98; Minnie Minoso, *Just Call Me Minnie: My Six Decades in Baseball* (Champaign, IL: Sagamore, 1994), 55–56.

## Chapter III

1. Letter to K. M. Landis, December 1943, File 1/7, *Integration: Correspondence and Clippings, BA MSS 67,*

on file, A. Bartlett Giamatti Library, National Baseball Hall of Fame and Museum, Cooperstown, NY.

2. For a discussion of the role of Judge Landis, see Norman L. Macht, "Does Baseball Deserve This Black Eye? A Dissent from the Universal Casting of Shame and Blame on Kenesaw Mountain Landis for Baseball's Failure to Sign Black Players Before 1946"; Richard Crepeau, "Landis, Baseball, and Racism—A Brief Comment"; Lee Lowenfish, "The Gentleman's Agreement and the Ferocious Gentleman Who Broke It"; and "Response by Norman Macht," *The Baseball Research Journal 38* (Summer, 2009): 26–35.

3. Carroll, *When to Stop the Cheering?*, 47–140; Jim Reisler, *Black Writers/Black Baseball: An Anthology of Articles from Black Sportswriters Who Covered the Negro Leagues* (Jefferson, NC: McFarland, 1994).

4. Reisler, *Black Writers/Black Baseball*, 33–56; David K. Wiggins, "Wendell Smith, the Pittsburgh Courier-Journal and the Campaign to Include Blacks in Organized Baseball, 1933–1945," *Journal of Sport History* 10 (Summer, 1983): 5–29; Wendell Smith, "Smitty's Sport Spurts: A Strange Tribe," *Pittsburgh Courier*, May 14, 1938.

5. Sam Lacy, "Sepia Stars Only Lukewarm Toward Campaign to Break Down Baseball Barriers," *Baltimore Afro-American*, August 12, 1939, 22; Snyder, *Shadow of the Senators*, 76–77; Luke, *Baltimore Elite Giants*, 100.

6. Fay Young, "Dustin' Off the News," *Chicago Defender*, August 16, 1941.

7. Joe Bostic, "In Re: Negroes in Big Leagues," *The People's Voice*, July 11, 1942.

8. Chester L. Washington, "Satchel's Back in Town," *Pittsburgh Courier*, May 9, 1936.

9. Ed Harris, "Nine Years Old, 50,000 Big," *Philadelphia Tribune*, August 7, 1941.

10. Carroll, *When to Stop the Cheering?*, 69–88; Reisler, *Black Writers/Black Baseball*. Several of the columns noted above are included in Reisler's anthology.

11. Carroll, *When to Stop the Cheering?*, 89–91, Wiggings, "Wendell Smith," *Journal of Sport History*.

12. Smith, *Pittsburgh Courier*, February 18, 1939, and February 25, 1939.

13. Ibid. The managerial interview series ran from July 15, 1939, to September 2, 1939. The order: Bill McKechnie, July 15; Bill Terry, July 22; Leo Durocher, July 29; Doc Prothro, August 5; Gabby Hartnett, August 12; Ray Blades, August 19; Casey Stengel, August 26; Pie Traynor, September 2.

14. Rogosin, *Invisible Men*, 206; Snyder, *Beyond the Shadow of the Senators*, 2; Timothy M. Gay, *Satch, Dizzy & Rapid Robert: The Wild Saga of Interracial Baseball Before Jackie Robinson* (New York: Simon & Schuster, 2010), 64–65.

15. Lester, *Black Baseball's National Showcase*, 107–09; Lanctot, *Negro League Baseball*, 220–23.

16. *Chicago Defender*, July 30, 1938 (quoted in Lester, *Black Baseball's National Showcase*, 107).

17. Art Rust, Jr., *Get That Nigger Off the Field: A Sparkling, Informal History of the Black Man in Baseball* (New York: Delacorte, 1976), 130.

18. "Ted Page," Holway, *Voices from the Great Black Baseball Leagues*, 155.

19. Lester, *Black Baseball's National Showcase*, 107–09; Lanctot, *Negro League Baseball*, 220–23; Levitt, *Ed Barrow*, 312–15; Alan H. Levy, *Joe McCarthy: Architect of the Yankee Dynasty* (Jefferson, NC: McFarland, 2005), 234, 247.

20. "No Good from Raising Race Issue," *The Sporting News*, August 6, 1942, 4.

21. "No Understanding Against Signing Negroes—Landis," *The Sporting News*, March 3, 1948; "MacPhail Sees Peril to Negro League Ball," July 29, 1942, File 1/21, *Integration: Correspondence and Clippings, BA MSS 67*, on file, A. Bartlett Giamatti Library, National Baseball Hall of Fame and Museum, Cooperstown, NY; Lanctot, *Negro League Baseball*, 233–34.

22. Fay Young, "Judge Landis' Decision—Bosh!" *Chicago Defender*, July 25, 1942.

23. Pietrusza, *Judge and Jury: Life and Times of Judge Kenesaw Mountain Landis*, 405–30.

24. Eddie Collins to William Harridge, January 6, 1943, File 1/4, *Integration: Correspondence and Clippings, BA MSS 67*, on file, A. Bartlett Giamatti Library, National Baseball Hall of Fame and Museum, Cooperstown, NY.

25. Clark Griffith to K. M. Landis, December 10, 1943; K.M. Landis to Clark Griffith, December 14, 1943, File 1/9, *Integration: Correspondence and Clippings, BA MSS 67*, on file, A. Bartlett Giamatti Library, National Baseball Hall of Fame and Museum, Cooperstown, NY.

26. Lester, *Black Baseball's National Showcase*, 208–10; Lanctot, *Negro League Baseball*, 244–46.

27. Murphy quoted in Lester, *Black Baseball's National Showcase*, 210.

28. Claude E. Barnett to K. M. Landis, November 26, 1943; Roy Wilkins to K. M. Landis, 26, 1943, File 1/8 *Integration: Correspondence and Clippings, BA MSS 67*, on file, A. Bartlett Giamatti Library, National Baseball Hall of Fame and Museum, Cooperstown, NY.

29. Snyder, *Beyond the Shadow of the Senators*, 178–180.

30. Lester, *Black Baseball's National Showcase*, 210; *Pittsburgh Courier*, December 11, 1943.

31. Sam Lacy to Eddie Collins and Larry MacPhail, March 3, 1945, File 1/12 *Integration: Correspondence and Clippings, BA MSS 67*, on file, A. Bartlett Giamatti Library, National Baseball Hall of Fame and Museum, Cooperstown, NY.

32. Marshall, *Baseball's Pivotal Era*, 3–98.

33. Ibid., Lawrence O'Conner to Sam Lacy, April 30, 1945, Larry MacPhail to William Harridge, June 2, 1945, File 1/12 *Integration: Correspondence and Clippings, BA MSS 67*, on file, A. Bartlett Giamatti Library, National Baseball Hall of Fame and Museum, Cooperstown, NY.

34. "Statement of L. (Larry) S. MacPhail, Bel Air, MD," Eighty-Second Congress, *Study of Monopoly Power: Hearings Before the Subcommittee On Study of Monopoly Power* (Washington, D.C.: United States Government Printing Office, 1952), 1062–65.

35. Extensive discussions of Rickey and MacPhail unavoidably figure in every book ever written about the integration of baseball. For just two outstanding examples, see Tygiel, *Baseball's Great Experiment* or Lanctot,

*Negro League Baseball.* For biographies, see Lowenfish, *Branch Rickey*; Warfield, *The Roaring Redhead: Larry MacPhail.*

36. "Rickey Claims That 15 Clubs Voted To Bar Negroes From the Majors," *New York Times*, February 18, 1948.

37. *New York Times*, February 24, 1948.

38. *New York Times*, February 18, 1948; Arthur Daley, "The Mahatma and the Redhead," *New York Times*, February 23, 1948; "MacPhail Brands as Lie Rickey's Statement," *New York Herald Tribune*, February 21, 1948.

39. Tygiel, *Baseball's Great Experiment*, 82–86.

40. Larry MacPhail to Albert B. Chandler, October 25, 1945, Memorandum on "The Negro in Baseball" enclosed in File 1/13 *Integration: Correspondence and Clippings, BA MSS 67*, on file, A. Bartlett Giamatti Library, National Baseball Hall of Fame and Museum, Cooperstown, NY.

41. "Report Of Major League Steering Committee For Submission to the National and American Leagues At Their Meetings in Chicago," Eighty-Second Congress, *Study of Monopoly Power*, 474–88. The portion considering the race issue is "E. Race Question," 483–84.

42. Cumberland Posey, "Posey's Points," *Pittsburgh Courier*; *Philadelphia Tribune*, March 25, 1944. The latter is quoted in Lester, *Black Baseball's National Showcase*, 210.

43. Carroll, *When to Stop the Cheering?*, 142; Manley and Hardwick, *Negro Baseball ... Before Integration*, 61–73; Heaphy (ed.), *Satchel Paige and Company*, 165–206.

44. Lanctot, *Negro League Baseball*, 118–52, 249; Rogosin, *Invisible Men*, 201; Snyder, *Beyond the Shadow of the Senators*, 1–32; "Buck Leonard," Holway, *Voices from the Great Black Baseball Leagues*, 261; Christopher Threston, *The Integration of Baseball in Philadelphia* (Jefferson NC: McFarland, 2003), 46–58.

45. Leroy (Satchel) Paige, *Maybe I'll Pitch Forever* (Lincoln: University of Nebraska Press, 1993; reprint of 1962 edition, published by Doubleday), 66.

46. "Dave Malarcher," Holway, *Voices from the Great Black Baseball Leagues*, 56.

47. "Joe Greene," Holway, *Voices from the Great Black Baseball Leagues*, 306; Holway, *Voices*, xiii; Bob Luke, *The Baltimore Elite Giants: Sport and Society in the Age of Negro League Baseball* (Baltimore: Johns Hopkins University Press, 2009), 70, 91; Stout, *Yankees Century*, 246.

48. Luke, *Baltimore Elite Giants*, 91; Rogosin, *Invisible Men*, 92–93; Snyder, *Beyond the Shadow of the Senators*, 1–32.

49. "Buck Leonard," Holway, *Voices from the Great Black Baseball Leagues*, 261; Fay Young, "Through the Years," *Chicago Defender*, July 14, 1945.

50. "Buck Leonard,"

51. Fay Young, "Big Leagues Scout 8 Negro Players," *Chicago Defender*, August 2, 1947.

## Chapter IV

1. Tye, *Satchel*, 77–80, 101–07; Rogosin, *Invisible Men*, 138–40; Terrie Aamodt, "Cracking a Chink in Jim Crow," Heaphy (ed.), *Satchel Paige and Company*, 54–72.

2. Tye, *Satchel*, 88–90; Aamodt, "Cracking a Chink in Jim Crow," Heaphy, ed., *Satchel Paige and Company*, 54–72; Lanctot, *Negro League Baseball*, 54.

3. Gay, *Satch, Dizzy & Rapid Robert*; Tye, *Satchel*, 77–107; Heaphy, *The Negro Leagues*.

4. Lanctot, *Negro League Baseball*, 230; Rogosin, *Invisible Men*, 124; Gay, *Satch, Dizzy & Rapid Robert*, 27–29; Paige, *Maybe I'll Pitch Forever*, 57; Leigh Montville, *The Big Bam: The Life and Times of Babe Ruth* (New York: Doubleday, 2006), 142–45.

5. Gay, *Satch, Dizzy & Rapid Robert*, 50–150; Tye, *Satchel*, 90–95; Ted Shane, "The Chocolate Rube Waddell," *Saturday Evening Post*, July 27, 1940.

6. Gay, *Satch, Dizzy & Rapid Robert*, 151–260; Marshall, *Baseball's Pivotal Era*, 84; Todd Anton and Bill Nowlin, eds. *When Baseball Went to War* (Chicago: Triumph Books, 2008), 103–110; Paige, *Maybe I'll Pitch Forever*, 87–92.

7. Wendell Smith, "The Sports Beat," *Pittsburgh Courier*, November 10, 1945; *The Sporting News*, October 30, 1946.

8. Gay. *Satch, Dizzy & Rapid Robert*, 278.

9. Virtue, *South of the Color Barrier*, 62–119; Marshall, *Baseball's Pivotal Era*, 45–63; *Pittsburgh Courier*, May 6, 1944.

10. Virtue, *South of the Color Barrier*, 115–40; Marshall, *Baseball's Pivotal Era*, 45–63.

11. Ibid.; Koppett, *History of Major League Baseball*, 220–29.

12. Virtue, *South of the Color Barrier*, 125–68; Adrian Burgos, Jr., *Playing America's Game: Baseball, Latinos, and the Color Line* (Berkeley: University of California Press, 2007), 151–56.

13. Virtue, *South of the Color Barrier*, 125–68; Marshall, *Baseball's Pivotal Era*, 45–100.

14. Ibid.; MacPhail, "Steering Committee Report," 82d Congress, *Study of Monopoly Power*, 474–88.

15. *New York Daily Worker*, March 23, 1942; Lester, *Black Baseball's National Showcase*, 173–74; "Sug Cornelius," Holway, *Voices from the Great Black Baseball Leagues*, 235–36.

16. *New York Daily Worker*, December 2, 1942; Lester, *Black Baseball's National Showcase*, 183; Rogosin, *Invisible Men*, 193–96; Joe Bostic, "Dodger Tryouts Blow at Jim Crow Baseball," *The People's Voice*, April 14, 1945 (included in Reisler, ed., *Black Writers/Black Baseball*); Lowenfish, *Branch Rickey*, 361–63.

17. Howard Bryant, *Shut Out: A Story of Race and Baseball in Boston* (New York: Routledge, 2002), 6–8, 31–33, 40–41, 112–13; Jerry M. Gutlon, *It Was Never About the Babe*, 95–98; Mark Armour, *Joe Cronin: A Life in Baseball* (Lincoln: University of Nebraska Press, 2010), 153–56.

18. Carroll, *When to Stop the Cheering?*, 69–125; Lester, *Black Baseball's National Showcase*, 172–279.

19. Carroll, *When to Stop the Cheering?*, 108; Dan Burley, "To Rickey, Stoneham, MacPhail: Straighten Up and Fly Right," *Amsterdam News*, August 4, 1945 (included in Reisler, ed., *Black Writers/Black Baseball*, 136).

20. Joe Bostic, "Dreamin'," *The People's Voice*, March

21, 1942 (included in Reisler, ed., *Black Writers/Black Baseball*, 77–79).

21. Chester L. Washington, "An Open Letter to Judge Landis," *Pittsburgh Courier*, May 30, 1942 (included in Reisler, ed., *Black Writers/Black Baseball*, 109–11).

22. Carroll, *When to Stop the Cheering?*, 141–58; Cumberland Posey, "Posey's Points," *Pittsburgh Courier*, June 27, 1942, March 27, 1943.

23. Carroll, *When to Stop the Cheering?*, 141–74; Wendell Smith, "The Sports Beat," *Pittsburgh Courier*, August 3, 1946; *Baltimore Afro-American*, April–September 1947; Luke, *Baltimore Elite Giants*, 106–07.

24. Dave Egan, "Baseball Manpower Shortage Solved," *Boston Record*, January 26, 1943; Shirley Povich, *All Those Mornings at the Post* (New York: Public Affairs, 2005); Lowenfish, *Branch Rickey*, 325; Snyder, *Beyond the Shadow of the Senators*, 1–32; Miscellaneous Clippings, File 1/21, *Integration: Correspondence and Clippings, BA MSS 67*, on file, A. Bartlett Giamatti Library, National Baseball Hall of Fame and Museum, Cooperstown, NY.

25. *New York Daily Worker*, June 8, 1942; Fur Dyers Union, Local 80, "Jim Crow Under Baseball Must Go," *Local 80 News*, File 1/3, *Integration: Correspondence and Clippings, BA MSS 67*, on file, A. Bartlett Giamatti Library, National Baseball Hall of Fame and Museum, Cooperstown, NY.

26. Lester, *Black Baseball's National Showcase*, 176–80; Carroll, *When to Stop the Cheering?*, 106–07; Kelly Rusinack, "Baseball on the Radical Agenda: The *Daily Worker* and *Sunday Worker* Journalistic Campaign to Desegregate Major League Baseball, 1933–1947," in Joseph Dorinson and Joram Warmund, eds., *Jackie Robinson: Race Sports, and the American Dream* (Armonk, NY: M. E. Sharpe, 1998), 75–85.

27. Hubert F. Julian to William Harridge, Telegram, April 10, 1945, File 1/3, *Integration: Correspondence and Clippings, BA MSS 67*, on file, A. Bartlett Giamatti Library, National Baseball Hall of Fame and Museum, Cooperstown, NY.

28. "Buck Leonard," Holway, *Voices from the Great Black Baseball Leagues*, 268–69.

29. Lester, *Black Baseball's National Showcase*, 208–10; Rogosin, *Invisible Men*, 185–86; Lowenfish, *Branch Rickey*, 470–74; MacPhail, "Steering Committee Report," 82nd Congress, *Study of Monopoly Power*, 483.

30. Wendell Smith, "Some Reds Always Want To Get Into the Act," *Pittsburgh Courier*, August 23, 1947.

31. Tygiel, *Baseball's Great Experiment*, 57–69; Dan Dodson, "The Integration of Negroes in Baseball," *Journal of Educational Sociology* 28 (October 1954): 73–82.

32. Larry MacPhail to Albert B. Chandler, October 25, 1945 (Enclosed: "The Negro in Baseball"), File 1/12, *Integration: Correspondence and Clippings, BA MSS 67*, on file, A. Bartlett Giamatti Library, National Baseball Hall of Fame and Museum, Cooperstown, NY.

33. Dan Daniel, "N.Y. Report Criticizes Negro Leagues in Probe of Organized Ball Color Bar," *The porting News*, November 29, 1945, 6.

34. *New York Times*, October 25, 1945; Dan Daniel, "Negro Player Issue Heads For Showdown," *The Sport-*ing News, November 1, 1945; Lanctot, *Negro League Baseball*, 252–99.

35. Lowenfish, *Branch Rickey*, 321–502; Marshall, *Baseball's Pivotal Era*, 120–66.

36. "John 'Buck' O'Neil," Fay Vincent, ed., *The Only Game In Town: Baseball Stars of the 1930s and 1940s Talk About the Game They Loved* (New York: Simon & Schuster, 2006), 94.

37. Leslie A. Heaphy, "Jackie Robinson and the 1945 Monarchs"; Jared Evan Furcolo Wheeler, "Jackie Robinson: The Desegregation of Baseball and the Fight for Civil Rights," Heaphy, ed., *Satchel Paige and Company*, 157–62; 179–89; Jonathon Eig, *Opening Day*.

38. Jonathan Eig, *Opening Day: The Story of Jackie Robinson's First Season* (New York: Simon & Schuster, 2008); Tygiel, *Baseball's Great Experiment*, 70–179; A. S. "Doc" Young, *Great Negro Baseball Stars: And How They Made the Major Leagues* (New York: A. S. Barnes), 17–49; Jackie Robinson, *I Never Had It Made: An Autobiography* (New York: Putnam, 1972), 26–70; J. G. Taylor Spink, "Rookie of the Year ... Jackie Robinson," *The Sporting News*, September 17, 1947, 3.

39. Red Barber, *1947: When All Hell Broke Loose in Baseball* (New York: Doubleday, 1982), 264.

40. "Club Heads Give Views," *New York Times*, October 24, 1945.

41. Clark Griffith to Albert B. Chandler, November 1, 1945, File 1/14, *Integration: Correspondence and Clippings, BA MSS 67*, on file, A. Bartlett Giamatti Library, National Baseball Hall of Fame and Museum, Cooperstown, NY.

42. Bill Veeck, with Ed Linn, *Veeck—as in Wreck: The Autobiography of Bill Veeck* (Chicago: University of Chicago Press, 1962), 170–80.

## Chapter V

1. Dan Daniel, "Over the Fence," *The Sporting News* (November 1, 1945): 12; Arthur Daley, "Happy Ribbed, Roasted and Fried at Merry-G-Round," *The Sporting News* (February 14, 1946): 13.

2. Young, *Great Negro Baseball Stars*, 10; Luke, *Most Famous Woman in Baseball*, 144; Peggy Pascoe, *What Comes Naturally: Miscegenation Law and the Making of Race in America* (Oxford: Oxford University Press, 2010).

3. Wendell Smith, "The Sports Beat," *Pittsburgh Courier*, November 10, 1945; Oscar E. Buhl, "Veeck Predicts Scramble for Colored Stars," *The Sporting News*, (July 16, 1947): 8; Wendell Smith, "Few, If Any, Colored Stars Ready to Join Majors, Says Negro Scribe," *The Sporting News* (January 12, 1949): 13.

4. Virtue, *South of the Color Barrier*, 100–19.

5. Art Carter, "Negro Baseball Players Star for Uncle Sam," *Negro Baseball Pictorial Yearbook* (1944). Copy on file, "Larry Doby" player file, National Baseball Hall of Fame and Museum, Cooperstown, NY.

6. Marshall, *Baseball's Pivotal Era*, 14–27; Todd Anton and Bill Nowlin, *When Baseball Went to War* (Chicago: Triumph Books, 2008).

7. Bill Veeck, with Ed Linn, *Veeck—as in Wreck: The Autobiography of Bill Veeck* (Chicago: University of Chicago Press, 1962), 175; Richard Ben Cramer, *Joe*

*DiMaggio: The Hero's Life* (New York: Simon & Schuster, 2000), 240–77.

8. Joseph Thomas Moore, *Pride Against Prejudice: The Biography of Larry Doby* (New York: Praeger, 1988), 89.

9. Veeck, *Veeck—as in Wreck*, 23–96, 170–72; Gerald Eskenazi, *Bill Veeck: A Baseball Legend* (New York: McGraw-Hill, 1988), 1–21; David M. Jordan, Larry R. Gerlach, and John P. Rossi, "A Baseball Myth Exploded: The Truth About Bill Veeck and the '43 Phillies," *The National Pastime* (1998): 3–13; Jules Tygiel, "Revisiting Bill Veeck and the 1943 Phillies," *The Baseball Research Journal* 35: 109–14. See also Paul Dickson, *Bill Veeck: Baseball's Greatest Maverick* (New York: Walker, 2012), 70–83.

10. Ibid., 97–131; Lou Boudreau with Ed Fitzgerald, *Player-Manager* (Boston: Little, Brown, 1949), 78; Young, *Great Negro Baseball Stars*, 9.

11. Veeck, *Veeck—as in Wreck*, 170–76; Eskenazi, *Bill Veeck*, 36–43; Dickson, *Bill Veeck*, 122–35.

12. Veeck, *Veeck—as in Wreck*, 171.

13. Ibid., 175; Moore, *Pride Against Prejudice*, 39–40; Young, *Great Negro Baseball Stars*, 50–56.

14. Eig, *Opening Day*, 180–190; Robinson, *I Never Had It Made*, 3–77; Jackie Robinson, *Baseball Has Done It* (Philadelphia: Lippincott, 1964), 1–75; Moore, *Pride Against Prejudice*, 39–63.

15. Moore, *Pride Against Prejudice*, 29–37; Rust, *"Get That Nigger Off the Field,"* 82.

16. Holway, ed. "Willie Wells," "Hilton Smith," "Newt Allen," *Voices from the Great Black Baseball Leagues*, 221, 103, 292; Hy Engel, "Starring a Habit with Larry Doby," *PM*, July 30, 1947. (included in Larry Doby file, A. Bartlett Giamatti Library, National Baseball Hall of Fame).

17. Veeck, *Veeck—as in Wreck*, 180.

18. Manley, *Negro Baseball ... Before Integration*, 61–95.

19. Veeck, *Veeck—as in Wreck*, 170–76; Lowenfish, *Branch Rickey*, 433; Tygiel, *Baseball's Great Experiment*, 211–19.

20. Manley, *Negro Baseball ... Before Integration*, 61–95; Luke, *Most Famous Woman in Baseball*, 88–89; Moore, *Pride Against Prejudice*, 40–41; Veeck, *Veeck—as in Wreck*, 176; J. G. Taylor Spink, "Doby's Play Makes the Eagles Scream," *The Sporting News,* October 20, 1948, 2.

21. Compiled from data gathered from the *Baseball Register* (St. Louis: C. C. Spink and Sons, 1946, 1947, 1948).

22. Tygiel, *Baseball's Great Experiment*, 47–179; Veeck, *Veeck—as in Wreck*, 170–80; Moore, *Pride Against Prejudice*, 39–65; Boudreau, *Player-Manager*, 103–06; Rick Swaine, *The Integration of Major League Baseball: A Team By Team History* (Jefferson, NC: McFarland, 2009), 48–61; Doc Goldstein, "Teeth Chattered in Cleveland Bow, Larry Doby Says," *The Sporting News*, November 12, 1947, 10.

23. Boudreau, *Player-Manager*, 53–56; Veeck, *Veeck—as in Wreck*, 154–55.

24. Young, *Great Negro Baseball Stars*, 57; Moore, *Pride Against Prejudice*, 46–47; Lou Boudreau, *Lou Boudreau: Covering All the Bases* (Champaign, IL: Sag-

amore, 1993), 96–98; Boudreau, *Player-Manager*, 105–08; "Larry Doby," Vincent, ed., *The Only Game in Town*, 171–92; "Player Joins Team Tomorrow," *New York Times*, July 4, 1947; "Doby Makes Debut As Indians Lose, 6–5," *New York Times*, July 6, 1947; "Larry Can Make Big Hit with Bat," *Cleveland Plain Dealer*, July 4, 1947.

25. Gordon Cobbledick, *Cleveland Plain-Dealer*, July 6, 1947, July 27, 1947; Moore, *Pride Against Prejudice*, 49.

26. Young, *Great Negro Baseball Stars*, 56–59; Moore, *Pride Against Prejudice*, 52–55; Boudreau, *Player-Manager,* 103–06; Marshall, *Baseball's Pivotal Era*, 144–48.

27. Young, *Great Negro Baseball Stars*, 55; Moore, *Pride Against Prejudice*, 61.

28. Veeck, *Veeck—as in Wreck*, 176–77.

29. "Once Again, That Negro Question," *The Sporting News*, July 16, 1947, 16.

30. J. Roy Stockton, "Muckerman Shouldn't Be Too Sad," *St. Louis Post Dispatch*, July 1947; Frederick G. Lieb, "Gates Rusting, Browns Rush in 2 Negro Players," St. Louis, July 1947. Both articles are preserved in volume 8 of the "1947 DeWitt Scrapbook," (BASCR 143 V. 8), held at the A. Bartlett Giamatti Library, National Baseball Hall of Fame and Museum, Cooperstown, NY. Both articles are newspaper clippings; no further information is provided. See also Young, *Great Negro Baseball Stars*, 108.

31. "Browns' Plight Reflects Player Shortage," *The Sporting News*, August 6, 1947, 12; Hank Thompson, "How I Wrecked My Life—How I Hope to Save It," *Sport* (December 1965): 46–51, 95–98; Tygiel, *Baseball's Great Experiment*, 220–22; Swaine, *Integration of Major League Baseball*, 62–70.

32. "Ese Hombre: Willard 'Home Run' Brown," John B. Holway, ed. *Black Diamonds: Life in the Negro Leagues from the Men Who Lived It* (Westport CT: Meckler, 1989), 107–18; Virtue, *South of the Color Barrier*, 82–83, 178–79; Young, *Great Negro Baseball Stars*, 140; "Othello Renfroe," *Voices from the Great Black Baseball Leagues*, 345.

33. Hank Thompson, "How I Wrecked My Life," *Sport*, 46–51, 95–98; "Othello Renfroe," *Voices from the Great Black Baseball Leagues*, 345.

34. *Pittsburgh Courier*, July 26, 1947; Wendell Smith, *Pittsburgh Courier*, August 30, 1947; Thompson, "How I Wrecked My Life," *Sport*, 46–51, 95–98.

35. "Home Run Brown," *Black Diamonds*, 107–18; Fredrick G. Lieb, "Browns Negro Players Bat Only .194 and .178," St. Louis, August 1947, *DeWitt Scrapbooks*, v.8; *New York Times*, July 17, July 19, July 23, 1947.

36. Wendell Smith, *Pittsburgh Courier,* August 30, 1947; Bill Roeder, *New York World Telegram*, April 12, 1951.

37. *Baltimore Afro-American*, August 9, 1947.

38. "Home Run Brown," *Black Diamonds*, 107–18.

39. Young, *Great Negro Baseball Stars*, 140–41; Thompson, "How I Wrecked My Life," *Sport*, 46–51, 95–98.

40. Thompson, "How I Wrecked My Life," *Sport*, 96.

41. Moore, *Pride Against Prejudice*, 67–69; Boudreau, *Player-Manager*, 103–22.

42. Boudreau, *Player-Manager*, 101; Veeck, *Veeck—*

*as in Wreck*, 178; Moore, *Pride Against Prejudice*, 67–72; Eskenazi, *Bill Veeck*, 37–41; Dickson, *Bill Veeck*, 122–35.

43. Ed McAuley, "Negro Spikes White Rival—and That's the Whole Story," *The Sporting News*, March 31, 1948, 3; Veeck, *Veeck—as in Wreck*, 179; Moore, *Pride Against Prejudice*, 73.

44. Boudreau, *Player-Manager*, 117–51.

45. Ibid., 177–78, 199–200, 214–15; Jack Ledden, "Hank's Tips, Lou's Bat Helped Doby Hit Over .300, Negro Star Says," *The Sporting News*, December 29, 1948, 8.

46. Veeck, *Veeck—as in Wreck*, 181–92; Young, *Great Negro Baseball Stars*, 75–80; Boudreau, *Player-Manager*, 161–66.

47. Paige, *Maybe I'll Pitch Forever*; Tyle, *Satchel*; John B. Holway, *Josh and Satch: The Life and Times Of Josh Gibson and Satchel Paige* (Westport CN: Meckler, 1991); Heaphy, ed. *Satchel Paige and Company*.

48. J. G. Taylor Spink, "Two Ill-Advised Moves," *The Sporting News*, July 14, 1948, 8; Veeck, *Veeck—as in Wreck*, 185; Dickson, *Bill Veeck*, 136–49.

49. Tom Meany, "$64 Question: Paige's Age," *New York Star*, July 21, 1948; Paige, *Maybe I'll Pitch Forever*, 198.

50. Paige, *Maybe I'll Pitch Forever*, 196–98; Veeck, *Veeck—as in Wreck*, 183–84; Boudreau, *Player-Manager*, 162–63.

51. Paige, *Maybe I'll Pitch Forever*, 7–11, 195–216; Veeck, *Veeck—as in Wreck*, 184–91; Boudreau, *Player-Manager*, 163–66.

52. Moore, *Pride Against Prejudice*, 15, 77–78; Young, *Great Negro Baseball Stars*, 75–80; Ed McAuley, "Life in the Majors with Satchel Paige," *The Sporting News*, September 22, 1948, p. 13; Tye, *Satchel*, 215–16.

53. Boudreau, *Player-Manager*, 235; Moore, *Pride Against Prejudice*, 82–83.

54. "Larry Doby," Vincent, ed. *The Only Game in Town*, 190.

55. Ibid., Tygiel, *Baseball's Great Experiment*, 239.

56. Veeck, *Veeck—as in Wreck*, 196–209; Eskenazi, *Bill Veeck*, 82–83; Paige, Maybe *I'll Pitch Forever*, 231–34.

57. "Doby And Robinson Shun Banquet League," *Ebony* (May 1949): 34–37; Bill Nunn, "Is There Trouble On The Tribe?" *The Sporting News*, September 12, 1953, 28; Moore, *Pride Against Prejudice*, 96–97; Hal Lebovitz, "Different Doby' Puts New Team Spirit In Injuns," *The Sporting News*, May 19, 1954, 9.

58. Edgar Munzel, "14 Negro Players Give Tribe Corner on Colored Talent," *The Sporting News*, April 13, 1949; Tygiel, *Baseball's Great Experiment*, 311; "Quota Talk Crops Up Again With Tribe," *The Sporting News*, September 12, 1953, 28; Minoso, *Just Call Me Minnie*, 42–57.

59. Larry Moffi and Jonathon Cronstadt, *Crossing the Line: Black Major Leaguers 1947–1959* (Lincoln: University of Nebraska Press, 1994), 41–44, 65–67; Minoso, *Just Call Me Minnie*; Young, *Great Negro Baseball Stars*, 169–73.

60. Minoso, *Just Call Me Minnie*, 132; Burgos, *Playing America's Game*, 194.

61. DuBois, *Souls of Black Folk*; Burgos, *Playing America's Game*, 194–96; Ruck, *Raceball*, 97–117;

Robert Boyle, "The Private World of the Negro Ballplayer," *Sports Illustrated*, March 21, 1960: 16–21, 75–84; "Readers Torn Over Tori," *USA Today Sports Weekly*, March 17–23, 2010: 3. Minoso quoted from Brent P. Kelley, *Voices from the Negro Leagues: Conversations with 52 Baseball Standouts* (Jefferson, NC: McFarland, 1998), 166–67.

62. Dan Daniel, "Greenberg Denies Offering Simpson," *The Sporting News*, May 28, 1951; Swaine, *Integration of Major League Baseball*, 56–59.

63. Tuttle, *Race Riot*; Isabell Wilkerson, *The Warmth of Other Suns: The Epic Story of America's Great Migration* (New York: Random House, 2010), 398.

64. *New York Daily Worker*, March 23, 1942; Lester, *Black Baseball's National Showcase*, 173–74.

65. Wilbert, *Arrival of the American League*; Asinof, *Eight Men Out*; Warren Brown, *The Chicago White Sox* (Kent, OH: Kent State University Press, 2007, facsimile of New York: G. P. Putnam's edition).

66. Minoso, *Just Call Me Minnie*, xiii-xv, 100; Swaine, *Integration of Major League Baseball*, 101–02.

67. Bill James, *Guide to Baseball Managers from 1870 to Today* (New York: Scribner, 1997), 195–99; Donald Honig, *The Man in the Dugout* (Lincoln: University of Nebraska Press, 1977), 118–43.

68. Honig, *Man in the Dugout*, 136–37.

69. Ibid., 140; Minoso, *Just Call Me Minnie*, 46–60; Irving Vaughan, "Sox Get Minoso, Lehner," *Chicago Daily Tribune*, May 1, 1951, 1; "Sox Beaten, 8–3," *Chicago Tribune*, May 2, 1951, 1; White Sox Get Minoso, Negro Ace, in Season's Biggest Player Trade," *New York Times*, May 1, 1951, 46.

70. Minoso, *Just Call Me Minnie*, 100–02; Edgar Munzei, "Yankees Tactics Stir White Sox to Vow of Reprisal," *The Sporting News*, June 1, 1955: 23; Gene Kessler, "Racial Prejudice Absent in Dust-Off Pitches," *The Sporting News*, June 8, 1955: 17; Moore, Pride Against Prejudice, 113–15.

71. Minoso, *Just Call Me Minnie*, 93–4; Honig, Man in the Dugout, 140–41.

72. James, Baseball Managers, 195–99.

73. Lloyd McGowan, "Royals Rodriguez Rookie Flash at 31," *The Sporting News*, August 8, 1951: 16; Minoso, *Just Call Me Minnie*, 53; "Bob Boyd," *When the Cheering Stops: Former Major Leaguers Talk About Their Game and Their Lives*, ed. Lee Heiman, Dave Weiner, and Bill Gutman (New York: Macmillan, 1990), 154.

74. Minoso, *Just Call Me Minnie*, 54, 66, 110; "Al Smith," *When the Cheering Stops*, 74; Swain, *Integration of Major League Baseball*, 56–59, 102-05.

## Interlude

1. A. S. (Doc) Young, "Negro Ball Fights Bravely for Life Against Big Odds," *The Sporting News*, August 7, 1957: 33.

2. Lawrence D. Hogan, *Shades of Glory: The Negro Leagues and the Story of African-American Baseball* (Washington D.C.: National Geographic, 2006), 266–379; Donn Rogosin, *Invisible Men: Life in Baseball's Negro Leagues* (Lincoln: University of Nebraska Press, 1983), 178–221; Leslie A. Heaphy, *The Negro Leagues 1869-1960* (Jefferson, NC: McFarland, 2003), 180–

224; Effa Manley and Leon Herbert Hardwick, *Negro Baseball ... Before Integration* (Haworth, NJ: St. Johann Press, 1976), 61–103; Brian Carroll, *When to Stop the Cheering?* (New York: Routledge, 2007), 69–174; Neil Lanctot, *Negro League Baseball: The Rise and Ruin of a Black Institution* (Philadelphia: University of Pennsylvania Press, 2004), 207–397; Robert W. Peterson, *Only the Ball Was White: Negro Baseball* (Englewood Cliffs, NJ: Prentice-Hall, 1970), 183–205; Dick Clark and Larry Lester, eds. *The Negro Leagues Book* (Cleveland: Society for American Baseball Research, 1994).

3. John P. Joy to Albert B. Chandler, November 2, 1945, File 1/11, *Integration: Correspondence and Clippings, BA MSS 67*, on file, A. Bartlett Giamatti Library, National Baseball Hall of Fame and Museum, Cooperstown, NY. Joy and his organization are very much a mystery. He appeared in various capacities from time to time over the next ten years, testifying before government commissions, taking out ads in the Chicago *Defender* offering franchises. His connections to the two functioning Negro Leagues is unknown.

4. Bob Luke, *The Most Famous Woman in Baseball: Effa Manley and the Negro Leagues* (Washington, D.C.: Potomac, 2011), 92, 136–39; Lanctot, *Negro League Baseball*, 337; Lester, *Black Baseball's National Showcase*, 317–20; Manley and Hardwick, *Negro Baseball Before Integration*, 92.

5. Negro American League of Professional Baseball Clubs, "Player's Contract," adopted 1947.

6. "Negro Loop Head Claims O. B. Refused Admission," *The Sporting News*, March 3, 1948: 18.

7. John P. Joy to Albert B. Chandler, November 2, 1945, File 1/11; J. B. Martin to Albert B. Chandler, August 1947, File 1/17; Effa Manley to Albert B. Chandler, April 24, 1946, File 1/15; *Integration: Correspondence and Clippings, BA MSS 67*, on file, A. Bartlett Giamatti Library, National Baseball Hall of Fame and Museum, Cooperstown, NY; Lanctot, *Negro League Baseball*, 282–87; Bob Luke, *The Baltimore Elite Giants* (Baltimore: Johns Hopkins University Press, 2009), 98–99; "Chandler Sees Martin, Wilson," *Chicago Defender*, January 26, 1946; "Negro Loop Head Claims O.B. Refused Admission," *The Sporting News*, March 3, 1948: 18.

8. Geri Stricker, "A Generation Too Early? Integration in the Short-Lived Interstate League of 1926," oral presentation, *Cooperstown Symposium on Baseball and American Culture*, Cooperstown NY, June 4, 2009.

9. Rogosin, *Invisible Men*, 185; Larry Lester, *Black Baseball's National Showcase: The East-West All-Star Game, 1933–1953* (Lincoln: University of Nebraska Press, 2001), 121–22; "Dave Malarcher," in John Holway, *Voices from the Great Black Baseball Leagues* (New York: Dodd, Mead, 1975), 54–55.

10. Bruce Adelson, *Brushing Back Jim Crow: The Integration of Minor-League Baseball in the American South* (Charlottesville: University of Virginia Press, 1999), 1–34; E. G. Brands, "Southern Circuits to Remain on 'All-White Basis,'" *The Sporting News*, August 6, 1947: 9.

11. Carroll, *When to Stop The Cheering?*, 144–49; Rogosin, *Invisible Men*, 113; Hogan, *Shades of Glory*, 358–63.

12. Jackie Robinson, "What's Wrong With Negro League Baseball?" *Ebony* (June 1948): 16–18.

13. Jackie Robinson, *I Never Had It Made: An Autobiography* (New York: Putnam, 1972); Lee Lowenfish, *Branch Rickey: Baseball's Ferocious Gentleman* (Lincoln: University of Nebraska Press, 2007), 321–502; William Marshall, *Baseball's Pivotal Era: 1945–1951* (Lexington: University Press of Kentucky, 1999), 120–66.

14. Carroll, *When to Stop The Cheering?*, 159–74; Lanctot, *Negro League Baseball*, 320–62.

15. Luke, *The Most Famous Woman in Baseball*, 143–45; "Mrs. Manley Calls Jackie Robinson 'Ungrateful,'" *Chicago Defender*, May 29, 1948; Wendell Smith, "Sports Beat," *Pittsburgh Courier*, November 20, 1948.

16. Manley and Hardwick, *Negro Baseball Before Integration*; Luke, *The Most Famous Woman in Baseball*; Rogosin, *Invisible Men*, 94.

17. Frank Robinson and Berry Stainback, *Extra Innings: The Grand-Slam Response to Al Campanis's Controversial Remarks About Blacks in Baseball* (New York: McGraw-Hill, 1988); Arlene Howard with Ralph Winbush, *Elston and Me: The Story of the First Black Yankee* (Columbia: University of Missouri Press, 2001), 159.

18. Stephen Jay Gould, *The Mismeasure Of Man*, 2d edition (New York: W. W. Norton, 1996), 63–104, 109–14; Frank Robinson, *Extra Innings*, 1.

19. Doc Young, "Negro Ball Fights Bravely for Life Against Big Odds," *The Sporting News*, August 7, 1957, 33.

## *Chapter VI*

1. Lerone Bennett Jr., *Before the Mayflower: A History of Black America* (Chicago: Johnson Publishing, 2007), 346–48; Juan Williams, *Eyes on the Prize: America's Civil Rights Years 1954–1965* (New York: Penguin, 1987), 1–36.

2. Dan Daniel, "Over The Fence: Negro Issue Fizzling Out," *The Sporting News*, August 20, 1947: 8.

3. Wendell Smith, "The Most Prejudiced Teams in Baseball," *Ebony* (May 1953): 111–20.

4. Williams, *Eyes on the Prize*, 1–90.

5. David Jordan, *The Athletics of Philadelphia: Connie Mack's White Elephants* (Jefferson NC: McFarland, 1999), 115–86.

6. Bruce Kuklick, *To Everything a Season: Shibe Park and Urban Philadelphia* (Princeton: Princeton University Press, 1991), 19–30.

7. Jordan, *Athletics of Philadelphia*, 115–29.

8. Ibid., 123; Kuklick, *To Everything a Season*, 73–77.

9. Kuklick, *To Everything a Season*, 82–94, 145–163.

10. Jordan, *Athletics of Philadelphia*, 140–186; Kuklick, *To Everything a Season*, 95–163; Harry T. Paxton "The Philadelphia A's Last Stand," *Saturday Evening Post*, June 12, 1954; Jeff Katz, *Kansas City A's and the Wrong Half of the Yankees*, 46–112.

11. Burgos, *Playing America's Game*, 85–86; Tom Swift, *Chief Bender's Burden: The Silent Struggle of a Baseball Star* (Lincoln: University of Nebraska Press, 2008); Christopher Threston, *Integration of Baseball*

*in Philadelphia*, 30–69; "Connie Mack," *The Sporting News*, August 27, 1947: 3; Jordan, *Athletics of Philadelphia*, 146.

12. "A's Sign Johnson as First Negro Scout," *The Sporting News*, February 7, 1951: 19; Johnson quotation on Mack from Rust, *Get That Nigger Off the Field*, 44. Story of Henry Aaron from Kevin Kerrane, *Dollar Sign on the Muscle* (New York: Avon, 1985), 63; Jordan, *Athletics of Philadelphia*, 152.

13. Moffi and Kronstadt, *Crossing the Line*, 103–04; Art Morrow, "A's Buy Trice; First Negro to Join Phila. Club," *Philadelphia Inquirer*, September 9, 1953, 47; "Athletics Call Up Trice of Ottawa," *New York Times*, September 9, 1953, 39.

14. Rollo Wilson, "Trice Bought by Philly Athletics," *Pittsburgh Courier*, September 12, 1953, 25.

15. Art Morrow, "A's, Browns Divide; Byrd Takes 2d, 2–0," *Philadelphia Inquirer*, September 14, 1953; Threston, *Integration of Baseball in Philadelphia*, 83–84.

16. "Johnson, A Negro, Athletics' Coach," *New York Times*, February 5, 1954, 25; Danny Peary, ed., *We Played the Game: Memories of Baseball's Greatest Era* (New York: Black Dog and Leventhal, 1994), 262–64.

17. Art Morrow, "Bob Trice Requests Return to Minors to 'Have Fun Pitching,'" *The Sporting News*, July 21, 1954: 31.

18. Moffi and Kronstadt, *Crossing The Line*, 122.

19. Wendell Smith, "What Are the Yankees Going To Do with Vic Power?" *Pittsburgh Courier*, October 17, 1953, 24.

20. Dan Daniel, "What About Vic Power? First Post-Season Poser for Yanks," *The Sporting News*, October 7, 1953: 7; "Yanks Faced With Problem in Power," *Pittsburgh Courier*, September 12, 1953, 25.

21. Joseph M. Sheehan, "Yanks Get Byrd and Eddie Robinson in 13-Man Deal With Athletics," *New York Times*, December 17, 1953, 57.

22. Frank Graham, Jr., "Power Proves His Case," *Sport* (August 1956): 44–47, 79; Peary, *We Played the Game*, 301–02.

23. Katz, *Kansas City A's and the Wrong Half of the Yankees*, 1–42.

24. Peary, *We Played the Game*, 241, 263, 303, 339; Graham, "Power Proves His Case," *Sport*, August 1956; Leonard Shecter, "Vic Power's New, Wonderful World," *Sport* (July 1966): 65–71; Robinson, *Baseball Has Done It*, 172–79.

25. Peary, *We Played the Game*, 301.

26. Peter Golenbeck, *Dynasty: The New York Yankees 1949–1964* (Englewood Cliffs NY: Prentice Hall, 1975), 201–02; Katz, *Kansas City A's and the Wrong Half of the Yankees*, 145–51.

27. Katz, *Kansas City A's and the Wrong Half of the Yankees*, 162–65; *Baseball Register: 1961*, 274.

28. Povich, *Washington Senators*, 67–72.

29. Ibid., 76–80; Wilbert, *Arrival of the American League*.

30. Povich, *Washington Senators*, 85–96; Deveaux, *The Washington Senators, 1901–1971*.

31. Threston, *Integration of Baseball in Philadelphia*, 37–69.

32. Snyder, *Beyond the Shadow of the Senators*, 1–12.

33. Ibid.

34. Ibid., 87–176; "Buck Leonard," *Voices from the Great Black Baseball Leagues*, ed. Holway, 250–78.

35. Snyder, *Beyond the Shadow of the Senators*, 87–176, 232.

36. Warfield, *Roaring Redhead*, 59.

37. Marshall, *Baseball's Pivotal Era*, 188; Bill Gilbert, *They Also Served: Baseball and the Home Front, 1941–1945* (New York: Crown), 14, 41–42.

38. Povich, *Washington Senators*, 200.

39. Ibid., 201–08; Deveaux, *Washington Senators*, 144–46; Snyder, *Beyond the Shadow of the Senators*, 68–78; Burgos, *Playing America's Game*, 150–60.

40. Burgos, *Playing America's Game*, 143–61; Ruck, *Raceball*, 72–84; Povich, *Washington Senators*, 206–08, 233; Bob Considine, "Ivory From Cuba," *Collier's* (August 1940): 9–24.

41. Burgos, *Playing America's Game*, 153–59.

42. "Buck Leonard," *Voices from the Great Black Baseball Leagues*, ed. Holway, 250–78; Snyder, *Beyond The Shadow Of The Senators*, 75–98.

43. Wendell Smith, "Branch Rickey Tells Courier," *Pittsburgh Courier*, November 3, 1945, 3.

44. Snyder, *Beyond the Shadow of the Senators*, 177–246; Carroll, *When to Stop the Cheering?*, 140–41.

45. Ibid., 180, 192; J. G. Taylor Spink, "Clark Griffith's 50 Golden Years in the American League," *The Sporting News*, July 23, 1952: 11–12; Dan Daniel, "Nats on Look-out for Negro Stars," *The Sporting News*, July 4, 1951: 11.

46. Bob Addie, "Winter Garden Denies Ban, But Nats' 7 Negroes Leave," *The Sporting News*, March 31, 1954: 17.

47. Swaine, *Integration of Major League Baseball*, 172–75; Shirley Povich, *Pittsburgh Courier*, August 29, 1952 (quoted in Tygiel, *Baseball's Great Experiment*, 293; Robinson, *Baseball Has Done It*, 188.

48. Moffi and Kronstadt, Crossing the Line, 116–17. I was so desperate for material on Paula, I lifted information from his Topps 1956 baseball card—#4. A primary source of sorts, I guess.

49. Moffi and Kronstadt, *Crossing the Line*, 229–35.

50. Ibid., 126–27; Deveaux, *Washington Senators*, 204.

51. Moffi and Kronstadt, *Crossing the Line*, 72–75, 165–66.

52. Quoted in Snyder, *Beyond the Shadow of the Senators*, 289.

53. Veeck, *Veeck—as in Wreck*, 223–29; Dickson, *Bill Veeck*, 184–206; Frederick G. Lieb, *Baltimore Orioles*, 173–78.

54. Veeck, *Veeck—as in Wreck*, 227–29; Lieb, *Baltimore Orioles*, 173–74; Tye, *Satchel*, 224–33.

55. Veeck, *Veeck—as in Wreck*, 281–94; Lieb, *Baltimore Orioles*, 172–82; Dickson, *Bill Veeck*, 207–17; Hugh Trader, Jr., "Shuffle-Off for Satch as Oriole Seen," *The Sporting News*, January 6, 1954: 19.

56. Tygiel, *Baseball's Great Experiment*, 121, 129, 313; Luke *Baltimore Elite Giants*; Adelson, *Brushing Back Jim Crow*, 100–02.

57. Luke *Baltimore Elite Giants*, 16–22, 77–79, 109–10, 134–59.

58. Edward C. Burke, "Orioles Sign Kryhoski and Heard," *Baltimore Sun*, February 16, 1954, 15; Lou Batter, "Heard," *Baltimore Sun*, February 25, 1954, 17; Ned

Burks, "Heard Sent to Portland," *Baltimore Sun,* June 7, 1954, 15; Moffi and Kronstadt, *Crossing the Line;* 109, 113–14.

59. Honig, *The Man in the Dugout,* 140–41; James, *Baseball Managers,* 196–98.

60. Honig, *The Man in the Dugout,* 140.

61. Edgar Munzell, "Boyd of White Sox Never Hit Under .352 in Negro Leagues," *The Sporting News,* March 14, 1951: 7–8; Doc Young quoted in Moffi and Kronstadt, *Crossing the Line,* 54; "Bob Boyd," in *When the Cheering Stops,* ed. Heiman et al., 153.

62. "Bob Boyd," in *When the Cheering Stops,* ed. Heiman et al., 145.

63. "Connie Johnson," in Kelley, *Voices from the Negro Leagues,* 119.

64. Rogosin, *Invisible Men,* 39, 76; Moffi and Kronstadt, *Crossing the Line,* 98–99.

65. Moffi and Kronstadt, *Crossing the Line,* 78–80, 109, 143–44, 165–66, 193–94.

66. Swaine, *Integration of Major League Baseball,* 73–74.

67. Howard, *Elston and Me,* 48.

68. Surdam, *Postwar Yankees;* Stout, *Yankees Century,* 85–262.

69. "No Negroes for Yanks," *The Sporting News,* August 6, 1947: 19; Warfield, *Roaring Redhead,* 171–207; Dan Daniel, "Dan Topping Denies Jim Crow Charge in Yankees' Failure to Call Up Power," *The Sporting News,* August 19, 1953: 4.

70. Dan Daniel, "Giants and Yanks Bombarding Dodgers' Lead in Negro Talent," *The Sporting News,* February 9, 1949: 1, 4; "Yanks Get 2 Negro Players," *New York Times,* July 20, 1950, 40.

71. Bill Madden, *Pride Of October: What It Was to Be Young and a Yankee* (New York: Warner Books, 2003), 149; John C. Hoffman, "Ernie Banks Played His First Game at 17," *The Sporting News,* July 20, 1955: 3.

72. Robert Shaplan, "The Yankees' Real Boss," *Sports Illustrated,* September 20, 1954; Dan Daniel, "Majors Must Balance Budget," *The Sporting News,* July 30, 1952, 1–2; Roger Kahn, *The Boys of Summer,* (New York: Harper and Row, 1971), 160; Stout, *Yankees Century,* 211, 232, 245–46.

73. Roscoe McGowen, "Dodger Star Entitled to Express Views, Declares O'Malley," Dan Daniel, "Jackie Off Base in TV Rap, Say Yankees," *The Sporting News,* December 10, 1952: 3; "Robinson Should Be Player—Not Crusader," *The Sporting News,* December 10, 1952: 12.

74. Mrs. Clara Jones, "Letter to the Editor: Yanks Want Negro Superman," *The Sporting News,* May 19, 1954: 14; Louis Effrat, "Yanks Purchase Contracts of Two Negro Players From Kansas City Club," *New York Times,* October 14, 1953, 37; Dan Daniel, "What About Vic Power?" *The Sporting News,* October 7, 1953: 7.

75. Madden, *Pride of October,* 145–61; Howard, *Elston and Me,* 18–45.

76. Howard, *Elston and Me,* 40.

77. Larry Lester, "J. L. Wilkinson: 'Only the Stars Come Out at Night,'" *Satchel Paige and Company,* ed. Heaphy, 110–143; Robert W. Creamer, *Stengel: His Life and Times* (New York: Simon & Schuster, 1984), 281–87; Howard, *Elston and Me,* 36–87.

78. Howard, *Elston and Me,* 40; Stout, *Yankee Century,* 254.

79. Howard, *Elston and Me,* 36–47; Madden, *Pride of October,* 151–56; Stout, *Yankees Century,* 253–55; Gollenbeck, *Dynasty,* 144–45; "Two More Hotels Admit Howard," *The Sporting News,* June 8, 1955.

80. Katz, *Kansas City A's and the Wrong Half of the Yankees,* 162–68, 173–79; Swaine, Integration of the Major Leagues, 187–88.

## Chapter VII

1. Bennett, Jr., *Before the Mayflower,* 587–92.

2. Thomas J. Sugrue, *The Origins of the Urban Crisis: Race and Inequality in Postwar Detroit* (Princeton: Princeton University Press, 1996), 17–32; Larry Lester, Sammy J. Miller, and Dick Clark, *Black Baseball in Detroit* (Charleston SC: Arcadia, 2000), 15.

3. Sugrue, *Origins of the Urban Crisis,* 33–88.

4. Ibid., 57–122; George Cantor, The *Tigers of '68: Baseball's Last Real Champions* (New York: Taylor, 1997), 47.

5. William M. Anderson, *The Detroit Tigers: A Pictorial Celebration of the Greatest Players and Moments in Tigers History* (Detroit: Wayne State University Press, 2008), 1–10; Lester, Miller and Clark, *Black Baseball in Detroit,* 7–108.

6. Anderson, *The Detroit Tigers,* 1–83; Falls, *The Detroit Tigers,* 1–106; Patrick Harrigan, *The Detroit Tigers: Club and Community,* 3–91.

7. Steven Watts, *The People's Tycoon: Henry Ford and the American Century* (New York: Random House, 2006), 30–54; Al Stump, *Cobb: A Biography* (Chapel Hill: Algonquin, 1994), 72–73, 160–61.

8. John Rosengren, *Hank Greenberg: The Hero of Heroes* (New York: New American Library, 2013).

9. Mark Theobold, "Briggs Manufacturing Company, 1909–1954; Detroit, Michigan (Coachbuilt.com, 2004).

10. Harrigan, *Detroit Tigers,* 40–65; Falls, *Detroit Tigers,* 55–106.

11. James Buckley Jr., *America's Classic Ballparks: A Collection of Images and Memorabilia* (San Diego: Thunder Bay, 2013), 69–94.

12. Lester, Miller, and Clark, *Black Baseball in Detroit,* 88–93; "Joe Greene," *Voices from the Great Black Baseball Leagues,* ed. Holway, 306.

13. Harrigan, *Detroit Tigers,* 59.

14. Lester, Miller, and Clark, *Black Baseball in Detroit,* 49; Theobold, "Briggs Manufacturing Company," (Coachbuilt.com).

15. Harrigan, *Detroit Tigers,* 58–62.

16. Hank Greenberg with Ira Berkow, *Hank Greenberg: The Story of My Life* (Chicago: Triumph Books, 1979), 83.

17. Harrigan, *Detroit Tigers,* 73–75; Falls, *Detroit Tigers,* 107–22; Lester, Miller, and Clark, *Black Baseball in Detroit.*

18. Swaine, *Integration of Major League Baseball,* 208–10; Moffi and Kronstadt, *Crossing the Line,* 219–20.

19. Harrigan, *Detroit Tigers,* 73–83.

20. Watson Spoelstra, "Exclusive Report on Tigers' Hiring Policy," *Michigan Chronicle,* June 14, 1958; Har-

rigan, *Detroit Tigers*, 83–85; Watson Spoelstra, "Tigers Insist They Will Use Negro 'If We Find a Good One,'" *The Sporting News*, May 5, 1958: 33.

21. Harrigan, *Detroit Tigers*, 85, quotation from personal interview.

22. Moffi and Kronstadt, *Crossing the Line*, 159–60; William M. Anderson, "Ozzie Virgil Breaks The Color Line with the Detroit Tigers," *Michigan History Magazine* (September/October 1997): 47–53.

23. Harrigan, *Detroit Tigers*, 84–85; David Maraniss, *Clemente: The Passion and Grace of Baseball's Last Hero* (New York: Simon & Schuster, 2006), 172; Willie Horton with Kevin Allen, *The People's Champion* (Wayne, MI: Immortal Investments, 2005), 127–29; Frank Robinson, *Late Innings*, 2.

24. "Tigers Get Virgil, Their First Negro," *New York Times*, June 6, 1958, 17; "Tigers' First Negro to Play 3rd Tonight," *Detroit Free Press*, June 6, 1958; "Ozzie Hits 1 for 5 In Tiger Debut," *Detroit Free Press*, June 7, 1958; Anderson, "Ozzie Virgil Breaks The Color Line," *Michigan History Magazine*, 47–53.

25. Burgos, *Playing America's Game*, 153–55, 180–82; Horton, *People's Champion*, 127–29.

26. Anderson, *Detroit Tigers*, 123; Harrigan, *Detroit Tigers*, 86.

27. Lawrence Casey, "Doby Calls Trade To Tigers 2nd Biggest Break of Career," *Michigan Chronicle*, April 4, 1959, Section two, 1; Horton, *People's Champion*, 131.

28. *Michigan Chronicle*, April 17 and 18, 1959.

29. Cantor, *Tigers of '68*, 89; Horton, *People's Champion*, 125–42; Harrigan, *Detroit Tigers*, 84–87.

30. Gutlon, *It Was Never About the Babe*.

31. Ibid., 67–134; Falls, *Detroit Tigers*, 28–29.

32. Gutlon, *It Was Never About the Babe*, 67–108; Bryant, *Shut Out*, 1–52; Ben Bradlee, Jr., *The Kid: The Immortal Life of Ted Williams* (New York: Little, Brown, 2013), 120–24.

33. Gutlon, *It Was Never About the Babe*, 68–87.

34. Eddie Collins to William Harridge, January 26, 1943, File 1/13 *Integration: Correspondence and Clippings, BA MSS 67*, at A. Bartlett Giamatti Research Center, National Baseball Hall of Fame and Museum, Cooperstown, NY.

35. Leigh Montville, *Ted Williams: The Biography of an American Hero* (New York: Broadway Books, 2004), 69–70; Dave Egan, "Baseball Manpower Shortage Solved," *Boston Daily Record*, January 26, 1943.

36. Gutlon, *It Was Never About the Babe*, 73–86, 185–88; Armour, *Joe Cronin*, 72–200.

37. Dave Egan, "What About Trio Seeking Sox Tryout?" *Boston Daily Record*, April 16, 1945.

38. Bryant, *Shut Out*, 28–41; Gutlon, *It Was Never About the Babe*, 91–101; Armour, *Joe Cronin*, 153–55; Glenn Stout, "Tryout and Fallout—Race, Jackie Robinson and the Red Sox," *Massachusetts Historical Review* 6 (2004).

39. Ted Williams, *My Turn At Bat: The Story of My Life* (New York: Simon & Schuster, 1969), 173–221.

40. Quoted in Bryant, *Shut Out*, 3.

41. Bryant, *Shut Out*, 45–47; Gutlon, *It Was Never About the Babe*, 99–101; Moffi and Kronstadt, *Crossing the Line*, 49–52; "Piper Davis," in Kelley, *Voices from the Negro Leagues*, 130.

42. Gutlon, *It Was Never About the Babe*, 109–34, 183–91.

43. Armour, *Joe Cronin*, 262–78.

44. Gutlon, *It Was Never About the Babe*, 71–74, 129; Bryant, *Shut Out*, 7–8.

45. Moffi and Kronstadt, *Crossing the Line*, 225–27.

46. Ibid., 210–12, Swaine, *Integration of the Major Leagues*, 90–94; Hy Hurwitz, "Red Sox May Ink Negro in Season or Two," *The Sporting News*, January 16, 1957: 18.

47. "First Negro With Red Sox Assigned Commuter's Role," *The Sporting News*, March 4, 1959: 8.

48. Herbert Tucker, *The Experiment*, April 18, 1959; Bryant, *Shut Out*, 1–3.

49. Egan, "Baseball Manpower Shortage Solved," *Boston Daily Record*, January 26, 1943.

50. "Red Sox Deny Bias," *New York Times*, April 14, 1949, 40; "Yawkey, Harris Called," *New York Times*, April 15, 1959, 38; "Bias Charge Is Denied," *New York Times*, April 22, 1959, 38.

51. Bryant, *Shut Out*, 52–54.

52. Dick Gordon, "Pumpsie Plunks Hits for Millers From Both Sides," *The Sporting News*, May 7, 1958: 35.

53. Moffi and Kronstadt, *Crossing the Line*, 210–12; Peary, ed. *We Played the Game*, 445–47.

54. Moffi and Kronstadt, *Crossing the Line*, 210–12; Bryant, *Shut Out*, 1–3.

55. Bryant, *Shut Out*, 66; Peary, ed. *We Played the Game*, 445–46.

56. Moffi and Kronstadt, *Crossing the Line*, 225–27; Mark Pattison and David Raglan (eds.), *Sock It To 'em Tigers: The Incredible Story of the 1968 Detroit Tigers* (Hanover, MA: Maple Street Press, 2008), 179–182.

57. Moffi and Kronstadt, *Crossing the Line*, 193–95.

## Chapter VIII

1. The Editors, "The Negro in American Sport: Round Table Discussion," *Sport*, 28–35; Robert Boyle, "Private World of the Negro Ballplayer," *Sports Illustrated* (March 21, 1960): 16–19, 74–84.

2. Boyle, "Private World of the Negro Ballplayer," *Sports Illustrated*, 74.

3. Ibid., quotations, 18. See also Burgos, *Playing America's Game*, 190–203; Ruck, *Raceball*, 49–117; Tim Wendel and Jose Luis Villegas, *Far from Home: Latino Baseball Players in America* (Washington, D.C.: National Geographic, 2008), 35–58.

4. Boyle, "Private World of the Negro Ballplayer," *Sports Illustrated*, 16.

5. Ibid., 16.

6. Ibid., 78.

7. Ibid., 74–78.

8. Ibid., 74; Howard, *Elston and Me*, 39.

9. Boyle, "Private World of the Negro Ballplayer," *Sports Illustrated*, 82–84.

10. Compiled from Swaine, *Integration of Major League Baseball*, 240–42; Moffi and Kronstadt, *Crossing the Line*.

11. Performance statistics compiled from "Leagues" section of *Baseball Reference.com*; Hall of Fame data from Baseball America, *The National Baseball Hall of*

*Fame Almanac*, ed. Will Lingo (Durham, NC: Baseball America, 2013).

12. Compiled from David S. Neft, et al, *The Sports Encyclopedia: Baseball*; transaction information from *Baseball Reference.com*, cross-checked against Swaine, *Integration of Major League Baseball*, 240–42; Moffi and Kronstadt, *Crossing the Line*.

13. Tygiel, *Baseball's Great Experiment*; Young, *Great Negro Baseball Stars*.

14. Jackie Robinson, *Baseball Has Done It*.

15. Frank Robinson, *Extra Innings*, quotation, 1.

16. *New York Times*, March 2, 1961; Malcolm X, *The Autobiography of Malcolm X*, as told to Alex Haley (New York: Ballantine, 1964); Bennett, *Before the Mayflower*, 378.

17. Boyle, "Private World of the Negro Ballplayer," *Sports Illustrated*, 78.

# Bibliography

## Books

Adelson, Bruce. *Brushing Back Jim Crow: The Integration of Minor-League Baseball in the American South.* Charlottesville: University of Virginia Press, 1999.

Anderson, William M. *The Detroit Tigers: A Pictorial Celebration of the Greatest Players and Moments in Tigers History.* Detroit, MI: Wayne State University Press, 2008.

Anton, Todd, and Bill Nowlin, eds. *When Baseball Went to War.* Chicago: Triumph, 2008.

Armour, Mark. *Joe Cronin: A Life in Baseball.* Lincoln: University of Nebraska Press, 2010.

Asinof, Eliot. *Eight Men Out: The Black Sox and the 1919 World Series.* New York: Holt, Rinehart, 1963.

Baldassaro, Lawrence, and Richard A. Johnson, eds. *The American Game: Baseball and Ethnicity.* Carbondale: Southern Illinois University Press, 2002.

Barber, Red. *1947: When All Hell Broke Loose in Baseball.* New York: Doubleday, 1982.

Bennett, Lerone, Jr. *Before the Mayflower: A History of Black America.* Chicago: Johnson Publishing, 2007.

Block, David. *Baseball Before We Knew It: A Search for the Roots of the Game.* Lincoln: University of Nebraska Press, 2005.

Boudreau, Lou, with Ed Fitzgerald. *Lou Boudreau: Covering All the Bases.* Champaign, IL: Sagamore, 1993.

_____. *Player-Manager.* Boston: Little, Brown, 1949.

Bradlee, Ben Jr. *The Kid: The Immortal Life of Ted Williams.* New York: Little, Brown, 2013.

Brown, Warren. *The Chicago White Sox.* Kent, OH: Kent State University Press, 2007, facsimile of New York: G. P. Putnam's edition.

Bryant, Howard. *Shut Out: A Story of Race and Baseball in Boston.* New York: Routledge, 2002.

Buckley, James Jr. *America's Classic Ballparks: A Collection of Images and Memorabilia.* San Diego, CA: Thunder Bay Press, 2013.

Burgos, Adrian Jr. *Playing America's Game: Baseball, Latinos, and the Color Line.* Berkeley: University of California Press, 2007.

Cantor, George. *The Tigers of '68: Baseball's Last Real Champions.* New York: Taylor Trade Publishing, 1997.

Carroll, Brian. *When to Stop the Cheering? The Black Press, the Black Community, and the Integration of Professional Baseball.* New York: Routledge, 2007.

Clark, Dick, and Larry Lester, eds. *The Negro Leagues Book.* Cleveland, OH: Society for American Baseball Research, 1994.

Clavin, Tom, and Danny Peary. *Roger Maris: Baseball's Reluctant Hero.* New York: Simon & Schuster, 2010.

Cottrell, Robert Charles. *The Best Pitcher in Baseball: The Life of Rube Foster, Negro League Giant.* New York: New York University Press, 2001.

Cramer, Richard Ben. *Joe DiMaggio: The Hero's Life.* New York: Simon & Schuster, 2000.

Creamer, Robert W. *Babe: The Legend Comes to Life.* New York: Simon & Schuster, 1974.

_____. *Stengel: His Life and Times.* New York: Simon & Schuster, 1984.

DeFord, Frank. *The Old Ball Game: How John McGraw, Christy Mathewson, and the New York Giants Created Modern Baseball.* New York: Grove Press, 2006.

DeValeria, Dennis, and Jeanne Burke DeValeria. *Honus Wagner: A Biography.* Pittsburgh: University of Pittsburgh Press, 1998.

Deveaux, Tom. *The Washington Senators: 1901–1971.* Jefferson NC: McFarland, 2001.

Dickson, Paul. *Bill Veeck: Baseball's Greatest Maverick.* New York: Walker, 2012.

Dixon, Phil S. *A Harvest on Freedom's Fields: Andrew "Rube" Foster.* Xlibris.com, 2010.

Dorinson, Joseph, and Joram Warmund, eds., *Jackie Robinson: Race Sports, and the American Dream.* Armonk, NY: M. E. Sharpe, 1998.

Dubois, W.E.B. *The Souls of Black Folk.* New York: Barnes and Noble, 2003. (Originally published in 1903.)

Eig, Jonathan. *Opening Day: The Story of Jackie Robinson's First Season.* New York: Simon & Schuster, 2008.

Eskenazi, Gerald. *Bill Veeck: A Baseball Legend.* New York: McGraw-Hill, 1988.

Falls, Joe. *The Detroit Tigers: An Illustrated History.* New York: Walker, 1989.

Farwell, Byron. *Over There: The United States in the Great War, 1917–1918*. New York: W.W. Norton, 1999.

Felber, Bill. *A Game of Brawl: The Orioles, the Beaneaters, and the Battle for the 1897 Pennant*. Lincoln: University of Nebraska Press, 2007.

Foner, Eric. *Reconstruction: America's Unfinished Revolution, 1863–1877*. New York: HarperCollins, 2002.

Franklin, John Hope. *From Slavery to Freedom: A History of Negro Americans*, 3rd ed. New York: Alfred A. Knopf, 1967.

Gay, Timothy M. *Satch, Dizzy & Rapid Robert: the Wild Saga of Interracial Baseball Before Jackie Robinson*. New York: Simon & Schuster, 2010.

Gilbert, Bill. *They Also Served: Baseball And the Home Front, 1941–1945*. New York: Crown, 1992.

Gillette, Gary, and Pete Palmer, eds. *The ESPN Baseball Encyclopedia*, 5th Edition. New York: Sterling Publishing, 2008.

Golenbock, Peter. *Dynasty: The New York Yankees 1949–1964*. Englewood Cliffs, NJ: Prentice Hall, 1975.

Goodwyn, Lawrence. *The Populist Moment: A Short History of the Agrarian Revolution in America*. Oxford: Oxford University Press, 1978.

Gould, Stephen Jay. *The Mismeasure of Man*, 2nd ed. New York: W.W. Norton, 1996.

Greenberg, Hank, with Ira Berkow. *Hank Greenberg: The Story of My Life*. Chicago: Triumph Books, 1979.

Gutlon, Jerry M. *It Was Never About the Babe: The Red Sox, Racism, Mismanagement, and the Curse of the Bambino*. New York: Skyhorse, 2009.

Harrigan, Patrick. *The Detroit Tigers: Club and Community*. Toronto: University of Toronto Press, 1997.

Heaphy, Leslie A. *The Negro Leagues, 1869–1960*. Jefferson, NC: McFarland, 2003.

_____, ed. *Satchel Paige and Company: Essays on the Kansas City Monarchs, Their Brightest Star, and the Negro Leagues*. Jefferson, NC: McFarland, 2007.

Heiman, Lee, Dave Weiner, and Bill Gutman, eds. *When the Cheering Stops: Former Major Leaguers Talk About Their Game and Their Lives*. New York: Macmillan, 1990.

Hogan, Lawrence D. *Shades of Glory: The Negro Leagues and the Story of African-American Baseball*. Washington D.C.: National Geographic, 2006.

Holway, John B., ed. *Black Diamonds: Life in the Negro Leagues from the Men Who Lived It*. Westport, CT: Meckler, 1989.

_____. *Blackball Stars: Negro League Pioneers*. Westport CT: Meckler, 1988.

_____. *Josh and Satch: The Life and Times of Josh Gibson and Satchel Paige*. Westport, CT: Meckler, 1991.

_____, ed. *Voices from the Great Black Baseball Leagues*. New York: Dodd, Mead, 1975.

Honig, Donald. *The Man in the Dugout*. Lincoln: University of Nebraska Press, 1977.

Horton, Willie, with Kevin Allen. *The People's Champion*. Wayne, MI: Immortal Investments Publishing, 2005.

Howard, Arlene, with Ralph Winbush. *Elston and Me: The Story of the First Black Yankee*. Columbia: University of Missouri Press, 2001.

Ignatiev, Noel. *How the Irish Became White*. New York: Routledge, 1995.

James, Bill. *Guide to Baseball Managers from 1870 to Today*. New York: Scribner, 1997.

_____. *The New Bill James Historical Baseball Abstract*. New York: Free Press, 2001.

Jordan, David. *The Athletics of Philadelphia: Connie Mack's White Elephants*. Jefferson NC: McFarland, 1999.

Kahn, Roger. *The Boys of Summer*. New York: Harper and Row, 1971.

Katz, Jeff. *The Kansas City A's and the Wrong Half of the Yankees*. Hingham, MA: Maple Street Press, 2007.

Kelley, Brent P. *Baseball's Bonus Babies: Conversations with 24 High-Priced Ballplayers Signed from 1953 to 1957*. Jefferson NC: McFarland, 2006.

_____. *Voices from the Negro Leagues: Conversations with 52 Baseball Standouts*. Jefferson, NC: McFarland, 1998.

Kerrane, Kevin. *Dollar Sign on the Muscle*. New York: Avon Books, 1984.

Kirwin, Bill, ed. *Out of the Shadows: African American Baseball from the Cuban Giants to Jackie Robinson*. Lincoln: University of Nebraska Press, 2005.

Koppett, Leonard. *Koppett's Concise History of Major League Baseball*. New York: Carroll and Graf, 2004.

Kuklick, Bruce. *To Everything a Season: Shibe Park and Urban Philadelphia*. Princeton, NJ: Princeton University Press, 1991.

Laing, Jeffrey Michael. *Bud Fowler: Baseball's First Black Professional*. Jefferson, NC: McFarland, 2013.

Lamster, Mark. *Spalding's World Tour: The Epic Adventure That Took Baseball Around the Globe*. New York: Public Affairs, 2006.

Lanctot, Neil. *Negro League Baseball: The Rise and Ruin of a Black Institution*. Philadelphia: University of Pennsylvania Press, 2004.

Lester, Larry. *Black Baseball's National Showcase: The East-West All Star Game, 1933–1953*. Lincoln: University of Nebraska Press, 2001.

Lester, Larry, Sammy J. Miller, and Dick Clark. *Black Baseball in Detroit*. Charleston, SC: Arcadia, 2000.

Levitt, Daniel R. *Ed Barrow: The Bulldog Who Built the Yankees' First Dynasty*. Lincoln: University of Nebraska Press, 2008.

Levy, Alan H. *Joe McCarthy: Architect of the Yankee Dynasty*. Jefferson, NC, McFarland, 2005.

Lewis, Franklin. *The Cleveland Indians*. Kent, OH: Kent State University Press, 2006; reprint, original New York: G. P. Putnam's Sons, 1949.

Lieb, Frederick J. *The Baltimore Orioles: The History of a Colorful Team in Baltimore and St. Louis*. New York: G. P. Putnam's Sons, 1955.

Lingo, Will, ed. *The National Baseball Hall of Fame Almanac*. Durham, NC: Baseball America, 2013.

Lowenfish, Lee. *Branch Rickey: Baseball's Ferocious Gentleman*. Lincoln: University of Nebraska Press, 2007.

_____. *The Imperfect Diamond: A History of Baseball's Labor Wars*. Lincoln: University of Nebraska Press, 1991.

Luke, Bob. *The Baltimore Elite Giants: Sport and Society in the Age of Negro League Baseball*. Baltimore: Johns Hopkins University Press, 2009.

_____. *The Most Famous Woman in Baseball: Effa Man-*

ley and the Negro Leagues. Washington, D.C.: Potomac Books, 2011.

Macht, Norman L. *Connie Mack and the Early Years of Baseball*. Lincoln: University of Nebraska Press, 2007.

Madden, Bill. *Pride of October: What It Was to Be Young and a Yankee*. New York: Warner Books, 2003.

Malcolm X. *The Autobiography of Malcolm X*. As told to Alex Haley. New York: Ballantine, 1964.

Manley, Effa, and Leon Herbert Hardwick. *Negro Baseball ... Before Integration*. Haworth, NJ: St. Johann Press, 1976.

Maraniss, David. *Clemente: The Passion and Grace of Baseball's Last Hero*. New York: Simon & Schuster, 2006.

Marshall, William. *Baseball's Pivotal Era: 1945–1951*. Lexington: University Press of Kentucky, 1999.

McWhirter, Cameron. *Red Summer: The Summer of 1919 and the Awakening of Black America*. New York: Henry Holt, 2011.

Meier, August, and Elliot Rudwick. *From Plantation to Ghetto*, 3rd ed. New York: Hill and Wang, 1976.

Minoso, Minnie. *Just Call Me Minnie: My Six Decades in Baseball*. Champaign, IL: Sagamore, 1994.

Moffi, Larry, and Jonathan Kronstadt. *Crossing the Line: Black Major Leaguers 1947–1959*. Lincoln: University of Nebraska Press, 1994.

Montville, Leigh. *The Big Bam: The Life and Times of Babe Ruth*. New York: Doubleday, 2006.

_____. *Ted Williams: The Biography of an American Hero*. New York: Broadway Books, 2004.

Moore, Joseph Thomas. *Pride Against Prejudice: The Biography of Larry Doby*. New York: Praeger, 1988.

Morgan, Edmund S. *American Slavery, American Freedom: The Ordeal of Colonial Virginia*. New York: W.W. Norton, 1975.

Neft, David S., Richard M. Cohen, and Michael L. Neft, eds. *The Sport Encyclopedia: Baseball 2006*. New York: St. Martin's Griffin, 2006.

*Negro Baseball Pictorial Yearbook*, 1944.

O'Neil, Buck. *I Was Right on Time: My Journey from the Negro Leagues to the Majors*. New York: Simon & Schuster, 1998.

Paige, Leroy (Satchel). *Maybe I'll Pitch Forever*. Lincoln: University of Nebraska Press, 1993, reprint of 1962 edition, published by Doubleday.

Painter, Nell Irvin. *Creating Black Americans: African-American History and Its Meanings, 1619 to the Present*. New York: Oxford University Press, 2007.

_____. *The History of White People*. New York: W.W. Norton, 2010.

Pascoe, Peggy. *What Comes Naturally: Miscegenation Law and the Making of Race in America*. Oxford: Oxford University Press, 2010.

Pattison, Mark and David Raglan, eds. *Sock It to 'em Tigers: The Incredible Story of the 1968 Detroit Tigers*. Hanover, MA: Maple Street Press, 2008.

Peary, Danny, ed. *We Played the Game: Memories of Baseball's Greatest Era*. New York: Black Dog and Leventhal, 1994.

Peterson, Robert. *Only the Ball Was White: A History of Legendary Black Players and All-Black Professional Teams*. New York: Oxford University Press, 1970.

Pietrusza, David. *Judge and Jury: The Life and Times of Judge Kenesaw Mountain Landis*. South Bend, IN: Diamond, 1998.

Povich, Shirley. *All Those Mornings at the Post*. New York: Public Affairs, 2005.

_____. *The Washington Senators: An Informal History*. New York: G. P. Putnam's Sons, 1954.

Rader, Benjamin G. *Baseball: A History of America's Game*, 3rd ed. Champaign: University of Illinois Press, 2008.

Reisler, Jim. *Babe Ruth: Launching the Legend*. New York: McGraw-Hill, 2004.

_____. *Black Writers/Black Baseball: An Anthology of Articles from Black Sportswriters Who Covered the Negro Leagues*. Jefferson, NC: McFarland, 1994.

Robinson, Frank, and Berry Stainback. *Extra Innings: The Grand-Slam Response to Al Campanis's Controversial Remarks about Blacks in Baseball*. New York: McGraw-Hill, 1988.

Robinson, Jackie. *Baseball Has Done It*. Philadelphia: Lippincott, 1964.

_____. *I Never Had It Made: An Autobiography*. New York: Putnam, 1972.

Rogosin, Donn. *Invisible Men: Life in Baseball's Negro Leagues*. Lincoln: University of Nebraska Press, 1983.

Rosengren, John. *Hank Greenberg: The Hero of Heroes*. New York: New American Library, 2013.

Ruck, Rob. *Raceball: How the Major Leagues Colonized the Black and Latin Game*. Boston: Beacon Press, 2011.

Rust, Art Jr. *"Get That Nigger Off the Field": A Sparkling, Informal History of the Black Man in Baseball*. New York: Delacorte, 1976.

Schwarz, Alan. *The Numbers Game: Baseball's Lifelong Fascination with Statistics*. New York: St. Martin's Griffin, 2004.

Snyder, Brad. *Beyond the Shadow of the Senators: the Untold Story of the Homestead Grays and the Integration of Baseball*. New York: McGraw-Hill, 2003.

Sowell, Mike. *The Pitch That Killed: The Story of Carl Mays, Ray Chapman, and the Pennant Race of 1920*. New York: Ivan R. Dee, 2004.

Stout, Glen. *Yankees Century: 100 Years of New York Yankees Baseball*. Boston: Houghton Mifflin, 2002.

Stump, Al. *Cobb: A Biography*. Chapel Hill, NC: Algonquin, 1994.

Sugrue, Thomas J. *The Origins of the Urban Crisis: Race and Inequality in Postwar Detroit*. Princeton: Princeton University Press, 1996.

_____. *Sweet Land of Liberty: The Forgotten Struggle for Civil Rights in the North*. New York: Random House, 2008.

Sullivan, Dean A., ed. Early *Innings: A Documentary History of Baseball, 1825–1908*. Lincoln: University of Nebraska Press, 1995.

Surdam, David G. *The Postwar Yankees: Baseball's Golden Age Revisited*. Lincoln: University of Nebraska Press, 2008.

Swaine, Rick. *The Integration of Major League Baseball: A Team by Team History*. Jefferson, NC: McFarland, 2009.

Swift, Tom. *Chief Bender's Burden: The Silent Struggle of a Baseball Star*. Lincoln: University of Nebraska Press, 2008.

Thorn, John, Pete Palmer, Michael Gershman, and David Pietrusza, eds. *Total Baseball: The Official Encyclopedia of Major League Baseball*, 5th ed. New York: Viking, 1997.

Threston, Christopher. *The Integration of Baseball in Philadelphia*. Jefferson NC: McFarland, 2003.

Trotter, Joe William, ed. *The Great Migration In Historical Perspective: New Dimensions of Race, Class, and Gender*. Bloomington: Indiana University Press, 1991.

Tuttle, William M., Jr. *Race Riot: Chicago in the Red Summer of 1919*. New York: Atheneum, 1970.

Tye, Larry. *Satchel: The Life and Times of an American Legend*. New York: Random House, 2009.

Tygiel, Jules. *Baseball's Great Experiment: Jackie Robinson and His Legacy*. Oxford: Oxford University Press, 2008.

_____. *Past Time: Baseball as History*. Oxford: Oxford University Press, 2001.

Veeck, Bill, with Ed Linn. *Veeck—as in Wreck: The Autobiography of Bill Veeck*. Chicago: University of Chicago Press, 1962.

Vincent, Fay, ed. *The Only Game in Town: Baseball Stars of the 1930s and 1940s Talk About the Game They Loved*. New York: Simon & Schuster, 2006.

Virtue, John. *South of the Color Barrier: How Jorge Pasquel and the Mexican League Pushed Baseball Toward Racial Integration*. Jefferson, NC: McFarland, 2008.

Walker, Fleetwood. *Our Home Colony: A Treatise on the Past, Present and Future of the Negro Race in America* (1898).

Warfield, Don. *The Roaring Redhead: Larry MacPhail—Baseball's Great Innovator*. South Bend, IN: Diamond Communications, 1987.

Washington, Booker T. *Up from Slavery*. New York: Barnes and Noble, 2003. (Originally published in 1901.)

Watts, Steven. *The People's Tycoon: Henry Ford and the American Century*. New York: Random House, 2006.

Wendell, Tim, and Jose Luis Villegas. *Far from Home: Latino Baseball Players in America*. Washington D.C.: National Geographic, 2008.

White, G. Edward. *Creating the National Pastime: Baseball Transforms Itself, 1903–1953*. Princeton, NJ: Princeton University Press, 1998.

White, Sol. *Sol White's History of Colored Base Ball: With Other Documents of the Early Black Game. 1886–1936,* Jerry Malloy, ed. Lincoln: University of Nebraska Press, 1995.

Wilbert, Warren N. *The Arrival of the American League: Ban Johnson and the 1901 Challenge to National League Monopoly*. Jefferson, NC: McFarland, 2007.

Wilkerson, Isabell. *The Warmth of Other Suns: The Epic Story of America's Great Migration*. New York: Random House, 2010.

Williams, Juan. *Eyes on the Prize: America's Civil Rights Years 1954–1965*. New York: Penguin, 1987.

Williams, Ted. *My Turn at Bat: The Story of My Life*. New York: Simon & Schuster, 1969.

Woodward, C. Vann. *Reunion and Reaction: The Compromise of 1877 and the End of Reconstruction*. Boston: Little, Brown, 1966.

_____. *The Strange Career of Jim Crow,* 2nd ed. London: Oxford University Press, 1966.

Young, A.S. "Doc." *Great Negro Baseball Stars: And How They Made the Major Leagues*. New York: A. S. Barnes, 1953.

## Important Journal Articles

Anderson, William M. "Ozzie Virgil Breaks the Color Line with the Detroit Tigers." *Michigan History Magazine* 75 (September/October 1997): 47–53.

Boyle, Robert. "The Private World of the Negro Ballplayer." *Sports Illustrated* 11 (March 21, 1960): 16–19, 74–84.

Bronson, Po and Ashley Merryman. "See Baby Discriminate." *Newsweek* (September 14, 2009): 52–60.

Considine, Bob. "Ivory From Cuba." *Collier's*, 106 (August 1940): 9–24.

Dodson, Dan. "The Integration of Negroes in Baseball." *Journal of Educational Sociology* 28 (October 1954): 73–82.

Graham, Frank Jr. "Power Proves His Case." *Sport* 25 (August 1956): 44–47, 79.

"Historically Speaking: Rube Foster." *Black Sports* (February 1972): 44–45.

Jordan, David M., Larry R. Gerlach, and John P. Rossi. "A Baseball Myth Exploded: The Truth About Bill Veeck and the '43 Phillies." *The National Pastime* 18 (1998): 3–13.

Macht, Norman L. "Does Baseball Deserve This Black Eye? A Dissent from the Universal Casting of Shame and Blame on Kenesaw Mountain Landis for Baseball's Failure to Sign Black Players Before 1946"; Richard Crepeau. "Landis, Baseball, and Racism—A Brief Comment"; Lee Lowenfish. "The Gentleman's Agreement and the Ferocious Gentleman Who Broke It"; and "Response by Norman Macht." *The Baseball Research Journal* 38, (Summer, 2009): 26–35.

"The Negro in American Sport: Round Table Discussion," *Sport* 29 (March 1960): 28–35.

Paxton, Harry T. "The Philadelphia A's Last Stand." *Saturday Evening Post* 134 (June 12, 1954).

"Readers Torn Over Tori." *USA Today Sports Weekly* (March 17–23, 2010): 3.

Robinson, Jackie. "What's Wrong with Negro League Baseball?" *Ebony* 3 (June 1948): 16–18.

Shane, Ted. "The Chocolate Rube Waddell." *The Saturday Evening Post* 120 (July 27, 1940).

Shecter, Leonard. "Vic Power's New, Wonderful World." *Sport* 35 (July 1966): 65–71.

Smith, Wendell. "The Most Prejudiced Teams in Baseball." *Ebony* 7 (May 1953); 111–120.

Stout, Glenn. "Tryout and Fallout—Race, Jackie Robinson and the Red Sox." *Massachusetts Historical Review* 6 (2004).

Theobold, Mark. "Briggs Manufacturing Company, 1909–1954; Detroit, Michigan." (Coachbuilt.com, 2004).

Thompson, Hank. "How I Wrecked My Life—How I Hope to Save It." *Sport* 40 (December 1965): 46–51, 95–98.

Tygiel, Jules. "Revisiting Bill Veeck and the 1943 Phillies." *The Baseball Research Journal* 35 (Summer, 2006): 109–114.

Wiggins, David K. "Wendell Smith, the Pittsburgh Courier-Journal and the Campaign to Include Blacks in Organized Baseball, 1933–1945." *Journal of Sport History* 10 (Summer, 1983): 5–29.

## Government Documents

Gibson, Campbell and Kay Young. "Historical Census Statistics on Population Totals by Race, 1790 to 1990..." United States Census. Working Paper No. 76. Washington, D.C.: U.S. Census Bureau, 2005.

"Organized Baseball—American League: Statements of profit and loss for year ending in 1952." Eighty-Second Congress, Study of Monopoly Power, Serial No. 1, Part 6: Organized Baseball. Washington, D.C.: United States Government Printing Office, 1952.

## Archival Holdings

Individual Player, Manager, and Official Files held at the A. Bartlett Giamatti Library, National Baseball Hall of Fame and Museum, Cooperstown, NY.

"Integration: Correspondence and Clippings" BA MSS 67, File 1/7, A. Bartlett Giamatti Library, National Baseball Hall of Fame and Museum, Cooperstown, NY.

"Jules Tygiel Papers, 1949–2008," BA MSS 34, A. Bartlett Giamatti Library, National Baseball Hall of Fame and Museum, Cooperstown, NY.

"1947 DeWitt Scrapbook," BASCR 143 V. 8, A. Bartlett Giamatti Library, National Baseball Hall of Fame and Museum, Cooperstown, NY.

## Newspapers and Magazines

*Baltimore Afro-American*, 1939–1947
*Baltimore Sun*, 1954
*Baseball Register*, 1946–1961
*Boston Daily Record*, 1943–1959
*Chicago Daily News*, 1938
*Chicago Daily Tribune*, 1951
*Chicago Defender*, 1919–1948
*Cleveland Plain Dealer*, 1947–1951
*Ebony*, 1948–1953
*The Freeman* (Indianapolis, IN), 1911–1917
*Michigan Chronicle* (Detroit, MI), 1958–1959
*Detroit Free Press*, June 6, 1958
*New York Daily Worker*, 1933–1947
*New York Herald Tribune*, 1948
*New York Star*, 1948
*New York Times*, 1945–1961
*Philadelphia Inquirer*, 1953–1954
*Philadelphia Tribune*, 1941–1944
*Pittsburgh Courier*, 1936–1953
*St. Louis Post-Dispatch*, 1947–1953
*Spalding's Baseball Guide and Record Book*, 1947–1954
*Sport*, 1956–1966
*The Sporting News*, 1942–1971
*Sports Illustrated*, 1954–1960
*Washington Post*, 1947–1955

## Online

Baseball-Reference.com, http://www.baseball-reference.com.

# Index